Materials and Components

of Interior Architecture

Eighth Edition

J. Rosemary Riggs

PEARSON

Boston Columbus Indianapolis New York San Francisco Upper Saddle River
Amsterdam Cape Town Dubai London Madrid Milan Munich Paris Montreal Toronto
Delhi Mexico City São Paulo Sydney Hong Kong Seoul Singapore Taipei Tokyo

Editorial Director: Vernon R. Anthony
Acquisitions Editor: Sara Eilert
Editorial Assistant: Doug Greive
Director of Marketing: David Gesell
Senior Marketing Coordinator: Alicia Wozniak
Marketing Assistant: Les Roberts
Associate Editor: Laura Weaver
Inhouse Production Liasion: Alicia Ritchey
Associate Managing Editor: Alexandrina Benedicto Wolf
Senior Manufacturing Buyer: Pat Tonneman
Art Director: Jayne Conte

Cover Designer: Karen Salzbach
Image Permission Coordinator: Mike Lackey
Cover image: Stephen Graham Photography
Content Developmental Editor: Barb Tucker,
  S4Carlisle Publishing Services
Full-Service Project Management: Diane Kohnen,
  S4Carlisle Publishing Services
Composition: S4Carlisle Publishing Services
Printer/Binder: LSC Communications
Cover Printer: LSC Communications
Text Font: Frutiger LT Std

Credits and acknowledgments borrowed from other sources and reproduced, with permission, in this textbook appear on the appropriate page within the text. Unless otherwise stated, all artwork has been provided by the author.

Library of Congress Cataloging-in-Publication Data

Riggs, J. Rosemary.
  Materials and components of interior architecture / J. Rosemary Riggs. — Eighth edition.
    pages cm
  Includes index.
  ISBN-13: 978-0-13-276915-0 (pbk. : alk. paper)
  ISBN-10: 0-13-276915-8 (pbk. : alk. paper) 1. Building materials. 2. Household appliances.
3. Plumbing—Equipment and supplies. 4. Interior decoration. I. Title.
  TA403.R525 2013
  698—dc23
                    2013001334

ISBN-13: 978-0-13-276915-0
ISBN-10:   0-13-276915-8

CONTENTS

What constitutes good design? This age-old question, when considered from a purely aesthetic viewpoint, can generate as many subjective responses as the number of individuals who answer it. When considered from a more objective perspective, however, a respondent might argue that a designed environment is good only when it delivers value by satisfying its end users' requirements. In other words, good design is what satisfies the needs of the people for whom the design is intended—whether it's the design of a product, a single room or an entire home, a conference room or a corporate headquarters, a trade show exhibit, even a university curriculum or a book's contents. It doesn't make a lot of difference how exceptional a design might appear; if it doesn't perform well, then it just isn't good design.

The Environment Group's Cary Johnson, FIIDA, argues that today's public expects, demands, and appreciates good design. "All one has to do is open the colorful advertising flyer for Target department stores to realize that our society has been exposed to and grabbed on to the notion of good design for everyone," he says. Indeed, gone are the days when cookie-cutter design ideas satisfy; design clients today want out-of-the-box thinking and innovative solutions that are custom-tailored to their own particular styles of working and living. More and more, they are also demanding solutions that are environmentally responsible, especially as the long-term, tangible benefits of sustainable design and building practices are more fully realized. Designers and architects, in particular, have a great potential to protect the Earth's natural environment, as they are the ones responsible for the majority of the world's built environments.

A plethora of products and materials, many of which are explored in this latest edition of *Materials and Components of Interior Architecture*, comprise the tools with which designers create stellar interiors. A comprehensive understanding of the information presented here is essential for any practitioner to achieve success. For it is the functionality of the individual elements within an environment that impacts the performance of the space as a whole—elements that must be carefully researched and specified, as well as properly installed, in order to achieve the desired results.

The well-known sustainable design architect William A. McDonough, FAIA, has often said, "Design is the first signal of human intention." If it is your intent to bring to every project the full scope of your abilities and passion for your work, then this book is an invaluable resource to take with you on your journey. Just as creative thinking is the hallmark of the architecture and design field, knowledge and research are the foundations upon which creativity proves its worth.

Katie Sosnowchik
Co-author, *Sustainable Commercial Interiors*

While teaching an introductory course in interior design, I noticed that the students usually chose paint or wallpaper for the walls and always used carpet on the floor, as though these were the only suitable treatments for walls and floors. I felt a need to break this cycle of thinking by exposing students to the fascinating world of materials—and so this book started to take shape.

I was unable to find a book that fully covered the exciting nonstructural materials available to the interior designer. Some authors concentrated on historical aspects of the home, both in architecture and furniture. Some emphasized upholstered furniture, draperies, and carpets; others stressed the principles and elements of design and color and the aesthetic values that make up a home. No one, however, concentrated on the "nuts and bolts" of interior design. Some books purporting to cover all types of flooring did not even mention wood floors, whereas others had only one or two paragraphs on the subject. This book covers a wide spectrum of these interior design issues.

Throughout this edition, for those particularly interested in environmental concerns, products and manufacturers are mentioned that are participating in some way in the recycling process. (See Chapter 1, "Environmental Concerns.") In particular, Chapter 1 should be of prime interest to those designers (most of us) who believe that the environment is precious and worth saving. Environmental responsibility and recycling are also ways to help cope with the growing landfill problems. In researching material for the "Environmental Concerns" chapter, a representative from a very environmentally conscious company told me that because she spends each day working on this problem, it has become a habit in her personal life and in the lives of other coworkers. This, of course, is the chapter's aim. At the end of the chapter, some companies are listed that are helping our environment, sometimes to their financial betterment, but not always.

In the past, the interior design profession dealt mainly with the more decorative aspects of design. Today it has become increasingly necessary for interior designers to be knowledgeable not only about the finishing materials used in the design field, but also about some structural materials as well. Many interior designers are working for—or with—architects, so it is important that they understand the properties and uses of all materials—thus, the *raison d'être* of this textbook. Together with the properties of materials, I also feel that students should know the historical background of the materials, as in the case of marble and the construction of wallcoverings. In the latter case, there is a considerable cost difference between various wallcoverings, and much of that difference is due to the methods of printing and the backing used. Knowledge of quality construction will help to convince consumers to use the more expensive (better-made) product. The section on wallcoverings includes background information on this subject supplied by the Wallcovering Organization.

In the case of decorative laminate, I found some interesting historical background and also current uses. For example, the old "Woodie" station wagon (1955) used laminate for the imitation wood on its sides. In addition, today most bowling alleys are surfaced with decorative laminate. The interiors of pleasure boats are often manufactured with laminate as well because of the product's durability, ease of maintenance, and resistance to salt. I also discovered some background on the beginnings of Jacuzzi and Moen.

Although most sales representatives realize that the interior design student of today is the customer of tomorrow, some still do not understand the scope of the interior design field. Many interior designers are women, and I have found that the ability to talk knowledgeably about materials earns the respect of both men and women in the profession. One sales rep actually said, "You really know what you are talking about."

Installation methods are discussed in this book because some contractors (luckily only a few) will use the cheapest method of installation, one that may not be the best for that particular job. These installation methods have been taken from information provided by manufacturers, associations, and institutions involved with each particular product. Knowledge of the correct installation procedures ensures a properly installed project. The Instructor's Manual provides many real-world examples of problems with products that have been improperly installed, and some installation problems are mentioned in this edition. Your instructor will probably describe some of his or her own experiences. In researching material for this eighth edition, I read technical journals to investigate various problems, such as yellowing in carpet, moisture in concrete slabs, and discoloration in vinyl flooring. Awareness of a potential problem before it occurs can prevent headaches in the future.

Maintenance information on many materials has also been included, because the cost of maintenance should be one of the deciding factors in product selection. What may be an inexpensive material at first may turn out to be the most expensive option over time because of high maintenance costs.

Most of the world uses the metric system. Because the U.S. government has stressed the importance of a transition to the metric system, designers will find increasing use of millimeters, meters, grams, and kilograms as measurements for length and weight. The wallcovering industry has already converted to metric or European measurements. Some manufacturers, particularly those who sell to Canada and other foreign countries, now list their products in two systems, inches and metric. Handy conversion tables of most of the measurements used in interior design are provided at the end of the book.

In doing my research and talking to many manufacturers, I have found a growing awareness of consumers' needs and wishes. Dependability is one thing the consumer requires, whether for a private home or a large commercial installation. Thus, many manufacturers offer warranties (e.g., one manufacturer offers a lifetime structural guarantee on its wood floor).

All disciplines have their own jargon. To communicate properly with contractors and architects, a designer must understand their jargon. Designers or prospective builders who have read and studied *Materials and Components of Interior Architecture* will be able to talk knowledgeably with architects and contractors about the uses of materials and their methods of installation. This understanding will also enable designers to decide for themselves which materials and methods are best for a given installation and avoid being influenced by the bias of salespeople.

One note about the spelling of *moulding:* The Architectural Woodwork Institute (AWI) uses this spelling, and the term is spelled this way in Canada, where this textbook is also used. The dictionary I consulted has both spellings. To be consistent I have used *moulding* throughout this book, as some companies even have that spelling in their corporate name.

Any question that a student has about products can easily be answered by using the Internet, and the information found will be up-to-date. There are so many changes in the names and ownership of companies that it is nearly impossible nowadays to keep pace without looking online.

In selecting products to mention, I have selected those that advertise in *Interior Design Magazine* and *Interiors & Sources,* especially in the *I & S Buyer's Guides*. I am also on the e-mail list of many companies who send me information about their latest products as soon as they appear on the market. Products that have received awards are also a good source of new and well-designed materials. Writing this edition in the midst of a global recession proved a little difficult. Some of the companies have actually gone out of business; others have merged with what used to be competitors and have changed their names.

This book can serve as a reference for designers who are already practicing, because it brings to their attention new materials on the market and improvements in current products, many of which have won awards in the years 2011 and 2012. A contractor, after reading this book, told me that contractors would also benefit from using it as a reference tool. Wherever possible, generic information has been used; however, when a product is unique to one manufacturer, that manufacturer's product has been used.

In arranging the subject matter, I placed the chapter on environmental concerns first, because all chapters on materials stress environmental concerns. The chapter on paint follows because all types of surfaces—floors, walls, and ceilings—may be painted. In this eighth edition I have also included wallcoverings in the paint chapter, as they are generally sold in paint stores. Then, starting from the bottom of a building, the logical progression starts with a chapter on carpets (Chapter 3). Carpet is the most common floor covering. Chapter 4 deals with all the other types of materials available for floors.

One comment on ceramic tile is needed here. Spain is the largest producer of ceramic tile, with Italy and Brazil also being large producers. However, I have not mentioned manufacturers of imported tile in this book because the scope of imported tile is too large. Students should be aware that many companies carrying ceramic tile also display imported tile, which can be ordered if desired. However, delivery may not be quite as easy as for domestically produced tile.

Many of the same materials used for flooring are also discussed in Chapter 5, but this time they are used on walls; the installation, finish, and maintenance vary, of course. Chapter 6 covers ceilings, areas that are usually either painted or ignored. Chapter 7 discusses all the other components that make up a well-designed room, including mouldings, doors, hardware, and hinges.

Chapter 8 explains the construction, structure, and design of fine cabinetry and could not have been written without the assistance of the Architectural Woodwork Institute. Although students may not construct cabinets themselves, they should be able to distinguish between good and bad construction and know what to look for in terms of quality. (The information presented in Chapter 8 also will come in handy for inspecting ready-made furniture because cabinets and furniture are constructed similarly.) Study of Chapter 8 will enable designers to provide rough drawings of cabinetry that is as economical as possible to construct. *Architectural Woodwork Standards,* Edition 1, 2009, should be consulted for precise drawings.

Chapter 9 discusses kitchens. With the background of the previous chapter, Chapter 9 enables a designer to make an intelligent selection of the appropriate cabinetry. Chapter 9 also covers the various appliances and the newest innovations in kitchen design. Chapter 10 describes bathrooms, both residential and institutional. One comment should be made about glass shower doors. I was building a new home and ordered a glass shower door. The salesman asked, "Where do you live?" which points to how building codes may differ even within one county. Chapters 9 and 10 were included because designers will be called on frequently to assist in the renovation of homes—including the very expensive areas of kitchens and bathrooms. These remodeling jobs will probably cost about 10 to 15 percent of the house's value. A full bath added to an older three-bedroom, one-bath house will not only guarantee recouping the cost of the improvements but will also increase the house's resale value.

A glossary of the words boldfaced in the text appears at the end of each chapter. This glossary can be used as an aid for students studying for exams. While compiling the index for this book, I realized that it can also be an aid in preparing for comprehensive exams, such as a final or the National Council for Interior Design Qualification (NCIDQ) exam. Thus, in the index I have listed (in parentheses) all the words in the chapter glossaries. I have done this for two reasons: First, the page number enables users to find the word (the usual purpose of an index); second, students can test themselves on whether they are familiar with the word and its meaning.

If one manufacturer seems to be given more emphasis than another in the text, it is not necessarily because its product is better than others on the market, but rather because the manufacturer has been extremely helpful in compiling this book (e.g., providing information and brochures, checking sections for accuracy, and, most important, providing photographs with which to illustrate the various sections). The photographs should not be glossed over as merely interesting illustrations but should be examined in detail as to how and where the material is used and the ambience it creates.

I am indebted to the many manufacturers and trade organizations that have so willingly sent me technical information, from which I have compiled up-to-date data. There are several associations that I wish to mention here who have allowed me to copy drawings and descriptions verbatim. Sherwin-Williams permitted me to use its training manual, which had easier-to-comprehend definitions than the ones in previous editions of this text. Sherwin-Williams also proofread the paint section. Thank you. The Wallcovering Association provided definitions for the various types of wallcovering. The Carpet and Rug Institute provided extensive information and granted permission to quote from its informative book, *Specifier's Handbook*. This handbook has been the basis for much of the information contained in Chapter 3. The National Oak Flooring Manufacturers Association (NOFMA) provides industry-wide standards for wood flooring installation. The Marble Institute of America reviewed the section on marble floors and walls, and the Tile Council of North America, the authority for all types of hard materials for floors and walls, provided the installation information for those materials. The Architectural Woodwork Institute supplied the information for Chapter 5, "Walls," and also for Chapter 8, "Cabinet Construction." Each of these associations is the recognized authority in its field. Thank you all for your help.

This textbook is a compilation of facts gathered with the help of high-speed Internet. I have tried to keep personal bias down to a minimum, but some may have crept in due to personal contact I had while building several houses for our own use. Many professionals also helped me ensure the accuracy and relevance of information presented in this text. For example, Robert Hanks of Bridgepoint Corporation realized that proper maintenance is vital to the durability of carpet, and Zach James of Sherwin-Williams was a great help in making sure that the information in Chapter 2 was current. (There have been many technical changes in that field due to environmental controls.)

Most of all, I would like to thank my husband, sculptor Frank Riggs, for serving as a house husband and for offering his support and encouragement. He also helped with some of the line drawings in the text. I am also grateful to him for not complaining about meals served at odd times during the writing of this edition (he is getting to be a better cook with each edition). Once I get on the computer, time is irrelevant.

Instructor Resources

All instructor resources can be downloaded from the Pearson Instructor Resources Website at www.pearsonhighered.com/irc.

J. Rosemary Riggs

For too many years, the fields of architecture and interior design have been treated as two separate disciplines involved in creating a pleasant living environment. The architect planned the exterior and interior of the home, often with little attention to where the furniture was to be placed. The interior designer had to contend with such things as walls that were not long enough to allow for placement of furniture, or heating vents placed directly under the bed or some other piece of furniture. On the other hand, designers would ruin the architect's designs by using the incorrect style of furniture, thereby spoiling the concept of the building.

Today, these problems are being resolved with many architects having interior designers on their staff, as is the case with the author of the Foreword. The result is that both disciplines cooperate from the very beginning of the project.

From the interior designer's point of view, this cooperation involves learning and appreciating the language and problems associated with architecture. The American Institute of Architects (AIA) is the professional organization for architects; the American Society of Interior Designers (ASID) and the International Interior Design Association (IIDA) are the professional organizations for interior designers. It is because of the professionalism of these organizations that the fields of architecture and interior design have gradually become aware of the need for closer cooperation. This book is dedicated to fostering that cooperation.

2 Lees Squared is a registered trademark of Mohawk Carpet Distribution, Inc.

3M is a registered trademark of the 3M Company

AccuGrain is a registered trademark of TT Technologies, Inc.

Aged Woods is a service mark of Jeffrey P. Horn

Alpha Base is a registered trademark of the Roppe Corporation

Anaglypta is a registered trademark of CMV Limited

Anystream 2000 is a registered trademark of the Speakman Company

Aquia is a trademark of Toto U.S.A., Inc.

ARGUS is a registered trademark of Pittsburg Corning Corporation

Armstrong is a registered trademark of AWI Licensing Company

Assurance Squared is a registered trademark of Mannington Mills, Inc.

Basic Coatings is a trademark of Betco Corporation

BioSpec is a registered trademark of Mannington Mills, Inc.

Brilliance is a registered trademark of the Masco Corporation

Classic-Craft is a registered trademark of Therma-Tru Corp.

Cleaner and Greener is a registered trademark of Leonardo Academy Inc.

Clorox is a registered trademark of The Clorox Company

Colonial Williamsburg is a registered service mark of The Colonial Williamsburg Foundation

Congoleum is a registered trademark of Congoleum Corporation

Core Weld is a registered trademark of Mannington Mills, Inc.

Corian is a registered trademark of E.I. du Pont de Nemours and Company

Cross-Grip is a registered trademark of Crossville, Inc.

Crossville is a registered trademark of Crossville, Inc.

cXc is a registered trademark of Milliken & Company

Decora is a registered trademark of Pittsburg Corning Corporation

DensArmor Plus is a trademark of Georgia-Pacific Gypsum LLC

DensGlass is a registered trademark of Georgia-Pacific Gypsum LLC

DensShield is a registered trademark of Georgia-Pacific Corporation

Designer Series is a registered trademark of Pella Corporation

DuPont is a registered trademark of E.I. du Pont de Nemours and Company

Durapalm is a registered trademark of Smith & Fong Company

Durasan is a registered trademark of National Gypsum Properties, LLC

Duroplex is a registered trademark of Dryvit Systems Inc.

Early Warning Effect is a registered trademark of RJF International Corporation

Easy Change is a registered trademark of Cutsforth Products, Inc.

ECOsurfaces is a registered trademark of Dodge Delaware Inc.

Elkay is a registered trademark of Elkay Manufacturing Company

Energy Star is a registered service mark of the Environmental Protection Agency

EverClean is a registered trademark of American Standard International Inc.

Everest is a registered trademark of Schlage Lock Company

EZ-Flex is a registered trademark of Chicago Metallic Corporation

FabriTRAK is a registered trademark of Fabri Trak Systems, Inc.

Faulux is a trademark of Dryvit Systems, Inc.

FiberFloor is a trademark of Tarkett Inc.

FloorScore is a registered trademark of Resilient Floor Covering Institute

FLUSHMATE is a registered trademark of the Sloan Valve Company

Focal Finish is a registered trademark of Focal Point Products, Inc.

Focal Point is a registered trademark of Focal Point Products, Inc.

Formglas is a registered trademark of Formglas Inc.

Formica is a registered trademark of The Diller Corporation

Frank Lloyd Wright Collection is a registered service mark of The Frank Lloyd Wright Foundation

Fresh Start is a trademark of Columbia Insurance Company

Gold Bond is a registered trademark of National Gypsum Properties, LLC

Green Sure is a registered trademark of The Sherwin-Williams Company

GREENGUARD Indoor Air Quality Certified is a registered certification mark of Air Quality Sciences, Inc.

H_2Okinetic is a registered trademark of Masco Corporation of Indiana

Harmony is a registered trademark of SWIMC, Inc.

i-ceilings is a registered trademark of AWI Licensing Company

iCore is a registered trademark of Mannington Mills, Inc.

iLevel Trus Joist Parallam PSL is a registered trademark of Weyerhaeuser NR Company

In2ition is a trademark of Masco Corporation of Indiana

Intersept is a registered trademark of Interface, Inc.

Jacuzzi is a registered trademark of Jacuzzi Inc.

Jenn-Air is a registered trademark of Maytag Properties, LLC

Johnsonite is a registered trademark of Johnsonite Inc.

Kallos is a registered trademark of Kohler Co.

Karbon is a registered trademark of Kohler Co.

Knape and Vogt is a registered trademark of Knape & Vogt Manufacturing Company

KOHLER is a registered trademark of Kohler Co.

Komotion is a registered trademark of Kohler Co.

Koroklear is a registered trademark of RJF International Corporation

Koroseal is a registered trademark of RJF International Corporation

Kotton is a registered trademark of Kohler Co.

Koverage is a registered trademark of Kohler Co.

Kurrent is a registered trademark of Kohler Co.

KWC Ono is a registered trademark of KWC AG

Environmental Concerns

In this chapter, you will:

- Analyze concepts and principles of sustainability related to building methods
- Identify environmentally focused organizations, systems, programs, and legal entities—and demonstrate knowledge of their functions
- Recognize the need for and methods related to improved workplace air quality worldwide, while appraising implications of design within a world context
- Demonstrate understanding of the need for industry-specific interior design regulations
- Relate the importance of federal laws related to energy conservation and indoor environmental quality

The Center for Environmental Study states:

> We stand at a crossroads. For the first time in history, we face the prospect of irreversible changes in our planet's life support systems. The growing human population and the by-products of our industrial and technological society threaten our planet's air, water, climate and biodiversity. These threats present a challenge to our society—to learn to live in harmony with our planet.

The World Resources Institute defines *sustainable development* as "growth that meets economic, social, and environmental needs without compromising the future of any one of them."

Members of the design community and the manufacturers they work with can, if they wish to, lead the way in helping save this country from overburdened landfills. This can be achieved in both the manufacturing process itself and in the disposal of the product once it is no longer needed. An example would be using linoleum instead of vinyl flooring. Linoleum is a product manufactured from natural materials and will, at the end of its use, gradually biodegrade.

Air Quality Issues

The increasing awareness of indoor air quality issues and the growing incidence of **sick building syndrome (SBS)** affecting worker comfort, well-being, and productivity highlight the vital need for improved workplace air quality worldwide. This syndrome is also commonly referred to as **building-related illness (BRI).**

Probably the best-known examples of environmental concerns are the precautions taken when dealing with asbestos. Before the mid-1980s, asbestos was among the ingredients used in the resilient flooring industry and in acoustical ceiling tiles. Since that time, this mineral has been proven injurious to health; therefore, the Resilient Floor Covering Institute (RFCI), a trade association of resilient flooring manufacturers, has developed a set of recommended work practices for the removal of resilient flooring, regardless of whether or not it contains asbestos. By following the RFCI's recommendations, contractors will ensure that the removal of an older resilient floor complies with the regulations established by the **Environmental Protection Agency (EPA)** and the **Occupational Safety and Health Administration (OSHA)** regarding the handling of asbestos-containing materials, should it be determined that removal is necessary.

Asbestos is hazardous to health when it becomes "friable," or free-floating and airborne, as in a dust form. However, asbestos used in resilient flooring manufactured prior to the mid-1980s is firmly encapsulated in the product because of the manufacturing process. The EPA has determined that encapsulated, or nonfriable, asbestos-containing products are not subject to extensive regulatory requirements as long as they remain in that state. Resilient flooring, either vinyl composition tile or sheet vinyl, is nonfriable provided that it is not sanded, sawed, or reduced to a powder by hand pressure.

To ensure that any asbestos present in resilient flooring does not become dislodged and friable, the RFCI has recommended work practices that specifically prohibit sanding, dry scraping, mechanically pulverizing, or beadblasting the resilient flooring or felt backing. In other words, workers should refrain from any procedure that produces dust.

Indoor Air Quality (IAQ)

The **indoor air quality (IAQ),** inside buildings, is affected by many factors. Many contemporary buildings are sealed environments in order to increase **HVAC** efficiency. This means that pollutants derived from such manufactured materials as synthetic fabrics, plywood, carpets, and paints are not cleared from the building.

Factors that can have a negative effect on health and comfort in buildings range from chemical and biological pollutants to occupant perceptions of specific stresses, such as temperature, humidity, artificial light, noise, and vibration. Sources of chemical indoor pollutants include outdoor air, the human body and human activities, emissions from building materials, furnishings and appliances, and the use of consumer products.

Microbial contamination is also a common indoor air quality issue. It is mostly related to the presence of humidity and moisture and is often linked to poor maintenance practices.[1]

INDOOR ENVIRONMENTAL QUALITY

The U.S. Environmental Protection Agency estimates that Americans spend about 90 percent of their day indoors, where the air quality can be significantly worse than outside. Indoor levels of pollutants may be two to five times higher, and occasionally more than 100 times higher, than outdoor levels. The Indoor Environmental Quality credit category promotes strategies that can improve indoor air as well as provide access to natural daylight and view and improve acoustics.[2]

A **NASA**-funded study directed by Dr. B. C. Wolverton, a 20-year veteran in horticultural research, found that the plants commonly used in interior plantscaping cleanse the air of many harmful pollutants, such as formaldehyde, benzene, and trichloroethylene. Common indoor plants may provide a valuable weapon in the fight against rising levels of indoor air pollution. The plants in your office or home are not only decorative, but NASA scientists have found them to be surprisingly useful in absorbing potentially harmful gases and cleaning the air inside modern buildings. The Plants for Clean Air Council recommends one potted plant for each 100 square feet of floor space.

When the air is too dry, people are susceptible to colds and flu. When the humidity is too high, people can develop other ailments. Through their natural processes of transpiration and evaporation, plants add moisture to the dry, overheated air often found in sealed office environments. At the same time, studies show that plants do not add moisture in significant amounts when the air is already moist. A study conducted at Washington State suggested that plants help regulate humidity. When plants were added to an office environment, the relative humidity stabilized within the recommended "healthy" range of 30 to 60 percent.

By using a professional plantscaping service, offices will have design uniformity throughout the workplace, plants in peak condition, and plants for correct light levels and HVAC conditions found in a particular workplace. TOPsiders Panel Mount Planters are aesthetically correct, 6" × 6" × 24" or 30" (this size provides proper scale and proportion for open plan systems), and are easily installed and taken down. TOPsiders have brackets for mounting on the tops, sides, and corners of partitions and are available in metal or marble finishes and 13 colors. (See Figure 1.1.)

FIGURE 1.1 Plants provide contrast to this interior. *Photo courtesy of August_0802/Shutterstock.*

Approaches to Environmental Issues

THE ENVIROSENSE CONSORTIUM

The Envirosense Consortium, Inc., is made up of companies working together to collect and share information through educational seminars and online resources, while moving forward to resolve issues related to indoor air quality and correlating environmental concerns. The Consortium focuses on a foundation of sustainable design and green building principles, particularly honing in on productivity of those who occupy commercial buildings.

The Consortium utilizes a strategy it identifies as a "Total Systems Approach," which integrates three primary aspects: product specification, building design, and construction. The impact of the systems on the biosphere is essential to the strategy. The Consortium provides seminars and a variety of online resources.[3]

CARPET AMERICA RECOVERY EFFORT (CARE)

The carpet industry is working to reduce its environmental footprint. The Carpet and Rug Institute (CRI) has developed three IAQ testing programs that minimize the potential of emissions from new carpet installations. The programs cover carpet, carpet cushion, and floor covering adhesive products. The goal for the programs is to help consumers with their buying decisions by identifying products that have been tested and meet stringent IAQ requirements.

CRI has culled data from 83 production facilities to detail methods being used by the carpet industry as it works to accomplish its goal of reducing its environmental footprint. These methods include decreasing overall energy consumption—including decreased reliance on "dirty fuels"—decreasing greenhouse gas emissions and other air pollutants, and decreasing water consumption. These methods have resulted in increased use of renewable energy sources. In addition, mills have invested in excess of $400 million to enhance sustainability, and action has been taken to expand the use of post-consumer waste materials in producing carpet.

CRI participates in the Carpet America Recovery Effort (CARE), which is a cooperative initiative between industry and the government. The work of this initiative centers on creating market-based resolutions related to reuse and recycling of post-consumer carpet.[4]

FIGURE 1.2 Green Seal emblem. *Courtesy of Green Seal Organization and Energy Star emblem.*

Green Seal

Green Seal, a nonprofit organization, works to educate purchasers, companies, and consumers in ways that will result in the development of a more sustainable planet. This organization focuses on an economy it identifies as a "Green Economy," which centers on renewability with minimal impact as it honors and protects the environment.

During the late 1980s, Green Seal recognized the absence of environmental certification programs in the United States, and it understood the need and desire of consumers to seek out green products. As a result, it moved forward to identify these products (see Figure 1.2) and provide environmental education.[5]

FIGURE 1.3 ENERGY STAR emblem. *Courtesy of the U.S. Environmental Protection Agency.*

ENERGY STAR

ENERGY STAR is a joint program of the U.S. Environmental Protection Agency and the U.S. Department of Energy that helps consumers save money and protect the environment through energy efficient products and practices. (See Figure 1.3.)

The results are in: Americans, with the help of ENERGY STAR, saved enough energy in 2009 to avoid greenhouse gas emissions equivalent to those from 30 million cars—all while saving nearly $17 billion on their utility bills. ENERGY STAR helps consumers make the energy efficient choice, without sacrificing features, style, or comfort.

Because a strategic approach to energy management can produce twice the savings—for the bottom line and for the environment—the EPA's ENERGY STAR partnership offers a proven energy management strategy that helps in measuring current energy performance, setting goals, tracking savings, and rewarding improvements.

The EPA provides an innovative energy performance rating system that businesses have already used for more than 130,000 buildings across the country. The EPA also recognizes top performing buildings and plants as ENERGY STAR Certified.[6]

LEED

LEED is an internationally recognized green building certification system, providing third-party verification that a building or community was designed and built using strategies aimed at improving performance across all the metrics that matter most: energy savings, water efficiency, CO_2 emissions reduction, improved indoor environmental quality, and stewardship of resources and sensitivity to their impacts.

Developed by the U.S. Green Building Council (USGBC), LEED provides building owners and operators a concise framework for identifying and implementing practical and measurable green building design, construction, operations, and maintenance solutions.

LEED is flexible enough to apply to all building types—commercial as well as residential. It works throughout the building lifecycle—design and construction, operations and maintenance, tenant fit out, and significant retrofit. And LEED for Neighborhood Development extends the benefits of LEED beyond the building footprint into the neighborhood it serves. The LEED green building certification program is a voluntary, consensus-based national rating system for buildings designed, constructed, and operated for improved environmental and human health performance. LEED addresses all building types and emphasizes state-of-the-art strategies in five areas: sustainable site development, water savings, energy efficiency, materials and resources selection, and indoor environmental quality.

LEED-certified buildings are designed to:

- Lower operating costs and increase asset value.
- Reduce waste sent to landfills.
- Conserve energy and water.
- Be healthier and safer for occupants.
- Reduce harmful greenhouse gas emissions.
- Qualify for tax rebates, zoning allowances, and other incentives in hundreds of cities.
- Demonstrate an owner's commitment to environmental stewardship and social responsibility.[7]

Environmentally Concerned Companies

The following companies, which manufacture products covered in this textbook, are all involved in recycling or preserving our planet in some way. Manufacturers of similar products may also be working on environmental concerns; specifiers who are concerned about the environment should check with other manufacturers as well.

AGED WOODS BRAND FLOORING

Aged Woods is precision-milled from old, destined-for-the-dump barn wood. Proper kiln-drying before milling assures a stable, bug-free floor. The look of these antique woods is natural resulting from a century or two of weathering and the signs of old-time craftsmen. Aged Woods floors add the rugged feel of Early America to residences, retail stores, restaurants, casinos, country clubs, and so on. (See Figure 1.4.) The authentic rustic character is unobtainable with new wood.[8]

FIGURE 1.4 Weathered Gray Barn Siding on the walls. *Photo courtesy of Aged Woods.*

SHAW INDUSTRIES

In 2009 the CARE Recycler of the Year Award was shared by Shaw Industries' Evergreen Nylon Recycling facility and the Los Angeles Fiber Company. From the time Shaw began operating the Evergreen plant in 2007, the company has recycled more than 220 million pounds of post-consumer Nylon 6 carpet and more than 36 million pounds of post-consumer carpet filler. In addition, significant fossil fuel usage was avoided through the plant's waste-to-energy processing.[9]

ENCORE INTERNATIONAL

The mission of Encore International is to utilize resources to protect the environment. Toward that end, the company is the largest user of scrap tire rubber in the nation. Each year, it converts more than 80 million pounds of tires into commercially used recycled rubber flooring. Due to the company's manufacturing process and responsiveness, its ECOsurfaces "recycled" rubber flooring has become widely recognized as a leader in rubber flooring.[10]

ECOkote 4341

ECOkote 4341 utilizes a renewable raw material and lacks heavy metals. As a result, it has garnered OMNOVA Solutions' E-CHEMISTRY designation. This designation recognizes a material's environmentally preferred qualities; it also illustrates OMNOVA's Vision 2014 goals to decrease operational environmental impact and increase availability of products offering sustainable features. The green, tri-bar "E" in the E-CHEMISTRY symbol featured on OMNOVA brands references the environmentally preferred qualities required for the product.[11]

KOHLER

KOHLER and many other manufacturers now produce toilets that flush 1.28 gallons of water or less, which can save a family of four as much as 16,500 gallons of water annually for each fixture—when compared to a 3.5 gallon toilet. Also available are water-conserving shower-heads and hand showers and faucets with low-flow aerators.

MILLIKEN

Milliken states that it is the only textile or carpet manufacturer that has garnered carbon negative status, as certified by the Leonardo Academy for Cleaner and Greener Energy and Emissions. As advised by Milliken, the term *carbon negative* means: "we capture and offset more carbon dioxide than we emit. We actually capture 10 times more CO_2 than we create globally—more than 10 million metric tons of it every year:

- Capturing CO_2 through the trees we plant and nurture in Milliken forests
- Offsetting it through use of alternative fuels
- Conducting energy audits, reducing consumption, and conserving energy."

Milliken advises that each product for which a spec is provided is carbon-neutral.[12]

MANNINGTON COMMERCIAL

Mannington Commercial is the first company certified to NSF's new American National Sustainability Assessment Standard for resilient floor covering.

tabrasa

tabrasa by Idea Paint is a water-based paint that can transform any working environment into a collaborative space with increased functionality that evokes creativity and impromptu teamwork. tabrasa transforms traditionally unusable office space into a dry-erase writing surface without seams, borders, or restrictions on size and placement.[13]

BENJAMIN MOORE

Benjamin Moore offers a completely acrylic interior latex primer sealer, which is a low-odor, low-**VOC,** spatter-resistant product. The company advises that this product is appropriate for facility management, commercial, and res A green building material.[14]

OCEANSIDE GLASSTILE

Oceanside Glasstile is made from a plentiful natural resource, silica sand. A significant quantity of the tile—as related to color—is developed from post-consumer recycled bottle glass and/or recycled glass that is culled from the company's manufacturing process. Another resource used by the company is glass from curbside recycling programs, glass that would alternatively likely find its way into landfills; Oceanside uses more than 2 million pounds of this glass each year.[15]

SHERWIN WILLIAMS

Sherwin Williams identifies two functions of the optimal green coating: the importance of delivering ultimate performance and the need to minimize impact on air quality. The company has created the GreenSure symbol as a guide to locating products that rise to the level of their highest green coating standard; these products meet or exceed regulatory requirements.[16]

TERAGREN FLOORING

Teragren flooring products are FloorScore certified. This certification indicates that the floors and adhesives have been tested for 78 **VOCs (volatile organic compounds)** and compliance with indoor air quality emissions. Teragren states that all of its select veneer and panels are SCS Indoor Advantage Gold-certified. As Teragren advises, this means these products are in compliance with California Special Environmental Requirements Specification 01350, which was developed to assure health as related to positive indoor air quality.[17]

THE WALLCOVERING ASSOCIATION

The Wallcovering Association began its work related to sustainability in 2008. In response to issues raised by its customers through such organizations as the United States Green Building Council (USGBC), the Wallcovering Association developed a comprehensive sustainability standard in conjunction with NSF International.[18]

glossary

Building-related illness (BRI). A variety of illnesses that have been attributed to toxic fumes inside a building.

Environmental Protection Agency (EPA). Organization that helps regulate environmental quality.

HVAC. Heating, ventilating, and air conditioning, almost always written using initials.

Indoor air quality (IAQ). The result of measuring the air inside a building for toxic emissions.

LEED. Leadership in Energy and Environmental Design.

NASA. National Aeronautics and Space Administration.

Occupational Safety and Health Administration (OSHA). Organization that regulates working conditions in businesses.

Sick building syndrome (SBS). The symptoms of an illness caused by toxic emissions inside a building.

Volatile organic compound (VOC). Toxic emissions from solvents in paints and other ingredients used in manufacturing.

endnotes

1. Envirosense Consortium, www.envirosense.org
2. EPA, www.epa.gov
3. Envirosense Consortium, www.envirosense.org
4. The Carpet and Rug Institute, www.carpet-rug.org
5. Green Seal, www.greenseal.org
6. LEED, www.usgbc.gov
7. Ibid.
8. Aged Woods, www.agedwoods.com
9. The Carpet and Rug Institute, www.carpet-rug.org
10. ECOREinternational, www.ecosurfaces.com
11. Omniva, www.omniva.com
12. Milliken Carpet, www.hospitalitycarpet.milliken.com
13. MDC, www.mdcwall.com
14. Benjamim Moore, www.benjaminmoore.com
15. Oceanside Glass Tile, www.ecohaus.com
16. Sherwin Williams, www.sherwinwilliams.com
17. Teragren, www.teragren.com
18. Wallcovering Association, www.wallcoverings.org

Paints and Wallcoverings

In this chapter, you will:

- Analyze the social and physical influences affecting historical changes in paint and its application

- Recognize the importance and components of flame-retardant paints, active devices that alert occupants to smoke, and devices that extinguish flames

- Explain the interaction of color with materials, texture, light, and form—and analyze the impact of color on interior environments

- Distinguish between solvent-based and water-based paint—and understand methods for applying paint to a variety of surfaces

- Discuss the importance of industry-specific regulations and federal law related to paints and wallcoverings

Paint can be thought of as pigments in a liquid medium, pigments that have been used to protect and decorate for tens of thousands of years. Even the earliest known humans living in caves used crude paints to create images that reflected the daily events of their lives.[1]

The earliest known paintings were found in the Lascaux caves in France and in the Altamira cave in Spain and date from as early as 15000 BCE. A thousand years later the Egyptians were making colors from soil and importing dyes such as indigo and madder. To this they added materials that are sometimes found in the paints that artists use: **gum arabic,** egg white, gelatin, and beeswax. The Egyptians also developed varnish from gum Arabic around 1000 BCE.

It is only since 1867 that prepared paints have been available on the American market. Originally, paint was used merely to decorate a home, as in the frescoes at Pompeii, and it is still used for that purpose today. Modern technology, however, has now made paint both a decorative *and* a protective finish. *Paint* is commonly defined as a substance that can be put on a surface to make a film, whether white, black, or colored. This definition has now been expanded to include clear films.

The colors used are also of great psychological importance. (See Figure 2.1.) A study by Johns Hopkins University showed that planned color environments greatly improved scholastic achievement. Most major paint companies now have color consultants who can work with designers on the selection of colors for schools, hospitals, and other commercial and industrial buildings. Today, paint is the most inexpensive method of changing the environment.

(a)

(b)

(c)

(d)

FIGURE 2.1 (a) Grey-blue gives a cool neutral background. (b) A green room has a cool ambience. (c) These vibrant colors give an active feeling to the room. (d) Yellow provides a warm cheery atmosphere. *Photos courtesy of The Glidden Company.*

Components of Paints

Lead was a major ingredient of paint from 1900 through the 1950s. Today's paint, though, represents a major departure from the paint of the early twentieth century. Recognizing the dangers of lead in paint, the Consumer Product Safety Commission has prohibited its use since 1978.[2]

Today's paint includes four basic ingredients:

1. **Pigments,** which give color to the coating.
2. **Binders,** which act like glue to hold the pigment particles together and provide washability/scrubbability, chemical resistance, durability, and other properties.
3. **Solvents,** which make the coating wet enough to spread on the surface.
4. **Additives,** which perform special functions.[3]

A typical coating product contains some or all of these ingredients. (See Figure 2.2.)

PIGMENTS

Pigments consist of powdered **solids** (such as *titanium oxides* and *silicates*) that give the coating its color and brightness qualities. These solids are important not only for their color, but also for their hiding ability. Generally speaking, the more pigment contained in a coating, the better it will hide, or obscure, the surface.[4]

Different pigments have different purposes. **Titanium dioxide** is the best white pigment for **hiding power. Extender** pigments, such as **calcium carbonate,** are inert. Masonry paints have a larger percentage of calcium carbonate than other paints. In flat paints, extenders improve sheen, uniformity, and touch-up capability. In eggshell and semi-gloss paints, extenders affect **gloss.**

BINDERS

Binders are liquid adhesives (such as **alkyd, resin,** latex, and **urethane**) that form a film of pigment particles on the surface. These sticky resins and other adhesives are the **vehicle** for binding the pigments to the surface, creating a strong and durable bond. Thus, the strength of the binder contributes to the useful life of the coating.[5]

Paints are generally classified as either solvent-based or water-based. Drying occurs when the water evaporates in water-base coatings, which are also known as latex coatings. Alkyds are coatings produced by reacting a drying oil with an alcohol.

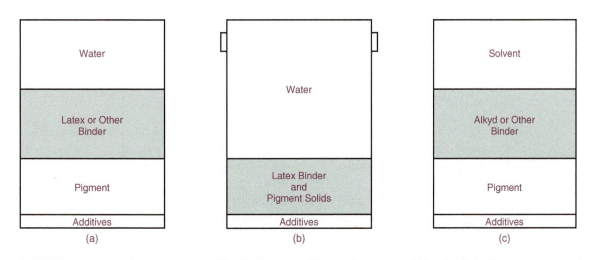

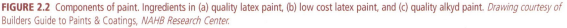

FIGURE 2.2 Components of paint. Ingredients in (a) quality latex paint, (b) low cost latex paint, and (c) quality alkyd paint. *Drawing courtesy of Builders Guide to Paints & Coatings, NAHB Research Center.*

Drying of the surface occurs by the evaporation of the solvent; curing of the resin occurs by oxidation.

SOLVENTS

Solvents are liquids (such as water and mineral spirits) that make the product easier to apply. Sometimes called *thinners*, solvents "carry" the other ingredients over the surface. Without solvents, the paint would be thick as molasses. The solvent helps the coating penetrate the surface and then evaporates as the coating dries.[6] Solvent-containing coatings can be used safely if overexposure is avoided and proper protective equipment is used.

The disposal of all types of coating materials is controlled by government regulations. Benjamin Moore has some useful tips for dealing with and disposing of leftover paint.

- Do not order more paint than is needed.

- Use all the paint you buy—an extra coat will give more protection.

- Leftover paint can be donated to a local charity, community beautification or service program, or neighborhood group that is assisting the elderly, disabled, or disadvantaged with the maintenance of their homes. Make sure the product you donate is in its original container with the label left intact.

- Leftover paint should *never* be poured down household sinks, toilets, or storm sewers. To dispose of latex paints, leave them to dry completely by removing the lid and allowing the water portion to evaporate. This should be done in an area that is away from children and animals. In most states, the container can then be disposed of in your household trash. Leave the lid off the can so that the disposal hauler can see that the paint is hardened.

- For disposal of solvent-based paints (alkyds or oil-based), contact the local or state government environmental control agency for disposal guidance.

ADDITIVES

Additives are special purpose ingredients (such as thickeners and mildewcides) that give the product extra performance features. The combination of these basic four ingredients is what creates a particular type and quality of coating.[7]

For example, mildewcides reduce mildew problems, which are a major cause of paint failure. Mildew is a fungus that thrives in good growing conditions—food, moisture, and warmth. Several mildew-cleaning solutions are available, the simplest of which is bleach and water.

To comply with the VOC emissions laws, more solids are being added, which makes the paint heavier bodied; therefore, it may take longer to dry. In many areas of the United States, the amount of VOC expressed in pounds of VOC per gallon is restricted.

Solvent-Based Paint

Solvent-based paints use a petroleum derivative (e.g., mineral spirits) as the solvent. These paints form a film through evaporation of the solvent and the **oxidation** of the resins. It takes longer for this type of paint to dry because the solvent takes between 24 and 48 hours to evaporate.[8]

Alkyds and oils are often used as the binder in solvent-based paints. Some people refer to paint by its binder, such as "oil" paint. Alkyds are coatings produced by reacting a drying oil acid with an alcohol. Drying of the surface occurs by the evaporation of a solvent; curing of the resin occurs by oxidation. The more oil there is in the formula, the longer it takes to dry, the better the wetting properties, and the better the elasticity.

Water-Based Paint

Water-based paints use water to make the paint easier to spread. Latex, **acrylic** latex, and vinyl acrylic are common binders found in water-based paints. When these paints are applied to a surface, the water evaporates, and individual resin particles become closely packed together. These resins unite to bind the pigment particles into a continuous film. Water-based paints dry when the water has evaporated, usually within four hours after application.[9]

Water-based latex paints perform well in a variety of weather conditions. Tiny pores permit water vapor to pass through dried latex paint film. This is often referenced as *breathability*, and it results in only small quantities of moisture being able to gather between the paint and the painted surface. Consumers who have had problems with peeling paint will likely find water-based latex paints a solution to their problems.[10]

A note of interest about latex: Latex paint is not made with latex rubber; in fact, the name *latex* is really just a decorative way to describe rubber-based paint. Latex paint is a carefully formulated polyvinyl material with acrylic resin and has never contained natural rubber, which is the allergen that causes allergic reactions. Therefore, people with sensitivity to latex products are in no danger of having a reaction to latex paint.[11]

Stain

Stains are coatings that also contain all four ingredients, but use a unique binder. The binder in stains causes the coating to penetrate deeply into the surface, leaving a thinner film on top. This extra-thin film allows the natural form of the surface to show through.

In addition to producing a thin film, stains have a low content of binder and pigment solids (in some cases as low as 14 percent), which results in a shorter life of the coating. Even so, stains are widely used on wood and other surfaces to show some of their natural beauty. Stains may be used for both interior and exterior applications. They are classified as either solid color or semi-transparent.

- Solid color stain permits the texture of wood to remain visible while hiding the grains so that the surface appears uniform.
- Semi-transparent stain allows both the texture and grain to remain visible.[12]

Non-grain raising (NGR) stains are more of a surface type of stain than a penetrating one but do not require sanding before application of the final coat. Both alcohol stains and NGRs are used industrially because of ease of application and fast-drying qualities.

Stain waxes do the staining and waxing in one process, penetrating the pores of the wood and allowing the natural grain to show, while providing the protective finish of wax. Real wood paneling may be finished with a stain wax provided that the surface of the wood will not be soiled.

Clear Coating

Some consumers do not want a paint or stain. Instead, they prefer a clear coating, one that has no noticeable pigment. This lack of pigment, however, does not necessarily result in a coated surface that remains unchanged in appearance, as the surface might appear lustrous or wet after an application of a clear coating.

Clear-coating products are often used when a consumer seeks additional protection for a surface. In this instance, a consumer might choose varnish or urethane. Urethanes, also known as polyurethanes, are often sought out due to their non-yellowing, stable qualities.

They can create a very strong film through a process such as moisture curing, which can occur through drying by solvent evaporation, or curing through reaction to water vapor, which requires relative **humidity** of greater than 20 percent.[13]

Government Regulations

Both the Occupational Safety and Health Administration (OSHA) and the Environmental Protection Agency (EPA) have strict rules governing not only the manufacture of paint, but also its application. Check the appropriate regulatory agency for the VOC limits in your area. Paint companies sell specially manufactured paints for sale in California, which has the strictest VOC regulations. Additional states are in the process of adopting these same regulations. Most paint companies have discontinued products that do not meet the new regulations and replaced them with VOC-compliant coatings.

Durability

Several paint companies have developed very durable acrylic latex paints.

Scuffmaster Armor is an exceptionally durable and cleanable multicolored or tone-on-tone water-based paint system for walls. Armor finishes blend durability and contemporary styling—providing an easily-customizable design option for demanding walls in commercial environments. Scuffmaster Armor is the only wall finish product made with polyurethane plastic. The result is a paint finish that withstands an incredible 25,000 ASTM scrub test cycle vs. only 3,900 scrubs for the leading water-based multicolor brand. Armor is also significantly more cleanable and stain-resistant than other multicolor products and ordinary acrylic latex paints.

Armor contains Microban antimicrobial product protection. This unique additive inhibits the growth of stain and odor-causing bacteria, mold, mildew, and other fungal growth on the dried paint film. Microban protection provides an added level of protection between cleanings but does not take the place of normal cleaning and disinfecting procedures and will not protect users or others against foodborne illness. Microban additives are EPA-registered for use in paint.

ScrubTough (ST) is a solid color eggshell paint that is over 20 times more durable than residential grade acrylic latex paint. ScrubTough excels in high traffic areas.[14]

PERMA-WHITE Mold & Mildew-Proof Interior Paint is a water-based paint specifically designed to withstand the harsh conditions of the moisture-prone areas in your home. Its unique formulation prevents mildew growth on the paint film even under the harshest conditions. This paint is self-priming, tintable to any color, and easy to apply; it also has a low odor.[15]

Gloss Ratings

The classification of paints according to gloss ratings depends on the surface's ability to bounce back varying amounts of light beamed on it. (See Figure 2.3.) These readings show the relative reflectance of the coated surface as compared with a smooth, flat mirror. The ratings in Table 2.1 measure the light reflectance of the surface only. Table 2.2 shows the percentage of light reflected by different hues and their different values.

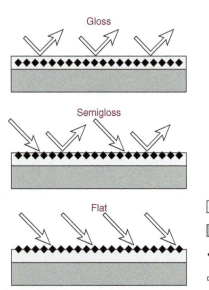

FIGURE 2.3 An illustration of how the pigment volume concentration affects the light reflectance. *Drawings courtesy of* Builders Guide to Paints and Coatings, *NAHB Research Center.*

Table 2.1 Standard Gloss Range for Architectural and Special Coatings

Name	Gloss Range	Test Method (ASTM D-523)
Flat	Below 15	85° meter*
Eggshell	5–20	60° meter
Satin	15–35	60° meter
Semi-gloss	30–65	60° meter
Gloss	Over 65	60° meter

*Angle at which light is reflected.

Source: Consumerism Subcommittee of the NPCA Scientific Committee acting with the Subcommittee D01.13 of the American Society for Testing and Materials (ASTM).

Table 2.2 Percentage of Light Reflected by Color

Color	Percentage of Light Reflected
White	89
Ivory	77
Canary yellow	77
Cream	77
Orchid	67
Cream grey	66
Sky blue	65
Buff	63
Pale green	59
Shell pink	55
Olive tan	43
Forest green	22
Coconut brown	16
Black	2

Lusters

A number of finishes, also known as **lusters,** are available in latex and alkyds. (See Table 2.3.) These finishes include:

- *Flat.* Flat paints offer the appearance of a very smooth, rich surface. They have the highest **pigment volume concentration (PVC),** are effective to meet the desire of little or no glare, and can withstand frequent washing. Flat paints are often used in libraries and guest rooms.

Table 2.3	Lusters Available in Exterior and Interior Paints		
Interior			**Exterior**
Alkyd	**Latex**		**Alkyd**
Gloss	Gloss		Gloss
Semi-gloss	Semi-gloss		Flat
Eggshell	Eggshell		
Satin	Satin		
Flat	Flat		
Velvet			

Source: Chart courtesy of Sherwin Williams, *Store Training and Reference* text.

- *"Eggshell," "Pearl," "Satin."* These paints offer greater reflection than flat paints, and surfaces where they are applied can generally tolerate only moderate scrubbing. Their PVC is lower than that of flat paint. These types of paints are often used in rooms where painted surfaces might need only a bit of washing.
- *Semi-gloss.* This paint type offers the appearance of a medium sheen, and it can be washed or scrubbed frequently. It has lower PVC than eggshell, and it is often used in kitchens and bathrooms.
- *Gloss or high gloss.* Consumers who seek very lustrous surfaces that can frequently be washed with ease will likely be drawn to this type of paint. It is a very low PVC product, and it will give rise to much more visible imperfections in surfaces.[16]
- *Enamel.* While the term **enamel** might at one time have identified a specific paint type, this distinction has become blurred since its use began. While once referencing a paint that was durable and provided a high-gloss finish for interior surfaces, current industry specifications now sometimes reference *flat enamels,* a term that refers to a flat appearance accomplished through specific additives. Manufacturers currently have come to frequently use the term *enamel* to reference a paint of higher quality, a product that will last longer and provide a smooth finish.[17] Enamels and other paints should be applied to a properly prepared surface. A glossy surface will not have **tooth** (the slight texture of a surface that provides good adhesion for subsequent coats of paint) and should be sanded with sandpaper or a liquid sanding material before the application of another coat of paint. Because of the VOC laws, latex enamels have been greatly improved; one advantage is that latex enamels do not yellow.

Primers

A primer is the first coat applied to the **substrate** to prepare for subsequent finishing coats and may have an alkyd or latex base. Some primers also serve as sealers and function on porous substrates such as some woods, and particularly on the paper used for **gypsum board.** These nonpenetrating sealers prevent the waste of paint caused by absorption of the porous materials and provide a good base for the final coats. Other primers are specially formulated for use on wood surfaces on which the natural dyes in the wood might cause unsightly stains. Some finish coats are self-priming, others require a separate primer. The manufacturers' specifications will provide this information.

The manufacturers have taken great efforts over the past few years to eliminate the odor in paint. Sherwin-Williams' Harmony product is based on a formula that works to decrease odors in the air. This formula, created without silica and utilizing the same technology as that in baking soda, provides greater durability and hide-ability, as well as ease in application. It is able to stand up to frequent washing while it maintains the capability of reducing ambient odors. Additionally, its antimicrobial properties resist mildew. Insofar as the duration during which Harmony will actively reduce odors, this is contingent upon the "concentration of the odors, the frequency of exposure and the amount of surface area being painted."[18]

Benjamin Moore Fresh Start QD-30 Stain Blocking Primer 202 is a general purpose solvent-thinned primer, sealer, and stain suppressor that:

- Has low odor.
- Effectively primes and seals charred or smoke-stained surfaces.
- Holds back water-soluble stains and most **"bleeding"** stains such as lipstick, crayon, and grease.
- Does not raise the grain of wood.
- Seals porous surfaces such as old flat wall paints and patches on previously painted surfaces.[19]

Manufacturers often formulate primers and finish coats that are intended to be used together as a system. It is good practice to use them together rather than choosing one manufacturer's primer and another manufacturer's topcoat.

Flame-Retardant Paints

Flame-retardant paints are for use in schools, hospitals, offices, factories, warehouses, homes, farms, or wherever there is a need for greater fire protection and lasting beauty. Most major paint companies manufacture a flame-retardant paint. Although they are not fireproof, they do reduce the flammability of the substrate.

For many commercial painting contracts, a Class A fire rating, defined as a **0-25 flame spread,** is required by law. Included in some technical data are the amounts of smoke developed and fuel contributed. More people die in fires from smoke inhalation than from the flames, so the smoke development figure may be more important than the flame spread figure.

When administered at normal film thickness, the majority of conventional paint systems will develop a Class A fire rating over a noncombustible, previously uncoated substrate. Substrates can provide a significant contribution to the overall flame-spread rating of the substrate and later coatings. Drywall contributes to a flame spread by a factor of about 10. Insofar as a substrate that burns easily, standard coatings will not provide efficacy in burn prevention, and flame spread of coating is enhanced by wood.[20]

Flame Control Coatings manufactures specialty coatings. The company offers two major product lines: flame-retardant paint and coatings and heat-resistant paint. The flame-retardant line, produced to meet building and fire codes, is made up of **fire retardant,** flame retardant, fire resistant, and **intumescent** paints and coatings. It also includes flame-retardant fabric coatings. This company's products are used in homes, restaurants, hospitals, and a variety of additional public buildings.

The company's Hi-Heat Coating line is designed to protect metal surfaces from corrosion and weather to 1,500°F; it provides high-temperature paints designed to create heat-resistant, durable finishes, protecting all types of metal surfaces from corrosion and weathering. This company also offers a number of fire-retardant paints, products that range from clear varnishes to flat, low, semi-, and high-gloss sheens.[21]

Varnish

Varnish is a transparent or pigmentless film applied to stained or unstained wood. Varnish dries and hardens by evaporation of the volatile solvents, oxidation of the oil, or both.

Where a hard, glossy finish that is impervious to moisture is needed, spar varnish is recommended for both outdoor and indoor use. In areas where moisture is not present, an alkyd varnish provides a slightly longer-lasting finish. Polyurethane is a synthetic resin used to make varnish resistant to both water and alcohol, thus making it usable as a finish on wood floors and tabletops. This type of varnish does not yellow or change color as much as conventional varnishes. The moisture-cured urethane varnishes are more durable but are also more expensive. Humidity must be rigidly controlled, because less than 30 percent humidity will cause too slow a curing time, and too high humidity will cause too fast a curing time, resulting in a bubbly surface. Where a satin finish is needed, the gloss varnish surface may be rubbed down with steel wool, or a satin varnish may be used.

Names of finishes do not seem to vary as much in opaque paints as they do in varnishes. One manufacturer will label varnish "dull" and another will call it "flat." Semi-gloss may also be called *satin* or *medium-rubbed-effect*, and high gloss may be called *gloss*. Remember that the paired names are synonymous.

Flame Control No. 166 Intumescent varnish is designed to be used on surfaces such as wood beams, columns, and ceiling panels, surfaces for which a maximum fire-rating finish—along with natural-wood appearance—is desired. As Flame Control No. 166 Intumescent varnish is softer than conventional coating, it is not designed to be used on hard-use areas such as shelving, doors, and floors.[22]

Varnish stains are pigmented and give a very superficial-colored protective surface to wood. They are used when a cheap, fast finish is wanted, but they never have the depth of color obtained with other stains. When the surface of a varnish stain is scratched, the natural wood color may show through.

Shellac

Shellac is a natural resin secreted by the lac bug. This secretion forms a protective cocoon for the developing lac bug larvae. The resin is harvested from tree branches, cleaned, and processed into dewaxed flakes which are then dissolved in denatured alcohol. It is available in clear, orange, and pigmented white. All dry to clear transparent films—the clear virtually colorless; the orange with an amber cast often preferred for antiques and for floors; and the pigmented white sometimes used as an undercoat on wood that is to be painted.

Shellac was the original glossy, transparent surface finish for furniture and was the finish used on what are now considered antiques. To experienced finishers and restorers of fine furniture the world over, shellac remains the finish of choice. One of the most elegant finishes for furniture, French polish, is done with shellac. Conservators and restorers of antiques continue to use shellac for refinishing antiques. And most importantly, its low toxicity makes it a perfect choice for items that come into contact with food or children's toys.

Shellac is often used as a sealer for knots and sappy streaks in new wood; porous surfaces before painting or papering; and hard-to-grip surfaces in need of priming. On a piece of furniture, shellac will turn white when exposed to water and/or heat. The urethane and oil varnishes have replaced shellac because they are not as quickly affected by heat and water.

Old shellac should never be used because as it ages its water resistance decreases and its drying time increases. When there is any doubt about the age of a particular can of shellac, it should be tested before it is used on a project. If the surface remains tacky, the shellac should be discarded in the proper manner because it may never harden.

One interesting note: A pharmaceutical shellac is used to coat pills so that they will dissolve slowly. Another grade of shellac is used to coat apples.

Lacquer

Lacquer is a paint that dries by solvent evaporation only and is applied by a spray gun. Lacquer may or may not contain pigments and is used commercially in the finishing of wood furniture and cabinets. A fine built-up finish may be achieved by many coats of lacquer, each of which is finely sanded before the subsequent coats.

Danish Oil

Danish Oil, which reinforces wood fibers beneath a surface, has been specially developed to provide a rich appearance without raising the woodgrain of interior woodwork. This oil creates a protective finish, one that will not wrinkle, peel, or crack. It is resistant to common chemicals and stains, as well as hot liquids and alcohol. Use of 700N Danish Oil is recommended for surfaces such as picture frames, gunstocks, paneling, wood doors and floors, and antiques. It also works for exterior wood not exposed to the sun.[23]

Novelty and Faux Finishes

Faux finishing is a painting technique used to create the illusion of texture on a wall. Faux finishes can be achieved by using sponges, special rollers, rags, and so on. The second color used is often of the same hue as the base and may be darker or lighter than the base. Most paint stores sell kits with a basecoat and a translucent color, opal or pearl **glaze,** or metallic such as gold, silver, or copper.

Several companies now manufacture commercial multicolored wall coatings. The finish consists of separate and distinct pigmented enamel particles suspended in an aqueous solution; the vehicle is a modified acrylate. These nonflammable coatings are sprayed over a special basecoat with a two-step final coat, often providing a textured surface.

Faulux finishes employ faux painting techniques for specific effects. They incorporate high-quality acrylics and enhancement agents and are derived from more than 2,000 scrub cycles, with an eye toward creating durable finishes that resist abrasion. The finishes are washable and Class A Flame Spread and Smoke Resistant. Additionally, they have very low VOCs.[24]

Duroplex is an interior textured acrylic wall finish designed to prevent mold and mildew. It was developed to provide abuse resistance and maximum longevity while providing extremely low long-term maintenance costs. Duroplex offers a 10-year warranty against surface mold and mildew growth, and the company states that it "contributes to a positive Indoor Air Quality (IAQ)." This product offers "a surface hardness that is 80% as hard as mild steel ... Class 'A' Flame Spread and Smoke Contribution rating." The company states that the product is "5 times less toxic than typical Type II vinyl wall covering under fire conditions." It is available in 86 standard colors and 25 textures in addition to custom color and texture options.[25]

Stenciling is a folk art form of wall painting that originated as an alternative to buying expensive rugs. Scenes of everyday life were cut into templates, then stenciled on walls and wood floors to create decorative patterns that actually resembled upscale wallpaper and rugs.

Color

Color is the least expensive way to dramatize, stylize, or personalize a home. Since colors affect us psychologically, they should be selected with this in mind. **Chroma** is the degree of saturation of a hue; a color at its full intensity has maximum chroma.

When studying paint chips, be sure to mask other colors on the same paint card. Otherwise, the eye will tend to blend all the colors together rather than see them individually. Another point to remember is that when matching a color, select a hue several shades lighter and of less intensity.

Reds and oranges will make a room exciting, and yellows, oranges, and reds will make a room seem brighter. A sunny room will appear cooler with greens, blues, and purples. To visually enlarge a room, choose white or yellow; conversely, to visually make a large room appear smaller, choose dark blues and dark brown. Blues and greens are peaceful hues. Notice the words *seem* and *appear* are used.

Sherwin Williams offers a very useful Color Visualizer on their Web site that can be used by homeowners and professionals alike. The visualizer allows the user to select from a broad palette of colors for different walls, trims, ceilings, accents, and upholstery colors. By just moving selected colors to these areas a whole room's color scheme can be seen. Glidden Paint Visualizer works on the same principle with various styles of rooms.

Application Methods

The four most common methods of applying paints are brush, roller, pad, and airless spray. Pads and rollers are do-it-yourself tools, although the roller may be used in remodeling if removal of furniture is impossible. Depending on the area, a combination of methods may be used. The best available equipment should be used, since poor-quality tools will result in a poor-quality paint job.

Whatever the material used for the bristles (hog hair or synthetic), brushes should have **flagged bristles** that help load the brush with more paint while helping the paint flow more smoothly. Cheap brushes have almost no flagging, which causes the paint to flow unevenly. Brushes are used for woodwork and for uneven surfaces, whereas rollers are used for walls and flat areas.

Spraying is used to cover large areas such as walls and ceilings in new homes, but especially for commercial interiors, where large expanses of surfaces require paint. Airless spraying uses fluid pressure. Most airless spraying uses undiluted paint, which provides better coverage but also uses more paint. All surrounding areas must be covered or masked to avoid overspray, and this masking time is always included in the painting contractor's estimates.

Spraying is 8 to 10 times faster than other methods of application. These figures refer to flat walls, but spraying is also an easier and more economical method of coating uneven or irregular surfaces than brushing, since it enables the paint to penetrate into the crevices. When spraying walls, the use of a roller immediately after spraying evens out the coat of paint.

Spraying is also the method used for finishing furniture and kitchen cabinets. For a clear finish on furniture and cabinets, heated lacquer is used, which dries quickly, cures to a hard film with heat, and produces fewer toxic emissions. Heated lacquer is formulated to be used without **reduction,** thus giving a better finished surface.

Surface Preparation

Surface preparation is the most important procedure to achieve a good paint finish. According to Sherwin-Williams "as high as 80% of all coating failures can be directly attributed to inadequate surface preparation that affects coating adhesion. Selection and implementation of proper surface preparation ensure coating adhesion to the substrate and prolong the service life of the coating system."

Renovation of buildings painted before the late 1950s must be done by a professional contractor trained in proper handling of lead-based paints. The new rules require lead-safe certification of renovators and companies that disturb six square feet of interior paint in a home, school, or day-care center built before 1978.

WOOD

Moisture is the major problem when painting wood. Between 5 to 10 percent moisture content is the proper range. Today most wood is **kiln-dried,** but exposure to high humidity may change that moisture content. Although knots in the wood are not technically a moisture problem, they do cause difficulties when the surface is to be painted, because the resin in the knots may bleed through the surface of the paint; therefore, a special knot sealer must be used. (See Table 2.4.)

All cracks and nail holes must be filled with a suitable wood putty or filler, which can be applied before or after priming according to instructions on the can or in the paint guides. Some woods with open pores require the use of paste wood filler. If a natural or painted finish is desired, the filler is diluted with a thinner; if the surface is to be stained, the filler is diluted with the stain.

If coarse sanding is required, it may be done at an angle to the grain; medium or fine sanding grits should always be used with the grain. Awkward places should never be sanded across the grain because the sanding marks will show up when the surface is stained.

PLASTER

When preparing a plaster wall for painting, it is necessary to ensure that the plaster is solid, has no cracks, and is smooth and level, since paint will only emphasize any problems. Badly cracked or loose plaster should be removed and repaired. *All* cracks, even if hairlines, must be repaired, since they will only enlarge with time. To achieve a smooth and level wall, the surface must be sanded with fine sandpaper; in addition, before the paint is applied, the fine dust must be brushed from the wall surface. Plaster is extremely porous, so a primer-sealer, which can be latex or alkyd, is required.

Table 2.4	Wood Classification According to Openness of Pores							
Softwood	Open Pores*	Color	Hardwood	Open Pores*	Color	Hardwood	Open Pores*	Color
Douglas-fir	No	Pale red	Ash, white	Yes	Light brown	Hickory	Yes	Light brown
Pine	No	Cream	Birch, yellow	No	Light brown	Maple	No	Light brown
Redwood	No	Dark brown	Cherry	No	Brown	Oak	Yes	Brown
			Chestnut	Yes	Light brown	Teak	Yes	Dark brown
			Elm	No	Brown	Walnut	Yes	Dark brown

*All wood with yes requires a filler due to open pores.

Source: www.fpl.fs.fed.us/documnts/fplgtr/fpl_gtr190.pdf

GYPSUM BOARD OR DRYWALL

On gypsum board, all seams must be taped, and nail or screw holes must be **set** and filled with spackling compound or joint cement; these filled areas should then be sanded. Care should be taken not to sand the paper areas too much because doing so causes the surface to be **abraded.** The abrasion may still be visible after the final coat has dried, particularly if the final coat has any gloss. Gypsum board may also have a texture applied, as described in Chapter 5, and the luster selected will be governed by the type of texture. Gypsum board must also be brushed clean of all fine dust particles before the primer is applied.

METAL

All loose rust, **mill scale,** and loose paint must be removed from metal before a primer is applied. There are many methods of accomplishing this removal. One of the most common and effective is sandblasting, in which fine silica particles are blown under pressure onto the surface of the metal. Small areas may be sanded by hand. For metals other than galvanized metal, the primer should be rust inhibitive and specially formulated for that specific metal.

MASONRY

Masonry usually has a porous surface and will not give a smooth topcoat unless block filler is used. Product analysis of block filler shows a much larger percentage of calcium carbonate than titanium dioxide. A gallon of masonry paint does not cover as large an area as a gallon of other types of paint, because the heavier calcium carbonate content acts as filler. One problem encountered with a masonry surface is **efflorescence,** which is a white powdery substance caused by an alkaline chemical reaction with water. An alkaline-resistant primer is necessary if this condition is present. However, the efflorescence must be removed before the primer is applied.

Writing Painting Specifications

The specifier should learn how to read the technical part of the product guide or find the same information on the label of the can. This is similar to the ingredients listed on food packaging.

The volume of solids is expressed as a percentage per gallon of paint. This percentage can vary from as much as 90 percent in some industrial coatings to almost 20 percent in architectural paints. If, for the sake of comparison, a uniform thickness of 1 1/2 **mils** is used, the higher percentage volume paint would cover 453 square feet and the lower percentage only 199 square feet. This, of course, means that more than twice as much paint of the lower volume would have to be purchased when compared with the higher volume. Thus, the paint that appears to be a bargain may turn out to cost more if the same result is to be achieved.

Painting specifications are a way of legally covering both parties in the contract between client and the painting contractor. There will be no misunderstanding of responsibility if the scope of the paint job is clearly spelled out, and most major paint companies include on their Web sites sample painting specifications covering terms of the contract. Some of these are more detailed than others. Table 2.5 will aid the designer in calculating the approximate time required to complete the painting contract.

A time limit and a penalty clause should be written into the contract. This time requirement is most important, because painting is the first finishing step in a project; if it is delayed, the completion date will be in jeopardy. The penalty clause provides for a deduction of a specific amount of money or a percentage for every day the contract is over the time limit.

Table 2.5	Coverage According to Method of Application	
Method	**Coverage per Hour**	
Brush	50–200 sq ft	
Roller	100–300 sq ft	
Spray	300–500 sq ft	

Information on surface preparation may be obtained from the individual paint companies. The problems created by incorrect surface treatment, priming, and finishing are *never* corrected by simply applying another coat of paint.

The method of application should be specified: brush, roller, or spray. The method must suit the material to be covered and the type of paint to be used. Moreover, primers or base coats must be compatible with both the surface to be covered and the final or topcoat. When writing painting specifications, items to be excluded are just as important as items to be included. If other contractors are present at the site, their work and materials must be protected from damage. One area should be designated as storage for all paint and equipment, and this area should have a temperature at or near 77°F, the ideal temperature for application of paints. The painting subcontractor should, on a daily basis, remove all combustible material from the premises.

The specifier should make certain that inspections are made before the application of each coat because these inspections will properly cover both client and contractor. If some revisions or corrections are to be made, they should also be written down and an inspection made before proceeding. Table 2.6 explains the average coat requirements for various interior surfaces.

Cleanup is the responsibility of the painting contractor. All windows and glass areas must be free of paint streaks or spatters. The area should be left ready for the succeeding contractor to begin work without any further cleaning.

Some states do not permit interior designers to sign a contract for clients, whereas other states do allow this. The designer should check state laws to see whether he or she or the client must be the contractual party.

Table 2.6	Average Coat Requirements for Interior Surfaces	
Surface	**Vehicle**	**Number of Coats**
Woodwork	Oil gloss paint	2–3 coats
	Semi-gloss paint	2–3 coats
Plaster	Alkyd flat	2–3 coats
Drywall	Alkyd flat	2–3 coats
	Vinyl latex	3 coats
Masonry	Vinyl latex	3 coats
Wood floor	Enamel	3 coats

USING THE MANUFACTURER'S PAINTING SPECIFICATION INFORMATION

All paint companies have different methods of presenting their descriptive literature, but a designer with the background material this chapter provides will soon be able to find the information needed. For example, first the material to be covered is listed, then the use of that material, and then the finish desired. Let's use wood as an example: The material is wood, but is it going to be used for exterior or interior work? Is it going to be left natural, stained, or painted? If interior, is it to be used on walls, ceilings, or floors? Each different use will require a product suitable for that purpose. Floors will obviously need a more durable finish than walls or ceilings.

Another category will be the final finish or luster—flat, semi-gloss, or gloss? Will you need an alkyd, a latex, or, for floor use, a urethane? This category is sometimes classified as the vehicle or generic type. The schedule then explains which primer or sealer is to be used for compatibility with the final coat. After the primer, the first coat is applied. This coat can also be used for the final coat or another product may be suggested. Drying time for the different methods of application may also be found in the descriptive literature. Two different times may be mentioned, one *dust free*, *tack free*, or *to touch*, meaning the length of time it takes before dust will not adhere to the freshly painted surface. Sometimes a quick-drying paint will have to be specified because of contaminants in the air. The second drying time is recoat time; this is important so that the application of the following coat can be scheduled.

The spreading rate per gallon will enable a specifier to calculate approximately how many gallons are needed for the job, thereby estimating material costs. Sometimes, in the more technical specifications, an analysis of the paint's contents is included both by weight and by volume. The most important percentage, however, is the volume amount, because the weight of solids can be manipulated, whereas volume cannot. This is the only way to compare one paint with another. The type and percentage of these ingredients makes paints differ in durability, application, and coverage. Some paint companies now have these percentages printed on the label of paint cans.

If paint is to be sprayed, there will be information on lowering the **viscosity** and, for other methods of application, the maximum reduction permitted without spoiling the paint job. Most catalogs also include a recommended thickness of film when dry, which is expressed as so many mils **DFT (dry film thickness).** This film can be checked with specially made gauges. The DFT cannot be specified by the number of coats. The film thickness of the total paint system is the important factor and not the film thickness per coat.

Troubleshooting Paint and Varnish Application

The ideal temperature for application of paints and varnishes is 77°F, but effective application can be achieved at temperatures ranging from 50°F and higher. This includes air temperature, surface temperature, and paint temperature. Cold affects viscosity, causing slower evaporation of the solvents, which results in sags and runs. High temperature lowers viscosity, also causing runs and sags. High humidity may cause less evaporation of the solvent, giving lower gloss and allowing dirt and dust to settle and adhere to the film. Ventilation must be provided when paints are being applied, but strong drafts will affect the uniformity of luster.

Today, most paints start with a base and the pigments are added according to charts provided to the store by the manufacturer. Sometimes it is necessary to change the hue of the mixed paint, and this can be done by judicious addition of certain pigments. It is vital that the designer be aware of the changes made by these additions. Any hue can now be matched by using a **spectrophotometer** that is hooked up to a computer, which can provide the necessary formula.

Wallpaper and Wallcovering

As wallpaper and wallcoverings are sold mainly in paint stores, this subject is covered within this chapter.

The Chinese mounted painted rice paper on walls as early as 200 BCE. Although mention of painted papers has been historically documented as early as 1507 in France, the oldest fragment of European wallpaper, from the year 1509, was found in Christ's College, Cambridge, England. This paper has a rather large-scale pattern adapted from contemporary damask. Seventeenth-century paper, whether painted or block printed, did not have a continuous pattern repeat and was printed on sheets rather than on a roll, as is the modern practice. The repetitive matching of today's papers is credited to Jean Papillon of France in the late seventeenth century. In the eighteenth century, England and France produced hand-printed papers that were both expensive and heavily taxed.

Leather was one of the original materials to be used as a covering for walls. The earliest decorated and painted leathers were introduced to Europe in the eleventh century by Arabs from Morocco and were popular in seventeenth-century Holland.

Flocked papers were used as early as 1620 in France. The design was printed with some kind of glue, which was then sprinkled heavily with finely chopped bits of silk and wool, creating a good imitation of damask or velvet. Flocked papers have been popular in recent decades but are less so now.

Scenic papers, many of them hand-painted Chinese papers, were used in the eighteenth century. Wallpapers were imported to the United States during the second quarter of the eighteenth century. Domestic manufacturing did not start until around 1800; even then, the quality was not equal to the fine imported papers.

After the Industrial Revolution, wallpaper became available to people of more moderate means, and the use of wallpaper became more widespread. In the late nineteenth and early twentieth centuries, William Morris stimulated interest in wallpapers and their designs. In the first half of the twentieth century, papers imitating textures and having the appearance of wood, marble, tiles, relief plasterwork, paneling, and moiré silk were in demand. In the late 1930s and 1940s, wallpaper was in style, but in the 1960s, 1970s, and 1990s painted walls were in fashion.

Today, designers are more discriminating with the use of wallpapers or, as they will be referred to from now on, *wallcoverings*. This change of name results from the fact that, although paper was the original material for wallcoverings, today's wallcoverings may be all paper, paper backed by cotton fabric, vinyl face with paper or cotton backing, or fabric with a paper backing. (See Basic Wallcovering Backings, p. 32.)

Most wallcoverings consist of three layers. Each layer provides a significant function. Beginning with the top surface and proceeding to the back, the layers are:

- **The decorative layer.** This is generally the thinnest layer and is made up of the inks applied to the top of the intermediate layer. This layer, which sometimes offers a protective polymer coating, is usually the factor that attracts the consumer to the wallpaper, as it provides the "decoration" for the wall.

- **The intermediate layer.** The decorative layer, which provides the background color for the wallpaper, is printed on the intermediate layer. The intermediate layer is often, but not always, white. It can be as thin as less than 1 mil and as thick as 10 mils (1 mil referencing 1/1000th of an inch).

- **The third layer.** This layer, which can be made of materials from woven fabrics to lightweight paper products, is the backing of the portion of wallcovering seated against the wall.

While those interested in purchasing wallcovering often focus on the surface, the backing is equally significant, particularly in consideration of function.[26]

CHARACTERISTICS OF WALLCOVERINGS

Wallcoverings are made of a variety of grounds and substrates, which provide their features, the most relevant of which are explained in the following list.

- **Washability.** The ability to endure occasional sponging with designated types of detergent solutions.

- **Scrubbability.** The ability to endure scrubbing with a brush and designated types of detergent solutions.

- **Stain resistance.** The ability to endure stain removal without showing significant change in material.

- **Abrasion resistance.** The ability to endure mechanical actions, such as scrubbing, rubbing, and scraping.

- **Colorfastness.** The ability to endure light exposure during a measured period of time, while resisting change or loss of color.

- **Peelability.** The ability of a decorative surface to resist dry peeling, while maintaining a continuous layer of the substrate to be used as a liner for hanging new wallcovering (though it must be noted that the covering must be scraped away prior to application of paint).

- **Strippability.** The ability to endure drystripping, while allowing for a minimum of paste or adhesive residue.

- **Prepasted.** An indication that the substrate has been treated with an adhesive activated by water.

It should be possible to determine strippability or peelability prior to purchase through a notation in a sample book or on a bolt label.[27] To assist consumers across the globe, a standard set of international wallcovering symbols has been established. (See Figure 2.4.)

PATTERNS

Today's wallcovering manufacturers produce pattern collections based on consumer responses to specific patterns and demand for certain styles, obtained through market research. Thus, designers can use these collections to create the desired atmosphere in a client's installation.

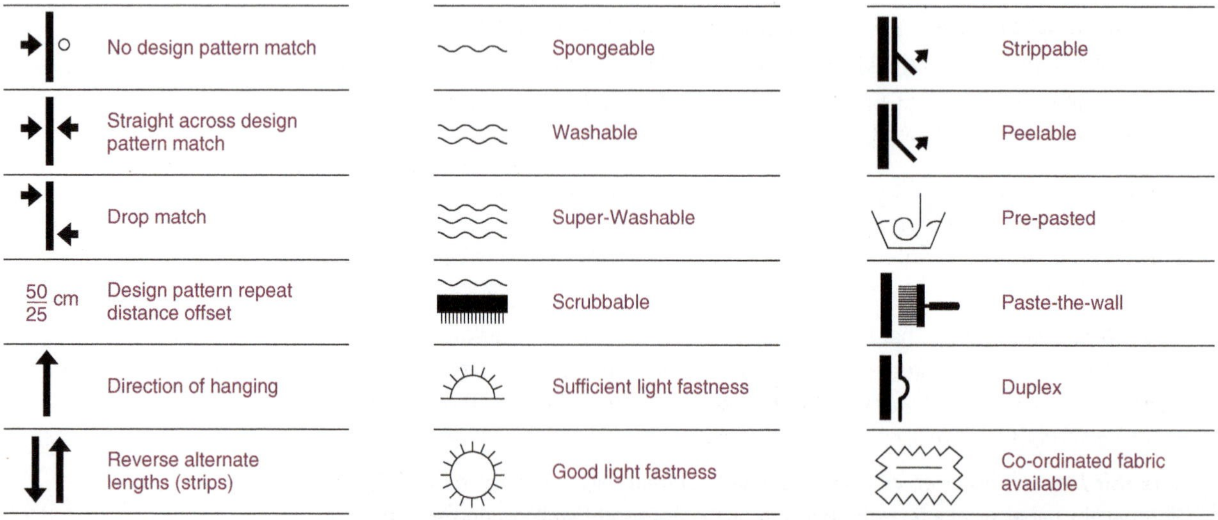

No design pattern match		Spongeable		Strippable		
Straight across design pattern match		Washable		Peelable		
Drop match		Super-Washable		Pre-pasted		
Design pattern repeat distance offset		Scrubbable		Paste-the-wall		
Direction of hanging		Sufficient light fastness		Duplex		
Reverse alternate lengths (strips)		Good light fastness		Co-ordinated fabric available		

FIGURE 2.4 International wallcovering symbols.

Many of the Early American designs were inspired by valuable brocades and tapestries that adorned the homes of wealthy individuals. Several contemporary companies have made arrangements with museums to produce historical designs. For example, Bradbury & Bradbury Art Wallpapers have meticulously researched historical collections from the last quarter of the nineteenth century through the Art Deco period.

Previous collections of Brunschwig & Fils have originated from such diverse sources as the Musee des Arts Decoratifs in Paris, the Royal Pavillion in Brighton, the Metropolitan Museum of Art in New York, Historic Deerfield in Massachusetts, and The Henry Francis Du Pont Winterthur Museum in Delaware.

Scalamandre produces wallpaper for the Preservation Society of Newport County and Prestwould Plantation. F. Schumacher & Company's licensors include Colonial Williamsburg, Historic Natchez, the National Trust for Historic Preservation, the Library of Congress, the Edith Wharton Restoration, and the Victorian Society. Thibaut Wallcoverings issues the Historic Homes of America collections based on samples from actual homes. Because Thibaut's papers are produced in large quantities, they are less expensive than the hand-screened prints mentioned previously, which are printed in smaller quantities.

Murals are large-scale, non-repeat, hand-screened papers done on a series of panels, usually installed above a chair rail. They may be scenic, floral, architectural, or graphic in nature. **Chinoiserie** murals are the perfect background for English-style furniture. Murals are sold in sets varying from two to six or more panels per set. Each panel is normally 28 inches in width and is printed on strips 10 to 12 feet in length. The height of the designs varies greatly, but most are somewhere between 4 and 8 feet. Some graphics go from ceiling to floor. Murals for rec rooms are also available.

For a French ambience, wallcoverings with delicate scrolls or lacy patterns are suitable for a formal background, whereas **toile-de-Jouy** and checks are appropriate for the French Country look. Wallcoverings for a formal English feeling range from symmetrical damasks to copies of English chintzes and embroideries.

Geometrics include both subtle and bold stripes and checks, as well as polka dots and circles. The colors used will dictate where these geometrics can be used.

Trompe l'oeil patterns are three–dimensional designs on paper. Examples of realistic designs are a cupboard with an open door displaying some books, a view from a window, or a niche with a shell top containing a piece of sculpture. These trompe l'oeil patterns are sold in a set.

DYE LOTS

During the manufacturing process, a pattern and dye-lot or run number is printed on each roll of wallcovering. The pattern number identifies a particular design and color. The dye-lot number represents a particular group of rolls that are printed on the same print run.

The dye-lot number will change each time there is a change in the printing process. Different dye-lot numbers could signal variables such as changes in tonal color, vinyl coating, and/or consistency of the embossing process being used during the production of wallcoverings. Any of these variables could show a slightly different color in the wallcoverings, sometimes visible only when two different dye-lots are compared with each other.

It is very important that the interior designer or installer check each individual roll in any wallcoverings shipment to ensure uniformity in color and pattern. It is also important to record pattern numbers and dye-lot or run numbers for future reference in case additional material is required.[28]

PATTERN MATCH

One significant aspect of preparing to hang wallcovering relates to pattern match. The major types of match to be considered are included in the following list.

- *Random match.* The pattern of strips will match, regardless of adjoining strip positions. It is sometimes preferred to reverse alternate strips in order to reduce negative visual effects, such as color or shading variations.

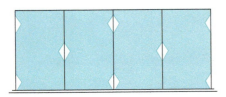

- *Straight-across match.* Due to design elements, all adjoining strips must be lined up to match and correctly repeat the pattern. All strips are the same at the ceiling line.
- *Drop match.* Two types of drop match are discussed in the following list:
  - *Half-drop match.* Design elements are set diagonally, so every other strip must be the same at the ceiling line. Numbering strips prior to hanging will help to alleviate confusion.
  - *Multiple-drop match.* Due to design elements, four or more strips are required for vertical design repetition.[29]

TYPES

Wallcovering textures include **embossed** papers, which hide any substrate unevenness; solid-color fabrics; and grasscloths. Embossed papers have a texture rolled into them during the manufacturing process. Care should be taken not to flatten the texture of embossed papers when hanging them.

Anaglypta is an embossed product made from paper that has been imported from England since the turn of the century. Designed to be painted, this wallcovering provides the textured appearance of sculptured plaster, hammered copper, or even hand-tooled Moroccan leather. Anaglypta is a highly textured wallcovering that is applied to the wall like any other product. Once painted, the surface becomes hard and durable. The advantage of Anaglypta is that not only is it used on newly constructed walls in residential and commercial interiors, but it may also be applied after minimal surface preparation. In older dwellings and Victorian restoration projects, Anaglypta provides the added advantage of stabilizing walls while covering moderate cracks and blemishes. **Friezes,** with ornate embossed designs, are part of the heavier Lincrusta line, the original extra-deep product. Low-relief and vinyl versions are also available.

Fabrics should be tightly woven, although burlap is frequently used as a texture. Walls are pasted with a nonstaining paste and the fabric, with the selvage removed, is brushed onto the paste.

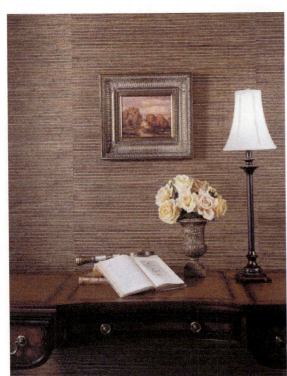

FIGURE 2.5 Grasscloth wallcoverings add interest and texture to a wall. *Photo courtesy of MDC Wallcoverings.*

- *Coated fabric.* Fabric substrate is coated with liquid vinyl or acrylic. The decorative layer is printed on the coating. This covering is often thought of as ideal in low-moisture areas, as it has great breathability.
- *Fabric-backed vinyl.* A substrate is laminated to a solid vinyl decorative surface. Type I fabric-backed vinyl is light duty and is generally most effective in locations such as hospitals, hotels, and offices. Type II fabric-backed vinyl is medium to heavy duty and is generally most effective in areas such as classrooms, hallways, and entryways.[30]

Custom Laminations, Inc. can apply a backing of paper to fabrics for wallcoverings, for upholstery, and for tablecloths. Their VKC Vinylizing is a clear film that is factory applied to the surface of your wallpaper. The colors, tone, and surface of your wallpaper are permanently locked in and protected forever. This means you can use the most beautiful wallpapers in the harshest of environments. Delicate, expensive papers can be used in bathrooms, kitchens, hallways, restaurants, or anywhere. This patented process comes with a three-year limited warranty. For all the benefits of VKC-FP Vinylizing wallpaper with a built-in flame retardant, use VKC-FP Vinylizing for Wallpaper. Wallcoverings processed with VKC-FP Vinylizing for Wallpaper will pass most flammability requirements.

Grasscloth, bamboo, and paper weaves are the natural choice for today's environmentally sensitive designers. With a wide array of textures, patterns, and color shadings, this sophisticated and elegant selection offers a style to complement any décor. (See Figure 2.5.) The designs truly harmonize pattern and texture with a quality that stimulates multiple sensory perceptions at once. These unique, very high-end wall treatments are ideal for specialty commercial projects such as boutique hotels and resorts, hotel ballrooms, restaurants, casinos, spas, cruise ships, conference or meeting rooms, executive offices, reception rooms or atriums, and high end retail. All patterns are crafted on 36-inch paper backing and meet the Class A fire rating.[31]

Flocked papers, as mentioned previously, are among the oldest papers on record. They are currently manufactured by modern methods but still resemble pile fabrics. One problem with flocked papers is that through abrasion or constant contact with the face of the paper, the flocking may be removed and a worn area will appear. A seam roller should never be used to press down seams because that also flattens the flocking.

Foils and mylars provide a mirrored effect with a pattern printed on the reflective surface; because of this high shine, the use of a lining paper is suggested to provide a smoother substrate. Foils conduct electricity if allowed to come in contact with exposed wires. Some older foils had a tendency to show rust spots in moist environments. This is why most "metallic" wallcoverings are presently made of mylar, a hard plastic film that offers an impressive appearance along with durability. Foils are used to best effect in well-lit rooms because the light reflects off the foil surface and enhances the effect of the wallcovering.

Kraft papers are usually hand–printed patterns on good-quality kraft paper similar to the type used for wrapping packages. Unless specially treated, these kraft papers absorb grease and oil stains, so care should be taken in placement (i.e., it might not be a good idea to use them in kitchens).

Leather is cut into designs or blocks (much like blocks of Spanish tiles) because the limited size of the hide prohibits the use of large pieces. The color of the surface varies within one hide and from one hide to another; therefore, a shaded effect is expected.

Coordinated or companion fabrics are used to create an unbroken appearance where wallcovering and draperies adjoin. (See Figure 2.6.) When using coordinated paper and fabric, the wallcovering should be hung first; then the draperies can be adjusted to line up with the pattern repeat of the wallcovering. The tendency is to call these companion fabrics *matching fabrics*, but this is incorrect. Paper or vinyl will absorb dyes in a different manner than will a fabric, and many problems will be resolved by strict avoidance of the word *matching*. One way of avoiding color differences is to use the actual fabric and have it paper backed for the wallcovering.

FIGURE 2.6 A good example of coordinating wallcovering and fabric. The Sweet Life Collection from Thibaut. *Photograph courtesy of Thibaut Wallcoverings.*

SURFACE PREPARATION

The secret to a good installation is surface preparation, because any little level discrepancy will be magnified after installation. Several manufacturers produce similar products.

Lining paper is an inexpensive blank paper recommended for use under foils and other fine quality papers. It absorbs excess moisture and makes a smoother finished wall surface. A heavier canvas liner is available for "bad walls."

Solid vinyl is made of a vinyl film laminated to a paper or fabric substrate. It is thought of as more durable than fabric-backed or paper-backed vinyls, due to application in a liquid form. High washability and scrubbability are also characteristic of solid vinyl.[32]

PRINTING OF WALLCOVERINGS

The most widely used print processes are surface, flexographic or flexo, gravure, and screen. Each is utilized to create a desired type of appearance, suitable to a specific range of uses.

Surface printing, which utilizes lightweight urethane print cylinders for production, is generally used to reproduce a stencil-like effect for use in styles such as traditional florals and juvenile or country motifs. The print design matches up to raised sections of the roller, which is cut away to leave behind the elevated design. Then ink is applied to the raised sections, and the ink is transferred from the design to wallcoverings. A different roller must be used for each color.

Flexographic printing, which can be used for dainty designs, is somewhat like surface printing; however, the cylinders are flexible and are often made with rubber. This type of printing is desirable for designs such as colonial and country.

Gravure printing, a photochemical process that involves pressure and the use of ink, relies on small ink reservoirs and provides an effect that can be described as photographic. It is the most costly of the printing manufacturing processes, as the costly photochemical process requires a copper-plated cylinder, but offers the designer the opportunity of achieving 25.4 microns (micrometers).[33]

Screen printing (flat screen) is frequently used for specialty and customized pieces. The process begins with flat mesh screens secured in a frame. The image section is placed onto the mesh screen, which is covered with a resist. The resist—frequently wax—provides a block against all openings within the screen, except those within the design image. Then a rubber squeegee is manipulated to move the ink across the screen. This pushes the ink through openings onto the wallcovering.

Screen printing (rotary screen) is often used for vinyl prints or designs requiring bright laydown of solid color, which developed as a replacement for hand screen printing. This is a high-speed production technique that involves ink fed into the inside core of a cylinder. An internal squeegee blade presses ink through the image section of the screen. Special ink must be utilized, and the process requires a heat tunnel to activate a blowing agent needed for the ink to expand in order to produce the desired three-dimensional appearance.[34]

There are several means by which a wallcovering can be hand printed. One of these methods is silk screening, which originated in Japan, evolving from the tradition of stencil printing on fabric. The intricate and detailed paper stencils used by printers were fragile and tore easily. To remedy this, strands of silk or human hair were glued to the stencil to increase its strength and durability. The process evolved to where printers stretched a piece of woven silk on a wood frame. The stencil was then glued directly onto the silk, thus creating the first "silk screen."

The following information from Bradbury & Bradbury explains the process of modern custom silk screening, as illustrated in Figure 2.7. Printing tables are 90 feet long and each holds six rolls of wallpaper. Metal rails along the side of the table have adjustable knobs which are set to the particular repeat of the pattern to be printed. A complex pattern for an average size Victorian room can require over 1,000 individual impressions.

Artwork is done by hand in the traditional manner by painting on acetate or cutting a stencil using a graphic arts film. A separate stencil must be prepared for each different color in the pattern, and all must align perfectly. Once a full repeat has been cut or painted by hand, computers aid in replicating the artwork.

Screen making is done by coating a silk screen with a photosensitive emulsion, essentially creating a large piece of film. The screen and artwork are sandwiched in a large vacuum frame and exposed to light. Areas exposed to the light become impervious; the other areas can be washed out. In the early days printers used silk on a wooden frame; today monofilament polyester is used on a titanium frame.

FIGURE 2.7 Process of silk screening. (a) Printing table. (b) Artwork done by hand. (c) An actual silk screen. (d) Paint being forced through the screen. *Photo courtesy of Bradbury & Bradbury Art Wallpapers.*

Paint is forced through the stencil using a plastic-bladed squeegee. The printer must skip every other repeat to prevent the silk screen frame from falling in wet ink. Each screen lays down one color. If a pattern has eight colors it must be printed eight times with eight different screens. (See Figure 2.8.)

Block printing is the process of producing a pattern on a wallcovering by means of wood blocks, into which the design is cut. For the most part, it has been replaced by silk screening.[35] (The block printing method is similar to the process used to make potato blocks in grade schools.)

Because silk screening and block printing are hand processes, a machinelike quality is not possible or perhaps even desirable. The pattern does not always meet at the seams as positively as does the roller–printed pattern. Matching should be exact in the 3- to 5-foot area above the floor, where it is most noticeable.

One of the best characteristics of the Duraprene-based line from Blumenthal is its great absorption of inks and surface dyes in patterning. The coverage and saturation is much deeper and better than standard vinyl printing, and the printing is much more stable. The feel of the product is also an added bonus. It is sumptuous and soft to the touch like brushed leather.

FIGURE 2.8 A collection of Persian-styled wall and ceiling papers that has been designed to capture the exotic feel of the "Luxurious East." *Photo courtesy of Bradbury & Bradbury Art Wallpapers.*

BASIC WALLCOVERING BACKINGS

As discussed earlier, while the wallcovering surface generally receives the most consumer attention, the backing must also be seriously considered. Types of backing include:

- **Paper.** Paper is generally utilized on vinyl-coated papers, paper-backed vinyls, and specialty products.
- **Woven fabric (scrim or osnaburg).** Scrim is utilized primarily in light-construction areas; osnaburg is utilized primarily in medium to heavy-usage areas.
- **Non-woven fabric.** This is created in a variety of grades in order to provide better printing techniques while maintaining strength.
- **Latex acrylic.** This is beneficial to provide improved handling and stability for fabric wallcoverings.[36]

Most machine-printed wallcoverings are **pretrimmed** at the factory, but the majority of handprints and handmade textures are untrimmed. This selvage (excess trimmed edge) should be removed from the wall and seams closed within one hour.

PACKAGING AND SIZES

Wallpaper comes in different lengths and widths; although usually priced by the single roll, it is packaged either as double or triple rolls. People may find this packaging versus pricing situation difficult to understand. However, wallpaper is packaged this way because double and triple rolls provide more usable wallpaper than single rolls. In addition, extra wallpaper allows for a margin of error during hanging and will help avoid the problem of finding the same dye lot or printing run when reordering to complete a project or if the wallpaper on the wall has been damaged and needs repair.

A basic reason for production in a variety of widths derives primarily from the variety of equipment among factories.

- Metric single rolls, also known as Euro rolls, provide 27 1/2 to 29 square feet. Double rolls provide 56 to 58 square feet.
- The American single roll, which generally has approximately 36 square feet of surface, is gradually being discontinued.[37]

When ordering handprints from a retail store, there are a few things one must know:

- There is a cutting charge if the wallcovering order requires a cut bolt.
- Buyers should remember the information on dye lots.
- Because these types of wallcovering are handmade there may be a design difference in positioning.

COMMERCIAL WALLCOVERINGS

Commercial wallcovering, also known as contract wallcovering, is made specifically for commercial use in buildings such as offices, hospitals, schools, apartments, and hotels. For this wider covering, it is important to hire a skilled professional paperhanger and helper. Commercial wallcovering is 52 or 54 inches wide and sold by the lineal yard, and it must be manufactured to meet or surpass physical and performance characteristics as specified in Federal Specification CCC-W408, characteristics related to abrasion and stain resistance, washability, scrubbability, flammability, and tear strength.[38]

Tensile strength is the single most important performance feature in commercial wallcovering. Abrasion resistance is important throughout but mainly in key areas such as outside corners.

As mentioned previously, mildew is a problem with walls. Whether using paint or wall-covering, the walls should be washed with a mixture of equal parts of household bleach and water. The correct paste or adhesive will help prevent mildew from forming under newly hung wallcovering. If proper precautions are not taken, any mildew that forms will permanently discolor the wallcovering. However, most adhesives contain an antifungal protection.

ESSEX 54" wallcoverings last three times longer than paint and may be specified in both Type I and Type II. ESSEX is available at 54" wide in Type I and Type II construction and is now available with 30 percent recycled content.

With plain textures, grasscloths, and suedes, it is advisable to reverse the direction of every other strip of wallcovering. This will provide a better finished appearance, particularly if one side of the wallcovering happens to be shaded a little more than the other.

Koroseal wallcoverings are produced using 100 percent water-based inks and cadmium-free materials. Koroseal and Vicrtex Wallcoverings feature Koroklear and Vicrklear topcoatings, providing stain and mildew resistance. Koroseal wallcoverings also have a built-in safety feature—Early Warning Effect—which gives off an odorless, colorless vapor when heated to 300 degrees, activating ionization smoke detectors.

Made with woven glass textile yarns that provide a textured finish, Texturglas wall finish strengthens, stabilizes, and protects new and existing walls. When coated with latex paint, the product does not trap moisture like conventional vinyl wallcoverings; the finish provides mold and mildew control and can be used to cover up problem surfaces. The material is reusable, recyclable, and emits no VOCs.

All textile wallcoverings have good acoustic qualities and good energy-saving insulation qualities. Textiles may be backed by paper, and the fiber content may be 100 percent jute or a combination of synthetics and wool and jute and/or linen and cotton. These textiles usually have a flame-spread rating of 25 or less.

Concourse, available from Eurotex Inc., is made of a wool-nylon blend and offers a woven flatweave texture, a texture very similar to that of wool. Concourse absorbs sound and is flameproof. It is often used as a backdrop for display and allows for display items, such as posters, to be attached with pushpins and sticky fabric strips.[39]

Sisal is another wallcovering that has high sound absorption and is static free. Rolls are either 4 or 8 feet wide and 100 feet long. Sisal has an extremely prickly texture, as opposed to the other textiles, but this roughness can be an asset, as in the following case: A school found that when students lined up outside the cafeteria, the wall against which they were standing became dirty and defaced by graffiti. Installation of sisal prevented both problems and reduced the noise level.

OMNOVA produces its vinyl wallcovering in several stages. Briefly, they are mixing, calendering, printing, and embossing. (Recently, they have expanded their printing repertoire to feature new inking systems that include metallics, pearlescent pigments, and interference inks.) During the final stage of production, a finish or topcoating is applied to the surface of the wallcovering. Several options of finish are available including a basic clear vinyl coating, our proprietary Prefixx stain-resistant topcoating, and Tedlar, a clear film laminate from DuPont.[40]

Some companies offer special-order printing of wallcoverings for a minimum order of 50 rolls or more. These prints may be designs already in a company's line or custom designs. Because such special orders involve hand printing, they are expensive; however, they may solve a particular design problem. In large public buildings, different colors of vinyl wallcovering are often used as a path finding aid for patrons. The different colors can indicate certain floors, or areas or departments within that floor.

SPECIALTY WALLCOVERINGS

For areas that experience light traffic or other special circumstances, specialty wallcoverings may be used. Though many specialty wallcoverings have been replaced by vinyl wallcoverings that approximate a similar look but provide greater durability, a variety of specialty wallcoverings are of historical significance and can still be produced by custom firms or specialty manufacturers.

- **String effects.** Wallcoverings with very fine vertical threads laminated to a paper substrate.
- **Acoustical.** Wallcoverings created mostly of human-made polyester and olefin fibers; tested for the Noise Reduction Coeeficient (NRC), it is frequently used in locations such as operable walls, panels, vertical surfaces, and areas where noise reduction is important; often used in restaurants, hallways, meeting rooms, theaters, and auditoriums.

POLYOLEFIN/SYNTHETIC TEXTILE WALLCOVERINGS

Polyolefin/synthetic textile wallcoverings, which are useful in high-traffic areas and are often made with polyolefin yarns, are generally hung with acrylic or paper backing. This type of wallcovering was created to provide the appearance of a natural textile but also provide strong abrasion and stain resistance.

- **Nonwoven.** Flexible, soft, and pill-resistant textile wallcovering made entirely of solution-dyed, short fibers mechanically interlocked into a continuous structure; completed with a heatset, latex back with an eye toward fiber lock; often used for tackable walls.
- **Woven.** Transparent textile wallcovering; allows sound travel through the material for absorption into a backerboard underneath; manufactured with continuous yarns woven perpendicular to one another in a warp/length and weft/width, which is similar to a grid pattern.
- **Digital borders, murals, and wallcoverings.** Permits expression of a variety of styles and designs, based on consumer choice.
- **Natural/organics.** Flexible, continuous rolled wallcoverings created from organic materials; can be produced as woven, nonwoven, or bonded finish and with or without a substrate/backing.
- **Cork/cork veneer.** Created by shaving cork veneer from cork planks or blocks and then laminating them to a plain or colored substrate; has variegated texture without a specific design or pattern; provides some sound resistance; often used to produce bulletin boards.
- **Grasscloth.** Created from woven native grasses bonded to a paper substrate.
- **Leather/suede.** Created from animal hide.
- **Jute.** Created of woody fibers from the inner bark of plant stems and can be woven into flexible material.
- **Silk.** Natural filament fiber from silkworms.
- **Wood surfaces.** Natural wood veneers.
- **Underliner.** Available in a variety of weights as a nonwoven product or plain paper stock; appropriate for use on most wall surfaces, including sheetrock, cinder block, paneling, and plaster; utilized to create a smooth surface for wallcovering installation.[41]

INSTALLATION

Before hanging any wallcovering, the walls must be sized. Sizing is a liquid applied to the wall surface that serves several purposes: It seals the surface against alkali, also known as hot spots; reduces absorption of the paste or adhesive to be used; and provides tooth for the wallcovering. The sizing must be compatible with the paste or adhesive used. There are many types of wallcovering adhesives, each formulated for various performance characteristics. Some adhesives are formulated for lightweight and delicate fabrics while others are designed to adhere heavyweight vinyl and acoustical coverings.

While all wallcovering adhesives are composed with some type of biocide system, wallcoverings are dissimilar in open-time, wet-tack, ease of application, and strippability. Adhesives are usually applied on the back of the wallcovering with a pasting machine or a roller.[42]

However, nonwoven acoustical wallcoverings require the adhesive to be applied to the wall using a brush or roller. Consult the manufacturer's installation instructions.

The major categories of adhesives are discussed in the following list:

- **Prepasted activators.** Generally thought of as cleaner and simpler in application than many other adhesives; valuable in matching patterns; designed to help in hanging prepasted wallcoverings through activation of existing adhesive.

- **Clear adhesives.** Starch-based; offer additional open time; offer simpler cleanup than that offered by clay-based adhesives; wheat or corn based.

- **Clay adhesives.** Generally more difficult to clean up than clear adhesives; starch-based; clay inserted as filler for purpose of increasing wet-tack; often used by retail consumers; thought of as higher level of wet-tack.

- **Vinyl-over-vinyl.** Like border adhesives, developed to bond to vinyl; contains synthetic polymers; may contain starch and other items to ease application; needs greater attention during application, due to permanence after drying; developed for purposes of hanging borders to wallcovers and hanging new wallcoverings to existing wallcoverings.[43]

Paste or adhesive is applied by means of a wide brush to the back of the wallcovering. Particular attention should be paid to the edges because this is where any curling will occur. The wallcovering is folded or **booked,** without creasing. This allows the moisture in the adhesive to be absorbed by the fabric substrate or backing, thus allowing for any shrinkage before the wallcovering is applied to the wall surface. Booking also makes an 8- or 9-foot strip easier to handle and transport from the pasting table.

MAINTENANCE

All stains or damage should be corrected immediately. Paper-faced wallcoverings should be tested to ascertain if the inks are permanent before cleaning fluids are applied. Vinyls may be scrubbed with a soft brush and water if they have been designated scrubbable. Foils are washed with warm water and wiped with a soft cloth to avoid any scratching. Hard water tends to leave a film on the reflective surfaces of foil.

Grasscloths, suedes, fabrics, sisal, and carpeting may be vacuumed to remove dust. Again, always follow the manufacturer's instructions for maintenance. Vinyl-covered walls should be washed at least once or twice a year. Grease and oils, in particular, should not be allowed to accumulate.

bibliography

Builders Guide to Paints and Coatings. Upper Marlboro, MD: NAHB Research Center in cooperation with Sherwin-Williams.

Entwisle, E. A. The Book of Wallpaper, A History and an Appreciation. Trowbridge, England: Redwood Press Ltd., 1970.

50,000 Years of Protection and Decoration: History of Paint and Color. Pittsburgh, PA: Pittsburgh Plate Glass Company.

Morgans, W. M. Outlines of Paint Technology. Vol 1 Painting and Coating Systems Guide. Cleveland: Sherwin-Williams, 2004–2005.

Schumacher. A Guide to Wallcoverings. New York: Schumacher.

S.T.A.R.T., Paint, Stains and Clear Coatings. Sherwin-Williams.

Wallcoverings Association, 401 North Michigan Avenue, Suite 2200, Chicago, Illinois 60611.

glossary

Abrade. To scrape or rub off a surface layer.

Acrylic. A synthetic resin used in high-performance water-based coatings.

Additives. One of the four major ingredients in paint. They have special properties as needed.

Alkyd. Synthetic resin modified with oil.

Binder. The solid ingredients in a coating that hold the pigment particles in suspension and attach them to the substrate. Consists of resins (e.g., oils, alkyd, latex). The nature and amount of binder determines many of the paint's performance properties—washability, toughness, adhesion, color retention, and so on.

Bleeding. When color penetrates through another coat of paint.

Booked. Wallpaper that has folded the pasted sides together in order to carry from the cutting table to the wall.

Calcium carbonate. An extender pigment.

Chinoiserie. (French) Refers to Chinese or Oriental designs or themes.

Chroma. A measurement of color; the degree of saturation of a hue.

DFT (dry film thickness). The mil thickness when coating has dried.

Efflorescence. A white alkaline powder deposited on the surface of stone, brick, plaster, or mortar caused by leaching of water.

Embossed. Paper covered with raised designs.

Enamel. Broad classification of paints that dry to a hard, usually glossy finish.

Extenders. Ingredients added to paint to increase coverage, reduce cost, achieve durability, and alter appearance. Less expensive than prime hiding pigments such as titanium dioxide.

Faux. French for "false" or "artificial" (pronounced fo). Includes marbling or other imitation finishes.

Fire retardant. A coating that (1) reduces flame spread, (2) resists ignition when exposed to high temperature, or (3) insulates the substrate and delays damage to the substrate.

Flagged bristles. Split ends.

Frieze. A type of wallcovering popular in the early 1900s. Generally a pictorial border which ran above the door height or, in dining rooms, above the plate rail.

Glaze. Clear medium that, when added to paint, makes the paint more transparent, giving depth to the desired faux finish.

Gloss. Luster. The ability of a surface to reflect light. Measured by determining the percentage of light reflected from a surface at certain angles. (See Table 2.1.)

Gum arabic. A solid resinous material that can be dissolved and will form a film when the solution is spread on a surface and the solvent is allowed to evaporate. Usually a yellow, orange, or clear solid.

Gypsum board. Thin slabs of plaster covered with a heavy-weight 100 percent recycled paper covering.

Hiding power. The ability of paint film to obscure the substrate to which it is applied. Measured by determining the minimum thickness at which film will completely obscure a black and white pattern.

Humidity. The amount of water vapor in the atmosphere.

Intumescent. A mechanism whereby fire-retardant paints protect the substrates to which they are applied. An intumescent paint puffs up when exposed to high temperatures, forming an insulating, protective layer over the substrate.

Kiln-dried. Lumber dried in an oven to a specific moisture content.

Luster. *See* **Gloss.**

Mill scale. An almost invisible surface scale of oxide formed when iron is heated.

Mils. Measurement of thickness of film. One one-thousandth of an inch. One mil equals 25.4 microns (micrometers).

Mural. A scene made up of several panels in sequence.

Non-grain raising (NGR). A type of stain.

Oxidation. Chemical reaction upon exposure to oxygen.

Pigment. Insoluble, finely ground material that gives paint its properties of color and hide.

Pigment volume concentration (PVC). When used in connection with paint, pigment volume concentration.

Pretrimmed. Materials in which selvages or edges have been removed.

Reduction. Lowering the viscosity of paint by the addition of a solvent or thinner.

Resin. A solid or semisolid material that deposits a film and is the actual film-forming ingredient in paint. Can be natural or synthetic. *See* **Gum arabic.**

Set. Countersunk below the surface of the gypsum board.

Solids. The part of the coating that remains on a surface after the vehicle has evaporated. The dried paint film.

Solvent. Any liquid that can dissolve a resin. Generally refers to the liquid portion of paints and coatings that evaporates as the coating dries.

Spectrophotometer. An instrument used for comparing the color intensities of different spectra.

Substrate. Any surface to which a coating is applied.

Tensile strength. Resistance of a material to tearing apart when under tension.

Titanium dioxide. A white pigment providing the greatest hiding power of all white pigments. It is nontoxic and nonreactive.

Toile-de-Jouy. *French.* Usually a monochromatic pastoral scene on a light colored cotton material.

Tooth. The slight texture of a surface that provides good adhesion for subsequent coats of paint.

Urethane. An important resin in the coatings industry.

Vehicle. Portion of a coating that includes all liquids and the binder.

Viscosity. The ease of flow in paint, e.g., water based paints flow more quickly than oil based paints.

0-25 flame spread. Lowest acceptable rating for commercial and public buildings.

endnotes

1. *History of Paints and Coatings. National Paint and Coatings Association,* www.paint.org

2. Wallcoverings Association, www.wallcoverings.org

3. S.T.A.R.T., *Paints, Stains and Clear Coatings,* Sherwin-Williams, p. 2.

4. Ibid.

5. Ibid.

6. Ibid.

7. Ibid.

8. Ibid.

9. Ibid.

10. Paint, www.paint.org

11. *Paints, Stains and Clear Coatings,* p. 6.

12. Ibid.

13. *Builders Guide to Paints and Coatings.* Upper Marlboro, MD: NAHB Research Center, 1993, pp.12 and 13.

14. Scuffmaster, www.scuffmaster.com

15. Rustoleum, www.rustoleum.com

16. *Builders Guide to Paints and Coatings,* pp. 12 and 13.

17. Ibid, p. 12.

18. Sherwin Williams, www.sherwin-williams.com

19. Benjamin Moore, www.benjaminmmoore.com

20. Sherwin Williams, www.sherwin-williams.com

21. Flame Control Coatings, www.flamecontrol.com

22. Ibid.

23. Log Home Supply, www.loghomesupply.com

24. Triarch Inc., www.triarchinc.com

25. Ibid.

26. Wallpaper Installer, www.wallpaperinstaller.com

27. Vinyl in Design, www.vinylindesign.com

28. MDC Wallcovering, www.mdcwall.com

29. Wallcoverings Association, www.wallcoverings.org

30. Ibid.

31. MDC Wallcovering, www.mdcwall.com

32. Doityourself, www.doityourself.com/stry/typesofwallpaper

33. Wallcoverings Association, www.wallcoverings.org

34. Doityourself, www.doityourself.com/stry/typesofprinting

35. Doityourself, www.doityourself.com/stry/decordictionary

36. Doityourself, www.doityourself.com/stry/wallcoveringbackings

37. Wallcoverings Association, www.wallcoverings.org

38. Doityourself, www.doityourself.com/stry/commercialwallcovers

39. Eurotex Inc., www.eurotexinc.com

40. Omnova, www.omnova.com

41. Doityourself, www.doityourself.com/stry/commercialwallcovers

42. Surface Materials, www.surfacematerials.com

43. Ibid.

3 Carpet

In this chapter, you will:

- Describe the social and physical influences affecting historical changes in carpet, including its composition and uses

- Discuss types of carpet and their fabrication and installation methods, as well as maintenance requirements

- Examine the importance of industry-specific regulations and federal law related to carpet

- Develop understanding of the importance and components of flame-retardant carpet fibers

- Recognize principles of acoustical elements, thermal systems, and telecommunication equipment as relevant to carpet and carpet cushion

History of Carpet

When and where carpets were first knotted is unknown, but it is generally believed that nomadic tribes in central Asia were some of the first rug weavers in areas known today as Turkey and Iran (Persia). The climate was very cold and the mountain ranges in these areas were perfect for raising sheep, the source of carpet wool. We know very little of early weavings, as the materials used were all perishable, and only a few rug fragments woven before the fifteenth century have survived.

Fortunately, while archeological excavations were ongoing in a valley of the Altai mountain range in lower Siberia during 1947–1949, a Russian archeologist, S. J. Rudenko, made an exciting discovery. He found an extremely well-preserved rug in a burial tomb that belonged to the prince of Altai, who lived in the fifth century BCE.

This rug, today called the Pazyryk carpet, survived in good condition on a lucky combination of circumstances. It appears that shortly after the prince's grave-mound was completed, it was plundered by robbers who tunneled into the mound and removed all the precious objects. However, they had no interest in the Pazyryk carpet and left it behind. Later, a torrent of water rushed into the opening the robbers made into the grave-mound and filled the chamber. The huge volume of water turned into ice, freezing the Pazyryk carpet until it was discovered 2,500 years later. Incredibly, the rug was well preserved. The design, dyes, and construction were all of the highest quality, indicating that the weaver was knowledgeable and experienced, and that rug weaving was at quite an accomplished level in the fifth century BCE.

The Pazyryk carpet measures 6' × 6'6" and is exhibited in the Hermitage Museum in St. Petersburg. The design has a large geometric center field area composed of squares and is framed by two main borders. One border features deer, and the other features warriors on horseback.

Additional historical carpets created during the sixteenth through eighteenth centuries still exist today and can be viewed in European museums. These immense pieces, which were woven with painstaking detail requiring thousands of work hours, were generally woven for royal palaces.

When Henry IV demanded, during the early seventeenth century, that a specific room be fitted in the Louvre for carpet weaving, this was an unprecedented royal mandate, one that resulted in the aesthetic aspect of royal taste being reflected in carpet—and the practical aspect of a proliferation of growth in the carpet-weaving industry.

Early significant contributions to the industry continued in Spain, where the Spanish were the first Europeans to create hand-tied **pile** rugs. During the eighteenth century, Thomas Whitty of Axminster, in England, developed the first loom machine capable of weaving carpets. By the nineteenth century in France, Joseph-Marie Jacquard had developed a method to produce patterned or figured weaving.[1]

In Colonial America, the first floor coverings were herbs, rushes, or sand spread on the floor. Later, rag rugs made from clothing scraps and hooked or braided mats were used. Affluent settlers, however, introduced America to prized Oriental rugs, which they brought with them to the New World. Oriental rugs may have as many as 500 to 600 knots per square inch and are named for the pattern and district where they are woven.

The first U.S. carpet mill was started in Philadelphia in 1791. America's most important historic contribution to the industry was the invention of the power loom by Erastus Bigelow in 1841. Years later, the first Brussels (looped-pile carpet) was made here, utilizing the **Jacquard** method of color pattern control. With further modification, the first **Wilton** carpets were also woven in the United States. By the late nineteenth century, a great deal of machinery and skilled labor found its way to the United States, and the roots of many of today's major carpet manufacturing firms were established.

For centuries, a handmade wool rug has been a status symbol. In the past, the high price of a wool rug or carpet was probably due to the tremendous labor involved; for example, an ancient weaver needed 900 days to complete an Oriental carpet.[2] It is interesting to note that whereas Europeans buy old Oriental rugs, Americans prefer to buy new ones.

Thus, carpets were originally for the wealthy. Today, because of modern technology, carpet is one product that gives more value for the money than in the past.

This chapter deals with carpet, defined as fabric used as a floor covering, rather than rugs (carpet cut into room or area dimensions and loose laid). Area rugs also include Oriental rugs, **Kilims, Rya** rugs, **Dhurries,** and American Indian rugs.

Note: According to historians, American Indians developed weaving traditions independently from other civilizations.

Much of the information on weaves, pile, and so on, may also apply to area rugs.

Area rugs are gaining in popularity because of the mobility of our population. Rugs can be used in many ways: as accents over existing carpet, to highlight a wood floor, or to spotlight area groupings.

Based in Dalton, Georgia, the Carpet and Rug Institute (CRI) is a nonprofit trade association representing the manufacturers of more than 95 percent of all carpet made in the United States, as well as their suppliers and service providers. It coordinates with other segments of the industry, such as distributors, retailers, and installers, to help increase consumers' satisfaction with carpet and to show them how carpet creates a better environment.

CRI is the leading source for science-based information and insight on how carpet and rugs create a better environment indoors. CRI's mission is to provide the carpet industry, its customers, and the public with facts that enable informed flooring choices. CRI offers considerable information about carpet selection, installation, and care and cleaning to consumers, as well as commercial and institutional users, at www.carpet-rug.org.[3]

Functions of Carpet

According to the CRI, the following are the primary features of carpet:

- **Comfort and warmth.** Carpet can often impart a more inviting feeling to a room than a hard surface would, and it offers a comfortable place where people can work, visit, or play. As a technical benefit, carpet offers R-value (thermal resistance). When utilized in colder seasons or climates, carpet actually aids in energy conservation, as it holds onto the heat it has absorbed.

- **Style and aesthetic benefits.** There is no limit to the impact carpet can impart to a living or work space. The panoply of color and style choices allow for ultimate personalization.

- **Protection.** A slip or fall can happen when least expected. Through its cushioning, carpet helps to guard against this possibility. If a slip or fall should occur, carpet can decrease the likelihood of harm, as it provides a soft spot to land.

- **Noise reduction.** Technologically advanced televisions, speaker phones, computers, and modern sound systems make our homes noisy places. Carpet helps absorb these sounds. Adding a cushion pad beneath your carpet reduces noise even further. Carpet also works as a sound barrier between levels by helping to block sound transmission to rooms below. And carpet on stairs helps mask the sound of constant foot traffic.

- **Economic benefits.** When appropriately cleaned and otherwise cared for, carpet offers a floor covering that can last for a substantial period of time, which means that the initial investment can provide a significant return.[4]

Construction Methods

Carpet construction has a substantial impact on variables relevant to installation. Tufted carpet is made up of the face yarn, primary backing fabric, and a binding compound. The face yarn can be **level** or **multi-level loop** pile, **cut pile,** or a combination of the two. A cut pile may also be **sculptured.** The binding compound is generally **SB** latex; however, it might also be PVC, fabric, or polyurethane—and the binding compound often includes a secondary fabric.

During the mid-twentieth century, tufting technology gave rise to the development of the broadloom tufting machine and the introduction of synthetic carpet yarn. The American carpet industry rapidly expanded from low-volume production of woven luxury products to mass production of quality, affordable goods. Carpet sales in the United States skyrocketed as a result of the advances in tufting, which means that today's carpet is affordable, but still provides high quality.[5]

In the beginning, carpet looms were only 27 inches wide. Today, most carpet is usually 12 feet wide, although some carpets come in 15-foot widths and carpet may be custom sized for large installations.

The CRI advises that 6-foot-width carpet is becoming more popular and is now being offered in a variety of designs and backing systems—with an eye toward performance needs. Experts point out advantages in transporting a 6-foot roll for structures such as high-rise buildings, where transporting a 12-foot roll would be expensive or impractical. While noting careful planning regarding additional seams, experts also allude to economy for hallways or similar narrow spaces.[6]

Another method of production is **modular carpet tiles,** available in 12″ × 12″ and 18″ × 18″ sizes, although 24″ × 24″ is occasionally used. Tiles that are 36″ × 36″ are rarely used. (See Figure 3.1.)

You can locate a line of products designed for entries and pathway systems through Lees Squared. The company states that appropriate placement of its FirstStep and StepUp **walk-off** products can result in reduction of soil and moisture entering a facility by as much as 91 percent—and can also provide a non-slip surface in a location where moisture is likely to be an issue. The company points out that these products can reduce maintenance costs and increase longevity for floor coverings traversed after entry, as it traps moisture.[7]

The main manufacturing processes in order of quantity of carpet produced are tufting, woven, needle-punch, and others. (See Figure 3.2.)

It is important to understand carpet construction in order to apply the variables that affect performance of a specific installation. Tufted carpet consists of the following components: the face yarn, which can be cut pile, loop pile, or a combination of cut and loop pile; primary backing fabric; a bonding compound, usually SB latex, but may be polyurethane, PVC, or fabric; and (often) a secondary backing fabric. The **gauge** of a carpet measures the density of the fibers.

The development of the broadloom tufting machine and the introduction of synthetic carpet yarns in the early 1950s transformed the American carpet industry from low-volume production of woven luxury products to mass production of high quality and comfortable, yet popularly priced, goods. The explosive growth of carpet sales in the United States in the ensuing years paralleled the continual development of tufting technology, the proliferation of high-speed tufting machines, and the development of synthetic carpet fibers and alternative backing systems. As a result, today's carpet is both better and less expensive.[8]

FIGURE 3.1 Installation and removal of carpet modules is easy, as shown in this photo. *Photo courtesy of Interface FLOR, LLC.*

Tufted

Wilton Weave

Velvet Weave

Axminster Weave

Knitted

FIGURE 3.2 Construction methods.

TUFTING

It is interesting to note that the art of tufting started in Dalton, Georgia, with hand-tufted bedspreads. This process gradually became mechanized and looms were widened to make tufted carpet. In a tufted piece of carpet, the back is woven first and then the face is tufted into it and backed with additional material. Tufting is a much faster process than the traditional weaving method and has greatly reduced the cost of carpet, thereby making it available to more buyers. The technique is fast, efficient, and simple. More than 90 percent of all carpet sold in the United States is tufted and 70 percent is made in Dalton, the Carpet Capital of the World.

WEAVING

Weaving is a fabric formation process used for manufacturing carpet in which **yarns** are interlaced to form cloth. The weaving loom interlaces lengthwise (warp) and widthwise (filling) yarns. **Pitch** is measured by the number of lengthwise warp yarns; in a 27″ width, the higher the number, the finer the weave. Carpet weaves are complex, often involving several sets of warps and filling yarns. The back and the face are produced simultaneously and as one unit. When describing an area rug, the term *tapestry weave* is sometimes used; however, sisal is always woven. **Velvet** carpets are the simplest of carpets to weave. They are made on a velvet loom that is not unlike the Wilton loom without the Jacquard unit. The rich appearance of velvets is due to their high pile density. Velvets can be cut or looped pile.

KNITTED

Knitted carpets were not made by machine until 1940. Their quality is generally high, depending on the yarns used and their density. Knitting a carpet involves at least three different facing yarns and perhaps a fourth for backing. Face yarns are knitted in with warp chains and weft-forming yarns in a simple knitting process. Variations of colors, yarns, and pile treatment (cut or looped, high or low) create design choices for knitted carpets. Knitting today is a speedy process that produces fine quality carpet.

Most knitted carpet is solid colored or tweed, although some machines have pattern devices. Both loop and cut pile surfaces are available.

NEEDLE-PUNCHED

Needle-punched carpet is often sought out for locker rooms, pool decks, patios, and other areas where great quantities of moisture are likely to collect. The manufacturing process for this type of carpet is generally accomplished through use of olefin staple yarn, a yarn that is solution dyed and colorfast. Barbed needles are used to punch a matted layer of short staple fibers into a spun, synthetic scrim. Through intertwining, a mat of surface fibers is formed. This mat, which looks like thick felt, is approximately 3/8" thick.[9]

AUBUSSON

Aubussons are flatly woven tapestries and carpets in silk or wool, named for the French town where they originated (circa 1500). Tapestries bear narratives or portraits, whereas carpets feature architectural designs in rich colors or flowers in muted pastels.

AXMINSTER AND WILTON

Axminster carpet is woven on an Axminster loom. Pile tufts are inserted individually from a variety of colored yarns arranged on wide spools, making possible the production of carpet and rugs in complex designs with many colors, such as Oriental design.[10]

Both carpets are woven; although the appearance of Axminster and Wilton carpets may be similar, the construction is very different. The Wilton looms have Jacquard pattern mechanisms that use punched cards to select pile height and yarn color. In a Wilton, unwanted yarn colors are buried under the surface of the carpet, limiting the color selection to five or six colors. The carpets are often patterned or have multilevel surfaces. The traditional fiber in Axminster and Wilton construction is wool, but a blend of 80 percent wool and 20 percent nylon is sometimes used. One way to distinguish between the two types is to roll them across the warp and weft. A Wilton will fold in both directions, whereas an Axminster will only fold in one.

It is critical when cleaning Axminster cut-pile carpet not to use spin bonnets, rotary brushes, or rotary extractors. The rotary action of this equipment can severely distort the pile yarn. In addition, the spin bonnet method can leave chemical residue which builds up in the carpet.[11]

The three Cs—color, comfort, and cost—are probably the major factors in residential carpet choice, whereas in commercial and institutional projects durability, traffic, cost, and ease of maintenance are more important features. The properties considered in carpet selection also include type of fiber, density of pile, depth of pile, method of construction, pattern, and cleanability.

Fibers

Fiber type is the major decision in selecting a carpet. Each fiber has its own characteristics, and modern technology has greatly improved the features of synthetic fibers. The cost and characteristics of the fiber need to be considered together so the final selection will fulfill the client's need. (See Table 3.1.)

The most prevalent natural fiber used in carpet is wool, but in some rare instances silk, linen, and cotton may be used. (See Figure 3.3.) Other natural fibers gaining in popularity are sisal and coir. Synthetic fibers are always more colorfast than natural fibers because to produce colored fibers, the dye can be introduced while the fiber is in its liquid state. Wool, in its natural state, is limited to off-white, black/grey, and various shades in between.

Carpet manufacturers do not produce the actual fibers described in this section, but rather buy the fibers from the various chemical companies.

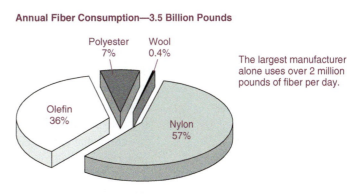

Annual Fiber Consumption—3.5 Billion Pounds

Polyester 7% · Wool 0.4% · Olefin 36% · Nylon 57%

The largest manufacturer alone uses over 2 million pounds of fiber per day.

FIGURE 3.3 Annual fiber consumption. *Courtesy of the Carpet and Rug Institute.*

NYLON

Nylon was introduced by DuPont in 1938 and accounts for nearly 90 percent of all carpet sold today. Nylon used to be designated by the generations, which basically went from one to five. Each generation had some type of improvement in the manufacturing process. However, nylon producers no longer use the generation label. Type 6 and Type 6,6 do not have the same chemical composition. Type 6,6 has a tighter molecular structure with more hydrogen bonding, better resistance to stains, enhanced resilience, and resistance to crushing and matting.

Table 3.1	*Fiber Performance in Carpet*				
	Nylon (Filament)	**Nylon (Staple)**	**Olefin (Filament)**	**Polyester (Staple)**	**Wool (Staple)**
Fiber Strength	Excellent	Excellent	Excellent	Excellent	Good
Appearance Retention	Excellent	Excellent	Fair	Fair	Excellent
Stain Resistant*	Very Good	Very Good	Excellent	Very Good	Very Good
Soil Resistant**	Very Good	Very Good	Fair	Good	Very Good
Cleaning	Very Good	Very Good	Very Good	Good	Very Good
Available Colors	Excellent	Excellent	Fair	Very Good	Fair
Pilling & Fuzzing	Excellent	Fair	Very Good	Fair	Fair
Resistance to Household Cleaners	Very Good	Very Good	Excellent	Very Good	Good

*Assuming nylon is treated with a stain-resistant chemical.

**Assuming treatment with a soil-resistant chemical.

Source: Fiber Performance chart courtesy of Mohawk Industries.

Sometimes the two terms **antistatic** and **conductive** are used improperly. Antistatic carpet will only work when the humidity is above 25 percent and is not permanent. In contrast, conductivity is a permanent property. Conductive fibers are capable of conducting electricity to ground. Most conductive fibers contain carbon, graphite, or stainless steel. Conductive carpets used by the computer industry are carbon-coated on the exterior of the fiber. External conductivity allows for static charges to make contact with the fiber's conductive element and then safely discharge to a ground source, such as an electrical conduit. Carbon fibers are inverted bi-component fibers.[12]

Lees states that the stain resistance quality of its Duracolor provides the capability to resist 99 percent of common stains. The company further states that Duracolor's stain-repelling characteristics differ from topical stain-resistance treatments, in that they are not worn away through time or heavy use, as they have been incorporated into the carpet fiber. Lees guarantees Duracolor for the life of the fiber.[13]

Milliken Carpet offers cXc (Carpet for Extreme Conditions), a carpet designed for health-care environments. The company references the high-performing technology applied in the production of its proprietary stain-blocking finish and face construction.[14]

When it comes to durability, there is little difference between bulked **continuous filaments** (BCF) or staple (spun) fibers. When carpet is manufactured with staple fiber, there will be initial **shedding** of shorter fibers. It will soon stop, depending on the amount of foot traffic and frequency of vacuuming. Wool is a naturally staple fiber; nylon and polyester can be staple or continuous filament; and olefin (polypropylene) is usually BCF.[15]

As a synthetic fiber, nylon absorbs little water; therefore, stains remain on the surface rather than penetrate the fiber itself. Dirt and soil are trapped between the filaments and are removed by proper cleaning methods. In addition, nylon has excellent abrasion resistance. The reason for worn or thin spots is that the yarn has been damaged physically by grit and soil ground into the carpet. This problem can be taken care of with proper maintenance.

WOOL

Wool has, for many years, represented the standard of quality against which all other carpet fibers are measured; this is still the case today to some degree. Most important are the aesthetics and inherent resilience of wool. The best wool for carpet comes from sheep that are raised in colder climates, such as New Zealand (domestic wools are too soft and fine for carpets). Although wool has a propensity for high **static electricity** generation, treatments are available to impart static-protection properties. Wool retains color for the life of the carpet despite wear and cleaning. It has good soil resistance because of its naturally high moisture content and has excellent pile resilience.

Wool gives good service. When price is no object, the best carpet fiber is wool. Wool blends, usually 80 percent wool and 20 percent nylon, have a larger market segment than a decade ago. Wool will stain or bleach in reaction to some spills, however, and is not as easy to clean as nylon.

It is difficult to ignite wool carpet, and wool carpet is self-extinguishable. Even after minor burn damage from sources such as cigarettes or fireplace embers, wool carpet is able to maintain its appearance. Bits of char can be whisked away. This is due to the fiber's high moisture content and protein elements.[16]

A combination of 80 percent goat hair and wool is used in Tretford USA cord carpet. This product is made from fusion-bonded construction, which can be cut in any direction without fraying or raveling, making it suitable for great floor graphics.

ACRYLIC

Acrylic is a manmade substance, similar in appearance and feel to wool. A plastic fiber made from acrylonitrile, acrylic became a substitute for wool in a number of carpets after the 1950s. The acrylic carpet had some advantages. It was less expensive than wool, resistant to mold and mildew, easy to dye in bright colors, fast drying, and fairly stain resistant.[17]

POLYESTER

While polyester is relatively inexpensive to manufacture, it does not provide a durable carpet. With each compression from a footstep or other source, the fibers are compressed. Because polyester fibers will not return to the original position after crushing, polyester carpets can quickly and permanently become matted.[18] This is why warranties for polyester carpets do not cover claims against matting or crushing.

OLEFIN

Because olefin (polypropylene) has colorfast qualities and is resistant to fading and acid-based stains, it is often laid in locations where resistance to chemicals and sunlight-fading are more critical than traffic durability. This fiber, which offers low levels of static electricity, can be purchased only as a solution dyed BCF fiber.[19]

COTTON

Cotton is an expensive natural fiber most often used for flat woven rugs such as Indian Dhurries.

SISAL AND COIR

Sisal, the world's strongest natural fiber, has its origins in Mexico, where the fiber is harvested from the leaves of the Henequin plant. Coir is also a natural fiber taken from the tough fibrous husk that surrounds the coconut. Because sisal and coir are natural fibers, there will be color variations when left undyed; however, several companies are dyeing, painting, or stenciling these fibers. In any event, the appearance of the color, whether natural or dyed, may change with direct sunlight. Both of these materials have bound edges.

SEAGRASS

Seagrass is the perennial grass of saltwater marshes cut from the plant. The plants are native to the monsoon climate of the Pacific basin. Reeds are thick and rigid. The nonporous skin is smooth to the touch and gives a slight natural sheen. Seagrass, as a natural fiber, characteristically absorbs atmospheric humidity and releases it, depending on climate conditions. This will cause the material to expand slightly in damp air and contract slightly in dry conditions. Waves and curling occur when the carpet is loosely laid. To eliminate curling of the carpet, roll the corners backwards, allow the carpet to lay flat, and place a few heavy books on the corners overnight. Little or no matting occurs due to the flat weave construction. The hard skin will not allow footmarks to develop. All seagrass carpets are backed with a natural rubber mat.

PAPER

The process used by Merida to produce paper products creates a strong natural durable fiber rug, one that feels soft and comfortable. The process is also utilized to create window and wall treatments. To achieve this process, Merida begins with virgin wood from sustainable managed forests in the United States. The process twists paper strips on a high-speed twister, which results in a paper cord. A wax emulsion is utilized to aid in smooth spinning, and this creates additional water resistance for the final product. The cord created through the spinning action is used in a weaving process, toward the end of a completed rug.[20]

JUTE

Jute is a soft, flexible, and hard wearing fiber that is well-suited to a natural area rug or floor covering material. Merida Meridian's distinctive 100 percent jute natural fiber rugs are woven in India and will resist wear and tear thanks to the abrasion-resistant properties of the fiber. Jute fiber is considered an eco-friendly material that is 100 percent biodegradable and recyclable. Jute yarns used in Merida's natural fiber area rugs are not dyed.[21]

Dyeing

Color is the most important aesthetic property of carpet. Designers should be familiar with the major methods of color application to carpet. Most residential carpet today is dyed using the piece-dyeing method, since manufacturers can store the plain or undyed carpet until a particular color is needed. Other methods may be used for special contract orders.

A carpet's color is derived from one of four dye methods. Each is explained here.

- *Jet-beck.* This is the most basic method. The dye is put into a vat with the carpet. Pressure is applied, which results in fast fiber penetration.

- *Kuster.* This method requires very careful control. The carpet moves along a conveyer belt as jets shoot computer-controlled color onto the fibers. Due to the inherent lack of control in this process, though, color can drift across a roll, resulting in sidematch shading. Carpet seaming will then not be possible, absent a visible color break at the seam line.

- *Atmospheric, also known as* **Beck.** This method, which is more time-consuming than some others, serves to eliminate issues with sidematch, as it distributes color evenly throughout the carpet. The carpet is "cooked" for several hours in a huge vat filled with hot dye.

- *Solution, also known as* **Yarn.** This method, often used to produce commercial carpet, also eliminates sidematch issues, and it provides the most colorfast product. To accomplish this method, yarn is dyed prior to being used to create carpet.[22]

The Easy Change program from Milliken allows the designer to (1) select a pattern; (2) decide on the changes, such as base, background, and accent colors; (3) request a computer image; and (4) request a carpet sample and then place the order.

Although floorcloths are mentioned in the section on wood floors in Chapter 4, the manner in which they are designed and constructed is appropriate for discussion here. In the past, heavy canvas was stretched and cut to size, then primed and stenciled or hand painted in a variety of patterns, and then sealed with oil. Today, extra-heavy canvas up to 12 feet wide is used and treated with a custom-developed flexible, non-yellowing protective coating to ensure longevity and prevent cracking. There are several contemporary companies and designers who have stock patterns but who also make floorcloths on commission.

Fabric Protectors

When discussing the different types of fabric protectors, it is important to keep in mind that some manufacturers are not anxious to divulge the contents of their protector. You may find some catch phrases which can be confusing when trying to decide what type of protector is used. Words such as *polymer*, *copolymer*, *hydrocarbon*, *aliphatic*, *chlorinated*, and even *metal cross-linked* have been used in describing fabric protectors. Although these words may have some relationship to protectors, you really only need to understand the three basic types of fabric protectors.

1. Colloidal silica, which fills pores, thus preventing soil from becoming embedded.

2. Silicones, which provide a water-repellent coating.

3. Fluorochemicals, which form an invisible shield on the fibers that helps prevent soil and stains from sticking.[23]

Another factor to consider for computer rooms and electronic offices is a backing engineered for control of electrostatic discharge **(ESD).**

Fire-retardant products are also used, especially in commercial installations where fire codes require such products. Wool self-extinguishes when the source of ignition is removed and merely chars, leaving only a cold ash which can be easily brushed away with no permanent scars; in contrast, synthetic fibers melt.

Antimicrobial Issues

All antimicrobial treatments are regulated by the United States Environmental Protection Agency. For EPA registration, these antimicrobial preservatives must undergo extensive toxicological assessments. The EPA Treated Articles Exemption (EPA PR Notice 2000-1) states that articles treated with an EPA-registered product may make claims only related to protection of the treated article against bacterial- or mold-related odors and staining. No implicit human health claims may be made unless the finished treated article (itself) is EPA registered. This EPA regulatory clarification is key in curbing overzealous marketing claims regarding the intended function of the antimicrobial treatment. Currently, there are no carpets registered as finished treated articles; therefore, no healthcare claims can be made or implied for carpets with these treatments.[24]

Intersept is a patented antimicrobial preservative against molds, **mildews,** bacteria, and odor-causing microorganisms. (See Figure 3.4.)

FIGURE 3.4 Intersept antimicrobial preservative. *Photo courtesy of Interface FLOR, LCC.*

Flammability Testing

It is extremely important for designers to realize the legal ramifications of flammability specifications because of possible damage and liability lawsuits. Designers should require carpet suppliers to submit written documentation of fire code compliance.

All carpet sold in the United States must meet the Federal Flammability Standards, but local and regional standards also exist. The local fire marshal has the authority to establish additional specific criteria, and should be consulted prior to writing specifications or purchasing carpet for a particular installation.

PILL TEST

Through FF1–70, the United States Department of Commerce (DOC), there is a requirement that carpets and large rugs (24 square feet or larger) for sale in the United States (whether manufactured in the country or imported) pass a small-scale ignition test, also known as the *Pill Test*.[25]

All fires have three distinct stages: ignition, flashover, and expansion. In the ignition stage, the fire has started but is contained in a small area of one room. Flashover occurs when the fire spreads beyond its point of origin and everything in the room is burning. In the expansion stage, the fire leaves the room and spreads over into other rooms or down a corridor. If the fire can be contained during the ignition stage, minimal damage will occur.

Another method for testing the flame resistance of carpet is the Steiner Tunnel Test (ASTM E-84). However, this test is being replaced by the Flooring Radiant Panel Test in most states because of greater accuracy.

FLOORING RADIANT PANEL TEST

This test is quite stringent, and local building and fire codes should be reviewed to determine when the test is required. Critical radiant flux limits for specific use areas where automatic sprinkler protection is not provided are detailed here.

- *Class I.* Average minimum of 0.45 watts per square centimeter within exits; access to exits (corridors) of healthcare facilities, including hospitals, nursing homes, and so on; and new construction detention and correctional facilities.

- *Class II.* Average minimum of 0.22 watts per square centimeter within exits; access to exits (corridors) of daycare centers, existing detention and correctional facilities, hotels, dormitories, and apartment buildings.[26]

Carpet Cushioning

A firm and resilient carpet cushion is necessary to form a good foundation for your carpet, increasing its comfort and extending its life by absorbing the impact of foot traffic. Carpet cushion also adds insulation and reduces noise.

SELECTING CUSHION/PAD

There are three basic types of cushion: **foam, sponge rubber,** and **fiber.** Each type is further subdivided into two or three varieties.

Foam

Foam comes in three varieties:

1. ***Prime urethane foam.*** This is a firmer version of the same cushioning used in upholstered furniture, mattresses, and automobile seats. Two liquid ingredients are combined to form a large mass of foam, which is then sliced into sheets for use as carpet cushion. There are three types of prime urethane carpet cushion: conventional prime, grafted prime, and densified prime cushion. Prime urethane foam grades are measured by density, or weight of the material per cubic foot.

2. ***Bonded urethane foam.*** Sometimes called *rebond,* this is formed by combining chopped and shredded pieces of foam into one solid piece. It frequently has a surface net for ease of installation and improved performance. Bonded foam grades are also measured by density. Rebond pad can cause yellowing of olefin carpet and stain-resistant nylon carpet. Rebond pad usually contains BHT (Butylated hydroxytoluene). BHT, a common preservative used in many plastics and even in bread, was removed from most olefin backings in 1985 because of yellowing of carpet fibers. Many cushion manufacturers have now also removed BHT from their products.

3. ***Mechanically frothed urethane foam.*** This is made with carpet backing machinery. Frothed urethane cushions are made from a process originally developed to apply cushioned backings to carpet. The urethane foam cushioning is applied to a sheet of nonwoven material, forming a carpet cushion product with a typically higher density and firmer feel.

Sponge Rubber

There are two specific types of sponge rubber carpet cushion. Grades for both are measured by weight in ounces per square yard.

1. ***Waffle sponge rubber.*** This is made by molding natural or synthetic rubber to a rippled or waffled surface. This variety produces a soft, resilient cushion whose luxurious feel is particularly useful for residences. Waffle rubber pad is often used improperly. The waffle part of the padding gives it a thickness that is mostly air; as a result, any of this type of padding rated less than 90 ounces is still too soft for today's carpets. Frequently, the rubber used to make this type of pad is held together with clay binders that break down with use.

2. ***Flat sponge rubber.*** This is a firm, dense cushion, which has a flat surface and is normally used in large-scale commercial applications and with loop type (or **berber**) carpet.

Fiber

There are two basic types of fiber carpet cushion: natural fiber and synthetic carpet fiber or felt. A third type, recycled textile fiber, is occasionally seen. The grade of fiber cushion is determined by its weight in ounces per square yard. Fiber cushions tend to have a firm "walk" or "feel."

1. ***Natural fibers.*** These include felt, horsehair, and jute. These are, of course, highly susceptible to rotting if over-wetted, odor development, and natural degradation. Some natural fiber cushions have been treated with a water-soluble dye that can stain a wet carpet. Fiber pads are used sometimes to limit the movement in an area rug. The key is density. Felt cushion density is by weight of ounces per square yard.

2. ***Synthetic fibers/synthetic felt.*** These include nylon, polyester, polypropylene, and acrylics, which are needle-punched into relatively dense cushions which have a firm feel and, as with other types of cushion, can be made in virtually any weight, to stand up under light, medium, or heavy traffic, which is how they are usually classified.

As can be seen from Table 3.2, the Carpet Cushion Council has established recommended minimum contract cushion criteria for three levels of traffic. Any cushion type and grade certified as meeting the CCC's guidelines can be expected to perform satisfactorily at that level under normal conditions, when used with a carpet made for the same specified traffic. To make proper selection easier, the various categories of cushioning have color-coded labels: red label for commercial, moderate traffic; green label for heavy traffic; and blue label for commercial, extra heavy traffic.

The quality of a carpet cushion is determined by density (the weight of one cubic foot of the cushion), not thickness and softness. If the cushion is too soft and thick, the carpet excessively flexes with traffic, the backing is put under enormous strain, and the carpet will delaminate. Foam pads should not lose more than half their height when you pinch them. The cushion under most residential carpet should be a thickness no greater than 7/16". (See Table 3.2.)

With urethane foam cushion, density is rated at pounds per cubic foot. For example, a 5-pound rebond pad would weigh 5 pounds per cubic foot. The CRI recommends a residential pad of at least 5 pounds and 3/8" thickness for light traffic (a living room), and a pad of 6.5 pounds and 3/8" for heavy traffic (hallways). These are minimum guidelines. Residential cushion should not be any thicker than 7/16". Berber carpet requires a firm cushion and is usually sold as "berber cushion."[27]

For commercial installations, the minimum should be 12 to 14 pounds with a thickness of 1/4" to 3/8".

Attached cushion is cushion material permanently bonded to the back of carpet and rugs by the manufacturer to provide additional dimensional stability, thickness, and padding. Materials used include polyurethane, sponge rubber, PVC, high-density foam, and latex.

Woven carpet must be installed over an extra-heavy super dense fiberpad or, in some cases, a heavy flat frothed foam.

The appropriate carpet cushion, or "pad," provides additional resilience, acoustical, and thermal qualities; comfort underfoot; and can extend the life of the carpet. Cushion should be selected according to the carpet manufacturer's requirements for thickness and density. Improper selection of carpet cushion can accelerate loss of carpet surface appearance, cause wrinkling and buckling, cause separation of the carpet seams, and cause a breakdown of the carpet structure itself. Improper cushion selection also may void applicable carpet manufacturer's warranties.

The type and thickness of cushion you need varies according to traffic levels and patterns. For example, bedrooms, dens, lounge areas, and other rooms with light or moderate traffic can use thicker and softer cushion, while living rooms, family rooms, hallways, stairs, and other heavy traffic areas require thinner, firmer cushion. Residential cut pile, cut and loop, or high-level loop carpet requires a resilient, firm cushion with a thickness of 7/16" or less. Be careful to avoid being influenced by the appearance of cushion, as it will no longer be viewed after installation.[28]

When you make your purchase, ask for installer recommendations. Many stores will suggest their professional installers or refer you to a specific installation firm. After making the purchase investment, you want to be certain the investment remains as valuable as possible—through proper installation.[29] In considering economy in your purchase, consider the long-term benefits, as well as the initial expense. The cushion selection is important, and inexpensive cushion could have a significant impact on the life of your carpet.

Special Notes

Radiant heating is becoming more widely used in certain sections of the country. In the case of radiant heating, you do not want a cushion that is an exceptionally effective insulator, but one that allows the heat from the subflooring to penetrate the carpet system and heat the room. A relatively thin, flat cellular sponge rubber or synthetic fiber cushion works well under these circumstances. Be sure to ask your customers if their room(s) have radiant heating.[30]

In an effort to prevent issues related to pet odors—and to provide easier spot removal— separate protective carpet liners are available. These liners, which can also be incorporated into the carpet through placement between the backing and cushion, are designed to prohibit, as much as possible, moisture from reaching the cushion. Invista's Stainmaster Carpet Cushion provides an example of this product type. It is designed to allow passage of moisture vapors and prohibit trapped moisture. Stainmaster Carpet Cushion features a breathable moisture barrier designed to catch spills and prevent them from seeping into cushion and sub-floor. Although it will catch the liquid, it will allow moisture vapors to pass through it so that no moisture is trapped underneath it.[31]

Carpet Specifications

Certain issues must be addressed to specify carpet, regardless of the installation site. Most of the critical decisions made during specification, including those for installation and maintenance, will determine the lifecycle of the carpet. The specifier should determine the expectation for the carpet and what the most important selection criteria are. A proper specification covers the key

Table 3.2	Minimum Recommended Requirements for Satisfactory Carpet Cushion Performance in Contract Installations

Types of Cushion	Class I Moderate Traffic
Commercial Application	**Office Buildings:** Executive or private offices; conference rooms **Health Care:** Executive, administrative **Schools:** Administration **Airports:** Administration **Retail:** Windows and display areas **Banks:** Executive areas **Hotels/Motels:** Sleeping rooms **Libraries/Museums:** Administration
Minimum recommended criteria for satisfactory carpet cushion performance in contract installations	

Fiber

Rubberized Hair	Wt. 40 oz.	Th: .27"	D = 12.3	
Rubberized Jute	Wt. 32 oz.	Th: .25"	D = 12.3	
Synthetic Fibers	Wt. 22 oz.	Th: .25"	D = 7.3	
Resinated Recycled Textile Fiber	Wt. 24 oz.	Th: .25"	D = 7.3	

Rubber

Flat Rubber	Wt. 62 oz.	Th: .150"	CR @ 25% = 3.0 psi min.	D = 21
Rippled Waffle	Wt. 56 oz.	Th: .270"	CR @ 25% = 0.7 psi min.	D = 15
Textured Flat Rubber	Wt. 56 oz.	Th: .220"	CR @ 25% = 1.0 psi min.	D = 18
Reinforced Rubber	Wt. 64 oz.	Th: .235"	CR @ 25% = 2.0 psi min.	D = 22
			CR @ 65% = 50.0 psi min.	

Polyurethane Foam

Grafted Prime Polyurethane*	D = 2.7	Th: .25"	CFD @ 65% = 2.5 psi min.
Densified Polyurethane*	D = 2.7	Th: .25"	CFD @ 65% = 2.4 psi min.
Bonded Polyurethane**	D = 5.0	Th: .375"	CFD @ 65% = 5.0 psi min.
Mechanically Frothed Polyurethane***	D = 13.0	Th: .30"	CFD @ 65% = 9.7 psi min.

Footnotes: Maximum thickness for any product is 3/8"
    D - Denotes Density in lbs./cu.ft.
    Oz. - Denotes weight in ounces/sq. yd.
    CR - Denotes Compression Resistance in lbs./sq. in
        as measured by ASTM D-3676
    CFD - Denotes Compression Force Deflection as
        measured by ASTM D-3574

All thicknesses, weights, and densities allow a .5% manufacturing tolerance
* = Polymer densities
** = Particle size not to exceed 1/2"
*** = Ash content = 50% max

Class II Heavy Traffic	Class III Extra Heavy Traffic
Office Buildings: Clerical areas, corridors (moderate traffic)	**Office Buildings:** Corridors (heavy traffic), cafeterias
Health Care: Patients' rooms, lounges	**Health Care:** Lobbies, corridors, nurses' stations
Schools: Dormitories and classrooms	**Schools:** Corridors, cafeterias
Retail: Minor aisles, boutiques, specialty	**Airports:** Corridors, public areas, ticketing areas
Banks: Lobbies, corridors (moderate traffic)	**Retail:** Major aisles, checkouts, supermarkets
Hotels/Motels: Corridors	**Banks:** Corridors (heavy traffic), teller windows
Libraries/Museums: Public Areas (moderate traffic)	**Hotels/Motels:** Lobbies and public areas
Convention Centers: Auditoriums	**Libraries/Museums:** Public Areas
	Country Clubs: Locker rooms, pro shops, dining areas
	Convention Centers: Corridors and lobbies
	Restaurants: Dining areas and lobbies

Class II Heavy Traffic			Class III Extra Heavy Traffic			
Wt. 40 oz.	Th: .3125"	D = 12.3	Wt. 50 oz.	Th: .375"	D = 11.1	
Wt. 40 oz.	Th: .25"	D = 12.3	Wt. 40 oz.	Th: .34"	D = 10.1	
Wt. 28 oz.	Th: .3125"	D = 7.3	Wt. 36 oz.	Th: .35"	D = 8.0	
Wt. 30 oz.	Th: .30"	D = 7.3	Wt. 38 oz.	Th: .375"	D = 8.0	

Wt. 62 oz.	Th: .150"	CR @ 25% = 3.0 psi min. D = 21	Wt. 62 oz.	Th: .150"	CR @ 25% = 4.0 psi min.	D = 26
Not Recommended for Use in This Class			Not Recommended for Use in This Class			
Wt. 64 oz.	Th: .235"	CR @ 25% = 1.5 psi min. D = 22	Wt. 80 oz.	Th: .250"	CR @ 25% = 1.75 psi min.	D = 26
Wt. 64 oz.	Th: .235"	CR @ 25% = 2.0 psi min. D = 22	Wt. 54 oz.	Th: .200"	CR @ 25% = 2.0 psi min.	D = 22
		CR @ 65% = 50.0 psi min.			CR @ 65% = 50.0 psi min.	

D = 3.2	Th: .25"	CFD @ 65% = 3.5 psi min.	D = 4.0	Th: .25"	CFD @ 65% = 5.0 psi min.
D = 3.5	Th: .25"	CFD @ 65% = 3.3 psi min.	D = 4.5	Th: .25"	CFD @ 65% = 4.8 psi min.
D = 6.5	Th: .25"	CFD @ 65% = 10.0 psi min.	D = 8.0	Th: .25"	CFD @ 65% = 8.0 psi min.
D = 15.0	Th: .223"	CFD @ 65% = 49.9 psi min.	D = 19.0	Th: .183"	CFD @ 65% = 30.5 psi min.

To help you compare various types of cushion, the Carpet Cushion Council has established recommended minimum contract cushion criteria for three levels of traffic. Any cushion type and grade certified as meeting CCC's guidelines for cushion being installed at a particular traffic level can be expected to perform satisfactorlly at that level under norm conditions, when used with a carpet made for the same specified traffic. Red Label; Commercial - Moderate Traffic • Green Label; Commercial - Heavy Traffic • Blue Label; Commercial - Extra Heavy Traffic.

Source: Table reprinted by permission of the Carpet Cushion Council.

FIGURE 3.5 East Brunswick Public Library, Consultant: Kimberly Bolan and Associates, LLC working with DEMCO Interiors Using the Theory Design from Milliken Carpet. *Photo courtesy of DEMCO, Inc.*

technical aspects—from sub-floor preparation, to choosing the proper cushion and method of installation, to post-installation cleanup—none of these can be overlooked in a successful installation. Consider the following basic issues to create a carpet specification:

Aesthetics. Texture, design/pattern, luster, appearance, or the "look" (see Figure 3.5)

- Business type: hospitality, retail, office, and so on
- Desired ambience
- Color selection parameters
- Flexible and functional
- Restricted: must match or blend with other furnishings
- Dark or bright ambient lighting
- Nature of lighting: fluorescent, incandescent, and so on
- Psychological/motivational factors

Functional considerations. Value, acoustics, ergonomics, safety, thermal insulation, low maintenance costs, flammability, static propensity, indoor air quality, lifecycle value

Appearance. Durability, wearability, cleanability, installability, color retention and fastness, texture retention, appearance retention

- Primary end-use considerations
- Traffic levels and patterns
- Wheeled traffic and ADA requirements
- Nature of regional soil
- Projected life span
- Projected quality of maintenance
- Government or building code requirements[32]

Aesthetic Considerations

Carpet is widely recognized for its excellent "first impression" of beauty, prestige, and dignity in any business or facility. Well-chosen carpet dramatically enhances the feeling of quality and distinction in interior design, a major consideration for hotels, restaurants, and corporate buildings. Carpet also has the ability to "de-institutionalize" a building, creating a "home-like" factor leading to improved patient and staff morale in healthcare facilities and improved student and teachers attitudes in schools. Carpet gives inhabitants a psychological "uplift."[33]

A realization in healthcare facilities that Alzheimer's patients can remember color differentiation better than numbers (according to the Alzheimer's Association) may be a consideration in any public facility. Color can provide an easily remembered visual link to a specific hall or wing. Brighter colors also aid in depth perception and differentiation of areas such as registration desks or main offices. Color is also a good way to differentiate a group or team area, or to differentiate between departments.[34]

Complete specifications for installations can be found on the Carpet & Rug Institute Web site in PDF files. They are contained in CRI 104—Standard for Installation Specification of Commercial Carpet and CRI 105—Standard for Installation of Residential Carpet.

PERFORMANCE

To clarify the difference between performance and construction specifications, performance specifications define what characteristics the carpet must deliver in use. In other words, performance specifications tell the manufacturer what the carpet must do without detailing how it must be made. By contrast, a construction specification tells the manufacturer, in very precise terms, how the carpet is to be manufactured without stipulating performance needs.

Specifying performance rather than construction can also take other important pressures off the specifier. For example, if the specifier does not regularly deal with carpet products, the latest technology and materials may be overlooked. The best, most economical product to ensure the desired performance may not be chosen.

Special requirements for different types of installation sites can be very complex and technical. For example, in window-wall architecture, fade resistance could be a matter of primary concern. In a hospital medical dispensary, stain resistance might be placed high on the list of performance priorities. Special static protection properties may be necessary for computer and data-processing areas.[35]

Measuring

Before estimating the amount of carpet needed for a particular job, there are several points that the designer needs to remember. First, if carpet is available in widths other than the usual 12 feet, then all the carpet must be of that width. DO NOT COMBINE DIFFERENT WIDTHS because of differences in dye lots. Second, the **nap** or pile of the carpet must be considered, and all pieces must have the nap running in the same direction (toward the entrance unless otherwise specified) or the seams will be obvious. Third, seaming and nap direction must be shown on all carpet seaming plans. Placement of furniture will often decide where seams should be placed. Seams should never be in the middle of high-traffic areas, such as at right angles to a doorway, across a hallway, or in front of often used office machines such as copiers and drinking fountains. In residential seaming layouts, seams must not be placed directly in front of seating areas.

Carpets that have to be seamed at right angles will also have an obvious seam; however, seams placed under a door are often necessary. The nap on stairs should run downward. The warp (nap) should always run in the longer direction.

The precise measuring of the carpet should be done by the installer on site, and a carpet seaming diagram should be submitted to the designer for approval. Nevertheless, the designer should understand how carpet measuring is done.

Carpet usually comes in 12-foot widths, but 6-foot, 9-foot, and 15-foot widths are sometimes available. Whatever width is selected, it will be necessary to piece or seam the carpet. This may entail purchasing slightly more yardage, because the fewer the seams, the better the appearance will be.

Although carpet comes in widths measured in feet, the amount ordered is always in square yards, so a square foot answer must be divided by 9 to arrive at the square yardage needed. (From experience, the author finds that when taking exams design students commonly make this error and as a result specify too much carpet.) However, the CRI has proposed a change to square feet, with the reasoning being that if carpet was sold by the square foot, it would be easier to make comparisons between other types of flooring materials which are priced by the square foot.

All measurers seem to have their own method of calculation. Some suggest using templates; others have complicated formulas. Some answers are very close with little waste, and others have few seams and much waste. The number of seams does depend on each job. A master bedroom may have a seam 1 foot in from a wall where a dresser, bed, or other piece of furniture is to be placed, because there the seam will not be visible, but in an art gallery the same seam placement would be unacceptable. Whichever method is used, the installer is responsible for the accuracy of the measurements.

In today's computerized design offices, programs are available to assist the designer in producing an economical yet viable plan. Some programs actually produce a floor plan with measurements, nap directions, and seam placements. The program can provide an estimate needed with the 12-foot width going across the room or at right angles. A pattern repeat can be programmed so the repeat is considered.

Problems

The following problems are associated with carpet.

CORNROWING

In **cornrowing,** the tufting machine is set to insert the prescribed number of face yarns in the back. As the carpet or rug is made, the face yarns will stand erect. After the carpet or rug is placed on the floor and is subjected to use, there will be considerable pressure placed on the individual face yarns. If the density is high enough, the surrounding tufts help to hold each other erect; however, if the density is too low, there is less support from the adjacent tufts and some of the tufts may be pushed over. With some tufts standing, and others crushed, the cornrow appearance is created. This is not considered a manufacturing defect.

DEPRESSIONS OR INDENTATIONS

The weight of heavy pieces of furniture can cause **indentations** in carpet. Some depressions may be permanent. Use furniture glides or cups under the legs of heavy pieces, or move your furniture a few inches backward or sideways so that the weight is not concentrated in one place. If depressions do occur, spritz the indentations with water in a spray bottle. Hold a hair dryer, set on medium, a few inches above the indentation. As the spot is drying use your fingers to gently work the pile upright and in the opposite direction.[36]

SHEDDING

Carpets made with spun fibers may shed loose bits of fiber left in the carpet from the manufacturing process. Removing these loose fibers does not affect the carpet life or quality. Because of the large micron size (>90 microns), these fibers are too large to become airborne or respirable (<4 microns).[37]

    With proper vacuuming, using a quality vacuum cleaner, most shedding disappears within the first year after installation.

MOLD AND MILDEW

These problems exist ONLY where there is excess moisture and dirt coupled with poor cleaning and maintenance habits. Mold growth can occur on any surface—from windowpanes to carpet—that is not properly maintained and when moisture is extreme. Eliminating sources of excessive moisture, such as water leaks, and controlling humidity greatly offset the potential for mold to grow.

MOTH AND BEETLE CONTROL

Most wool and wool-blend carpet made in the United States is permanently treated to prevent moth damage. Carpet and rugs made of manmade (synthetic) fibers are naturally resistant to insects. Synthetic carpet fiber is not a food source, and is resistant to beetles, commonly called carpet beetles. However, beetles already in the home may lay eggs in the carpet pile and hatch in 8 to 15 days. For assistance in removing beetles or other insects, contact a professional pest control specialist.

RIPPLES AND BUCKLINGS

Ripples and buckling in carpet are most often caused by the failure to adequately stretch the carpet using a power stretcher, the use of an inappropriate or failed cushion, or excessive temperature and/or humidity. Ripples can be a combination of any of the previously noted deficiencies. If ripples or buckles develop, consult your carpet retailer. Generally, the problem can be corrected by a qualified carpet installer re-stretching the carpet with a power stretcher.

SHADING, PILE REVERSAL, "WATERMARKING," OR "POOLING"

Shading is not a change in color, but a change in pile direction (pile reversal) that sometimes appears randomly in a carpet or rug. All pile yarn carpet is subject to pile reversal; however, it is most likely to be observed in smooth surfaced, densely constructed, plush-type qualities. This phenomenon is difficult, if not impossible, to predict or prevent. Pile reversal creates a permanent change in the carpet's appearance caused by the difference in the way light reflects off the sides and tip of a yarn as the pile lays in different directions. Shaded areas appear light from one direction and dark from another direction. After a period of use, carpet may look as though water has spilled on sections of the carpet, hence the term *watermarking*. Other terms also commonly used to describe pile reversal are *pooling*, *shading*, and *highlighting*.[38]

Some changes can be expected after the carpet is used. The traffic areas will appear a little different from the adjacent, unwalked-on areas. This difference is because the carpet pile has been compressed by the pressure from footsteps. Vacuuming and brushing will help to raise the crushed pile. An occasional vacuuming, however, cannot equalize the continual compressing of the carpet. The end user will have to work to keep the pile erect. Vacuuming and brushing the pile all in one direction, or professional cleaning, may temporarily improve the condition. This changes only the top portion of the pile, however, and shading will soon redevelop. With some plush carpet, vacuum cleaner marks and footsteps may show after the carpet has been freshly cleaned.

SPROUTING

Occasionally, a tuft will rise above the pile surface of a carpet. This is called **sprouting.** The best way to correct these is just to snip off these tufts level with other tufts. DO NOT PULL THEM OUT!

STAIN-RESISTANT CARPET

Almost all of the carpet manufactured today has finishes that make it more stain- and soil-resistant. Although stain-resistant carpet is easier to maintain, it still requires care. Remove spots as soon as something is spilled or tracked on the carpet. If spills or soil are allowed to remain, they may become permanent.

STATIC ELECTRICITY

Static electricity is caused by the rubbing together of two different types of materials: carpet face fibers and shoe sole materials. Most carpets have some type of treatments built into them that will eliminate the static electricity problem. Moisture in the air will help the problem; however, it may produce condensation on window glass in colder climates.

YELLOWING

Yellowing in light-colored carpet can be caused by a variety of outside influences, such as pollutants from heating fuels, changes in alkalinity, cleaning solutions, and atmospheric or environmental contaminants. All **carpet yellowing** may not be removable; however, the use of acetic acid (white vinegar), citrus acid, or tartaric acid is often successful in reversing yellowing. In some cases, the use of an alkaline detergent solution prior to the use of these acid rinses may cause permanent yellowing. A solution of one part white vinegar mixed with one part water is recommended for consumer use. If yellowing persists or is widespread, contact a carpet cleaning professional.

Installation

Before beginning the actual installation procedures, there are several preliminary facts that need to be mentioned in order to start a good installation.[39]

STORAGE

Store carpet and related materials in a climate-controlled, dry space. Protect carpet from soil, dust, moisture, and other contaminants and store on a flat surface. Stacking heavy objects on top of carpet rolls or stacking more than three rolls is prohibited.

HANDLING

Transport carpet in a manner that prevents damage and distortion. Bending or folding individual carpet rolls or cuts from rolls is not recommended. When bending or folding is unavoidable for delivery purposes, the carpet is required to be unrolled and allowed to lie flat immediately upon arrival at the installation site.

SHOP DRAWINGS

The carpet shop drawing is required to contain specific information about the job, such as the following:

- Name of the job, owner, and installation company. On new construction the name of the general contractor and architectural firm are required.
- Building address.
- Date of drawing.
- Scale.
- Floor number and location in building.
- Compass direction on each sheet.
- Drawing for each area to be carpeted (color coding is preferable).
- Construction of substrate for each area.
- Required floor preparation, materials, and quantities.
- Type of installation for each area.
- Quantities of carpet needed for each area, including roll length requirements, pattern repeat, manufacturer installation sequencing, and cut list.
- Exact notations where dye-lot changes occur.
- Excess material in each area and how it is to be used.
- Seam layout of each area.
- Allowed tolerance created by cutting carpet 3 to 4 inches (75 to 100 mm) longer than the area measurement.
- Carpet pile direction for each area.
- Name of manufacturer, style, backing system, and color of carpet for each area.
- Large-scale drawings showing treatment of step areas or other detail work.
- Location and type of expansion joints and edge transitions.
- Type of wall base in each area.[40]

Your commercial carpet installation is a significant investment, both in monetary terms and overall facility image. It is important to implement a maintenance program from the beginning. A consistent and effective carpet maintenance program can maintain the initial facility image and dramatically extend the life of your monetary investment.

The International Certified Floorcovering Installers Association is an organization of flooring professionals whose purpose is to identify, train, and certify flooring installers according to skill and knowledge and to provide the industry with educational programs that enhance the ultimate goal of customer satisfaction.[41]

The Association's test also covers written OSHA, EPA, and CRI-104 and CRI-105 knowledge.[42]

- **Residential I (R-1).** Minimum two years experience; possesses the ability to install residential entry-level carpet.

- **Residential II (R-2).** Minimum four years experience; possesses the ability to install residential carpets and patterns of a more difficult level.

- **Commercial I (C-1).** Minimum of two years experience; possesses the ability to install commercial entry-level carpets.

- **Commercial II (C-2).** Minimum of four years experience; possesses the ability and knowledge to install commercial carpets and patterns of a more difficult level.

- **Master Installer.** Minimum of 10 years experience; possesses the ability to install woven carpets, handsew, and work with the most difficult products.

The International Certified Carpet Installers now also have similar requirements for other types of materials (e.g., tile, wood, and laminate).

The best carpet installer available should always be used.

METHODS OF INSTALLATION

There are three main types of carpet installation. In some situations, the one used will be dictated by the specifier. Table 3.3 provides the advantages and best uses for each type of installation.

Table 3.3   Different Methods of Carpet Installation

Stretch-In Method	Direct Glue-Down Method	Double Glue-Down Method
Allows for better comfort underfoot and better acoustical properties, for example, higher-impact noise ratings and higher **noise-reduction coefficients (NRCs)** in instances of installation with separate cushion	Takes advantage of more durable seams, due to a lack of vertical flexing	Provides the dual benefit of direct glue-down carpet stability with the cushioning benefits of stretch-in installation
Increases R-value (thermal insulation)	Eases access to utility-related lines—such as telephone and electrical lines—below the floor	Enhances performance, comfort, and appearance
Provides installation for floors that cannot be glued down	Eliminates, as much as possible, seam-peaking	Provides greater ease in inlay and carpet-border tasks
More easily matches and addresses issues with seam repair	Provides intricate inlay and border options	Suitable in areas where wheeled traffic is likely to occur
Generally has lower removal costs than if it were an adhered installation	Decreases expense, when possible	Ideal for locations where restrictions related to area size are not an issue
Should be avoided in locations such as ramps and inclines, in locations with office-systems furniture and demountable partitions, in locations with a high likelihood of heavy rolling traffic, in locations where extreme humidity is likely, and in instances when carpet has a unitary backing or other backing for which only glue-down installation is intended	Suitable where rolling traffic is likely, such as ramp areas, in buildings where HVAC systems are likely to be turned off for great periods of time (with an eye toward decreasing buckling as much as possible), and in locations where restrictions related to area size are not an issue	
	Note: Be certain to avoid glue-down installation in no-restretch settings.	

Source: CRI Web site, www.carpet-rug.org

All of TacFast's technologies are based on detachable systems of attachment. Many of the TacFast flooring products feature a free-floating substrate with a hook element covering its surface (the LocPlate Products) and a flooring surface with a loop fabric covering the underside. The flooring surface is attached to the hook substrate by engaging the hooks and loops, creating a mechanical bond that holds the flooring surface in place securely, yet is releasable.

All TacFast flooring products are composed of two parts:

1. A substrate that has a hook surface; and

2. A surface material which has a loop fabric covering its entire underside.[43]

Lees Squared produces a releasable adhesive system under the product name Self Lock. This is a patented, factory-applied system for modular carpet. Because the manufacturing process results in the adhesive being placed on the back of the module, it is possible to lay the modules quickly. Lees Squared recommends this product for raised floors, as well as in locations where use of adhesive and chair pads is undesirable. The company states that the system "prevents shifting even at pivot points, on ramps and under rolling chairs." The company further advises that the tiles may be taken up repeatedly, with no loss of bonding strength. This system is suitable for use with the majority of cable systems. It does not cause damage to flat wire when tugged away from the floor.

The Super Self Lock has been designed for use in locations such as convention centers, retail environments, and airports, areas that will certainly see tremendous wheel and foot traffic.[44]

The CRI finds that most complaints about wrinkling or buckling in **tackless (strip)** installations result from inadequate stretch during initial installation or from cushion that does not provide adequate support for the carpet. Adequate stretch can only be obtained by the use of power stretchers.

Another problem is the separation from the floor in a glue-down installation caused by an insufficient amount of carpet floor adhesive.

Because of their heavy backing, carpet tiles may also be loose laid. Carpet modules can be freely rotated and/or replaced without detracting from the overall like-new appearance of the installation, particularly in the healthcare, institutional, retail, and hospitality areas, with their heavy use and traffic. This type of installation also eliminates restretching problems, with no movement of pattern-type carpet or bordering. It is also useful in furnishing the upper floors of tall buildings, where delivering heavy, cumbersome rolls of broadloom may present a problem. (This is particularly true in the case of refurbishing when construction cranes and elevators used to lift the original carpets are no longer available.)

Coir and sisal are highly absorbent; therefore, for at least 24 hours prior to installing, they should be allowed to acclimate to the humidity and temperature of the room in which they will be placed. The direct glue-down procedure is the best method of wall-to-wall installation for coir and sisal if there are no great fluctuations in humidity or temperature. If these conditions exist, then loose-laying is suggested.[45]

CLEANING AND MAINTENANCE

Your commercial carpet installation is a significant investment, both in monetary terms and overall facility image. It is important to implement a maintenance program from the beginning. A consistent and effective carpet maintenance program can maintain the initial facility image and dramatically extend the life of your monetary investment.

The appearance of carpet depends upon several factors: color, pattern, density, fiber, and a viable carpet maintenance program. In order to keep carpet products performing their best, designing and implementing a comprehensive maintenance plan is very important. Great care should be taken when choosing carpet colors, patterns, and textures. These features, combined with fiber quality and construction standards engineered to meet performance requirements, are important factors.[46]

Carpet is the only textile product on which people walk. This is why carpet construction, or performance, and installation specifications are so critical. The third critical specification is maintenance.

Specification of any one of these three elements without knowledge or consideration of the other two increases the risk that the carpet will not perform up to potential or expectation.

Even properly specified carpet can wear out or appear to be worn out if it is not maintained adequately. Dirt is unsightly but it can also be abrasive. As foot traffic deposits soil and causes the pile yarns to flex, embedded grit cuts the face fibers. The carpet begins to lose density and resilience. Threadbare spots appear and the carpet wears out. Moreover, allowing soil to build up and to spread may give the carpet a worn out appearance even if the face fibers are essentially intact.

If carpet is not vacuum cleaned regularly, the dirt builds up and begins to spread. To guard against buildup, a well-planned program is essential in commercial installations with their high traffic loads. Planned maintenance is the key to extending the life expectancy of carpet. The maintenance plan is no less important than the initial carpet specification and installation.

MAINTENANCE PLAN AND SCHEDULE

There is a big difference between cleaning carpet and maintaining carpet. Cleaning is the removal of apparent soil. For many commercial carpet owners, cleaning takes place irregularly, on an "as needed" basis, and is merely to maintain carpet's daily appearance at a consistent level of cleanliness. Soiling, however, is a cumulative process which, if allowed to go too far, cannot easily be reversed. A customized comprehensive carpet care program consists of five elements:

1. **Soil containment.** Isolation of soil entering the building using mats at entrances.
2. **Vacuuming.** Scheduled frequency for removal of dry soil using a CRI-approved "Green Label/Seal of Approval Vacuum."
3. **Spot and spill removal system.** Using professional spot removal techniques.
4. **Interim cleaning.** Scheduled frequency appearance cleaning for all traffic areas.
5. **Restorative cleaning.** Scheduled frequency deep cleaning to remove residues and trapped soils.

There are some conditions where appearance change must be expected. In areas where the oily material from asphalt sealers is tracked into the building, carpet and other flooring may become yellowed over time. Check the traffic lanes often for slight dulling of color; this indicates a buildup of soil. It is virtually impossible to remove all of this material once it has penetrated the fiber of any carpet. Entrance mats and scheduled cleaning can reduce this phenomenon. (See Figure 3.6.) Areas where large amounts of sandy soil

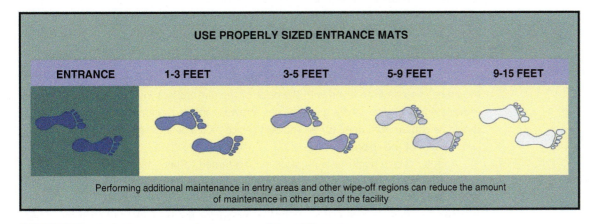

FIGURE 3.6 Properly sized entrance mats. *Drawing courtesy of Carpet & Rug Institute.*

enter the building may become dull in appearance over time. This is due to abrasion of the fiber surface, affecting the reflection of light. Frequent vacuuming helps to minimize this problem.[47]

The maintenance plan should be developed as the carpet specifications are being considered. (In fact, a plan should be prepared in case the carpet is installed prior to completion of construction.) One point that is often overlooked in carpet maintenance is minimizing the immediate sources of soil around the perimeter of the building by keeping sidewalks, parking lots, and garages adjacent to the building as clean as possible.

When preparing the maintenance plan, keep in mind that one of the advantages of carpet compared to hard floors is that carpet localizes soil. Carpet tends to catch and hold soil and spills where they occur instead of allowing them to spread quickly. This feature of carpet suggests that the best maintenance plan will identify in advance the most likely areas for soiling and spilling. The plan will specify maintenance schedules and procedures for these areas, as well as the remainder of the carpet.

Specifically, heavy traffic areas, like entrances and lobbies, will not only require the most substantial carpet, they will probably have to be vacuumed once a day. In some instances, greasy motor oil from parking lots should be anticipated.

Kitchen smoke in restaurants and cafeterias will contribute heavily to overall soiling. Stains and spills in restaurants and hospitals will be very common. Routine procedures for attending to these as quickly as possible are necessary.

Whatever the nature of the installation, it is wise to anticipate dealing with soil from the very first day the carpet is installed. Otherwise, abrasive dirt may build up faster than it can be handled.[48]

For seagrass, periodic cleaning of the surface with a high suction vacuum is needed. The nonstatic, no-pile surface does not trap dirt and dust. Remove liquid spills immediately to avoid spots. Fiber seal is recommended in high spill areas. For spot and overall cleaning, use dry cleaning powder such as the Host Carpet Cleaning System, which is readily available through the yellow page listings.

DAILY AND PERIODIC PROCEDURES

Two elements essential to an efficient maintenance program are (1) daily procedures encompassing both regular vacuuming and spot cleaning, and (2) scheduled overall cleaning to remove discoloring grime and to refresh the pile.

Overall, grime not only causes discoloration, it presents another undesirable quality. Carpet that is not cleaned and reconditioned regularly, no matter how faithfully it is vacuumed, will tend to permanently crush and mat down. As greases present in smoke, or pollutants in the air, settle on the carpet, pile yarns may become gummy enough to stick to each other and flatten in use. Matted carpet appears to be worn out, even if there is no real pile loss. Obviously, carpet which must be replaced because it *looks* worn out is no less costly than carpet which must be replaced because it *is* worn out!

COLOR AS A MAINTENANCE FACTOR

The color of the carpet can contribute significantly to minimizing the appearance of dirt, particularly for entrances and lobbies, which get the bulk of tracked-in soil. If possible, colors should be chosen which blend with the color of the dirt brought in from outside. Since the most common dirt colors are greys, beiges, browns, and reds, carpet colors for entrances should be chosen from these tones. The best choice would be a tweed coloration combining two or more of the colors.

Another choice might be a multicolored, patterned carpet which would provide additional visual interest while helping camouflage dirt and spills until they can be removed. Such highly patterned carpet is a popular choice for hotel lobbies and restaurants.

Lighter, more delicate colors are best reserved for inside spaces (e.g., offices, guest rooms, lounges) where soiling rates are obviously lower and the danger of accidental spills is more remote.

PREVENTATIVE MEASURES

Preventative measures consist of minimizing the debris that is tracked in from outside and protecting carpet from moisture and dirt that is already inside the building. This is largely accomplished with the use of mats—outside and inside. Using both types of mats at entrances and other areas helps prevent excessive soiling on carpet.

Outside mats scrape debris off of shoes that have the capability to track in that material. Use soil-removal mats that have a coarse texture, are able to brush soil from shoes, and hold large amounts of soil in their pile.

Inside mats remove smaller particles of dirt as well as oils and other liquids that can be tracked in from outside. Use water-absorbent mats to prevent tracked-in moisture from getting to the carpet. Mats that extend for 6 to 15 feet inside the entrance will trap 80 percent of soil and moisture from the first five or six steps. Another way to prevent soiling using mats is by placing protective mats around food stations, water coolers, elevators, and stair thresholds to prevent moisture and dirt from becoming ground into carpet.

For mats to continue to trap soil, they should be cleaned on a regular basis, more frequently than the carpet. If accumulated soil is not removed, the mat will become overloaded and cannot prevent soil from entering the building.

Other preventive tips include restricting food and beverage consumption to specific areas, requiring lids on drinks or oversized cups, and placing trashcans in easily accessible areas. In addition, keeping parking lots, sidewalks, and entrances clean will cut down on the tracking in of debris.[49]

Note: The area underneath a desk should be protected by a chair mat. These areas are sometimes considered low traffic areas; however, the chair rollers can create damage due to the concentration of pressure and wear.

Carpeting of entryways is recommended. One example of an entryway system is Mannington Commercial's Ruffian and Ruffian Ridgework, which provides a two-step system— the initial sturdy grooves stepped on initially and the scraper tile next underfoot. The scraper tile provides a "network of deep channels that act as reservoirs to catch and hold water, dry soil and larger debris." This system traps oil and fine dirt particles, which can be removed upon cleaning.[50]

As elevators experience tremendous floor traffic and soiling, carpeting of elevators is also recommended, regardless of the choice to carpet an entrance lobby. Removable carpets can be quite beneficial, as they allow for easier cleaning. Double-sided tape can provide safety benefits for elevators.[51] It is wiser to have soil wiped off on the elevator carpet rather than having it tracked over the carpet elsewhere.

It is common to have two sets of walk-off mats and removable carpets available. Because they take such heavy abuse, one set is kept in place while the other is being cleaned. If walk-off mats are not regularly cleaned (weekly or semiweekly), they become a source of soil and lose their effect.[52]

Another method of dirt control in commercial buildings is to use a recessed mat or grating inside exterior doors. These gratings feature a system of self-cleaning recessed treads that are closely spaced to prevent the smallest heel from catching, yet allow dirt and sand to collect below the surface. The grate removes easily for cleaning.

In the residential carpet industry, soiling problems may occur related to products used by family members. For example, in a teenager's room acne medicine may spill on the carpet; in another room plant food, aerosols, or furniture polish may be the culprit. In bathrooms a toilet bowl cleaner or a dandruff shampoo can cause a dark brown stain, often with a blue fringe. Urine is also a culprit in small area discoloration. These spots begin at the backing and progress upward over a period of time. They may be dull yellow or even red. The characteristic ammonia like odor will be present for only a few hours, and it is replaced by a musty odor. Bleach can be a problem in the laundry area, or it may be tracked in from the swimming pool. Dimethysulfoxide, otherwise known as DMSO, is widely used for relief of pain from arthritis, back problems, athletic injuries, and other muscular aches. It is a clear liquid with an odor similar to garlic and causes rapid loss of color on carpet due to its solvent action.

VACUUMING SCHEDULES AND EQUIPMENT

For years, the CRI was hearing complaints about carpet being hard to maintain. So naturally, they did what any professional association would do; they began asking, "Why?" Upon testing a few vacuum cleaners in a closed, stainless-steel chamber with carpet on the floor and a measured amount of soiling, they found that most vacuum cleaners didn't harm the carpet, but neither did they trap and retain soil very efficiently. Many of those vacuums were removing soil from the carpet, where it was doing no harm in terms of human health, and were flinging it into the air where it became part of the airborne soil burden.

The CRI contacted the equipment manufacturers and told them what they found. Most of the vacuum manufacturers did the right thing by re-engineering their equipment to make it more efficient. Today, the CRI has a listing of Green Label Seal of Approval vacuums on their Web site.

CRI began certifying carpet cleaning with its Green Label Vacuum program. While Green Label Vacuum certified products are still commercially available, future plans include merging vacuums into the Seal of Approval program while still maintaining Green Label status. Vacuums will be required to show cleaning effectiveness and appearance retention, but also must meet an air quality test that ensures the dust and dirt collected by the vacuum stays within the bag and canister.[53]

Further, closed-chamber tests conducted by Lees Commercial Carpets demonstrates that using a CRI Green Label/Seal of Approval/vacuum on carpet for only four minutes results in a 10-fold reduction in airborne dust burdens compared to a non-Green Label vacuum. Think about the implications of that statement—less dust to breathe and less dust spread over furnishings and fixtures that has to be removed. That's a win-win situation for professionals.[54]

According to the CRI,

Of all the carpet maintenance procedures, vacuuming takes the most time and attention, yet is the most cost effective. The carpet should be inspected for spots during vacuuming. Spots should be removed as soon as possible. The longer they are allowed to set, the more permanent they may become.

The following is a normal vacuuming schedule:

- High traffic—Vacuum daily
- Medium traffic—Vacuum twice weekly
- Light traffic—Vacuum weekly

This broad guide recommends minimum schedules only. To reduce this general rule to specifics, some definitions will be useful. Track-off areas are where a carpet collects foot soil tracked in from the outdoors or from hard surfaced floors indoors. Funnel areas are where foot traffic is squeezed into or through a concentrated area, such as a doorway, stairwell, or in front of a drinking fountain, vending machine, and so on. These areas can be identified in advance of soiling. Planned vacuuming in these areas, *even when soil is not visible*, will help prevent soil buildup. Also, it will help focus maintenance attention on the places where it is known that soil will be tracked.

In the final analysis, an adequate schedule must be based on the individual installation and its own traffic load and soiling rate. For example, soil may accumulate so rapidly at entrances (track-off areas) that carpet at those locations will have to be vacuumed several times a day. In another instance, rooms may be entered directly from an uncarpeted corridor. Under those circumstances, even light traffic may cause heavy soiling, and the carpet may have to be vacuumed several times a week. Only experience will tell whether more frequent vacuuming is indicated.[55]

SPOT REMOVAL

Identification and immediate action are the keys to effective spot removal procedures. To minimize time and effort, it is helpful to know what causes a spot so that treatment can begin without guesswork. In most installations, spot identification may not be difficult because the possibilities are limited. In others, it could be a real problem.

A drug-dispensing area in hospitals, for example, is susceptible to hundreds of spotting and staining agents. Employees must be instructed to report spills as they occur and to identify the spilled material.

It is also important to clean up spills as quickly as possible. The longer a spot sets, the more difficult it may be to remove. If it sets too long, it might react with the carpet dyes and cause permanent discoloration. Hence, an alert staff and a well-stocked spot removal kit are important to a good carpet maintenance program. Always test a cleaning agent to determine its effect upon the carpet dye, fibers, and the spot before applying larger amounts.

IMPORTANCE OF THE MAINTENANCE PLAN

There are many factors that will influence the frequency of cleaning, but a maintenance plan should be in effect before the traffic areas start to show discoloration. If the traffic areas are allowed to become excessively soiled, on-location cleaning may not remove sufficient soil to restore them to an acceptable level. The high-use areas must be cleaned more frequently in order to maintain a satisfactory overall appearance.

DEEP CLEANING

Periodic deep cleaning is required to remove oily materials that have become bonded to the carpet fibers, as well as to collect dirt particles that have been pushed into the space between fibers and onto the fibers by the pressure of foot traffic. There are five main methods that are used to clean carpet (vacuuming, shampooing, dry-cleaning, foam cleaning, and bonnet), although there are many variations on the basic methods, multiple names for the same process, and various combinations of methods. Operator training and experience are needed to use any of the methods successfully.

Of all cleaning methods, those that focus on shampooing are generally thought of as the least effective. To accomplish the shampooing, specific types of detergent are administered to the carpet and then agitated by a cleaning machine designed for this purpose. The shampoo is often removed through vacuuming. While this method offers the benefit of pleasant fragrance and improved appearance, this effect is generally transitory, as these benefits diminish in time—and they fail to address dirt particles and microbes left behind in the carpet.

Consumers who are frustrated by the drying time required for the shampooing method will likely appreciate the dry-cleaning method, through which a specially developed cleaning powder is worked into the carpet. The powder attracts the dirt particles, and then the particles and powder are vacuumed from the carpet.

For a method that incorporates elements of the shampooing and dry-cleaning methods, consumers might wish to try the foam cleaning method. Only a minimal quantity of water is required, and a foam detergent attracts the soil, which clings to the detergent. After application and the appropriate procedure to work the detergent into the carpet, a vacuum is swept across the surface.

A dry-cleaning method used almost exclusively in commercial buildings is the bonnet method. In contrast to residential cleaning methods, which have been developed with a focus on dirt removal, the bonnet method has been developed with a focus on maintaining or restoring carpet appearance. The bonnet method is accomplished through application of a chemical detergent to the carpet and use of an absorbent pad on a rotary shampoo machine. Consumers should note that this method can cause serious damage to fibers used to create most residential carpets.[56]

Beware of the bargain carpet cleaning companies that will clean a whole house for a ridiculously low price. They often hire untrained people and, in the case of water extraction, may soak the carpet so it takes a long time to dry completely, especially in high-humidity areas. The time invested in developing a plan for carpet maintenance will pay off in longer use from the carpet. *Cleaning should be done before the carpet shows signs of soil.* It is essential that the manufacturer's recommendations be followed, especially if guarantees and liabilities are involved.

bibliography

Bridgepoint Corporation. *Protector Course*. Salt Lake City, UT: Bridgepoint Corporation, 2008.

Burlington Industries, Inc. *Carpet Maintenance Guide for Hospitals and Health Care Facilities*. King of Prussia, PA: Burlington Industries Inc., Carpet Division, 1987.

The Carpet and Rug Institute. *Carpet Specifier's Handbook*. Dalton, GA: The Carpet and Rug Institute, 2008.

Monsanto Contract Fibers. *Concepts Ideas for Specifiers*. Atlanta, GA: Monsanto Fiber and Intermediates Co.

Revere, Glen. *All About Carpets*. Blue Ridge Summit, PA: TAB Books Inc., 1988.

Reznikoff, C. S. *Specifications for Commercial Interiors*. Whitney, NY: Library of Design, an imprint of Watson-Guptil Publications, a division of Billboard Publications, 1989.

The Wool Bureau, New York, NY.

glossary

Antistatic. A nonpermanent type of static dissipation.

Axminster. Pile tufts inserted from spools of colored yarns, making possible an almost endless variety of geometric or floral patterns.

Berber. A looped pile rug originating in North Africa; may be patterned or natural colored. Today, berbers are mostly textured natural earth tones.

Carpet yellowing. An unwanted change of color.

Conductive. Carpet with fibers capable of conducting electricity to ground.

Continuous filaments. Continuous strand of synthetic fiber extruded in yarn form without the need for spinning that all natural fibers require.

Cornrowing. A characteristic that should be expected in carpet with higher tufts and lower density pile, resulting in the pile laying flat.

Cut pile. A pile surface created by cutting the loops of yarn in a tufted, woven, or fusion-bonded carpet.

Dhurrie. A reversible tapestry woven, flat rug with no pile. Originally from India; today it comes mostly in pastel colors.

ESD. Electrostatic discharge; to be considered around computers.

Fiber. The material, natural or man-made, from which carpets are made.

Foam. One of the types of carpet padding.

Gauge. The distance between needles in tufted carpets as measured in fractions of an inch; therefore, gauge is also the number of yarn ends across the width of the carpet.

Indentations. Marks left in the carpet from heavy pieces of furniture remaining in one place.

Jacquard. An apparatus on a carpet-weaving loom that produces patterns from colored yarns. The pattern information is contained on perforated cards. The holes in the cards activate the mechanism that selects the color to be raised to the pile surface.

Kilim. A flat-woven, or pileless, rug.

Level loop. A carpet style having all tufts in a loop form and of substantially the same level.

Mildew. A discoloration caused by fungi.

Modular carpet tiles. Carpet precut into 18" or 24" squares or other suitable dimensions.

Multi-level loop. A carpet with some tufts that are substantially longer than others. Gives a sculptured appearance or pattern.

Nap. Carpet or rug pile surface.

Noise-reduction coefficient (NRC). The average percentage of sound reduction at various Hertz levels.

Pile. The yarns that are looped or cut on the surface of the carpet.

Pitch. Number of lengthwise warp yarns in a 27" width.

Ripples. Waves caused by either improper stretching or humidity.

Rya. A Scandinavian hand-woven rug with a deep resilient, comparatively flat pile. Usually of abstract design.

SB. Styrene butadiene.

Sculptured. A patterned carpet made by using high and low areas, cut at an angle.

Shading. Apparent color difference between areas of the same carpet. The physical cause is the difference between the cut end luster and side luster of fibers.

Shedding. Normal process of excess yarns coming to the surface in a freshly installed carpet.

Sponge rubber. One of the three types of carpet padding.

Sprouting. Protrusion of individual tuft or yarn ends above the pile surface. May be clipped with scissors.

Static electricity. A situation in which shoe friction against carpet fiber causes production of an electrostatic charge that is discharged from carpet to person to conductive ground (e.g., a doorknob).

Tackless (strip). Narrow lengths of wood or metal containing either two or three rows of angled pins on which carpet is stretched and secured in a stretch-in installation.

Velvet. Woven carpet made on a loom similar to a Wilton loom but lacking the Jacquard mechanism. These carpets are generally level loop, level cut/loop, or plush, in solid or tweed colors.

Walk-off. Mats on which most of the exterior soil is deposited.

Wilton. Carpet woven on a loom with a Jacquard mechanism, which utilizes a series of punched cards to select pile height and yarn color.

Yarns. A continuous strand composed of fibers or filaments used in the production of carpet and other fabrics.

endnotes

1. *Brief History of the Pazyryk Carpet,* Chicago, IL: Peerless Imported Rugs.
2. Adapted from Wool Bureau Library, Vol. 6, Rugs and Carpet (boldface added).
3. Carpet & Rug Institute, www.carpet-rug.org
4. Ibid.
5. Ibid.
6. Ibid.
7. Lees Carpet, www.leescarpet.com
8. CRI, www.carpet-rug.org
9. Carpet Buyers Handbook, www.carpetbuyershandbook.com
10. CRI, www.carpet-rug.org
11. Super Steamer, www.supersteamer.com
12. Static Smart, www.staticsmart.com
13. Lees Carpet, www.leescarpet.com
14. Millikencarpet.com
15. CRI, www.carpet-rug.org
16. Renaissance Flooring Inc., www.flooringarizona.com
17. A+Systems, www.asystems.in/other_products.html
18. Carpet Super Site, www.carpetsupersite.com/carpet_comparison.htm
19. Carpet Buyers Handbook, www.carpetbuyershandbook.com
20. Merida Meridian, www.meridameridian.com
21. CRI, www.carpet-rug.org
22. Carpet Guru, www.carpetguru.com
23. Bridgepoint Corporation *Protector Course*, Salt Lake City, UT, p. 11.
24. CRI, www.carpet-rug.org
25. Ibid.
26. Ibid.
27. Carpet Cushion Council, www.carpetcushion.org/types
28. CRI, www.carpet-rug.org
29. Carpet Cushion Council, www.carpetcushion.org
30. Carpet Cushion Council, www.carpetcushion.org/types
31. Bene-Clean, www.beneclene.com
32. CRI, www.carpet-rug.org
33. Ibid.
34. Ibid.
35. Ibid.
36. Ibid.
37. Ibid.
38. Ibid.
39. Ibid.
40. Ibid.
41. Ibid.
42. Certified Flooring Installers, www.cfi-installers.org
43. TacFast, www.tacfast.com
44. Lees Carpet, www.leescarpet.com
45. CRI, www.carpet.rug.org
46. Ibid.
47. Ibid.
48. CRI, www.carpet-rug.org
49. Ibid.
50. Mannington Carpet, www.mannington.com
51. Constantine Carpet, www.constantine-carpet.com
52. Carpet & Rug Institute, *Specifier's Handbook*, p. 56.
53. Carpet & Rug, www.carpet-rug.org/pdf_word_docs/
54. Clean Link, www.cleanlink.com
55. Carpet & Rug Institute, www.carpet-rug.org
56. Wise Geek, www.wisegeek.com

4 Floors

In this chapter, you will:

- Describe the social and physical influences affecting historical changes in carpet, including its composition and uses
- Recognize types of flooring materials and their fabrication and installation methods, as well as maintenance requirements
- Identify relevant aspects of design related to flooring—and apply appropriate and necessary information to address these design aspects
- Identify the importance of industry-specific regulations related to floors
- Demonstrate understanding of the composition of various types of wood—and the relevance of each to flooring selection, installation, and maintenance

Wood

Wood was used in ancient times for flooring. According to the Bible, Solomon's Temple had a floor of fir; the Romans, in contrast, used wood on only the upper floors of their buildings and stone on the main floor. These stone floors persisted throughout the Dark Ages. In peasant homes, of course, a dirt floor was spread with straw; however, heavy, wide oak planks predominated in larger domestic structures. The term *ground floor* has its roots in the fact that the ground floor of a structure was once the ground, the dirt, the earth.[1] Clearly, this term has a different meaning today.

The first wood floors, called puncheon floors, were made of split logs, flat side up, fitted edge to edge, and smoothed with an ax or an adz. When saws became available to cut the wood into planks, white pine plank flooring of great widths was used during the U.S. Colonial period and was pegged in place. These early hardwood floors were not sanded or finished, since the pine would be polished smooth simply by regular traffic.

Initially, fine wood flooring came into vogue in Europe, where only the wealthiest in society could afford such flooring. Parquet floors were among the wealthy class's favorite wood-flooring surfaces, as they were stunning and offered many patterns. While only the wealthy were able to enjoy fine wood floors in European homes, this was not the case in North America, where a plentiful supply of timber flooded the market.

Until the late 1900s, hardwood floors were created by hand. Mass production in factories then became prevalent. For less expensive homes, hardwood plank became the most common type of flooring. Due to incorrect installation and lack of care, though, very few of these early floors are still in existence today.[2]

Partially because hardwood floors were thought of as lacking longevity, carpet quickly usurped the place of hardwood. By the 1920s and 1930s, cork and linoleum became popular. Even so, hardwood floors remained in the marketplace, due to their durability. After World War II, however, hardwood floors were often hidden beneath carpet, which became quite popular.

By the late twentieth century, hardwood floors enjoyed a resurgence in the residential flooring marketplace. Once again, consumers began to show their appreciation of the hardwood floor's appearance and durability. By 2012, the National Wood Flooring Association (NWFA) stated that hardwood floors were responsible for 10 percent of flooring sales. Recycled and reclaimed wood had niched comfortably back into the marketplace.[3]

In eighteenth- and early nineteenth-century America, sand was frequently spread over the wood floor to absorb dirt and moisture. Later, the wealthy stained these floors and then covered them with Oriental rugs; in more modest homes, the floors were left either bare or covered by homemade rugs. When renovating an old pine plank floor, pay particular attention to the knots, which are much harder than the surrounding wood. They have a tendency to protrude above the level of the worn floor and must be sanded to give a smoother surface. In some early floors that have not been renovated, it is possible to trip over these knots because they extend so far above the level of the floors. In the early nineteenth century, **stenciling** was done directly on the floor in imitation of rugs, parquet floors, marble, and tile. Painted floors and **floorcloths** came to be highly regarded until the carpet industry spelled the decline of floorcloths in the 1830s and 1840s. These floorcloths are now making a comeback.

Parquetry and **marquetry** were used in France starting in the early 1700s, with one of the most famous examples of this period being the beautiful parquet floor at the Palace of Versailles. In 1885, the invention of a machine capable of making a **tongue-and-groove** (often referred to as t & g) in the edge of the wood and the use of **kilns** combined to produce a draft-proof hardwood floor.

In the Victorian era, inlaid border patterns using contrasting light and dark wood were put together in an intricate manner. (See Figure 4.1.) End-grain wood was even used to pave streets at the beginning of the twentieth century. In the early 1920s, unit block flooring was introduced; this made parquet floors more reasonably priced, because each piece did not have to be laid down individually, but rather in one block.

Also contributing to the current popularity of wood floors are manufacturers' warranties, which vary from 5 to 25 years.

Wood is divided into two broad categories: **hardwoods** from deciduous trees, which lose their leaves in winter, and softwoods, from conifers or evergreens. In reality, there is an overlapping of hardness because some woods from evergreens are harder than those from broad-leafed trees. The harder woods will, of course, be more durable. This durability, together with

FIGURE 4.1 This inlay includes the following woods: maple, white oak, merbau, and black walnut. *Photo courtesy of Czar Floors, Inc.*

color and texture, must be considered in both flooring and furniture construction. Ease of finish should also be considered when the wood will have an applied finish.

There are two types of oak used in flooring: white oak and red oak. The heartwood and sapwood of red oak are similar in appearance, which is light-colored with a reddish tone. It is slightly redder in color than white oak, which can have a white to cream to light brown color. The grain of red oak is open, and also somewhat coarser (and therefore more porous), than that of white oak, which tends to have longer rays.

Both red oak and white oak are quite dense and stiff. Both have great shock resistance, and both are durable. White oak, though, is a bit harder and resists fungi and insects quite well, due to its high tannic acid content.[4]

Weight is usually a good indicator of the relative strength of wood. Because wood is a natural material, it absorbs or eliminates moisture depending on the humidity to which it is exposed. Most shrinkage or swelling occurs in the width of the wood; the amount depends on the manner of the cut. Quarter sawn woods are the least troublesome.

Warping is the tendency of wood to twist or bend when drying. Warping may occur as a **bow, crook, twist,** or **cup.** (See Figure 4.2.) The moisture problem can be minimized by using kiln-dried lumber. In the kiln drying process, wood is stacked in an oven so heated air can circulate around each plank and thus render a uniform moisture content. Between 7 to 8 percent moisture content is acceptable in wood used for making floors and furniture, whereas 12 to 19 percent is acceptable for construction grades of wood.

Hardwood naturally contracts and loses moisture upon exposure to very dry air. In high humidity, however, the wood might expand, due to increased moisture in the air. A humidifier can be used in the winter to provide a stable relative humidity in the range of 25 to 35 percent. An air conditioner performs the same function in the summer. The Hardwood Information Center advises that hardwood flooring be stored for one week or longer in the location where installation is intended, which will allow the wood to "reach a balance with the surroundings."[5]

Wood is composed of many cells that run vertically, thus giving wood its straight grain. At frequent intervals, **medullary rays** thread their way between and at right angles to the vertical cells. These rays are most noticeable in plain oak and beech.

Consider the circular rings of trees. Some of the giant sequoias of California and the ancient oaks of Great Britain have been dated by rings showing hundreds of years of growth. These rings show the seasonal growth and comprise springwood (formed early in the growing season) and summer wood or late wood. In some trees, such as ash or oak, the different times of growth are very obvious, whereas in others, such as birch and maple, the seasonal growth is more blended. When there is an obvious difference in growth times, there is also a difference in weight and hardness. The faster-growing trees, usually those in more moderate

Warp

Deflection of One Corner

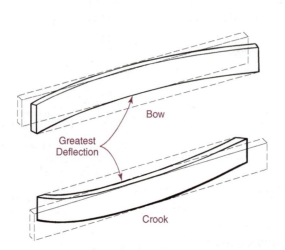
Bow

Greatest Deflection

Twist

Crook

Deflection

Cup

FIGURE 4.2 Warp should be avoided in flooring projects.

climates, are softer than the same trees grown in northern areas, where the growing season is shorter. Next to the bark is the sapwood, which contains the food cells and is usually lighter in color. Heartwood contains the currently inactive cells and is slightly darker because of chemical substances that are part of the cell walls.

Figure is the pattern of the wood fibers; the wood **grain** is determined by the arrangement of the cells and fibers. Some grains are straight and others are patterned; this characteristic is enhanced by the method of cutting the boards.

There are two principal methods of cutting lumber. One is called plain sawn for hardwoods and flat grained for softwoods. The second is **quarter sawn** for hardwoods or edge grained for softwoods. When referring to maple as a flooring material, the term *edge grained* is used, although maple is a hardwood. Oak is quarter sawn, but fir cut in the same manner is called vertical grain. Interior designers will probably be dealing mainly with hardwoods, so, with the exceptions just noted, the terms *plain sawn* and *quarter sawn* will be used henceforth. Each method has its own advantages: Plain sawn is the cheapest, easiest, and most economical use of wood, whereas quarter sawn gives less distortion of wood from shrinkage or warping.

Each method of cutting gives a different appearance to wood. Plain sawing gives a cathedral or pointed-arch effect, whereas quarter sawing gives more of a straight-line appearance. Saw mills cut logs into boards producing 80 percent plain to 20 percent quartered lumber. Quartered oak flooring, therefore, is extremely hard to find and is expensive. Most production is mixed cuts. (See Figure 4.3.)

Veneer is a very thin sheet of wood varying in thickness from 1/8 inch to 1/100 inch. Wood more than 1/4 inch thick is no longer considered veneer. The manner in which the veneer is cut also gives different patterns. The three methods are rotary sliced, flat sliced, and quarter sliced. (These are discussed in more detail in Chapter 5.) **Laminated or engineered wood** is used for some floors and is a sandwich with an uneven number of sheets of veneer, layered at right angles to prevent warping, with the better veneers on the face. (See Figure 4.4.) Water-resistant glue should be used for bonding the layers together, and the sandwich is placed in a hot press in which pressure of 150 to 300 pounds per square inch (**psi**) is applied. Heat around 250°F permanently sets the adhesive and bonds the layers together into a single strong panel.

Laminated **prefinished** floors are less affected by humidity and are therefore considered more stable. Only laminated wood floors may be installed below grade; however, the manufacturer's installation procedures must be followed exactly. Laminated products expand little, so they may be fitted close to a vertical surface. It is predicted that laminated wood flooring sales will more than double in the next five years, because strong environmental trends are leading consumers to these products.

Grades of oak are determined by appearance alone. Flooring that is generally free of defects is known as clear although it may contain **burls,** streaks, and pinworm holes. Select is almost clear, but this grade contains more of the natural characteristics, including knots and other marks. The common grades have more marking than either of the other two grades and are often specified because of these natural features and the character they bring to the flooring.

Although oak is the predominant wood used for flooring, maple, walnut, teak, and cherry are also used. Any wood can be used for any floor.

NEW PRODUCTS AND TRENDS

A new trend in hardwood floors has led to the popularity of hand-scraped and distressed hardwood floors, particularly in posh locations. During early hardwood-flooring history, floors were often

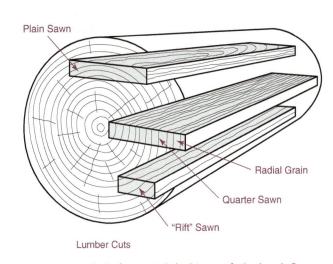

FIGURE 4.3 Methods of sawing include plain sawn for hardwoods, flat grained for softwoods, quarter sawn for hardwoods, and edge grained for softwoods.

Plain Sawn

Radial Grain

Quarter Sawn

"Rift" Sawn

Lumber Cuts

Solid Wood
Milled from one piece of wood into boards that are three-quarters of an inch thick.

• Should not install below grade, as moisture makes it expand and contract.

Engineered Wood
Constructed of multiple layers of crossgrain wood that are bonded together.

• Designed for installation at any house level including below grade.

FIGURE 4.4 Solid wood and engineered wood. This illustration not only shows the difference between solid wood and engineered wood but also shows a tongue-in-groove joint. *Drawing courtesy of Armstrong World Industries.*

hand-scraped on location in order to flatten them. Today, sanding methods have made hand-scraping an option (rather than a requirement) that is generally chosen for its proclivity to supply a unique appearance.[6]

The difference between hand-scraped and distressed is that hand-scraped is done by hand and distressed is done by machine to imitate the look of hand-scraped. However, the distressed flooring can show repetitive marks.

Consumers sometimes seek out the attractive appearance of flooring such as Durapalm, which is developed from many layers of palm. This type of flooring can be installed through glue-down and nail-down methods, depending on the consumer's needs and preference.[7]

Dark-stained flooring is another popular trend right now. There are many dark-stained bamboo options available that give homeowners a rich look within their home. This dark flooring is especially stunning in kitchens. On the other end of the spectrum, lighter flooring (almost white) is also very popular. The lighter option is typically found with a maple or hardwood floor and stained bamboos. See Table 4.1 for a comparison of different hardwood flooring brands.[8]

Table 4.1 Hardwood Flooring Brand Comparison

Hardwood Flooring Brand	Solid Strips and Planks	Prefinished Engineered Planks	Longstrip Engineered Planks	Exotic Species	Hand-Scraped Floors	Glueless Installation
Anderson Hardwood Floors	—	Yes	—	Yes	Yes	—
Award Hardwood Floors	Yes	Yes	Yes	Yes	—	Yes
BR-111	Yes	Yes	—	Yes	—	—
Bruce Hardwood Floors	Yes	Yes	Yes	Yes	—	Yes
Capella Wood Floors	—	Yes	—	—	—	—
Columbia Flooring	Yes	Yes	Yes	Yes	Yes	Yes
Hartco Wood Flooring	Yes	Yes	—	Yes	—	—
HomerWood Hardwood Floors	Yes	—	—	—	Yes	—
Kahrs Wood Flooring	—	Yes	Yes	Yes	—	Yes
Kentucky Wood Floors	Yes	Yes	—	Yes	—	—
Lauzon Hardwood Flooring	Yes	Yes	Yes	Yes	—	—
Mannington Wood Floors	—	Yes	—	Yes	Yes	Yes
Mercier Wood Flooring	Yes	Yes	—	Yes	—	—
Mirage Wood Floors	Yes	Yes	—	Yes	—	—
Mohawk Hardwood Flooring	Yes	Yes	Yes	Yes	Yes	Yes
Mullican Flooring	Yes	—	—	Yes	Yes	—
Muskoka Hardwood Flooring	Yes	Yes	—	Yes	—	—
Robbins Hardwood Flooring	Yes	Yes	—	Yes	—	—
Shaw Hardwood Floors	Yes	Yes	Yes	Yes	Yes	Yes
Somerset Hardwood Flooring	Yes	—	—	Yes	Yes	—
Tarkett Wood Floors	Yes	Yes	Yes	Yes	Yes	—

Source: From Floor Facts website, www.floorfacts.com/hardwood-flooring-comparison.asp. Used with permission.

TYPES OF WOOD FLOORING

The three different types of wood flooring are strip, random plank, and parquet.

Strip Flooring

Strip flooring is described by plank width and thickness. Its width, but not its thickness, remains constant. Strip flooring ranges in thickness from 5/16" to 3/4" wide and is available exclusively in widths of 1 1/2", 2", and 2 1/4".[9]

Usually 2 1/4"-wide strip flooring is tongue-and-grooved on both sides and ends. This type of flooring is most commonly made of oak, although other woods may be used, such as teak and maple. Strip flooring may be laid parallel to the wall or diagonally. Gymnasium floors are always constructed of maple but require a special type of installation that provides a slight "give" to the floor. Strip flooring is used above levels only and is not recommended for concrete slabs.

Another variation of plank, strip, and parquet flooring is acrylic impregnated flooring. Liquid acrylic is evenly forced into the pore structure of select hardwood, and then is permanently hardened. The finish, therefore, is as deep as the wood itself, is highly resistant to abrasion and impact, never requires refinishing, and is easy to repair and maintain. Dyes and fire retardants may be added to the acrylic, if required. The stain penetrates throughout the wood; therefore, worn areas need only to be retouched with a topcoat. The floor never needs sanding, staining, or refinishing. Acrylic impregnated hardwood is over 50 percent more crushproof than non-impregnated flooring. With all these impregnated woods, it must be remembered that the color cannot be changed because it has penetrated the whole depth of the wood. This can be an asset or a liability, depending on the purchaser's requirements.

Regular strip flooring is sold by the board foot and 5 percent waste allowance is added to the total ordered.

Random Plank

Plank flooring is 3 to 8 inches wide; most installations comprise three different sizes. The widths selected should correspond to the dimensions of the room to keep the flooring in proper scale: narrower ones for the smaller rooms and wider ones for the larger rooms. Random plank comes with a **square** or **beveled** edge (see Figure 4.5) and may be factory finished or finished after installation.

Plank floors also have a tongue-and-groove side. The prefinished tongue-and-groove disguises any shrinkage, because the V-joint becomes a fraction wider; with a square edge, however, the crack caused by shrinkage is more obvious. (This is why it is important that all wood be stored in the climatic conditions that will prevail at the installation site. Proper storage conditions will allow the wood to absorb or dissipate moisture and reach stable moisture content.) A white finish will also emphasize any shrinkage. In the past, some plank floors were installed using wooden pegs or plugs. A hole (or several holes for a wide plank) was drilled about 1 1/2 to 2 inches from the end of the plank. A **dowel** was pounded into the floor joist and glued into place. Any excess dowel was then cut and sanded flush with the floor. Often, these plugs were constructed of a contrasting wood and became a decorative feature of plank flooring. Today it is recommended that, because of its width, plank flooring be screwed to the floor, then the screws should be countersunk; short dowels of walnut, other contrasting wood, or even brass are then glued in to cover the screw for decorative purposes only.

Unfortunately, some prefinished floors may have plugs made of plastic, which seems incongruous in a wood floor. Another decorative joining procedure used in the past was the butterfly or key, where a dovetail-shaped piece of wood was used at the end joint of two boards. Plank flooring can also be of different species, which creates an interesting color combination.

For those desiring the authentic look of an old floor, Aged Woods has recycled antique planks with varying amounts of character (i.e., knots and knot holes, nail holes, flat and vertical

Edge and End Detail
Special milling on the edges of each individual board to create visual effects.

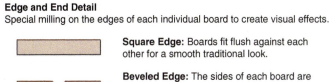

Square Edge: Boards fit flush against each other for a smooth traditional look.

Beveled Edge: The sides of each board are sanded or angled to create grooves, or an outline effect around each board.

Eased Edge or Micro-Beveled Edge: Edges are slightly angled where they meet to create a less apparent outline.

FIGURE 4.5 Edge and end detail. *Drawing courtesy of Armstrong Flooring.*

grain pattern, cracks and occasional insect marks, and **patina,** a dark, rich coloring). Aged Woods supplies oak, chestnut, pine, hemlock, and poplar in various finishes for the old appearance. These are reclaimed wood from buildings that are going to be torn down.

Plank flooring is sold by the square foot, and a 5 percent waste allowance is generally added to the total square footage.

Parquet

Parquet comprises individual pieces of wood, called **"billets."** These are generally made of oak, from 3/8 to 3/4 inch thick, joined together to form a variety of patterns. These small pieces are held together by various methods: a **metal spline,** gluing to a mesh of paper, or gluing to a form of cheesecloth. Sizes vary from 9 to 19 inches square.

There are many parquet patterns and most manufacturers make a similar variety of patterns, although the names may vary. One company will name a pattern Jeffersonian, another Monticello or Mt. Vernon, but they are variations of the same pattern. This particular design is made with a central block surrounded by **pickets** on all four sides. The center may be made of solid wood, a laminated block, five or six strips all in the same direction, or a standard unit of four **sets.**

Designers need a word of warning about using some parquet patterns that may have direction (for example, the herringbone pattern). Depending on whether the pieces are laid parallel to the wall or at an angle, a client may see L's, zigzags, or arrows. The important thing to consider is the client's expectations.

To reduce expansion problems caused by moisture, the oak flooring industry has developed several types of parquets. The laminated or engineered block is a product that displays far less expansion and contraction with moisture changes and, therefore, can be successfully installed below grade in basements and in humid climates. It can even fit tight to vertical obstructions. Blocks can be glued directly to the concrete with several types of adhesive, which the industry is making VOC compliant. One concern in the past has been a laminated block's ability to be sanded and refinished. Because the face layer is oak, with proper maintenance the initial service life can be expected to be 20 to 30 years. Any of the laminated products on the market today can be sanded and refinished (at least twice) using proper techniques and equipment, so the expected life of a laminated block floor is 60 to 90 years.

Parquet flooring is packed in cartons with a specific number of square feet. When ordering parquet flooring, only whole cartons are shipped, so the allowance for cutting may be taken care of with the balance of the carton.

All the parquet woods mentioned in this section are quarter sawn or plain sawn, but some species are cut across the growth rings (end grained). End-grain patterns are formed by small cross-cut pieces attached into blocks or strips with the end grain exposed. The thickness may vary from 1 inch to 4 inches, depending on the manufacturer. One-and-a-half inches of end-grain block have insulating qualities equal to 23 inches of concrete. Some end-grain block floors are still in place after more than 40 years of heavy industrial use. These blocks absorb noise and vibration and have been installed in museums and libraries.

Figure 4.6 illustrates the differences between *on, above,* and *below grade.* Above grade is not a problem for installation of wood floors, because no moisture is present. As mentioned earlier, moisture is the major cause of problems with wood. On grade means that the concrete floor is in contact with the ground. The floor usually has drainage gravel as a base, covered by a polyethylene film to prevent moisture from migrating to the surface. The concrete is then poured on top of this polyethylene sheet. Below grade means a basement floor in which the presence of moisture is an even greater problem. All freshly poured concrete should be allowed to **cure** for 30 to 60 days.

The National Oak Flooring Manufacturers Association (NOFMA) recommends testing for excessive moisture in several areas of each room on both old and new slabs. When tests show too much moisture in the slab, do not install hardwood floors. For a moist slab, wait until it dries naturally or accelerate

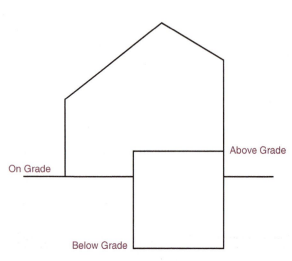

Above Grade

On Grade

Below Grade

FIGURE 4.6 Grade levels.

drying with heat and ventilation; then test again. (If moisture is still present, consult a specialist in this field to avoid flooring problems.)

There are two tests for moisture: rubber mat and polyethylene film.

1. **The rubber mat test.** Lay a smooth, noncorrugated rubber mat on the slab, place a weight on top to prevent moisture from escaping, and allow the mat to remain for 24 hours. If the covered area shows water marks when the mat is removed, too much moisture is present. This test is not effective if the slab surface is other than light in color originally.

2. **The polyethylene film test.** Tape a one-foot square of 6 mil clear polyethylene film to the slab, sealing all edges with plastic moisture resistant tape. If, after 24 hours, there is no "clouding" or drops of moisture on the underside of the film, the slab can be considered dry enough to install wood floors.

Particleboard is a panel product composed of a composite of cellulosic particles of a variety of sizes. A synthetic resin or binder is used to bind these particles through heat and pressure. Processes can be altered in order to create products for a number of applications, and additives can provide methods of improving performance, such as enhancement of moisture resistance and increase in dimensional stability and fire retardancy.[10] Particleboard underlayment is a product used widely as a substrate for floors in residential construction. Flooring manufacturers always specify the type of underlayment to be used with their products.

Substrates must be clean (free of dust, grease, or oil stains), dry, and level. As stressed in Chapter 3 and repeated throughout this book, SURFACE PREPARATION IS EXTREMELY IMPORTANT! The completed floor is only as good as the substrate. Any high spots should be ground down and low spots filled using the correct leveling compound. One floor installer related a story about a client who complained of a loose wood floor installed over a slab. When the loose wood was removed, not only did the wood come up, but the material used as filler for the low spots was attached to it. The person who leveled the floor had used the wrong leveling compound.

Two types of patching compounds are available for use under flooring: gypsum and portland cement. Whichever type is used, antimicrobial agents must be added to prevent mold and mildew growth.

Solid strip products are nailed down, and parquet products are glued down. Laminated planks are the only product that can be either nailed or glued.

The National Oak Flooring Manufacturers Association suggests that several factors may contribute to an unsatisfactory installation. First, the wood floor should be scheduled at the end of construction. Because most other work is completed, the floors will not be abused. The building should now be dry, with any moisture introduced during construction gone. Second, a substrate of 5/8" or thicker plywood or 1" × 6" edge boards is preferred. A thicker, well-fastened substrate provides the better installation. Third, the wood flooring should be well nailed; there should be no skimping on the number of nails per strip, plank, and so on.

Walls are never used as a starting point for installation because they are never truly square. Wood parquet must always be installed in a pyramid or stair-step sequence, rather than in rows, to avoid a misaligned pattern (see Figure 4.7). Parquet may also be laid parallel, or at a 45° angle, to the wall.

Reducer strips may be used at the doorway if there is a difference in level between two areas, and they are available to match the wood floor. Most wood floor **mastics** take about 24 hours to dry; therefore, no one must walk on the floor or place furniture in the room during that period. Laminated planks must be rolled with a 150-pound roller before the adhesive sets. An unfinished wood floor is sanded with the grain using progressively finer grits until the floor is smooth and has an almost shiny

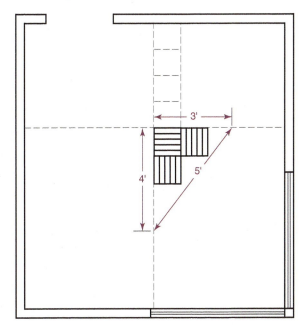

FIGURE 4.7 Method of laying parquet.

appearance. After vacuuming to eliminate any dust particles, finishing materials specifically manufactured for use on wood floors are applied. For open-grained wood such as oak, a filler with or without stain may be used after sanding to provide a more highly reflective surface. Often there is a preference for natural-color hardwood floors, but stain may be used to bring out the grain or produce a darker tone. When a very light finish is wanted, the wood may be bleached or pickled. If a white floor is needed, a laminated wood floor is better because such floors are less likely to expand and contract (problems that show up as dark lines).

The following are some common finishes used with wood flooring:

- **Oil-modified urethane.** A petroleum base containing a blend of plasticizers, resins, and additional film-forming ingredients; most common surface finish; easy to apply; solvent-based polyurethane that ambers with age; available in a variety of sheens

- **Moisture-cured urethane.** Solvent-based polyurethane available in ambering and non-yellowing; should be applied by a professional, due to difficulty of application and intense odor; more durable and moisture resistant than many other surface finishes; usually available in gloss or satin; cured through absorption of small amounts of moisture vapor; relative humidity critical in curing process

- **Water-based urethane.** Made from plasticizers, a blend of synthetic resins and additional film-forming components; usually more expensive than other urethanes; provides non-yellowing finish; available in a variety of sheens; dries in approximately two hours; lighter odor than oil-modified finishes; creates moisture-resistant, durable surface

- **Conversion-varnish sealers (Swedish finishes).** Alcohol-based, two-component, acid-curing product; originated in Sweden

- **Penetrating sealers.** Solvent-based; made of linseed or tongue oil; additional ingredients mixed in to aid in hardness and faster drying; frequently has color; often used for staining and sealing wood floors; spread across floor for purpose of allowing penetration into flooring surface

- **Paste wax.** Applied in thin coats after sealer or stain applied; buffed to required sheen; oldest—and often thought of as the best—finish, as it is the least expensive and the simplest to apply, repair, and care for; wax penetrates stain and is in the wood, resulting in wear to the wood, rather than the finish

- **Varnish.** Made of vinyl-alkyd; now generally thought of as replacement for older varnish types made of vegetable oils; was more frequently used prior to availability of urethane finishes

- **Lacquer.** Should NOT be used; flammable and incompatible

- **Shellac.** Natural shellac made of wax and other ingredients—and rarely used for topcoating; dewaxed shellac becoming popular as a wood floor sealer[11]

Prefinished flooring is available in the following finishes:

- **Acrylic-impregnated.** Made of acrylic monomers, which are forced into the wood's cell structure; offers greater hardness; finished through wearlayer placed over wood

- **Acrylic-urethane.** Made with ingredients similar—but not identical—to those of polyurethane; provides advantages similar to those of polyurethane

- **Aluminum oxide.** Consists of particles placed into polyurethane finish for the purpose of enhancing the wearlayer's abrasion resistance; widely used with high grades of hardwoods

- **Ceramic.** Based on technology addressing use of ceramics to increase wearlayer's abrasion resistance

- **Polyurethane.** Used as wearlayer; strong, long-lasting, clear finish

- **UV-cured.** Polyurethane finishes cured with ultraviolet light, rather than heat; finished at factory[12]

MAINTENANCE

Eight steps on a floor surface are needed to remove sand or dirt from the bottom of shoes. Walk-off or tracking mats should be used at all exterior doors. General housekeeping prolongs the life of a wood floor. The main problem with maintenance of any floor is grit, which can be removed by dust mop, broom, or vacuum.

Another problem is indentations caused by heels, especially women's high heels. A 125-pound woman wearing high heels can exert as much as 2,000 pounds per square inch; therefore, indentations should be expected. Round-headed chair glides and narrow wheels on furniture legs are also damaging, as they can scratch or permanently dent the floor. In their Consumer Flooring Guide, Congoleum has the following information on how to protect against indentations and furniture damage:

- Make sure furniture legs have large surface, nonstaining floor protectors.

- Replace small, narrow metal or dome-shaped glides with smooth, flat glides that are flat on the floor. Glides should be equipped with self-adhesive felt pads to avoid scratching the surface of the floor. The pads should be checked periodically for grit and wear and replaced when necessary. Heavy furniture or appliances should be equipped with flat, nonstaining composition furniture casters or cups of appropriate size—available square from 1 1/2" to 2 5/8" and round from 1 3/8" to 1 5/8".

- Moveable appliances and furniture should be equipped with easily swiveling casters. They should be at least 2" in diameter with nonstaining hard rubber treads with a minimum 3/4" flat surface width. Do not use ball-shaped casters.

- Place mats at outside entrances to prevent dirt, grit, and soil from being tracked onto the floor. Use 100 percent latex-backed mats (labeled nonstaining), because some rubber-backed mats or carpets may permanently discolor your floor.[13]

While only a few floor types require waxing, if this is needed for the floor you are working with, be certain to allow a thin wax coat to dry and then harden prior to use of an electric bristle brush buffer. To determine whether the floor you are working with has been waxed, drip a water drop onto the floor, then wait for about 20 minutes. If you see a white spot, or if the water soaks in immediately, the floor has a wax finish.[14]

To remove grease, dirt, and scuffmarks from a floor with a wax finish, you should use a solvent wax remover from time to time. Be certain to select a product designed for use on wood floors.

Certain chemicals in wood oxidize in strong light, causing the wood to change color; therefore, rugs or area rugs should be moved periodically.

Wood and water do not mix. No matter what claims the manufacturer makes for the wood finish, water must never be poured onto the floor intentionally. A damp-mop is fine for non-waxed polyurethane and other surface finishes in good condition. However, wax-coated finishes should NEVER be cleaned with water, not even with a damp-mop. (*Wood Floor Care Guide* is available from the Oak Flooring Institute, an affiliate of NOFMA.)

Many manufacturers sell a line of maintenance products specially prepared for their own products. Custom finishes, such as polyurethane and Swedish, should NOT be waxed. Manufacturers of acrylic wood provide special cleaning materials for their products.

If cracks appear in the wood floor, they are probably caused by lack of humidity and can be reduced by installing a humidifier.

Wood floors can be refinished. The old method was to sand the floor with a power sander, which created dust throughout the area. Basic Coating's TyKote Recoating system is the easiest and proven way to refinish Aluminum Oxide Factory Finished flooring. TyKote is a revolutionary way to prepare commercial, residential, and sports wood floors for recoating. All dust, mess, and equipment associated with screening are eliminated when using TyKote. Applied in a liquid state, TyKote acts as an intermediate bonding layer between the existing floor and the new topcoat.

Basic has reinvented the wood floor recoating process. This innovative system makes it easier to give your customers beautiful floors in less time and with less dust and mess. The fast and easy-to-use three-step process means wood floors can be recoated in one night, and you can be back in business the next day.[15]

Bamboo and Palm

Bamboo, a member of the grass family, has soared to great popularity as a floor-covering product. Bamboo floors are created from timber bamboo. Because this bamboo matures in a time frame shorter than five years, it is thought of as plentiful, renewable, sustainable, and readily available.

For production, the bamboo is initially split into strips. Then it is dried in a kiln. When dry, the strips are joined and laminated, which creates multi-ply bamboo hardwood. During this production process, boric acid is applied to the bamboo to provide protection from insects.

One example of a plywood paneling and flooring product is Smith and Fong's Plyboo, which is manufactured in China. This product, which can be installed, finished, and cared for just as other hardwood floors can be, is often used for commercial and residential flooring.[16]

Teragren bamboo flooring, which may be installed over radiant heat, supplies the protection of a seven-coat finish and offers a substantial warranty.[17] It has undergone testing for 78 volatile organic compounds, is FloorScore-certified, and can be easily maintained through cleaning with a recommended product.

Most companies produce products that use a formaldehyde-free adhesive, and those products with formaldehyde produce a lower formaldehyde that even the California laws permit.

While you might have heard the term *coconut wood flooring,* it is incorrect to refer to this flooring as a wood. Instead, it is created from a member of the palm family. This type of flooring has a very distinctive appearance and is generally thought of as a very high-end flooring. The process for harvesting palm for flooring calls for the palm to reach the end of its coconut-bearing cycle prior to being cut down. It is then replaced by new coconut palms. Like bamboo, coconut palm is sustainable and grows very quickly, growing to maturity in about six years.[18]

The finish is either a UV-applied polyurethane or aluminum oxide and resists 20,000 revolutions on the **taber test.** PVA-C formaldehyde-free glue is used and the finish is also formaldehyde free. Plyboo is available in horizontal and vertical grains, prefinished or unfinished.

INSTALLATION

Bamboo hardwood floors can be floated, nailed, or glued. They may also be floated over slab or radiant heat systems. Bamboo flooring should be allowed to acclimatize on site for at least three days. Each plank should be laid out separately during the acclimatizing process. The method of installation is similar to other wood tongue-and-groove planks.

Laminate

Pergo Inc. is credited with developing the idea for the **laminate floor** in 1977. This flooring arrived in the European market in 1984; by 2004, Pergo was offering its premium hardwood product in the United States.[19]

Laminate flooring is actually a composite that's designed to endure more-than-average wear and tear. A direct-pressure manufacturing process fuses four layers into one extremely hard surface. The four layers are:

1. **Back layer.** Reinforced with melamine; provides moisture resistance and structural stability

2. **Fiberboard core.** Extremely dense core board; has edge-sealing treatment designed to offer greater structural stability

3. **Decorative layer.** Extremely elaborate photo to provide specific appearance; provides laminate look of tile or wood

4. **Wearlayer.** Seals out moisture; resists wear, fading, and staining; provides clear, strong finish[20]

Other laminate floors may vary in core and surface. (See Figure 4.8.)

INSTALLATION

The following items are important to keep in mind when installing laminate flooring:

- Keep the planks within a 30°F temperature range.

- Whisper 3-N-1 underlayment (high-density PE/PP foam) provides a vapor barrier (no additional films required).

- Keep 5/16" expansion/contraction space around walls, doors, columns, and so on.[21]

- As a final step of installation, use Core Weld on all end and side joints.

FIGURE 4.8 ICORE II from Mannington Commercial. *Photo courtesy of Mannington Commercial.*

MAINTENANCE

Many businesses and individuals select laminate flooring due to its easy maintenance, which results generally from this product's composition, its manufacturing process—and specifically, from the product's use of aluminum oxide, which is extremely hard.

The majority of manufacturers offer directions and kits for cleaning their laminate floor products. Be certain to check with the manufacturer or seller to determine appropriate cleaning methods for the laminate you have selected—not only so you can properly care for your floor, but also with an eye toward maintaining the product's warranty.

For the most part, manufacturers' maintenance kits include a terry cloth mop and a cleaning solution to be sprayed onto the mop-head prior to use on the floor. For all laminate floors, it is generally recommended that owners sweep, vacuum, and dust mop their floors on a daily basis.[22]

Grout

As most of the hard surface materials that follow require the use of **grout** to finish the floor, it is introduced before discussion of those materials. Grout is the material used to fill the joints between hard surface materials. The type of grout employed, if any, depends on which variety of tile is being used. Therefore, not only is the type of grout important, but also the spacing of the tile. Proper joint placement is crucial so both sides of the room have equal size pieces. The use of crack isolation membranes in thin-bed installations is necessary to prevent cracks in the substrate from cracking marble or ceramic tiles installed over them.

According to the Tile Council of America, there are many different forms of grouting materials available to meet the requirements of the different kinds of tile and types of exposure. Portland cement, the base of most grouts, can be modified to provide such qualities as whiteness, mildew resistance, uniformity, hardness, flexibility, and water retention. ANSI A108.10, A118.6, and A118.7 should be referenced for installation instructions and material specifications. Epoxies, furans, silicone rubber, and other types of non-cement-based grouts have qualities not available with cement grouts, but their use requires the installer to have special skills. These materials are also generally more expensive than cement-based grouts.[23]

Commercial portland cement grout for floors is usually grey (but colors are available) and is designed for use with ceramic **mosaics,** quarry, and paver tile. Damp curing, the process of keeping the grout moist and covered for several days, is required and results in a much stronger grout. For areas that must be opened for traffic as quickly as possible, there are quick-set grout additives. (See Table 4.2.)

Grouts with sand are not used with highly reflective tiles, because the roughness of the grout is not compatible with the high gloss. For glazed tiles, unsanded grout or mastic grout is used. Special grouts that are chemical resistant; fungus and mildew resistant; or of a latex composition are used when movement is anticipated. Grout sealers form an invisible barrier that is resistant to moisture and stains while allowing vapor to escape.

Marble

Marble, due to its exquisite appearance, has long been in great demand as a material for a variety of surfaces, including floors, fireplace facings, hearths, windowsills, foyers, walls, floors, and countertops. This material, which naturally occurs in mountainous areas across the globe, is actually a **metamorphic** rock. Most marble used today is mined from quarries in Spain, Italy, and China.[24]

Pressure and/or heat created the metamorphic change that turned limestone debris into marble. Today all rocks that can take a polish come under the heading of marble. Dolomitic limestone ("hard" limestone), although technically limestone, is known commercially as marble. Travertine and onyx are related stones. Travertine is more important for flooring purposes because it is easier to work; onyx is brittle and is mostly relegated to decorative uses. Serpentine is of a different chemical makeup, but because it can be polished, it is classified as marble. Serpentine is not sensitive to citric acid and other kitchen spills. All of the aforementioned stones are calcareous.

The minerals that result from impurities give marble a wide variety of colors. The colored veins of marble are as varied and numerous as the areas from which it is quarried. One famous type, Carrara marble, is pure white. Michelangelo used this marble for many of his sculptures. Other Carrara marble may have black, grey, or brownish veining. The name *verd antique* is applied to marbles of prevailing green color, which consists chiefly of serpentine, a hydrous magnesium silicate. Verd antiques are highly decorative stones; at times, the green is interspersed with streaks or veins of red and white. The pinks, reds, yellows, and browns are caused by the presence of iron oxides, whereas the blacks, greys, and blue-greys result from bituminous deposits. Silicate, chlorite, and mica provide the green colors.

Marble is the most ancient of all finished materials currently in use today. Some authorities believe that the onyx marble of Algeria was employed by the Egyptians as early as 475 BCE. Biblical references show that marble was used in King Solomon's Temple at Jerusalem, as well as in the palace of Sushun more than one thousand years before Christ. Parian marble from the Aegean Sea was found in the ruins of ancient Troy.

Pentelic marble was used in the Parthenon in Athens and is still available today. Phidias used this marble for the frieze of the Parthenon; portions of this frieze known as the **Elgin Marbles** are intact today and are on display at the British Museum. Makrana marble, a white marble, was used in the Taj Mahal in India. Inside the Taj Mahal sunlight filters through marble screens as delicate as lace and the white marble walls are richly decorated with floral designs in onyx, jasper, carnelian, and other semiprecious stones.

Knoxville, Tennessee, was known at the turn of the twentieth century as the marble capital of the United States. Marble is found in many eastern states, from Vermont to Georgia, and in some western states. The Georgia Marble Company ranks as the world's largest producer of marble products. Dolomitic marble is quarried in Tennessee and Idaho. The famous Yule Quarry in Marble, Colorado (from which came the columns of the Lincoln Memorial and the massive block forming the Tomb of the Unknown Soldier), has been reopened. The white marble from this quarry may be the purest marble in the world.

Marble floors were used in the Baroque and Rococo periods in Europe. During the French empire, black and white marble squares were used, and they remain a popular pattern for marble floors today. In the formal halls of Georgian homes, the marble floors were appropriate for mahogany tables and chairs. In his Barcelona Pavilion, Mies Van der Rohe used great slabs of marble as freestanding partitions. Today, marble is used for furniture, floors, and interior and exterior walls.

The Marble Institute of America offers numerous continuing education system (CES) courses for design professionals, most of which are approved by the American Institute of Architects. The one-hour course on sustainable design offers an introduction to the sustainability movement and information regarding the choice of natural stone in contributing to sustainable design solutions. The learning objectives established for the course are as follows:

- Recall several objectives of sustainable design

- Understand some characteristics of genuine stone and their relevance to sustainable design

- Identify ways to reduce environmental impacts when selecting and sourcing genuine stone

- Explain how genuine stone was used to support sustainable design goals, upon reviewing case study examples[25]

CHARACTERISTICS OF MARBLE

Marble does not come in sheets (slabs) and must be quarried. There are three principal quarrying methods utilized today. The first is by drilling holes and thus outlining the block. Then wedges are driven into the holes and the blocks are split from the surrounding rock. The second method uses wire saws. A long steel cable with diamond teeth is passed over the stone with downward pressure, cutting the block of stone free from the deposit. The third method employs a large chain saw-type machine to saw the stone free from the deposit. Marble chips are used in the production of **terrazzo, agglomerated** marble tiles, and cast polymer products.

Marble is a relatively heavy and expensive material for use on floors because of the necessity of using the conventional thick-bed installation method. Fiberglass and epoxy resins employed as a backing hold delicate stones together during fabrication, shipment, and installation. This mass-produced method allows expensive decorative stone to be furnished more economically than with conventional methods (i.e., permanent stone liners also known as backer slabs).

The following properties need to be considered for marble floors:

- *Density.* Averages 0.1 pound per cubic inch. This figure may be used to calculate the weight of the marble.

- *Water absorption.* Measured by total immersion of a 2-inch cube for 48 hours and varies from 0.1 to 0.2 percent, which is less than that for other natural stones. The maximum absorption as established by **ASTM** C503 is 0.20 percent.

- *Abrasion resistance.* Measured by a scuffing method that removes surface particles similar to the action of foot traffic. Abrasion resistance for commercial flooring should be at least a hardness value of 10, as measured by ASTM C241. The Marble Institute of America (MIA) recommends a hardness value of 12. This value is not necessary for single-family homes.

Table 4.2 | Grout Guide

These guidelines cannot address every installation. The type and size of tile, service level, climatic conditions, tile spacing, and individual manufacturer's recommendations are all factors that should be considered when selecting the proper grout.

W = Wall Use F = Floor Use	Jobsite Mix (Sanded)	Grouts Containing Portland Cement		
		Standard Unsanded Cement Grout A118.6 (4)	Standard Sanded Cement Grout A118.6 (4)	Polymer Modified Unsanded Tile Grout A118.7 (4, 9)
Tile Type				
Glazed Wall Tile (7)		W	W	W
Glazed Floor Tile (7)	W, F	W, F	W, F	W, F
Ceramic Mosaics	W, F	W, F	W, F	W, F
Quarry, Paver, and Packing House Tile (8)	W, F		W, F	
Large Unit Porcelain or Vitreous Tile (8)	W, F	W, F	W, F	W, F
Dimension Stone (7, 8) (including Agglomerates)	W, F	W, F	W, F	W, F
Use				
Dry/Limited Water Exposure	W, F	W, F	W, F	W, F
Wet Areas (10)	W, F	W, F	W, F	W, F
Exteriors (8, 9, 10)	W, F	W, F	W, F	W, F
Performance	(Note: There are five performance ratings, from Best [A] to Minimal [E])			
Suggested Joint Widths (5)	1/8" to 5/8"	1/16" to 1/8"	1/8" to 5/8"	1/16" to 1/8"
Stain Resistance	E	D	D	C
Crack Resistance	E	D	D	C
Color Availability	D	B	B	B

Notes:

(1) Mainly used for chemical resistant properties.

(2) Special tools needed for proper application. Silicone, urethane, and modified polyvinylchloride used in pregrouted ceramic tile sheets. Silicone grout should not be used on kitchen countertops or other food preparation surfaces unless it meets the requirements of FDA Regulation No. 21, CFE 177.2600.

(3) Special cleaning procedures and materials recommended.

(4) Follow manufacturer's directions.

(5) Joint widths are only guidelines. Individual grout manufacturer's products may vary. Consult manufacturers' instructions.

(6) Epoxies are recommended for prolonged temperatures up to 140°F, high-temperature-resistant epoxies and furans up to 350°F.

(7) Some types of glazed ceramic tiles, polished marble, marble agglomerates, and granite can be permanently scratched or damaged when grouted with sanded grout formulas. DO NOT use sanded grout or add sand to grout when grouting polished marble, marbled agglomerates, and ceramic wall tiles with soft glazes. Check the tile or marble manufacturer's literature and test grout on a separate sample area prior to grouting.

(8) Some types of ceramic tiles and dimension stone may be permanently stained when grouted with pigmented grout of a contrasting color. WHITE GROUT IS BEST SUITED FOR GROUTING WHITE OR LIGHT-COLORED MARBLE OR GRANITE.

(9) Latex modification may be required in areas subject to freezing temperatures. Consult grout manufacturer for recommended products and methods.

(10) Colored cementitious grouts may darken when wet.

Source: Courtesy of Tile Council of North America.

Polymer Modified Sanded Tile Grout A118.7 (4, 9)	Modified Epoxy Emulsion A118.8 (4)	100% Solid Epoxy A118.3 (1, 3, 4, 6)	Furan A118.5 (1, 3, 4, 6)	Silicone Urethane (2, 4)	Mastic Grout (3, 4)
W		W		W	W
W, F	W, F	W, F			W, F
W, F	W, F	W, F		W	W, F
W, F	W, F	W, F	W,		
W, F	W, F	W, F	F	W	W, F
W, F	W, F				
W, F	W, F	W, F	W, F	W, F	W, F
W, F	W, F	W, F	W, F	W, F	
W, F	W, F	W, F (4)	W, F (4)	W, F	
1/8" to 5/8"	1/16" to 5/8"	1/16" to 5/8"	3/8" to 5/8"	1/16" to 1/4"	1/16" to 1/4"
C	C	A	A	A	B
C	C	B	C	A	C
B	B	B	Black only	B	B

Marble is also classified A through C, according to the fabrication methods considered necessary and acceptable in each instance, as based on standard trade practice.

A polished finish reflects light and emphasizes the color and marking of the material. The polished finish may be used in residential installations, but not for commercial installations. The biggest problem with a polished floor is that the shine is removed in the traffic area but the edges retain the shine, emphasizing the difference in the two areas. A honed surface, in contrast, is satin smooth with little light reflection. Therefore, a honed finish is preferred for floors, stair treads, thresholds, and other locations where heavy traffic will wear off the polished finish.

When using marble or any other natural stone, the weight of these materials must be calculated to ensure that the substrate is strong enough to support the extra weight. This is where 3/8" thick marbles come into use. Especially in remodeling, the floor is probably not constructed to bear heavy stones. Substrates must meet a maximum deflection of 1/180 of span. The stiffer the substrate, the longer lasting the finished floor. Substrates that have measurable deflection will fail.

Two of the materials used to help provide rigidity to a stable substrate are a cementitious backer unit (CBU) and glass water-resistant gypsum backer board.

CBU—which is meant to be applied directly to metal wall studs, subfloors, and wood—is a backing and underlayment product that can be used in wet or dry locations. You can bond ceramic tile to CBU through use of dry-set, latex/polymer modified portland cement mortar or epoxy; to do this, be certain to follow instructions from the manufacturer of the backer board. For interior installation and material specifications, see **ANSI** (American National Standards Institute) A108.11 and ANSI A118.9 or ASTM C. 1325. For a backer board that conforms to ASTM C1178, you can use Coated Glass Mat Water-Resistant Gypsum Backer Board.[26]

A crack-suppression membrane allows the stone setting bed to span cracks and narrow expansion joints without the fear of the stone floor following the crack. There are, of course, limits to which crack suppression membranes can work.

Large stone medallions have been a popular decorative element used in grand residences for thousands of years. Reserved for princes and prelates in the past, these incredible pieces are now available to those working within a more modest budget.

Walker Zanger offers medallions handcrafted in Italy and the United States to the industry's highest standards. All medallions are fully assembled for ease of installation.[27]

Mosaic medallions are crafted from thousands of different chips of stone, painstakingly combined to form a brilliant pattern, and mounted on sheets for easy installation.

Medallions are created by hand-cutting pieces of stone and terracotta, and carefully fitting them together to form the design. This process is a rare art, practiced only by a few workshops in Italy.

Water-jet medallions take advantage of modern technology. The stone is cut by a super pressurized stream of water that is controlled by a computer programmed with the shapes that comprise the design. This process allows for incredible precision. Installed, water-jet cut medallions create a seamless design.

INSTALLATION

Several associations are responsible for codes and standards based on the consensus of their membership. The natural stones, such as marble, travertine, and slate, use the specifications and test methods contained in the ASTM Manual, Section 4, Construction; Volume 04.08, Soil and Rock; Building Stones. The ceramic tile industry uses ANSI A108 for installation specifications.

Because marble is the first hard surface material covered in this book, installation methods will be discussed in detail. The same methods are used for all natural stones, ceramic tile, quarry tile, and other types of hard surface materials. (See Table 4.3.)

Setting materials account for only 10 percent of installation costs, but account for 90 percent of problems; therefore, proper specification and professional installation is crucial and will eliminate most problems. Skinning, a film that forms on the surface of the setting materials and causes improper bonding, is a common cause of installation failure for all setting materials. To cure this problem, the application tool should be used again to break up the skin.

Portland cement **mortar** is a mixture of portland cement and sand. According to the Tile Council of North America the proportion of portland cement to sand is 1:5 for floors and, for walls, portland cement, sand, and lime in proportions of 1:5:1/2 to 1:7:1. Portland cement mortar is appropriate for most surfaces and typical installations.

The Tile Council of North America also states a mortar bed, up to 2″ in thickness, helps with precise slopes or planes in the finished tile work on floors and walls. To enhance performance properties, the mortar bed may utilize a latex/redisperable polymer—as directed by the manufacturer—as a part of the liquid portion or the entire liquid portion.

There are two methods for installing ceramic tiles with a portland cement mortar bed on walls, ceilings, and floors. Both methods are equally effective.

1. As explained in ANSI A108.1A, the tile may be set on a mortar bed that is still workable. Absorptive ceramic tiles must be soaked before setting on a mortar bed that is still workable when using a neat portland cement bond coat.

2. As explained in ANSI A108.1B, the tile may be set on a cured mortar bed with dry-set or latex/polymer modified portland cement mortar.

> Portland cement mortars can be bonded to concrete floors; backed with membranes and reinforced with wire mesh or metal lath; or applied on metal lath over open studding on walls. They are structurally strong, are not affected by prolonged contact with water, and can be used to **plumb** and square surfaces installed by others.
>
> Suitable backings, when properly prepared are: brick or cement masonry, concrete, wood or steel stud frame, rough wood floors, plywood floors, foam insulation board, gypsum board, and gypsum plaster. The one-coat method may be used over masonry, plaster, or other solid backing that provides firm anchorage for metal lath.
>
> Complete installation and material specifications are contained in ANSI A108.1A, A108.1B, and A108.1C.[28]

Thick-set or thick-bed *must* be used for setting materials of uneven thickness such as natural flagstone and slate. It may also be used for hard-surfaced materials of uniform thickness. Tiles are placed on the mortar and tapped into place until the surface is level. The mortar used on floors is a mixture of portland cement and sand, roughly in proportions of 1:6.

The Tile Council of North America states:

> Dry-set mortar is a mixture of Portland cement with sand and additives imparting water retentivity which is used as a bond coat for setting tile.
>
> Dry-set mortar is suitable for **thin-set** installations of ceramic tile over a variety of surfaces. It is used in one layer, as thin as 3/32″, after tiles are embedded, has excellent water and impact resistance, is water-cleanable, nonflammable, good for exterior work, and does not require soaking of the tile.
>
> Dry-set mortar is available as a factory-sanded mortar to which only water need be added. Cured dry-set mortar is not affected by prolonged contact with water but does not form a water barrier. It is not a setting bed and is not intended to be used in truing or leveling the work of others.
>
> Suitable backings, when properly prepared, include plumb and true masonry, concrete, gypsum board, cementitious backer units, fiber-cement underlayment, coated glass mat water-resistant gypsum backer board, cementitious coated foam backer board, cured Portland mortar beds, brick, ceramic tile and dimension stone . . .
>
> Complete installation and material specifications are contained in ANSI A108.5 and ANSI A118.1.[29]

Another thin-set method is to use an adhesive that is spread with a trowel. The trowel is used not only for spreading, by using the flat edge for continuous coverage, but also as a metering device for determining the proper amount of adhesive. Oil-based adhesives should be avoided when installing marble because they stain the marble. Again, it must be repeated that thin-bed should be used only where the substrate is solid and level.

Table 4.3 | Floor Tiling Installation Guide

Performance-Level Requirement Guide and Selection Table

Based on results from ASTM Test Method C-627 "Standard Test Method for Evaluating Ceramic Floor Tile Installation Systems Using the Robinson Type Floor Tester." All methods are material dependent; performance rating should not exceed rating of weakest component. Consult each material manufacturer for individual component rating.

Service Requirements

Find required performance level and choose installation method that meets or exceeds it. Performance results are based on ceramic tile meeting ANSI A137.1, or tile designated by tile manufacturer.

	FLOOR TYPE—Numbers refer to Handbook Method numbers			
	Concrete	**Page**	**Wood**	**Page**
Extra Heavy: Extra heavy and high-impact use in food plants, dairies, breweries, and kitchens. Requires quarry tile, packing house tile, or tile designated by tile manufacturer. (Passes ASTM C 627 cycles 1 through 14.)	F101, F102, F111 F112, F113, F114 F115, F116, F121 F125[i], F125A[i] F131, F132 F133, F134, F205	17, 17, 18 19, 19, 20 20, 20, 22 23, 23 24, 24 25, 25, 21		
Heavy: Shopping malls, stores, commercial kitchens, work areas, laboratories, auto showrooms and service areas, shipping/receiving, and exterior decks. (Passes ASTM C627 cycles 1 through 12.)	F103, F111, F112 F113, F121	17, 18, 19 19, 22	F143[a, 9]	33
Moderate: Normal commercial and light institutional use in public space of restaurants and hospitals. (Passes ASTM C627 cycles 1 through 10.)	F112, F115 F122[c], F200 RH110, RH111 RH115, RH116	19, 20 22, 21 26, 27 27, 28	F121, F141, F145	22, 32, 32
Light: Light commercial use in office space, reception areas, kitchens, and bathrooms. (Passes ASTM C627 cycles 1 through 6.)	F122[c]	22	F143[a], F144[b, e&f] F146, F150[h] F160, F175, F180 RH122 RH130[h], RH135[e&f]	33, 34 35, 33 34, 36, 39 29 29, 30

Residential:
Kitchens, bathrooms, and foyers. (Passes ASTM C627 cycles 1 through 3.)

F116[j]	20	F142, F144 · 32, 34
TR711[d]	61	F147, F170 · 36, 35
F135	26	F148, F149 · 37, 37
		F150[h], F151, F152 · 33, 37, 38
		F155, F180, F185 · 38, 39, 40
		RH130[h], RH135 · 29, 30
		RH140 · 31

Notes:

Consideration must also be given to (1) wear properties of surface of tile selected, (2) tile size, (3) coefficient of friction.

Unglazed Standard Grade tile will give satisfactory wear or abrasion resistance in installations listed. Glazed tile or soft body decorative unglazed tile should have the manufacturer's approval for intended use. Color, pattern, surface texture, and glaze hardness must be considered in determining tile acceptability on a particular floor.

Selection Table Notes:

Tests to determine Performance-Levels utilized representative products meeting recognized industry standards:

a. ANSI A118.3 epoxy mortar and grout.

b. Data in Selection Table based on tests conducted by Tile Council of North America, except data for F144 Method, which is based on test results from an independent laboratory.

c. ANSI A118.4 latex-portland cement mortar and grout.

d. Tile bonded to existing resilient flooring with epoxy adhesive.

e. 7/163-minimum-thick cementitious backer unit or minimum 1/4"-thick fiber-cement underlayment tested.

f. Minimum 1/43 thick cementitious backer unit can be used for residential applications over 19/323 minimum thick subfloor; minimum 1/43 thick cementitious backer unit can be used for light commercial applications over minimum 23/323 thick subfloor.

g. Requires tile designated by tile manufacturers as suitable for the rating.

h. Requires minimum 19/323 exterior glue plywood underlayment for light rating; 15/32" exterior glue plywood underlayment may be used for residential rating.

i. Requires membrane designated by membrane manufacturer as suitable for the rating.

j. F116 with epoxy is extra heavy while F116 with organic adhesive is rated residential.

Source: Courtesy of the Tile Council of North America.

Almost all marble and granite tile produced today are manufactured for use with a joint, and are furnished with a slight **chamfer** (bevel) at the junction of the face and edge.

MAINTENANCE

The booklet *Care & Cleaning for Natural Stone Surfaces,* available from the Marble Institute of America, Inc. (Appendix B), provides maintenance recommendations for all natural stones, including marble, granite, limestone, onyx, and slate. According to the institute, which serves the Dimension Stone Industry, a spill on a stone surface should be blotted with a paper towel immediately. Do not wipe the area, as it will spread the spill. Flush the area with plain water and mild soap and rinse several times. Dry the area with a soft cloth. Repeat as necessary. Identifying the type of stain on the stone surface is the key to removing it. Sometimes the location and color of the stain in proximity to possible culprits will make identification easier (i.e., plants, food service area, cosmetics, etc.). Surface stains can often be removed by cleaning with an appropriate cleaning product or household chemical. Deep-seated or stubborn stains may require using a poultice or calling in a professional.[30]

Terrazzo

Terrazzo was developed by the Venetians in the sixteenth century and is still used to this day. Terrazzo as we know it today, however, was not produced until after the development of portland cement in the eighteenth century.

Terrazzo, which is made of granite, quartz, glass, marble, and other appropriate chips, is a composite material that is precast, which means it is poured into place. This material is utilized for floor and wall treatments. (See Figure 4.9.) A principal goal of terrazzo use is to create a surface that is smooth and uniformly textured. To achieve this purpose, terrazzo is generally cured, ground, and polished, though other processes may also be used. The various types of terrazzo include:

- *Standard terrazzo.* Usually consists of small chip sizes; most popular type of terrazzo
- *Venetian terrazzo.* Consists of larger chip sizes

FIGURE 4.9 Solid colored Key Resin terrazzo was used on the stairs and multi colors were used in the lobby of a High School. *Photograph courtesy of Michael McBride of Abingdon Industries.*

- *Palladian.* Consists of thin marble slabs that have been randomly fractured; sometimes includes terrazzo joints between slabs

- *Structural terrazzo.* Placed by terrazzo contractor as 4 inches of 4,000 psi concrete plus cementitious terrazzo topping

- *Rustic terrazzo.* Consists of a **matrix** that has been depressed to expose chips; uniformly textured

- *Resinous matrices.* A terrazzo system consisting of chemical or resinous materials; sometimes consists of resinous materials added to portland cement to achieve great resistance to harmful items, such as alkalis and acids; usually made up of small chips applied in thin cross-sections

INSTALLATION

The National Terrazzo and Mosaic Association (NTMA) specifies three binder types for use in anchoring marble chips or other terrazzo floor **aggregates:** a portland cement product, a polyacrylic modified portland cement, and an epoxy or polyester system. While all three are used to accomplish the goal of anchoring the aggregate, treatment of each differs.[31]

Divider strips of brass, zinc, or plastic are attached to the substrate and are used for several purposes: as expansion joints to take care of any minor movement; as dividers when different colors are poured in adjacent areas; and as enhancements of a design motif, logo, or trademark.

Because of the labor involved in a monolithic installation, terrazzo tiles consisting of portland cement with an aggregate of marble chips may be used.

When cementitious terrazzo tiles are used, they may be installed using the thin-set method or other cement mortar methods. Wausau Tile is the only domestic manufacturer of cementitious precast terrazzo tile, available in 12", 16", and 24" square by 5/8" thick, in both square and chamfered edges. Wausau terrazzo floor tiles can be installed by one or two installation methods. With the tile set method, chamfered edge tiles are set with 1/16" to 3/16" joints, and then grouted. With the new tight-joint method, square-edge tiles are set with a 1/16" minus joint, then grouted flush and ground and polished on the job for a monolithic look. The size of the chips may be large or small, or a mixture of sizes. The finish may be polished or slip-resistant.

Agglomerated marble tiles consist of 90 to 95 percent marble chips, combined with 5 to 10 percent resins and formed into blocks in a vacuum chamber. They are available as floor tile or marble wall veneers. Agglomerated marble sometimes is classified as cast marble, but the term *cast* is also used to describe a polyester product containing ground marble.

MAINTENANCE

Moisture, which is placed into terrazzo products during the composition, curing, grinding, grouting, and polishing stages, is of substantial consideration when dealing with this product. On the one hand, the quantity of moisture is clearly tied to proper installation. On the other hand, as this moisture will dissipate, and as it will evaporate through the surface after finishing, it's important to minimize the evaporation to as great a degree as possible. Toward that end, the terrazzo should be sealed with a product that will penetrate the surface. Even though this sealer adds to curing time, it is an important step, and the time required for curing will be well worth the wait. This is not the only way time is on your side with terrazzo products. When maintained properly, terrazzo surfaces will grow more and more beautiful as time passes.[32]

In order to provide terrazzo maintenance, you'll need to know the type of binder used for anchoring, as the maintenance method will be based on the anchoring used. Overall, the NTMA advises that scrubbing powders with water-soluble inorganic salts and soaps and scrubbing powders containing crystallizing salts or water-soluble inorganic salts should be avoided in terrazzo maintenance, as alkaline content can cause **spalling**[33] through penetrating pores and breakage as they dry and expand. (This is similar to the problem that occurs with cement floors.) The NTMA has an excellent booklet titled *The Care of Terrazzo.*

After the initial cleaning, the terrazzo floor should be allowed to dry and then sealed with a water-based sealer in the acrylic family especially designed for terrazzo use. The Underwriters Laboratories classification of this sealer should include slip-resistance with a coefficient of friction rating of minimum 0.5.

The NTMA recommends the following maintenance plan for terrazzo floors:

1. Sweeping each day with a yarn-wick brush that has been treated with a sweeping compound

2. Damp-mopping each week with a neutral cleanser for lightly soiled floors

3. Mechanical buffing with a neutral cleaner for heavily soiled floors (Be certain to mop residue away with clean water prior to drying and buff with a dry brush after drying.)

4. Stripping away old sealer and finishing coats—then resealing clean floors—twice each year

Note that the same process used for removing stains from marble should be used for terrazzo.[34]

Travertine

Travertine, which is primarily used for floor and wall tile, is a dense form of limestone. It generally occurs naturally in banded layers. While most travertine is cream or white, this stone is also available in a variety of peach and brown tones. Travertine is often used in bathrooms, dens, and kitchens.[35]

MAINTENANCE

The maintenance of travertine is the same as for marble.

Granite

Granite is an excellent choice for kitchen countertops, floors, and other heavily used surfaces. Granite is an igneous rock, which means it was once molten and formed as it cooled deep within the Earth. Minerals within granite typically appear as small flecks throughout the stone, creating a "salt and pepper" look. Other types have veining similar to marble. Granite is a dense-grained, hard stone. It can be highly polished or finished in a variety of other ways. A broad spectrum of color is available. Granite, quarried from the mountains of Italy, the United States, India, Brazil, China, and dozens of other countries around the world, is one of the most popular natural stones in the market.[36]

Granite consists of chiefly three minerals—quartz, alkali feldspar, and plagioclase feldspar—which make granite white, pink, and light grey. Granite also contains other minerals which account for buff, beige, red, blue, green, and black; however, within these colors, the variegations run from light to dark. The color grey, for example, may be light, medium, or dark, or vary between dark and purplish grey or dark and greenish grey. It is important to see an actual sample of the type of granite to be used.

The National Building Granite Quarries Association (NBGQA) recommends submitting duplicate 12" × 12" samples to show the full range of color, texture, and finish. The designer retains one set and the other is returned to the granite supplier for reference.

In addition to color, finish is important. The following are the most popular.

- *A **polished surface finish**.* Considered the smoothest and nicest, it is shiny and reflective, and it brings forth the character of the stone. Consumers appreciate the visibility of the stone's crystal structure and deep color.

- *A **satin surface finish**.* Considered a mid-range finish, it is relatively new to the market. The gloss is light; it is not shiny like a polished finish, nor is it matte like a honed granite finish.

- *A **honed surface finish**.* Considered more flattering than a full-gloss finish, it provides a smooth, matte, nonreflecting surface. This is accomplished through ending the finishing process before the buffing stage. The result is a smooth surface without reflection, one that, when perfect, has no scratch marks. When there is a likelihood of great foot traffic or water being tracked across a surface, this finish is highly desirable.[37]

The method of veneered construction used to make thinner and lighter-weight marble squares is also used with granite, and for the same reasons. When a feeling of permanence and stability is needed, granite is a good choice; therefore, granite is often used in banking institutions.

INSTALLATION

Honed granite is installed using the same methods as for marble. When more textured finishes are specified and when the granite has not been cut to a definite size, a mortar joint is used.

MAINTENANCE

Granite floors, particularly those with rougher surfaces, require ordinary maintenance by means of a brush or vacuum cleaner. The more highly finished granite surfaces should be maintained in the same manner as marble.

Flagstone

Flagstone is defined as thin slabs of stone used for paving walks, driveways, patios, and so on. It was used on the floors in Tudor England (1485–1603). Flagstone is generally fine-grained **sandstone, bluestone, quartzite,** or slate, but thin slabs of other stones may be used. One-inch-thick bluestone flagging in a random multiple pattern compares favorably in price to premium vinyl tiles. Flagstone stones are siliceous and very durable because they are composed mainly of silica or quartzlike particles.

Flagstone stone may be irregularly shaped, the way it was when quarried, varying in size from 1 to 4 square feet, or the edges may be sawn to give a more formal appearance. Thickness may vary from 1/2 inch to 4 inches; therefore, the flagstone *must* be set in a thick mortar base to produce a level surface.

The extra thickness of the flagstone must be considered when positioning floor joists. One client had flagstones drawn and specified on her blueprints. The carpenter misread the plans, however, and assumed that it was to be a flagstone patterned floor and not the real thing. The client arrived at the house one day to discover that the entryway did not have the lowered floor necessary to fit the extra thickness of the stone. The contractor had to cut all the floor joists for the hall area, lower them 4 inches, and then put in additional bracing and supports in the basement—a costly error.

Another point to remember with flagstones is that the surface is usually uneven because it comes from naturally cleaved rock; therefore, flagstones are not suitable for use under tables and chairs. In addition, an entrance hall of flagstones is very durable; however, the stone needs to be protected from grease which can be absorbed into the stones.

The grout used in setting flagstones is a sand portland cement type and fills all areas where flagstones adjoin.

MAINTENANCE

Flagstones are relatively easy to clean with mild acidic cleaning solutions. There are sealing compounds on the market that make flagstones **impervious** to any staining and wear. These compounds are available in gloss and matte finishes and protect the treated surface against the deteriorating effects of weathering, salts, acids, alkalis, oil, and grease. The gloss finish does seem to give an unnatural shiny appearance to the stone; however, where the impervious quality rather than the aesthetic quality is important, these sealers may be used. Vacuuming will remove dust and siliceous material from the surface and a damp-mop will remove any other soil from the sealed surface.

Slate

Slate was also used as a flooring material in Tudor England. In seventeenth-century France, slate was combined with bands of wood. Slate is a very fine-grained metamorphic rock cleaved from sedimentary rock shale. One characteristic of slate is that this cleavage allows the rock to be split easily into thin slabs. The most common colors for slate range from grey to black, but green, brown, and red are also available. In areas of heavy traffic, honed black slate tends to show the natural scuffing of shoes, and the scratches give the black slate a slightly greyish appearance. All stones will eventually show this scuffing; therefore, highly polished stones should be avoided as a flooring material. While slate used to come mainly from Vermont, most of the slate in this country is now imported from India and China. The current trend seems to be the Chinese slate called China Lotus, a light greenish-brown stone with strong gold influences in the stones.

Different finishes are available in slate, as in other stones.

- *Natural cleft finish.* Stone naturally occurring within the ground generally occurs in layers. When it is separated along a natural seam, the resulting stone is a natural cleft surface.
- *Sand sawn finish.* Stone surface that remains unchanged after coming from a gang saw is identified as having this finish. The finish is granular and smooth; it offers a variety of textures and grades.
- *Honed finish.* This finish is extremely fine and smooth.[38]

The standard thickness of sawed flooring slate is 1/2 inch. Also available are 3/4 inch and 1 inch thicknesses, which are suitable for both interior and exterior use. One-half-inch slate weighs 7 1/2 pounds per square foot, 3/4-inch weighs 11 1/4 pounds, and 1-inch weighs 15 pounds. The absorption rate of slate is 0.23 percent. One-quarter-inch slate is used for interior foyers in homes and commercial buildings using the thin-set method. This thickness is an excellent remodeling item over wood or slab and gives a rug-level effect when it adjoins carpet. One-quarter-inch slate weighs only 3 3/4 pounds per square foot.

Sealers usually darken the slate and give a glossy appearance. Natural cleft finish and sand sawn rubbed finish may be sealed suitably; however, sealers may not adhere nor give a desirable appearance to machine gauged or honed finish. It is important that care be taken in selecting a treatment that is slip-resistant.[39]

INSTALLATION

As can be seen from the preceding types, slate is available for both thin-set and thick-set applications. When thin-set mastic or adhesive is used, a 1/4″ × 1/4″ notched trowel held at a 45° angle is suggested.

Several points need to be remembered with both types of installations. If grout is used with slate (the spacing should be 3/8″ minimum), it is important that any excess be cleaned off immediately, because grout that has dried on the slate surface will probably never come off. If grout is not used, the slate tiles are butted against each other. Joint lines are staggered so no lines are more than 2 to 3 feet long in a straight line.

Thick-bed installation is similar to that for flagstones. All joints should be 3/8″ wide flush joints and should be **pointed** with 1:2 cement mix the same day the floor is laid to make the joints and setting bed **monolithic.**

MAINTENANCE

The maintenance guidelines for marble apply to slate as well.

Ceramic Tile

Because ceramic tile was one of the most durable materials used by ancient civilizations, archaeologists have discovered that thin slabs of fired clay, decorated and glazed, originated in Egypt about 4700 BCE. Tile was, and is often, used in Spanish architecture to such a degree that a Spanish expression for poverty is "to have a house without tiles." The Spanish also use decorative ceramic tiles on the **risers** of stairs. The Romans used fired clay pipes to carry water and sewage and used terracotta to construct and decorate their public and private buildings.

In England, many abbeys had mosaic tile floors. The European cathedrals of the twelfth century also had tile floors. In ancient times, tiles were used to make pictures on the walls, and these patterns were spread over many tiles. A good example is the representation of bulls and dragons in the Ishtar Gate from Babylon, which is now in the Pergamon Museum in Berlin. Later, each tile was decorated with intricate patterns, or four tiles were used to form a complete pattern. Eighteenth- and nineteenth-century tiles used a combination of these two design types.

Tiles were named after the city where they originated: Faience with its striking opaque glazes, from Faenza in Italy; Majolica, with bright decorations, from Majorca, Spain; and Delft tiles, from the town of Delft in Holland. Delft tiles, with their blue and white designs, are known worldwide.

Production tiles are made by two methods: dust press and extruded. Floor and wall tiles for interior use are produced by the dust-press method. The clay mixture is forced into steel dies under heavy pressure and fired at very high temperatures to form **bisque,** a tile ready to be glazed. These tiles are then sprayed with a surface glaze and fired at a lower temperature than before. This second firing fuses the glaze to the tile. The dust-press method produces distinct shapes and sizes.

The second production method is an extruded or ram process in which the clay is mixed to form a thick mud and is then forced through a die. This process forms a slightly rougher-looking and larger tile, which is glazed in the same manner as the dust-process tiles. The temperature and proportions of the ingredients dictate the tile use: walls, floors, interior or exterior, and residential or commercial.

Seneca Tiles, Inc., has a line called Seneca Handmold, which is an authentic hand-formed clay tile characterized by irregular edges, corners, and surface variations. Rich tones and inviting textures enhance both traditional and contemporary interiors.[40]

Water absorption tests are valuable in determining the likely stain resistance of unglazed tile. A tile high in water absorption will likely have the least stain resistance. The converse

Table 4.4	Porosity Variances
Type	**Water Absorption Rate**
Impervious	0.5% or less
Vitreous	More than 0.5% but less than 3%
Semivitreous	More than 3% but less than 7%
Nonvitreous	More than 7%

is also true, in that a tile low in water absorption is likely to have greater stain resistance. (See Table 4.4.)

Porcelain tiles are composed of feldspar, kaolin, and ball clays, and at least one manufacturer has stated that the tiles are fired at temperatures greater than 2200°F, which results in a viscous liquid phase leading to crystallization. The tile color occurs as a result of body stains being added. Because porcelain tiles are generally thought of as virtually the strongest and least penetrable available—approximately 33 percent stronger than glazed tiles—they are often purchased for use in retail and heavy commercial-use locations. An additional advantage of this tile type is that it provides a frost-proof product that offers an airy, expansive feel.[41]

Because of the low absorption rate of porcelain tiles, bond-promoting additives are added to the mortars and grouts.

Many types of finishes and patterns are available in ceramic tiles, ranging from a very shiny, highly reflective glaze to a dull matte finish and even an unglazed impervious tile. Tiles may be solid color or hand painted with designs.

The surface texture of the ceramic tile relates to the reflectance qualities. For example, a perfectly smooth tile will have a much higher reflectance rate than a rough surface tile, although both tiles have identical glazes. Ceramic tiles are available in many different shapes and sizes. Instead of the traditional 4 1/4″ × 4 1/4″ tile, 8″, 12″, and even 18″ square tiles are used widely. (See Figure 4.10.)

Highly glazed tiles are not recommended for floor use for two reasons: First, the surface can become extremely slippery when wet; second, some wearing and scratching can occur over a time, depending on type of use. Of course, if moisture and wear are not a problem, then glazed tiles may be used.

ASTM C-1028-89 has established the dynamometer pull meter method for determining the static coefficient of friction of ceramic tile and other similar surfaces. The higher the coefficient, the less likely slippage will occur. Of course, a variety of factors can affect slip-resistance, include a person's stride, the amount of wear on the sole of a shoe, and the presence of foreign material. ANSI has not established a standard value for coefficient of friction, but OSHA has an industry standard rating of 0.50 for slip-resistant surfaces. Likewise, the Americans with Disability Act (ADA) recommends a static coefficient rating of 0.60 for accessible routes and 0.80 for ramps.[42]

Authorities state that the raised-point texture of Cross-Grip has resulted in the highest performance rating available from the National Restaurant Association's testing for slip-resistance.[43]

Most ceramic tile companies produce a raised-dome surface tile that can be detected underfoot and by cane contact (which meets the guidelines set by the ADA). Its yellow color serves as a caution for platform and curb edges.

When ceramic or quarry tiles are used on a floor, the floor is usually finished with a **base** or combination trim tile having a **bullnose** at the top and a **cove** at the bottom in the same material as the floor tiles. If ceramic tiles are to be continued onto the wall surface, a cove base is used. (See Figure 4.11.)

FIGURE 4.10 Three different size Rosso Tuscan Clay tiles are shown here in combination: 3″ × 3″, 3″ × 16″, and 16″ × 16″. *Photograph courtesy of Crossville Inc.*

CERAMIC MOSAIC TILE

Mosaic has been associated with a variety of civilizations. Archeological digs have unearthed gorgeous examples of mosaic across the globe. One of the first known uses of mosaic consisted of terracotta cones affixed to a background surface to provide an artistic appearance. Slightly later appearances of mosaic included pavement with a random mosaic design accomplished through use of a variety of stone colors. The Greek civilization was the first known to have utilized pebbles as art, creating works that featured elaborate scenes depicting animals and people.

Tesserae, pieces created for mosaic, were developed by 200 BCE. Many of these pieces were quite small, and through their use, artists were able to approximate the appearance of a painting. The tesserae were developed from stone, such as marble, because the mosaics created from these pieces were often used for floor coverings, and glass was not sufficiently durable for this purpose. Still, mosaic was also used on other surfaces, and small pieces of terracotta and other ceramic pottery were often added to a mosaic to supply additional colors. For surfaces other than floors, pieces of glass were also used in mosaic art.[44]

By definition of the Tile Council of America (TCA):

- **Mounted tile.** Assembled into units or sheets through use of material appropriate for handling and installation; can be edge-mounted, back-mounted, or face-mounted (see ANSI A137.1); exposure to bonding surfaces of the tile body should allow for 80 percent coverage of the bond mortar in dry areas and 95 percent coverage in wet areas

- **Back and edge-mounted.** Assembled with fiber mesh, perforated paper polyurethane, resin, or other bonding material; bonding material applied to back edge of tile

- **Clear film-faced.** Assembled through removing clear plastic adhesive film from face after final set

- **Paper-faced.** Assembled through wetting and removing paper from face of tile through use of water-soluble adhesives; tile then adjusted before final set

When determining which tile to choose, it is important to note that tile manufacturers are charged with providing information as to whether specific assemblies are designed to be installed in exterior areas, swimming pools, or other wet locations. You should note that a paper-mounted mosaic is not suitable for wet locations.[45]

A paver tile has the same composition and physical properties as a mosaic tile, but it is thicker and has a facial area of more than 6 square inches.

INSTALLATION

The Handbook for Ceramic Tile Installation is published by the Tile Council of America, Inc., every year. (Table 4.2 is from this publication.) The designer can choose the correct tile installation for every type of floor use and specify a *Handbook* method number, grout, and setting method. The *Handbook* is also a guide in developing job specifications. As can be seen from Table 4.2, ceramic tile for floor use may be installed by both thick- and thin-set methods.

When ordering any tile, 2 percent extra of each color and size should be added for the owner's use. This will allow immediate replacement of damaged tiles, and the color will match exactly.

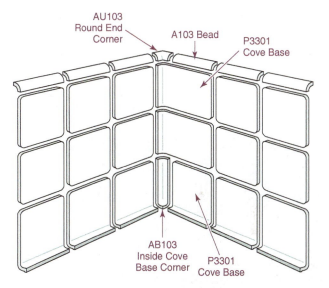

FIGURE 4.11 Line drawings. *Courtesy of Crossville Tile.*

Other Types of Tile

Another tile option to consider is the fiber-optic floor, which mixes function and fashion. It offers the lovely look of a high-end tile floor, but it also includes an embedded fiber-optic display. Possibilities for the fiber-optic design are limitless, and some businesses choose to display their logos through use of this type of floor.[46]

If you're looking for a sleek statement for your walls, you might want to consider stainless steel, which is becoming a popular option. Crossville's Stainless Steel Series offers an expansive variety of shapes, sizes, and textures, suitable for business and residential use.[47]

Most **ESD** floors are rendered electrically conductive by adding, blending, or weaving carbon and graphite into standard flooring materials. Vinyl tile is made conductive by adding conductive carbon chips or veins into the vinyl raw materials used in standard vinyl flooring. Carpets are made conductive by weaving in thousands of carbon-coated conductive fibers. Rubber is made conductive by adding either carbon powder or chemicals that reduce electrical resistance of regular rubber flooring. Epoxy coating manufacturers utilize several different methods for making the coatings conductive, including fiber technology, conductive aggregate additives, carbon and graphite particulate blending, and sometimes a combination of several in the same coating.[48]

Pregrouted tiles usually come in sheets of up to 2.14 square feet that have already been grouted with an elastomeric material such as silicone, urethane, or polyvinyl chloride (**PVC**) rubber, each of which is engineered for its intended use. The perimeter of these factory pregrouted sheets may include all or part of the grout between sheets, or no grout. Field-applied perimeter grouting should be of the same elastomeric materials used in the factory-pregrouted sheets or as recommended by the manufacturer. Pregrouted tiles save on labor costs because the only grouting necessary is between the sheets, rather than between individual tiles.

Slip-resistant tiles contain abrasive particles that are part of the tile. Other methods of slip-resistance may be achieved by grooves or patterns on the face of the tile.

Some tiles are self-spacing because they are molded with **lugs.** Other means of spacing are achieved by using plastic spacers to ensure alignment of tiles and an even grout area.

QUARRY TILE

Quarry tile is unglazed tile made by the extrusion process from natural clay or shales with the color throughout the body. Depending on the geographic area where the clays are mined, the colors will vary from the warm brown-red to warm beige. The face of a quarry tile may be solid colored, variegated with light and dark within the same tile, or flashed, in which the edges of the tile are a darker color than the center. A quarry tile is extruded in a 1/2-inch-thick ribbon and then cut to size. The qualities of the clays and temperatures at which they are fired (up to 2000°F) provide a variety of finished products. Quarry tiles are generally considered stain resistant but not stain proof.

The rugged, unglazed surface of quarry tiles develops an attractive patina with wear. An abrasive grit surface is available for installations in which slip-resistance is important. Most quarry tiles are manufactured unglazed to retain the natural quality of the tile, but some quarry tile is available glazed.

Seneca Tiles prides itself in utilizing ancient methods that require great art and craft. The company states that, due to the requirements of mass production, most manufacturers have given up these methods. Seneca Tiles states that its insistence in utilizing these ancient methods results in maintaining the natural characteristics of glazes and clays, giving rise to a fine, beautiful product.[49] (See Figure 4.12.)

FIGURE 4.12 Notice how the contrasting grout of this quarry tile makes the pattern stand out, whereas if the grout had matched the color of the tile it would give a blended look. *Photo courtesy of Seneca Tile.*

Installation

Quarry tiles may be installed by either thick- or thin-set methods. The grout is either a sanded portland cement mix or an epoxy grout with a silica filler. It is the responsibility of the tile installer to remove all excess grout as part of the contract.

Maintenance

Ceramic or quarry tiles may be cleaned with a damp-mop if the soil is light, or with water and a detergent if the soil is heavier. Tile and grout are two different materials, with grout being the more porous. Any soil that is likely to stain the grout should be removed as soon as possible.

MEXICAN OR SALTILLO TILE

In Mexican or saltillo tile, clay, taken directly from the ground, is shaped by hand into forms. Saltillo tile differs from ceramic and quarry tile in that the proportion of ingredients in the clay is not measured. The clay form is allowed to dry in the sun until it is firm enough to be transported to the kiln. Because Mexican tile is a product of families working together, it is common to find a child's hand print or a dog or cat paw imprinted in the surface of the tile. Leaf prints may also be noticed, in which a leaf drifted down when the tile was drying. These slight imperfections are part of the charm of using saltillo tile. Mexican tile is often named for the town in which it is made, thus the name *Saltillo*, the capital of Coahuila, Mexico. Today, Mexican factories are producing more consistent quality tiles.

Because of the uneven thickness of Mexican tile, it should be installed using the thick-set method. If it is being used in a greenhouse or similar area where drainage is possible, Mexican tile may be laid in a bed of sand, which will adapt to any unevenness of the tile. All cracks or joints are then filled with sand.

Saltillo tile is extremely porous—the most porous of all tile—because of its natural qualities. If the tiles are not sealed in the factory (and most are not), a "grout release" *must* be sponged, sprayed, or rolled on. Another method of preventing the grout from staining the tile is to use a sealer before grouting. It is recommended that one of the many new sealer/finish products, which allow the combination of linseed oil and wax into one process application, be used. Additional coats can be applied to provide a matte or a gloss finish. The more coats applied, the higher the gloss will appear. The benefits are cost, labor, and an environmentally friendly finish.

Maintenance

A Mexican tile floor should be kept free of dust and dirt by sweeping or vacuuming and, when the floor shows signs of wear, applying another coat of wax or sealer/finish and buff. Traffic areas may need to be touched up frequently with wax or sealer.

GLASS TILE

An example of glass tile is Crossville Tile's Water Crystal Mosaics, which the company states incorporates current high-tech production with ancient glass-making. The tiles produced by Crossville Tile are 13/16" square and 5/16" thick for strength and durability. They are sheet mounted on 11 1/2" × 11 1/2" sheets.[50]

Maintenance

Simple cleaning with clean water and a sponge or mop should suffice. Any oily deposits should be removed by using soap and water and then rinsing with clean water.

Glass Block

One example of how glass block is used in flooring is IBP's GlassWalk system. The IBP system includes laminate structural glass units with a top layer tempered for impact resistance and a heat-strengthened bottom layer, bonded with a clear resin interlayer. In this easy-to-install system, the prefabricated glass block units are set in an extruded aluminum two-way hollow grid sized to fit the glass floor unit.[51]

Glass block is made of four ingredients: broken glass called culletsand, soda ash, and limestone. Ingredients are measured and heated until the mixture is a liquid, which is then poured into molds to form a half of the glass block. The two halves are heated and pressed together to form the completed block.

Concrete

According to the Portland Cement Association, although the terms *cement* and *concrete* often are used interchangeably, cement is actually an ingredient of concrete. In other words, there is no such thing as a cement sidewalk, or a cement mixer; the proper terms are *concrete sidewalk* and *concrete mixer*. Concrete is basically a mixture of aggregates and paste. The aggregates are sand and gravel or crushed stone; the paste is water and portland cement. Concrete gets stronger as it gets older. Portland cement is not a brand name, but the generic term for the type of cement used in virtually all concrete, just as stainless is a type of steel and sterling a type of silver. Cement comprises from 10 to 15 percent of the concrete mix, by volume. Through a process called *hydration*, the cement and water harden and bind the aggregates into a rocklike mass. This hardening process continues for years, meaning that concrete gets stronger as it gets older.

Curing is one of the most important steps in concrete construction, because proper curing greatly increases concrete strength and durability. Concrete hardens as a result of hydration: the chemical reaction between cement and water. However, hydration occurs only if water is available and if the concrete's temperature stays within a suitable range.[52]

Maintenance for interiors is difficult, unless the surface has been treated with a floor sealer specially manufactured to produce a dust-free floor. Color may be added when the concrete is mixed, or it may be dusted on the surface during the finishing operation. It can be colored by the application of a chemical stain. This stain is often called *acid stain*, even though acid is not the ingredient that colors the concrete. Instead, a chemical reaction actually does the coloring. A concrete floor looks less like an unfinished floor or substrate if it is stamped and/or colored into squares. In addition, any cracking is more likely to occur in these stamped grooves and be less visible. Several pattern products are available to mark the surface of the **plastic** concrete, so it imitates the shapes and patterns of brick or natural stone.

Dark-colored concrete floors are used in passive solar homes because the large mass absorbs the rays of the sun during the day and radiates the heat back at night.

Concrete floors may be painted with an epoxy, polyurethane, or acrylic paint. Generally, epoxy paints are the best for adhesion.

MAINTENANCE

Because cured concrete can sometimes absorb harmful chemicals, prewetting must be done before using any cleaning solution. Synthetic detergent should be used because soap will react with the lime and cause a scum.

Exposed Aggregate

When an exposed aggregate floor is specified, the type of aggregate used is extremely important because it is visible on the finished floor. River stone gives a smooth rounded texture. Today, the river stone effect may be achieved by tumbling stones in a drum to remove sharp edges.

INSTALLATION

While the concrete is still plastic, the selected aggregate is pressed or rolled into the surface. Removal of the cement paste by means of water from a hose when the concrete is partially hardened will expose the aggregate and display the decorative surface. For interior use, most of the aggregate should be approximately the same size and color, but other values within that hue may also be used, with a scattering of white and black stones.

One drawback to the use of exposed aggregate is that, like any other hard-surfaced material, exposed aggregate is not sound absorbent and is hard on the feet during prolonged standing.

A clear polyurethane finish specially formulated for masonry surfaces can be applied. This finish brings out the natural color of the stone, similar to the way a wet stone has more color than a dry one. Coated exposed aggregate seldom seems to become soiled. A vacuum brush used for wood floors will pick up any loose dirt from between the stones.

Brick

Prehistoric man made brick from dried mud, but he soon discovered that when mixed with straw, the shaped brick could withstand the elements. In fact, kiln-burned brick made by the Babylonians 6,000 years ago still exists. Sun-dried brick, or **adobe,** dates from around 5000 BCE and is still used in some areas of the southwestern United States, but with some modern-day materials added. Fired bricks and kilns first appeared between 2500 and 2000 BCE in Mesopotamia and India, but the art was lost around 1700 BCE. Fired brick was not used again until 300 BCE.

The earliest recorded use of brick is in the Bible: The Egyptians made the Israelites work "in mortar and in brick" (Exodus 1:14). There was a limitless supply of clay from the bed of the Nile River. Sun-baked brick was used in the Tower of Babel and in the wall surrounding the city of Babylon.

The Chinese used brick in the third century BCE for building part of the Great Wall. The Romans used sun-dried bricks until about 14 CE, when they started using bricks burnt in kilns. The Romans took this knowledge of brick making to Europe and Britain; however, after they left in 410 CE, the art died out and was not restored until the eleventh and thirteenth centuries.

The first brick buildings in the United States were built in Jamestown, Virginia, by British settlers, and on Manhattan Island by the Dutch. Bricks used in Virginia were probably made locally because there are records of brick being exported in 1621. Of course, the Aztecs of Mexico and Central America also used adobe bricks for building purposes.

Until about the mid-1850s, brick was molded by hand, but from then on it was made using mechanical means. Bricks are made by mixing clay and shale with water and are formed, while plastic, into rectangular shapes with either solid or hollow cores.

During the process of heating the bricks, the clay loses its water content and becomes rigid; however, it is not chemically changed. During the higher temperatures used in burning, the brick undergoes a molecular change: The grains fuse, closing all pores, and the brick becomes vitrified or impervious.

The color of brick depends on three factors: chemical composition of the clay, method of firing control, and temperature of the kiln. A red color comes from the oxidation of iron to form iron oxide. Lighter colors (the salmon colors) are the result of underburning. The higher the temperature, the harder the brick. Harder bricks have lower absorption potential and higher compressive strength than softer ones. Generally, the denser the brick and the lower the absorption, the easier it is to clean and maintain. Flooring brick, used in such places as factories, where floors receive heavy use, is hard and dense.

INSTALLATION

For areas in which spilled liquids are likely, such as in a kitchen or bathroom, a mortared installation is appropriate. When installing over a wood frame floor, a thin brick paver may be selected to reduce the additional dead weight of the floor assembly. Brick pavers weigh approximately 10 pounds per square foot (psf) per inch of thickness.

Pavers are laid in a conventional manner in a 1/2-inch wet mortar bed with mortar joints. When the joints are thumbprint hard, they are **tooled,** compacting the mortar into a tight, water-resistant joint. Where moisture is not a problem, a mortarless method may be used.

Patterns used should be interlocking to ensure a secure floor.

MAINTENANCE

Brick may be vacuumed, swept, damp-mopped, or spray buffed.

Linoleum

Linoleum, a mainstay floor covering for over 100 years, is derived from two Latin words: *Linum* (linen) and *Oleum* (oil). Linoleum was invented in 1860 by the English rubber manufacturer, Sir Frederick Walton Marmoleum (natural linoleum). It's one of the few flooring products made almost entirely from natural raw materials—it's composed of linseed oil (from flax seed), rosins (from pine), and wood flour (a waste produced by the lumber industry), all calendered onto a natural jute backing. The colors are made from environmentally responsible pigments and even the adhesives used to install Marmoleum are natural, safe, and environmentally friendly. Marmoleum is a sustainable choice in flooring: because of its natural properties, it actually becomes stronger over its life, so it will last a long time. At the end of its useful life, it's biodegradable!

In addition, because of its antistatic properties, Marmoleum stays cleaner than other floors and tends to repel dust and dirt. Dusting or damp-mopping is usually all the care it needs. Further, Marmoleum is naturally antimicrobial and will inhibit the growth of harmful microorganisms, including dust mites and the MRSA strains of bacteria.[53]

It is only sensitive to alkaline solutions, which dissolve the linseed oil and dry out the material. Linoleum is a tough yet visually striking floor covering, highly resistant to heavy rolling loads and foot traffic. Because linoleum is a natural organic product, its performance is enhanced by time, as exposure to air serves to harden and increase its durability. Although linoleum continues to harden over time, the floor remains quiet and comfortable under foot.

Forbo offers Marmoleum global 2 with Topshield, which is made of a strong, long-lasting primer and top layer to provide resistance to dirt and scuffs. Forbo states that the topcoat can be renovated.

INSTALLATION

The installation of linoleum should always follow the manufacturer's specifications, including the selection of what type of adhesive to use and how to finish the seams. If you are using linoleum sheets, vinyl sheets, or specialty sheet flooring, the seams should be welded using a colored linoleum rod that is melted along the seam. Heat welding blocks the penetration of dirt and moisture.

MAINTENANCE

Linoleum flooring can best be maintained by simply sweeping or vacuuming the loose dirt and dust. A damp-mop with plain water or water with a small amount of mild detergent can be used for more cleaning power. Small scratches and ingrained dirt can be buffed out using a nylon brush or nonabrasive cleaning pad.

Asphalt Tile

Dark-colored asphalt flooring was developed in the United States in the 1920s. Like linoleum, however, asphalt tile is a flooring material that has been gradually phased out because of advanced technology. Asphalt tile was very inexpensive, but it was not resistant to stains and could be softened by mineral oils or animal fats. The individual tiles were brittle and had poor recovery from indentation. Asphalt tile may still be found in some older homes.

Vinyl Composition Tile

For consumers seeking a less expensive, durable option for floor tile, one with color pigments that are insoluble in water and resistant to light and cleaning agents, vinyl composition tile (VCT) can be a logical choice. This tile is made of organic binder filler, inorganic fillers, and pigments.[54]

Armstrong offers SafeWalks VCT, which it states is resistant to slips. According to the company, the flooring meets the requirements for static coefficient of friction established by the Americans with Disabilities Act.

Vinyl composition tiles were once made with asbestos. In recent years, however, asbestos has been proven to have adverse health effects, so VCTs are no longer made with asbestos fibers. Therefore, there are no health hazards now.

Note: The Occupational Safety and Health Administration has provided rigid rules for safely removing old vinyl asbestos floors.

The thickness, or **gauge,** as it is sometimes called, of VCTs is 3/32 inch, or 1/8 inch. For commercial and better residential installations, the 1/8-inch gauge should be used.

The advantages of vinyl composition tile are that it (1) is inexpensive, (2) is easy to install and maintain, (3) may be installed on any grade, (4) resists acids and alkalis, and (5) withstands strong cleaning compounds. The disadvantages are that it (1) has low impact resistance, (2) has poor noise absorption, and (3) is semiporous as compared with solid vinyls and solid rubber.

INSTALLATION

Vinyl composition, vinyl, and some other tiles are all installed using the thin-set method. The most important step in this installation procedure is to be sure the substrate is smooth and level. With thinner tile, any discrepancies in the substrate will be visible on the tile's surface. In a residential installation of thinner tile, a newly installed floor developed a wavy and bumpy appearance after only several weeks, because the wood substrate had not been sanded.

Materials and the installation site should be at a minimum temperature of 65°F for 48 hours before, during, and after installation. The substrate is troweled with the manufacturer's suggested adhesive and, as with the installation of parquet floors, the walls should not be used as a starting point.

MAINTENANCE

Initial Maintenance

- After application, do not place heavy equipment or furniture on the floor for 48 hours. Do not wash or scrub the floor for five days.
- After the floor has dried, make certain it is clean. Then apply three to five coats of a quality cross-linked acrylic floor finish.

Regular Care and Maintenance (after initial cleaning and polishing)

- Use a soft push broom or treated dust mop, and clean frequently.

- Immediately upon noticing spills or stains, remove them. Use a diluted, neutral detergent for damp-mopping. If heavy soiling occurs, use an automatic floor machine for light scrubbing.

- Use clean water for rinsing. Do not allow any foot traffic until the floor is completely dry.

- Provide protection and restore gloss through high-speed burnishing or spray-buffing.[55]

- Many of the same maintenance procedures may apply for commercial installations of other types of vinyl floors. See the manufacturer's specifications.

Solid Vinyl

Solid vinyl tile is really not all vinyl. It has a lower percentage of fillers and a higher percentage of PVC than vinyl composition tiles. It usually consists of a fiberglass—reinforced backing on which the pattern is printed. The final coat may be either clear vinyl or vinyl with urethane. The latter is tougher and wears longer. Sizes are 12", 18", and 24" square.

MAINTENANCE

Maintenance is the same as for vinyl composition tile.

Pure Vinyl Tile

Pure vinyl tiles are homogeneous or, in other words, pure vinyl with few, if any, fillers, featuring the same color throughout the tile. Vinyl tiles have a higher resistance to abrasive wear than VCT. They are available in faux-stone finishes, marble, travertine, brick, and slate. Pure vinyl tiles are also used as feature strips or for borders. Borders should be of approximately the same width at all walls.

Two examples of pure vinyl tile are Mannington's Assurance II and Assurance Squared. These tiles, which are manufactured with an embossing texture to provide drainage, are useful in locations such as business entries, laboratories, and operating rooms.[56]

Vinyl wall base effectively trims off a floor installation and helps hide minor wall and floor irregularities. Its distinctive profile consists of a reclining curvature at the top and a descending thin toe line that conforms snugly to the wall and floor. Some vinyl cove bases can be hand-formed to make the corners, whereas others come with both inside and outside corners preformed. The cove wall base comes either in 20-foot rolls or 48-inch strips in 2 1/4-inch or 4-inch heights.

INSTALLATION

Pure vinyl tiles are installed with a specified adhesive and are laid in a pyramid shape.

MAINTENANCE

Mannington advises that color-coded synthetic cleaning pads that are used for many commercial products should not be used for its Mannington Assurance II and Assurance Squared products. Rather, the manufacturer recommends that a soft brush (e.g., 3M # 53 brush or equivalent) be periodically used to make sure that the embossed areas of the flooring are deep cleaned.[57]

Periodically sweeping with a soft broom or vacuum will prevent the build-up of dust and dirt. Spills should be cleaned immediately. Damp-mopping with a mild detergent is sufficient for slightly soiled floors, whereas scrubbing with a brush or machine is used for heavy soil. Soap-based cleaners should not be used because they can leave a dulling film. The floor should be rinsed with clean water after cleaning. However, the floor should never be flooded, and excess dirty water should be removed with a mop or wet vacuum. No-wax floors can be damaged by intense heat, lighted cigarettes, and rubber or foam-backed mats or rugs. If stubborn stains persist, they should be rubbed with alcohol or lighter fluid.

Rubber

Rubber flooring is now made of 100 percent synthetic rubber. Rolls of rubber flooring are 4 foot wide and rubber tiles are 9-, 12-, 18-, 20-, 36-, and 39-inch squares, depending on manufacturer. Thickness varies from 3/32 to 3/16 inch. The tiles are usually marble or travertine patterned, and are laid at right angles to each other. They may be laid below grade and are extremely sound absorbent. Stair treads are being made of rubber to comply with the California building code, which calls for a clearly contrasting color on the stair tread in public buildings.

Although available with a smooth surface, multilevel rubber flooring (raised discs or pastilles, solid or duo-colored squares, or even rhythmic curves) has become increasingly popular where excessive dirt or excessive moisture is likely to be tracked inside. Raised portions have beveled edges, causing the dirt to drop down below the surface, which reduces abrasion on the wear surface. The same thing happens with water; most of it flows below the wear surface. Although the original purpose of this type of rubber tile was to reduce wear from moisture or dirt, rubber floors are now used to meet the minimum requirements of the Americans with Disabilities Act (ADA). Rubber flooring is considered an ideal product for public areas because it offers excellent traction.

One brand of rubber flooring, ECOshapes, provides a relatively easy way to create the appearance of a custom floor design. ECOshapes are available in a variety of shapes and colors, so they can be configured to provide a desired appearance.[58]

Johnsonite Tactile Warning Strips include "an underfoot or tactile warning" to point out hazardous areas, such as platforms and open stairwells. Durable strips of this type are often used in locations such as offices, shopping malls, healthcare facilities, malls, schools, and airports. Their product meets the requirements set forth by Section A117.1-1986, Accessible Warnings on Walking Surfaces. When tactile warning strip material is used, it should extend across the full width of the hazardous area at a continuous depth of 3 feet prior to the hazard.[59] Several other manufacturers have similar warning surfaces for the visually impaired.

Many large office buildings have no source of daylight in stairwells or hallways. When an emergency evacuation of the building is necessary, many times the electricity is not working and exit signs and stairwells are in the dark. As a result of the first World Trade Center bombing, Johnsonite pioneered the SAFE-T-FIRST System which integrates color with Permalight self-illuminating technology in vinyl or rubber flooring products and accessories, such as exit signs and directional arrows. (See Figure 4.13.) Johnsonite has received many awards for this extensive product offering which includes rubber cove base, vinyl handrail tape, and even disc inserts for raised disc flooring.

Roppe uses Alpha Base, which combines their wall base with an innovative "signage" capacity for such wording as "In Case of Fire Use Stairs," "Fire Exit," and so on. In case of fire, the first thing building occupants are often instructed to do is to "get close to the floor" in order to avoid dangerous, impeding smoke. When this happens, standard signs are often invisible. It is ideal for schools, hospitals, dormitories, public buildings—anywhere you need to show exits and escape routes.

These two products may have saved many lives in the September 11, 2001, attacks on the World Trade Center and the Pentagon. The author heard one survival story from the Pentagon in which 12 people held hands and crawled along the floor in order to get to safety.

FIGURE 4.13 The Safe-T-First System in light from Johnsonite. The system has won many design awards. It is visible in light and sudden darkness. *Photographs courtesy of Johnsonite.*

MAINTENANCE

Proper maintenance is essential to the appearance and wear life of rubber tiles. The tile should be swept and mopped daily with a neutral pH detergent.

New rubber floor should not be cleaned for a minimum period of 72 hours after installation to ensure proper adhesive curing. Stripping a new rubber floor may not be required unless the end user intends to apply an acrylic floor finish. If buffing is the end user's preferred method of maintenance, stripping will remove the internal waxes which continuously bloom to the surface of the tile. Typically, a wax containing detergent is used to clean the tile for a period of 90 days to allow the waxes to uniformly bloom prior to routine buffing of the tile. The equipment used to buff rubber floor tiles should never exceed 350 rpm.

Sheet Vinyl

Sheet vinyl manufacturers have greatly improved not only the quality but also the designs of their products. Precise information regarding construction is a trade secret, but the following information is generic to the industry.

Sheet vinyl comes in widths of 6 feet, 6 feet 6 inches, 9 feet, and 12 feet and is manufactured by two methods—inlaid or rotogravure. Most inlaid sheet vinyls are made of thousands of tiny vinyl granules built up layer by layer, and then fused with heat and pressure. The result is a resilient, hefty flooring with a noticeable depth of color and a crafted look. Some sheet vinyls have extra layers of foam cushioning to provide comfort underfoot and muffle footsteps and other noises. Color chips are distributed throughout the depth of the wear surface. A fibrous backing will produce a lightweight flexible flooring that virtually eliminates tearing and creasing and the telegraphing of irregularities from the old flooring to the new.

Armstrong identifies three categories of vinyl sheet flooring:

1. ***Heterogeneous.*** A layered, designed, high-performance structure that is flexible, easy to maintain, and easy to install.

2. ***Homogeneous.*** A flooring sheet-form system that is uniform in structure and composition; usually consists of vinyl plastic resins, plasticizers, fillers, pigments, and

stabilizers; meets the requirements of ASTM F 1913, Standard Specification for Sheet Vinyl Floor Covering without Backing (and is sometimes called unbacked vinyl sheet flooring).

3. **Inlaid sheet flooring.** Decorative floor surfacing material in which the design is formed by color areas set into the surface; the design may or may not extend to the backing.[60]

Rotovinyls are made by a rotogravure process that combines photography and printing. Almost anything that can be photographed can be reproduced on a rotovinyl floor. The printed layer is protected by a topping (called the wearlayer) of vinyl resin (PVC) either alone or in combination with urethane. Vinyl resin composition often produces a gloss surface, whereas urethane creates a high-sheen result. A mechanical buffer with a lamb's wool pad will bring back the satin gloss of the vinyl resin composition wearlayers. Urethane wearlayer flooring should not be buffed. All rotovinyls are made with an inner core of foamed or expanded vinyl, which means they are cushioned to some extent. At the lower end of the price scale, cushioning may be thin. Most sheet vinyls are flexible enough to be coved up the **toe space** to form their own base (check manufacturers' specifications).

The wearlayer is the final, protective topcoat on sheet vinyl or vinyl tile flooring products. Usually consisting of clear vinyl or urethane, wearlayers enable the flooring to resist scuffs, stains, and other evidence of wear. The thicker the wearlayer, the better the protection against the effects of foot traffic, dirt, and overall daily use. Generally, for residential rotogravure products, those with the thickest wearlayers often have long-term warranties. There is a definite distinction, however, between residential and commercial flooring. Product characteristics, maintenance, and warranties vary considerably.

For residential installations, high gloss finishes are still available, but the trend seems to be patterns that copy natural materials, such as stone, wood, marble, and slate. The warranties, ranging from 5 to 11 years and more, cover manufacturing defects and wear.

The multi-level embossed sheet vinyl flooring has become increasingly popular where excessive dirt or excessive moisture is likely to be tracked inside. Lonseal has many different configurations including large or small raised discs, squares, cobblestone effect, and even a deeply grooved "sound wave" pattern. Raised portions have beveled edges, causing the dirt to drop down below the wear surface, which reduces the abrasion on the wear surface. The same thing happens with water; most of it flows below the wear surface and makes the floor more slip-resistant. For a transitional flooring between indoors and outdoors, Londeck can be heat-welded to achieve a watertight, weatherproof surface. All Lonseal floors exceed requirements of the Americans with Disabilities Act (ADA).

FiberFloor is a new kind of resilient flooring. New to North America, but popular in Europe for over a decade, FiberFloor combines a cushiony feel with carefree maintenance and exceptional durability. A unique balanced construction allows the floor to lay flat and stay flat. No glue is required![61]

The company offering BioSpec MD homogeneous sheet flooring with MCare antimicrobial and Quantum Guard finish states that this product decreases deterioration resulting from staining, odor, and premature degradation. The company advises that the product offers a Quantum Guard HP finish, so that the requirement for polishing during a long period of time will be eliminated. The company also states that this patented finish contains a urethane aluminum oxide topcoat, which is cured through a UV process.[62]

INSTALLATION

Seaming methods vary from manufacturer to manufacturer, depending on the product and its application. Installation may be a perimeter-bond system stretched over the floor and secured only at the edges. The other—a full-adhered system—is set in a full bed of mastic. The correct trowel notch size is important with resilient floors. The latter type should be rolled with a weighted roller to eliminate air pockets and form a good bond between the backing and the adhesive.

Installing new flooring over an existing floor is preferable to removal, particularly if it is known that the existing floor contains asbestos. As noted in Chapter 1 and previously in the vinyl asbestos section of this chapter, removal of old floor coverings or adhesives that might contain asbestos requires, in some states, a trained asbestos abatement contractor, whether or not the asbestos is friable.

The old floor must be fully adhered. A perimeter-bonded system must not be covered. When covering a textured or embossed surface, a manufacturer-recommended embossing leveler must be used. Asphalt tiles or asphalt adhesive must not be covered, because asphalt eats through vinyl.

Furniture should be equipped with the proper load-bearing devices; otherwise, indentations will mar the vinyl surface. Static load limitations vary for each product. Refer to each manufacturer's information. (See Figure 4.14.)

Heavy refrigerators and kitchen or office equipment should not be dragged across the floor, because this will damage and tear the surface. These items should be "walked" across the floor on a piece of wood or on Masonite runways. Runways must be used even if using an appliance dolly. Furniture should be equipped with flat bearing surfaces or wide rubber rollers.

It is not unusual to experience discoloration issues with resilient flooring. These issues can arise in a variety of ways. For example, they can develop from the product itself. They can also develop from above or below the product surface. Logically, these issues will result in the most readily visible damage on light-colored material, and it should be noted that an inlaid product will generally discolor face-down, whereas a rotogravure product is likely to stain more easily from the back.[63]

A synthetic polyurethane patch sometimes used for filling voids on the surface of wood panels will also cause discoloration in the shape of the patch. This problem can also be avoided by using an underlayment grade of plywood. If there are dark pieces of wood or bark in wafer board and oriented strand board (OSB), they will cause staining. The use of construction adhesives to cement underlayments of substrates is a major cause of discoloration. Rubber-backed mats may cause staining, and coco fiber mats may cause scratches.

MAINTENANCE

Remember that no-wax does not mean NO maintenance. Congoleum's information on resilient sheet flooring is probably applicable to most similar type flooring.

Protect and do not disturb the sealed seams for at least 16 hours after seam sealer application to ensure a proper seam bond. Permanent damage may result if seam sealer is stepped on or disturbed before it is dry.

TYPE OF LOAD	KENTILE FLOORS INC. RECOMMENDS	KENTILE FLOORS INC. DOES NOT RECOMMEND	TYPE
HEAVY FURNITURE, more or less permanently located, should have composition furniture cups under the legs to prevent them from cutting the floor.	Right  — Wide Bearing Surfaces Save Floors	Wrong  — Small Bearing Surfaces Dent Floors	Composition Furniture Cups 
FREQUENTLY MOVED FURNITURE requires casters. Desk chairs are a good example. Casters should be 2" in diameter with soft rubber treads at least 3/4" wide and with easy swiveling ball bearing action. For heavier items that must be moved frequently, consult the caster manufacturers as to the suitable size of equipment that should be used.	Right 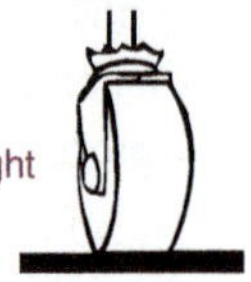 — Rubber Rollers Save Floors	Wrong  — Hard Rollers Mark Floors	Rubber Wheel Casters 
LIGHT FURNITURE should be equipped with glides having a smooth, flat base with rounded edges and a flexible pin to maintain flat contact with the floor. They should be from 1¼" to 1½" dia., depending upon weight of load they must carry. For furniture with slanted legs apply guides parallel to the floor rather than slanted ends of legs.	Right 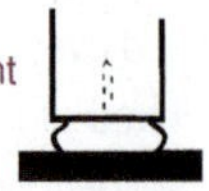 — Use Flat Bearing Surfaces	Wrong  — Remove Small Metal Domes	Flat Glides With Flexible Shank 

FIGURE 4.14 Static load.

Keep traffic to a minimum during the first 48 hours on all resilient sheet and tile floors to allow the adhesive to harden.

Furniture should not be placed on the floor until the adhesive has had adequate time to dry (at least 24 hours).[64]

Cork

Cork is the name given to the bark of the cork oak, a tree from the beech family, characteristic of western Mediterranean countries. The bark acts as a protective shell to the harsh climate changes and numerous fires affecting the region. To get the bark, cork trees are stripped of their bark every 9 to 14 years; the tree is never cut and the habitat remains undisturbed. The properties of cork are derived naturally from the structure and chemical composition of the inner cells. Each cubic centimeter of cork's honeycomb structure contains between 30 to 50 million cells.

Hence, cork provides:

- **Insulation.** Due to its low density, cork has excellent acoustical and thermal insulating characteristics, as 90 percent of the tissue is made of gaseous matter.
- **Resiliency.** Cork quickly returns to its original shape after it is released from pressure.
- **Impermeability.** The seal Suberin is a waxy substance, which stops gases and liquids from penetrating cork.
- **Hypoallergenic qualities.** Because cork does not absorb dust, it is valuable for use in locations where allergy issues are a concern.
- **Durability.** Due to the fact that cork is not as affected by friction as some other hard surfaces, this material is quite durable.
- **Fire retardant qualities.** Due to its composition, cork is a natural fire retardant. It will not release toxic gases or spread flames in instances of combustion.

Cork granules are used to produce cork floor tiles. These granules are often culled from low-quality bark and unconsumed product within the wine-cork production process. The floor tile created from these granules is bound with resins; it is molded through application of heat and pressure to meet the intended density. It is possible to coat cork wearlayers with acrylic product or urethane. These layers can also be varnished or waxed. From 2000–2010, technology was honed within the **floating floor** industry to adapt cork flooring to an efficacious and highly desirable product.[65]

Cork today can be found in many products and applications from the wine bottle stopper to the insulation panels of the NASA space shuttle. Frank Lloyd Wright, in 1937, used cork as a decorative durable flooring material in his renowned Falling Waters house in Pennsylvania, making him one of the first American architects to do so.

INSTALLATION

Cork is a wood product; therefore, floor tiles should be acclimatized to the site for 72 hours before installation. Because of cork's natural qualities, no two tiles are identical in pattern or color. Pieces may vary slightly in color, tone, and grain configuration. It is the installer's or client's responsibility to mix colors and patterns in an acceptable manner. The cork tiles should be shuffled to get the desired aesthetic mix. Only those substrate materials and adhesives specified by the manufacturer of the cork flooring should be used. Expansion and contraction, resulting from climatic conditions, will occur, so an approximate 1/8" to 1/4" space around the perimeter of the room must be allowed for. This space is covered by a base.

Natural Cork provided the following information on installation on a concrete substrate: "Check concrete slab for moisture by chipping quarter size sections 1/8" deep in several places and applying two drops of 3% phenolphalein in alcohol solution (readily available at drug stores) with a dropper in each section. If solution turns red, too much moisture is present for safe installation of Cork Parquet." A calcium chloride test is also acceptable.

MAINTENANCE

Walk-off mats should be used, provided they do not have a rubber back, which may cause permanent discoloration. (See Figure 3.6.) Furniture guards should also be used. Spills should be picked up immediately; wet spills or water should not be allowed to stand on the cork floor. With factory-refinished cork parquet tiles and Planks Plus, a high-quality hardwood floor polyurethane cleaner should be used in accordance with the manufacturer's instructions. When the finish begins to show wear, the floor should be cleaned and one of Natural Cork's recommended topcoat finishes should be used.

Formed-in-Place or Poured Floors

Formed-in-place floors come in cans and are applied at the site in a seamless installation. The basis of the "canned floors" may be urethane, epoxy, polyester, or vinyl, but they are all applied the same way. First, as with all other floor installations, the surface must be clean, dry, and level. Second, a base coat of any of the aforementioned materials is applied to the substrate according to manufacturer's directions. Third, colored plastic chips are sprinkled or sprayed on the base and several coats of the base material are applied for the wearlayer.

Formed-in-place poured floors seem popular in veterinary offices, where a nonskid and easily cleaned surface is desirable. Such floors can also be coved up a base like sheet vinyl, which eliminates cracks between the floor and base. Of course, this type of flooring may be used in any area where cleanliness is paramount.

MAINTENANCE

Maintenance is the same as that for sheet vinyl.

bibliography

Berendsen, A. *Tiles: A General History*. New York: Viking Press, 1967.

Byrne, M. *Setting Tile*. Newton, CT: Taunton Press, 1996.

Oak Flooring Institute. *Hardwood Flooring Finishing/Refinishing Manual*. Memphis, TN: Oak Flooring Institute, 1986.

Oak Flooring Institute. *Wood Floor Care Guide*. Memphis, TN: Oak Flooring Institute, 2004.

Tile Council of America. *2010 Handbook for Ceramic Tile Installation*. Anderson, SC.

glossary

Adobe. Unburnt, sun-dried brick.

Agglomerate. Marble chips and **spalls** of various sizes, bonded together with a resin.

Aggregate. The solid material in concrete, mortar, or grout.

ANSI. American National Standards Institute.

ASTM. American Society for Testing and Materials.

Base. A board or moulding at the base of a wall that comes in contact with the floor; protects the wall from damage.

Beveled. In wood flooring, the top edge is cut at a 45° angle.

Billets. Small pieces of wood making up a parquet pattern.

Bisque. Once-fired clay.

Bluestone. A hard sandstone of characteristic blue, grey, and buff colors, quarried in New York and Pennsylvania.

Bow. Longitudinal curvature of lumber.

Bullnose. A convex rounded edge on tile.

Burl. An abnormal growth or protuberance on a tree, resulting in a very patterned area.

Chamfer. Tile with a slight beveled edge.

Cove. A concave rounded edge on tile.

Crook. The warp of a board edge from the straight line drawn between the two ends.

Cup. Deviation of the face of a board from a plane.

Cure. Maintaining the humidity and temperature of freshly poured concrete for a period of time to keep water present so the concrete hydrates or hardens properly.

Dowel. Round wooden rod to join two pieces of wood.

Elgin Marbles. (Pronounced with a hard "g"). Name given to portions of the frieze of the Parthenon. Lord Elgin, the British Ambassador to Turkey from 1799 to 1802, persuaded the Turkish government in Athens to allow him to remove the frieze of the Parthenon to the British Museum in London to prevent further damage.

ESD. The rapid, spontaneous transfer of electrostatic charge induced by a high electrostatic field.

Figure. The pattern of wood fibers.

Floating floor. A wood floor that is not attached to the substrate; rather, it is merely laid on top.

Floorcloths. Painted canvas used in the early 1800s.

Gauge. Thickness of tile.

Grain. Arrangement of the fibers of the wood.

Grout. Material used to fill in the spaces between tiles.

Hardwood. Wood from trees that lose their leaves.

Impervious. Less than 0.5 percent absorption rate.

Kiln. An oven for controlled drying of lumber or firing of tile.

Laminate floor. Same construction as a decorative laminate, only specially made for flooring.

Laminated or engineered wood. Bonding of two or more layers of material.

Lugs. A projection attached to the edges of a ceramic tile to provide equal spacing of the tiles.

Marquetry. Veneered inlaid material in wood flooring that has been fitted in various patterns and glued to a common background.

Mastic. An adhesive compound.

Matrix. The mortar part of the mix.

Medullary rays. Ribbons of tissue extending from the pitch to the bark of a tree, particularly noticeable in oak.

Metal spline. Thin metal wire holding strips of parquet together.

Metamorphic. Changes occurring in appearance and structure of rock caused by heat and/or pressure.

Monolithic. Grout and mortar base become one mass.

Mortar. A plastic mixture of cementitious materials, with water and fine aggregates.

Mosaic. A small size tile, ceramic or marble, usually 1 inch or 2 inch square, used to form patterns.

Nonvitreous. Tile that absorbs more than 7 percent moisture.

Parquetry. Inlaid solid wood flooring, usually set in simple geometric patterns.

Patina. Soft sheen achieved by continuous use.

Pickets. Wood strips pointed at both ends, used in parquet floors in patterns such as Monticello.

Plastic. Still pliable and soft, not hardened.

Plumb. Exactly vertical.

Pointed. Act of filling joints with mortar.

Prefinished. Factory finished, referring to wood floors.

Prefinished flooring. Wood floors that have been factory finished before they are installed.

psi. Pounds per square inch.

PVC. Polyvinyl chloride. A water-insoluble thermoplastic resin used as a coating on sheet vinyl floors.

Quarter sawn. Wood sliced in quarters lengthwise that shows the grain of the wood to best advantage.

Quartzite. A compact granular rock, composed of quartzite crystals usually so firmly cemented as to make the mass homogeneous. Color range is wide.

Reducer strip. A tapered piece of wood used at the joining of two dissimilar materials to compensate for difference of thickness.

Riser. The vertical part of a stair.

Sandstone. Sedimentary rock composed of sand-sized grains naturally cemented from mineral materials.

Semivitreous. Three percent, but not more than 7 percent, moisture absorption.

Sets. Groups of parquet set at right angles to each other, usually four in a set.

Spall. A fragment or chip, in this case of marble.

Spalling. Flaking of floor because of expansion of components.

Square. Edges cut at right angles to each other.

Stenciling. Method of decorating or printing a design by painting through a cut-out pattern.

Taber test. Scientific method to measure the amount of wear a surface can take before it is worn out.

Terrazzo. Marble chips of similar size combined with a binder that holds the marble chips together. This binder may be cementitious or noncementitious (epoxy resin).

Thin-set. The method of installing tile with a bonding material that is usually 3/32" to 1/8" in thickness. In certain geographical areas, the term *thin-set* may be used interchangeably for dry-set portland cement mortar.

Toe space. Area at the base of furniture or cabinets that is inset to accommodate the toes.

Tongue-and-groove. A wood joint providing a positive alignment.

Tooled. A mortar joint that has been finished by a shaped tool while the mortar is plastic.

Twist. A spiral distortion of lumber.

Veneer. A very thin sheet of wood varying in thickness from 1/8 to 1/100 inch.

Vitreous. Moisture absorption of 0.5 percent to less than 3 percent.

endnotes

1. Find Any Floor, www.findanyfloor.com
2. Ibid.
3. Ibid.
4. County Floors, www.countyfloors.com
5. Hardwood Information Center, www.hardwoodinfo.com
6. Flooring Trends, www.flooringtrends.com
7. Durapalm, www.durapalm.com
8. Designs by BSB, www.designsbybsb.com
9. Bane Clene, www.baneclene.com
10. Composite Panel Association, www.pbmdf.com
11. Wood Floors On Line, www.woodfloorsonline.com
12. Ibid.
13. Congoleum, "Maintenance & Warranty Information," *Consumer Flooring Guide*, www.congoleum.com/care
14. Sustainable Future, www.sustainable-future.com
15. Basic Coatings, www.basiccoatings.com
16. Plyboo, www.plyboo.com
17. Ibid.
18. Coconut Floorings, www.coconutfloorings.com
19. Pergo, www.pergo.com
20. Flooring Biz, www.flooringbiz.com
21. Mannington icore, www.manningtonicore.com
22. Flooring Guide, www.flooringguide.com
23. Tile Council of America, *Handbook for Ceramic Tile Installation*, Clemson, SC, 2009, p. 7
24. Precision Stone, www.precision-stone.com
25. Marble Institute of America, www.marble-institute.com
26. Tile Council of America, *Handbook for Ceramic Tile Installation*, Clemson, SC, 2009, p. 7
27. Walker Zanger.Medallion Collection, www.walkerzanger.com
28. Tile Council of America, *Handbook for Ceramic Tile Installation*, Clemson, SC, 2009, p. 5.
29. Ibid.
30. Marble Institute of America, www.marble-institute.com
31. National Terrazzo Manufacturers Association, www.ntma.com
32. Ibid.
33. Bane Clene, www.baneclene.com
34. National Terrazzo Manufacturers Association, www.ntma.com
35. Impamerica, www.impamerica.com
36. Marble and Granite, www.marblegranite.com
37. Natural Stone Interiors, www.natural-stone.com
38. Building Stone Institute, www.buildingstoneinstitute.org
39. Structural Slate, www.structuralslate.com
40. Seneca Tile, www.senecatiles.com
41. Letter from Crossville Tile, Crossville, TE
42. Homeowners Florida Tile, www.homeowners.floridatile.com
43. Crossville Tile, www.crossvilleinc.com
44. Mozaico, www.mozaico.net
45. Tile Council of North America, *Handbook for Ceramic Tile Installation*, Clemson, SC, 2009, p. 10
46. Fiberoptics Floors Inc., www.fiberworks.com
47. Crossville Inc., www.crossvilleinc.com
48. Anti Static Flooring, www.staticworx.com
49. Laticrete, www.laticrete.com
50. The Natural Abode, www.thenaturalabode.com
51. Seneca Tile, www.senecatiles.com
52. Portland Cement, www.cement.org
53. Natural Abode, www.naturalabode.com
54. Armstrong World Industries, www.armstrong.com
55. Ibid.
56. Ibid.
57. Ibid.
58. ECO Surfaces, www.ecosurfaces.com
59. Johnsonite, www.johnsonite.com
60. Armstrong World Industries, www.armstrong.com
61. Tarkett, www.tarkettna.com
62. Mannington, www.mannington.com
63. Floor Biz, www.floorbiz.com
64. Congoleum, www.congoleum.com
65. Cork Innovations, www.corkinnovations.com

Walls

In this chapter, you will:

- Analyze the social and physical influences affecting historical changes in materials for walls
- Describe types of wall materials, their fabrication and installation methods, and their maintenance requirements
- Develop an understanding of the nature and value of integrated design practices as related to walls
- Recognize the principles of natural lighting design related to walls
- Determine appropriate wall components to provide optimal security

In floors, the weight of flooring material is spread over a large area; however, when these same materials are used on walls, they create a heavy dead load. Thus, walls—whether constructed or veneered with granite, stone, or brick—must have a foundation prepared to withstand this additional weight. **Compressive strength** is also important for wall installation materials.

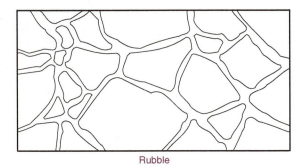
Rubble

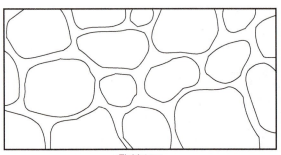
Ashlar

Fieldstone

FIGURE 5.1 Types of stonework.

There are two types of walls: load bearing and nonbearing. Interior designers need to know the difference between the two. **Load-bearing** walls are those that support an imposed load in addition to their own weight; a nonbearing wall is just designed for utilitarian or aesthetic purposes. The architect deals with both, but the interior designer probably deals primarily with nonbearing walls. A load-bearing wall should never be removed or altered without consulting an architect or engineer.

Stone

Most interior designers do not specify stone walls except maybe for fireplaces; however, it is important to understand the various patterns. A stone wall, in a residence, is usually a veneer and may be constructed of any type of stone. **Rubble** is uncut stone or stone that has not been cut into a rectangular shape. **Ashlar** is stone that is precut to provide enough uniformity to allow some regularity in assembly. The rubble masonry is less formal, requires the use of more **mortar,** and is not as strong as the other types of **bonds** because of the irregularly shaped bonds. Uniform mortar joints are a mark of a skilled worker. **Fieldstone** or **cobble** has a more rounded feeling than does ashlar or rubble (Figure 5.1).

MAINTENANCE

Stonework should be cleaned with a stiff brush and clean water. If stains are difficult to remove, soapy water may be used, followed by a clean-water rinse. Stonework should be cleaned by sponging during construction, which facilitates final cleaning. The acids used to clean brick should never be used on stone walls.

Regular maintenance of these walls consists of brushing or vacuuming to remove dust. It is important to remember that, generally, igneous types of stones are impervious; in contrast, sedimentary and metamorphic stones are more susceptible to stains. Stone walls should not be installed where grease or any substance that may stain the stone is present.

StoneLite panels (see Figure 5.2) are composite wall panels made up of a thin natural stone veneer reinforced with an aluminum honeycomb backing. The stone veneer can be almost any stone including granite, marble, or limestone.[1]

FIGURE 5.2 Drawing of StoneLite panels versus solid stone. *Courtesy of Stone Panels Inc.*

Granite

Granite is used wherever a feeling of stability and permanence is desired, which is probably why one sees so much granite in banks and similar institutions. The properties of granite were mentioned in Chapter 4. Granite for walls may be polished, or honed, because abrasion is not a problem with walls.

INSTALLATION

Anchors, **cramps,** dowels, and other anchoring devices should be type 304 stainless steel or suitable **nonferrous** metal. A portland cement sand mortar is used and, where applicable, a sealant is used for pointing the joints.

MAINTENANCE

If required, granite walls may be washed with a weak detergent solution and rinsed with clear water. The walls should be buffed with a lamb's wool pad to restore shine.

Marble

Marble has the same elegant and formal properties whether used for walls or for floors. According to the Marble Institute of America, interior marble wall facing may be installed by mechanical fastening devices utilizing nonstaining anchors, angles, dowels, pins, cramps, and plaster spots, or in a mortar setting bed to secure smaller units to interior vertical surfaces. The overall dimensions of the marble determine the setting method. Resilient cushions are used to maintain joint widths, which are then pointed with white cement or other approved material.

In addition to the traditional sizes, new thin marble veneers that are backed with lighter weight materials have less weight per square foot and, depending on job conditions, may be set in either a conventional full mortar bed or by any of the several newer thin-bed systems.

MAINTENANCE

Maintenance is the same as that for marble floors.

Travertine

When travertine is used in wall applications, it is not necessary to fill the voids. Unfilled travertine gives an interesting texture to the wall surface; however, for a perfectly smooth installation, filling is required. Like flooring, wall applications of travertine may be filled with a clear, translucent epoxy or an opaque epoxy matching the color of the travertine. Filled travertine does tend to have less sheen on the opaque filled area than on the solid area. The surface of the travertine may be left in its rough state, providing texture; it may be cut and sanded; or it may be ground smooth.

INSTALLATION

Installation methods of travertine are the same as for marble.

Brick

Brick is used for both exterior and interior walls, and the surface of the brick may be smooth, rough, or grooved. Bricks with these surface textures create interesting wall designs with interesting shadows. Bricks are available in whites, yellows, greys, reds, and browns and may

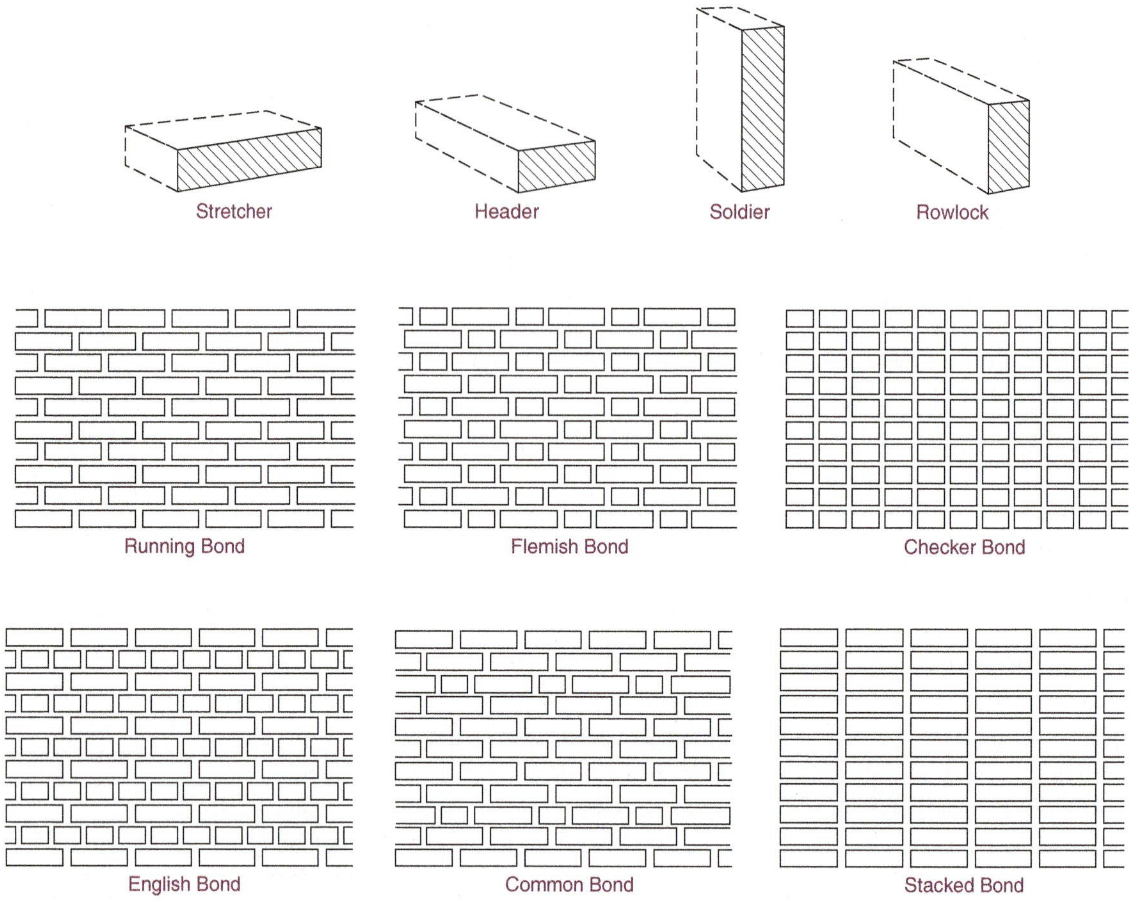

Stretcher

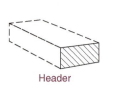
Header

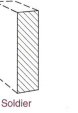
Soldier

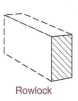
Rowlock

Running Bond

Flemish Bond

Checker Bond

English Bond

Common Bond

Stacked Bond

FIGURE 5.3 Stretchers, headers, and bonds.

be ordered in special sizes or shapes. Firebrick is used for lining boilers and fireplaces and is made of special fire-resistant clays.

The standard brick size is 3 3/4" wide by 8" long and 2 1/4" high. Bricks laid to expose the long side in a horizontal position are called **stretchers;** vertically, they are called **soldiers.** When the ends of the bricks show horizontally, the bricks are called **headers,** but vertically they are called **rowlocks** (see Figure 5.3). A bond is the arrangement of bricks in rows or **courses.** A common bond is defined as bricks placed end to end in a stretcher course with vertical joints of one course centered on the bricks in the next course. Every sixth or seventh course is made up of headers and stretchers. These headers provide structural bonding as well as a pattern. A bond without headers is called a running bond. It is interesting to note that in some historical digs of buildings dating from the 1880s, it is possible to discover the nationality of the builders of brick walls (e.g., English and Flemish, as well as several other European nationalities).

Masonry walls may be hollow masonry, where both sides of the wall are visible, or they may be veneered. When both sides are visible, the **header course** ties the two sides together. A veneered wall is attached to the backing by means of metal ties. (See Figure 5.4.)

The joints in a wall installation are extremely important because they create shadows and special design effects. The joints of a brick wall are normally 3/8" thick. The mortar for these joints consists of a mixture of portland cement, hydrated lime, and sand. The mortar serves four functions:

1. It bonds the brick units together and seals the spaces between them.

2. It compensates for dimensional variations in the units.

3. It bonds to reinforcing steel and therefore causes the steel to act as an integral part of the wall.

4. It provides a decorative effect on the wall surface by creating shadow or color lines.

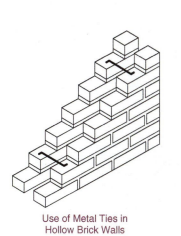

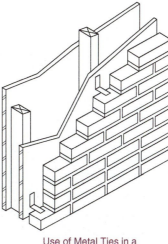

Use of Metal Ties in
Hollow Brick Walls

Use of Metal Ties in a
Brick Veneer Wall

Use of Headers in a Hollow Brick
Wall Visible from Both Sides

FIGURE 5.4 Brick wall construction.

Mortar joint finishes fall into two classes: troweled and tooled joints. In the troweled joint, the excess mortar is simply cut off (**struck**) with a trowel and finished with the trowel. For the tooled joint, a special tool other than the trowel is used to compress and shape the mortar in the joint.

INSTALLATION

Brick and concrete blocks are both installed by masons. Bricks are placed in a bed of mortar; mortar is then laid on the top surface of the previous course, or row, to cover all edges. The mortar joints may be any of the types shown in Figure 5.5.

MAINTENANCE

The major problem with finishing brick walls is the **mortar stain,** which occurs even if the mason is skilled and careful. To remove mortar stain, the walls are cleaned of surplus mortar and dirt; then scrubbed with a solution of trisodium phosphate, household detergent, and water; and then rinsed with water under pressure. If stains are not removed with this treatment, a solution of muriatic acid and water is used. The acid should be poured into the water, and not vice versa, to avoid a dangerous reaction. Just the bricks themselves should be scrubbed. The solution should not be allowed to dry but should be rinsed immediately with clean water. For cleaning light-colored bricks, a more diluted solution of muriatic acid and water should be used to prevent burning.

Regular maintenance for bricks includes brushing and vacuuming to remove dust that may have adhered to the rough surface. Masonry walls that may come in contact with grease, such as in kitchens, should be either impervious or sealed to prevent penetration of the grease.

Flush	Raked	Stripped
Struck	Weathered	Concave or Rodded
V Joint	Beaded Flush May Also Be Inset	Shoved

FIGURE 5.5 Mortar joints.

Concrete

Light-transmitting concrete, known also as translucent concrete, is literally the brightest concrete development in recent years. Strands of optical fibers are cast by the thousands into concrete to transmit light, either natural or artificial, into all spaces surrounding the resulting

FIGURE 5.6 Translucent concrete. *Courtesy of Optics.org.*

translucent panels. (See Figure 5.6.) The material can be used in a variety of architectural and interior design applications, such as wall cladding and dividers.

Originally developed by a Hungarian architect in 2001, light-transmitting concrete is produced by adding 4 to 5 percent optical fibers (by volume) into the concrete mixture.[2]

Currently, many architects of contemporary buildings, particularly in the commercial, industrial, and educational fields, are leaving poured concrete walls exposed on the interior. The forms used for these walls may be patterned or smooth, and this texture is reflected on the interior surface. The ties that hold the forms together may leave holes that, if properly placed, may provide a grid design. From the interior designer's point of view, a poured concrete wall is a *fait accompli*. The surface may be left with the outline of the forms showing, patterned or plain, or it may be treated by the following methods to give a different surface appearance: bush hammering, acid etching, or sandblasting. Bush hammering is done with a power tool that provides an exposed aggregate face by removing the sand-cement matrix and exposing the aggregate. Sandblasting provides a textured surface. Bush hammering produces the heaviest texture, whereas the texture from sandblasting depends on the amount and coarseness of sand used. Acid etching just removes the surface.

If concrete is left in its natural poured state, the main problem facing the designer is using materials and accessories that will be compatible with cast concrete. Obviously, such materials need to imply weight and a substantial feeling, rather than delicacy or formality. The massive feeling can be overcome, however, by plastering over the concrete.

Concrete Block

Concrete block is a hollow concrete masonry unit (CMU) composed of portland cement and suitable aggregates. Walls of this type are found in homes, but they are more frequently used in commercial and educational interiors. There are several problems with concrete block.

It has extremely poor insulating qualities if used on an exterior wall; if used on an outside wall and moisture is present, **efflorescence** will form. It also has a fairly rough surface that is difficult to paint, although coverage may be accomplished by using a specially formulated paint and a long-nap roller.

INSTALLATION

The mason erects a concrete block wall in a similar manner to a brick one and is often visible from both sides; therefore, the joints need to be finished on both sides of the block. Concrete block may be erected in either a running bond pattern or stacked (running bond is the stronger).

MAINTENANCE

Acid is not used to remove mortar smears or droppings, as with brick. Instead, excess mortar should be allowed to dry and then is chipped off. Rubbing the wall with a small piece of concrete block will remove practically all the mortar. For painting instructions, see Chapter 2.

Glass Block

In the 1920s and 1930s, glass block seemed to be used only in bathrooms and on the sides of front doors; today, however, modern technology and the innovation of architects and designers have led to a revival and growth of its use in a variety of design environments. Although glass block must only be used for non-load-bearing installations, creative designers have nonetheless found many appealing uses for it.

Glass block, by definition, is composed of two halves of pressed glass fused together. The hollow in the center is partially **evacuated,** which provides a partial vacuum with good insulating qualities. The construction of the block is such that designs may be imprinted on both the inside and the outside of the glass surfaces. In all of their applications, glass blocks permit the control of light—natural or artificial, day or night—for function and drama. Thermal transmission, noise, dust, and drafts may also be controlled. For curved panel radius minimums refer to Table 5.1.

Pittsburgh Corning Corporation, the only American manufacturer of glass block, produces a variety of styles that may be used for both exterior and interior purposes. (See Figure 5.7.)

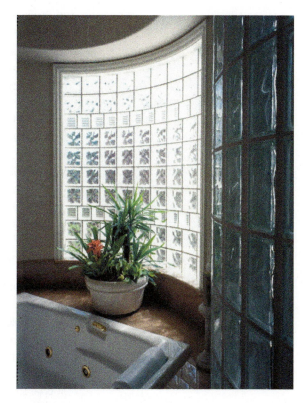

FIGURE 5.7 Private residence. Blocks used are Argus Parallel Flutes and Decora pattern. *Photograph courtesy of Pittsburgh Corning Glass Block.*

Table 5.1	Radius Minimums for Curved Panel Construction			
Block Size	**Outside Radius in Inches**	**Number Blocks in 90° Arc**	**Joint Thickness in Inches**	
			Inside	**Outside**
6 x 6	52 1/2	13	1/8	5/8
4 x 8	36	13	1/8	5/8
8 x 8	69	13	1/8	5/8
12 x 12	102 1/2	13	1/8	5/8

Source: Courtesy of Pittsburgh Corning Corporation.

LightWise Architectural Systems Blast-Resistant Glass Block Panels let in light while providing privacy and protection from various levels of blast. They are the perfect choice for high-risk buildings such as military facilities, airports, government offices, embassies, courthouses, correctional facilities, arenas, financial centers, offices, and other high-profile public and retail spaces.

Vistabrik is a desirable product for a structure that is likely to be the subject of security issues. The company that produces Vistabrik states that the product offers low maintenance and replacement expense, and it is "highly resistant to impact, bullets, and fire." The company also states that the product "features low distortion transparency for clear observation through sturdy, 3-inch thick glass block partitions into areas where visual supervision is a must."[3]

Solar Wall Tubes are perfect for commercial building walls where you want to bring in light without compromising the masonry look and feel of the building. The Glass Block Solar Wall Tube's mirror-like finish magnifies and reflects the light and solves many design issues related to single or double glass block installations in multi **wythe** wall construction. It allows the architectural look of single or double glass blocks on both sides of a thick wall. It also provides a visually aesthetic look in the hollow area between the glass blocks. The sturdiness of the metal tube prevents any loading from above the opening from being transferred to the glass block.[4]

Privacy considerations and aesthetics are key in block choice. The VUE pattern, which is clear, provides excellent light transmission while maintaining privacy. Opal glass block, which works well in a variety of settings from schools, hospitals, and libraries to public buildings and residences, diffuses daylight; however, it allows optimal enjoyment of light during late afternoon. Its opal appearance provides a highly desired aesthetic, while its functional aspects provide the security and privacy of glass block.

A standard glass block is 3 7/8" thick; the Thinline Series units are 3 1/8" thick. Glass block is available in 6", 8", and 12" squares, and some styles come in 4" × 8" and 6" × 8" rectangular blocks. Thinline block has the additional advantage of 20 percent less weight.

INSTALLATION

The mortar-bearing surfaces of glass block have a coating that acts as a bond between the block and the mortar. Additionally, the coating acts as an expansion-contraction mechanism for each block. An optimum mortar mix is one part portland cement, one-half part lime, and four parts sand. Panel reinforcing strips are used in horizontal joints every 16 to 24 inches of height, depending on which thickness of block is used. Expansion strips are used adjacent to **jambs** and **heads.** Joints are struck while plastic and excess mortar are removed immediately. Mortar should be removed from the face of the block with a damp cloth before final set occurs. For easier cleaning of glass block showers, use a non-mildew-forming silicone or acrylic sealer to coat the mortar joints.

Prefabricated panels with or without ventilation are also available.

MAINTENANCE

Ease of maintenance is one of the attractive features of block. Mortar or dirt on the face of glass block may be removed by the use of water, but not with abrasives (steel wool, wire brush, or acid).

Plaster

The Egyptians and ancient Greeks used plaster walls that they painted with murals. The frescoes of early times were painted on wet plaster, which absorbed the pigment so it dried as an integral part of the plaster. The frescoes of Michelangelo's Sistine Chapel still retain their original brilliant color after 400 years. Historically, plaster was also used for intricate mouldings and decorations. Today, plaster-covered walls are used only in commercial installations and expensive custom-built homes, because applications are expensive in comparison to **drywall.**

Lath is the foundation of a plaster wall. In the pyramids in Egypt, the lath was made of intertwined reeds. The construction of the half-timbered homes of the English Tudor period is often referred to as daub and wattle (the daub being the plaster and the wattle the lath), this time a woven framework of saplings and reeds. When restoration work is done on houses built in the United States prior to the 1930s, the lath will probably be found to be thin wood strips nailed to the studs about 3/8" apart.

Modern lath is gypsum board, metal, or masonry block. The gypsum lath consists of a core of gypsum plaster between two layers of specially formulated, absorbent, 100 percent recycled paper. The gypsum lath is 3/8" or 1/2" thick, 16" wide by 48" long, and is applied horizontally with the joints staggered between courses. Other sizes are also available. Special types of gypsum lath may have holes drilled in them for extra adhesion or have a sheet of aluminum foil on one side for insulating purposes.

Metal lath, expanded metal that is nailed to the studs, is used not only for flat areas but also for curved surfaces and forms. The **scratch coat** is troweled on and some plaster is squeezed through the mesh to form the mechanical bond, whereas the bond with gypsum board is formed by means of **suction.** Beads or formed pieces of metal are placed at exterior corners and around casings to provide a hard edge that will not be damaged by traffic.

Surface finishes called *veneer plaster* are on the market; they create the upscale look of solid plaster at a lower cost. Veneer plaster has high resistance to cracking, nails popping, impact, and abrasion failure, and is particularly suited to accommodate wall situations where light conditions require smooth even expanses of wall.

One example of veneer plaster is National Gypsum's Gold Bond BRAND Uni-Kal Veneer Plaster, which offers a long-lasting surface that resists abrasion when it is applied in a thin coat and troweled to an even finish. This single-component veneer plaster can be controlled to provide a number of textured finishes.[5]

Joints are reinforced with fiberglass webbing; steel corners and **casing beads** protect corners. An alkali-resistant primer formulated for use over new plaster should be used if the surface is to be painted. If a gypsum board wall is already installed, a plaster bonding agent must be applied before using the veneer plaster, which is then applied in two coats.

Plaster used to be troweled on the lath in three different coats. The first coat bonded to the lath; the second was the brown coat; and the third, the finish coat, was very smooth. The first two coats were left with a texture to provide tooth. A three-coat plaster job is still done sometimes; however, two coats or even one may now be enough to complete the finished surface.

As mentioned in Chapter 2, because of its extreme porosity, plaster must be sealed before proceeding with other finishes.

Gypsum Board

Gypsum board has the same construction as gypsum board lath. Sheets are normally 4 feet wide and 8 feet long, but they may be obtained in lengths up to 16 feet. The long edges are usually tapered; with a beveled edge, sometimes the short sides are also coated with the paper.

The term *drywall* originated to differentiate between plaster or "wet wall" construction and any dry material, such as gypsum board, plywood, or other prefabricated materials that do not require the use of plaster or mortar. In some areas of the United States the term *drywall* is synonymous with *gypsum board*.

Another term mistakenly used as a synonym for *drywall* is Sheetrock, a registered trademark of the U.S. Gypsum Company for its brand of gypsum board. The term *gypsum wallboard* implies use on walls only, whereas most gypsum board companies now produce a type of reinforced gypsum board specially designed for ceilings, which can withstand deflection. All gypsum board companies produce their product with 100 percent recycled paper on both the face and the back of the board.

An example of gypsum board is Gold Bond BRAND Sta-Smooth Gypsum Board, which offers two-edge configurations that can relieve joint deformity issues arising as a result of damaged gypsum board edges, twisted framing, highs and lows in temperature and humidity, and weak alignment. This drywall system is easy to apply, and it is appropriate for use in drywall systems where conventional types of gypsum board are to be used. Regular Sta-Smooth boards are available in 1/2" thicknesses, 4' wide, and in customary gypsum board lengths. The Sta-Smooth System is also composed of ProForm BRAND Quick Set Setting Compounds, a hardening-type taping compound, and regular ProForm tape and finishing compounds.[6]

Some edges are square; the square edge is designed to be a base for a fabric covering or wallpaper, paneling, or tile. The square edge also can be used where an exposed joint is desired for a paneled effect. Tapered, round-edge gypsum board can be used for walls and ceilings in both new construction and remodeling. It is designed to reduce the beading and ridging problems commonly associated with standard-type gypsum board.

Several types of specialty gypsum wallboards are available: those for fire-resistant purposes; those for abrasion resistance; those for mold/mildew resistance; those for use as a vapor retarder barrier on exterior walls; or those for radius construction.

Sheetrock Brand Flexible gypsum panels are much more flexible than standard panels of the same thickness, making them ideal for use anywhere a tight radius is required. These gypsum panels permit quick and easy construction of curved walls, ceilings, arches, and stairways. Tapered edges allow easy final decoration. They have a noncombustible gypsum core encased in 100 percent recycled face and back paper.[7]

In new construction, 1/2" thickness is recommended for single-layer application; for laminated two-ply applications, two 3/8" thick sheets are used. The horizontal method of application is best adapted to rooms in which full-length sheets can be used, because horizontal application minimizes the number of vertical joints. Today, screws are used rather than nails, because screws can be installed by automatic screw guns and will not pull loose or "pop." Screws are placed a maximum of 12 inches on center (o.c.) on ceilings and 16 inches o.c. on walls where framing members are 16 inches o.c. Screws should be spaced a maximum of 12 inches o.c. on walls and ceilings where framing members are 24 inches o.c. In both cases, the screw heads should be slightly below the surface. A very good drywall installation may also have an adhesive applied to the studs before installing the panels, in which case screws may be farther apart.

If, however, nails are used, the spacing is slightly different. Nails should be spaced a maximum of 7 inches o.c. on ceilings and 8 inches o.c. on walls along framing supports. The ceilings are done first and then the walls.

A thorough inspection of the studs should be made before application of the gypsum board to ensure that all warped studs are replaced. If this is not done, the final appearance of the plaster board will be rippled. Of course, this problem is not present when metal studs are used (e.g., in commercial construction).

After all the sheets have been installed, the outside corners are protected by a metal corner or bead, which is either right angled or curved. The bead is manufactured with strong, paper tape that is laminated to a sturdy, rust-resistant metal form. It provides superior resistance to edge cracking and chipping, resulting in corners that stay beautiful despite normal building movement and everyday wear-and-tear.[8] Trim strips are available for a **reveal** effect.

Joint cement, spackling compound, or, as it is called in the trade, "mud," is applied to all joints with a 5" wide spackling knife. Tape is placed to cover the joint and is pressed into the mud. (*All* seams or joints must be taped regardless of length; otherwise, cracks will soon appear.) The outside beads have joint cement feathered to meet the edge. Another layer of compound is applied, **feathering** the outer edges. After drying, the compound is sanded and a third coat is applied, with the feathering extending beyond the previous coats. All screw holes are filled with joint cement and sanded smooth. Care must be taken to sand only the area that has been coated with joint cement, because sanding the paper layer will result in a roughness that will be visible, particularly when a painted semi-gloss or gloss finish is applied. In fact, the Gypsum Association suggests a thin skim coat of joint compound should be applied over the entire surface to provide a uniform surface for these paints. The drywall installer should be informed of the final finish so that attention can be paid to special finishing.

The surface of the gypsum board may be left smooth, ready for painting or a wallcovering, or it may have some type of texture applied. The latter is done for several reasons. Aesthetically, a texture may eliminate glare and is likely to hide any surface discrepancies caused by warping studs and/or finishing of joints. The lightest texture available is called an orange peel (the surface has the texture of the skin of an orange). Another finish is a skip-troweled surface: After the texture has been sprayed on, a metal trowel is used to flatten some areas. The heaviest texture is a heavily stippled or troweled appearance, similar to rough-finished plaster. A texture is preferred whenever there is a **raking light** on the wall surface; the texture helps hide surface discrepancies.

When water may be present, such as in bathrooms and kitchens, most building codes require the use of a water-resistant gypsum board. Its facing paper is colored light green so as to make it readily distinguishable from regular gypsum wallboard. Moisture-prone areas like basements and bathrooms call for highly mold-resistant interior gypsum panels.

DensArmor Plus panels are ideal for moisture-prone interior walls, such as those found in basements and residential bathrooms. These non-paper-faced fiberglass mat drywall panels are also ideal for commercial pre-rock installations.

DensArmor Plus panels feature a fiberglass mat surface on both the front and the back for the best in interior protection from moisture currently available. The moisture-resistant fiberglass mats make DensArmor Plus panels the ideal replacement for paper-faced greenboard. A revolutionary departure from traditional wallboard, the face of DensArmor Plus panels finishes in the same steps as paper-faced wallboard and offers superior performance in resisting mold. Georgia-Pacific Gypsum has earned two GREENGUARD certifications: GREENGUARD Indoor Air Quality Certified and GREENGUARD Children & Schools Certified for low emissions for the DensArmor Plus family of interior panels and ToughRock gypsum board. In addition, DensArmor Plus Interior Panels, DensShield Tile Backer, and DensGlass Shaftliner have been GREENGUARD recognized as microbial-resistant.[9]

In association with ceramic tile, special water-resistant tile backers are used. If a pliant wallcovering is to be used, all plasterboard must be sealed or sized, because the paper of the gypsum board and the backing of the wallcovering could become bonded, making the wallcovering impossible to remove.

Another type of gypsum board features fabric or vinyl wallcovering plastic in a variety of simulated finishes, including wood grains and other textures. This type of gypsum board can be applied directly by adhesive to the studs or as a finish layer over a preexisting wall. The edges may be square or beveled. Wood or metal trim must be applied at both the floor and ceiling to create a finished edge. National Gypsum manufactures Durasan, a prefinished panel in which no work such as taping, joint finishing, sanding, or painting are required. Thirty-yard rolls of the face material are available for columns and other curved surfaces.

Tambours

Tambours are vertical slats of any material attached to a flexible backing, as in the front of a roll-top desk. The slats may be solid wood or hardboard. Other materials, such as wood veneer, bamboo, high-pressure laminate, metal, metallic mylar, melamine, melamine/mylar, and real glass mirror, are laminated to a tempered hardboard core with a flexible brown fabric backing approximately 3/16" thick overall. Slats are cut 1/2 to 1 inch o.c. with the angle of the groove varying between 30° and 90°. Depending on the face material and use, dimensions vary from 18 inches wide by 15 inches long for roll-top desks, to 48 inches by 120 inches long. Because of their flexibility, tambours are used for curved walls as well as for roll-up doors in kitchen appliance garages.

INSTALLATION

The method of installation depends on the surface to which the tambour is to be attached. A special adhesive is usually required, and the manufacturers' instructions should always be followed.

Wood

When selecting a wood or veneer, designers should ascertain whether it comes from a renewable source. It is possible for some woods to be sustainable with proper management.

Wood is a good natural insulator because of the millions of tiny air cells within its cellular structure. For equal thickness, it is 4 times as efficient an insulator as cinder block, 6 times as efficient as brick, 15 times as efficient as stone, 400 times as efficient as steel, and 1,770 times as efficient as aluminum. The production of the final wood product is also energy efficient: One ton of wood requires 1,510 kilowatt-hours to manufacture, whereas one ton of rolled steel requires 12,000 kilowatt-hours, and one ton of aluminum requires 67,200 kilowatt-hours.

Wood for walls comes in two different forms: solid wood strips (dimensional lumber) and plywood. Solid wood may be used on the walls of residences, but it is not usually used for commercial applications, unless treated, because of the fire and building code restrictions. For residences, redwood, cedar, and knotty pine are the most commonly used woods, but walnut, pecan, and many others may also be used.

There are several grades of redwood from which to choose. The finest grade of redwood is Clear All Heart, with the graded face of each piece free of knots. Clear All Heart gives a solid red color, whereas Clear redwood—also top quality—contains some cream-colored sapwood and may also have small knots. Although the cream-colored sapwood may be attractive to some, to others its random appearance is bothersome; therefore, the clients need to know the difference in appearance as well as cost between Clear All Heart and Clear. B Heart is an economical all-heartwood grade containing a limited number of tight knots and other characteristics not permitted in Clear or Clear All Heart. B Grade is similar to B Heart except that it permits sapwood as well as heartwood.

Redwood is available in vertical grain, which has straight vertical lines, and flat grain, which is cut at a tangent to the annual growth rings, exposing a face surface that appears highly figured or marbled. Smooth-faced redwood is referred to as surfaced; saw-textured lumber has a rough, textured appearance.

There are two types of cedar: aromatic cedar, which is used for mothproof closets, and regular cedar, which is used for both interior and exterior walls. Another soft wood frequently used for residential interiors is knotty pine, in which knots are part of the desired effect (unlike the top grade redwood).

Boards may be anywhere from 4 to 12 inches wide, with tongue-and-groove for an interlocking joint or **shiplap** for an overlapping joint. The tongue-and-groove may have the beveled edges for a V-joint or may be rounded or even elaborately moulded for a more decorative effect. Shiplap boards come with their top edges beveled to form a V-joint or with straight edges to form a narrow slot at the seams.

Square-edged boards are used in contemporary settings and may be board and batten, board on board, reverse board and batten, or contemporary vertical. (See Figure 5.8.) Board and batten consists of wide boards spaced about 1 inch apart; a narrow 1″ × 2″ strip of batten is nailed on top to cover the 1-inch gap. Board on board is similar to board and batten except that both pieces of wood are the same width.

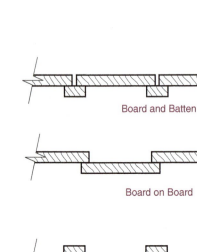

Board and Batten

Board on Board

Reverse Board and Batten

Contemporary Vertical Batten and Board

FIGURE 5.8 Board and batten.

Reverse board and batten has a narrow strip under the joint or gap. In contemporary vertical installations, the battens are sometimes placed on edge between the wider boards. For acoustical control, boards are often placed on edge and spaced about 2 to 3 inches apart on an acoustical substrate.

The National Oak Flooring Manufacturer's Association (NOFMA) suggests using oak flooring on walls and ceilings. It is now possible to obtain a Class A, 0 to 25 flame spread rating (often required in commercial structures) by job-site application of an intumescent coating. Beveled oak strip flooring gives a three-dimensional effect when installed on a wall.

Several companies manufacture paneling that comes prepackaged in boxes containing approximately 64 square feet. The longest pieces are 8 feet and the shortest 2 feet, with beveled edges and tongue-and-grooved sides and ends. This type of paneling, although more expensive than regular strips, eliminates waste in a conventional 8-foot-high room.

The latest wood for walls, woven Durapalm, gives a three-dimensional look to the wall. (See Figure 5.9.)

FIGURE 5.9 Woven Durapalm gives an interesting texture to the wall. *Photograph courtesy of Smith & Fong.*

INSTALLATION

Wood may be installed horizontally, vertically, or diagonally. Each type of installation will give a completely different feeling to the room. Horizontal planking will appear to lengthen a room and draw the ceiling down, whereas vertical planking adds height to a room and is more formal. Diagonal installations appear a little more active and should be used with discretion or as a focal point of a room. Diagonal or herringbone patterns look best on walls with few doors or windows. Each application method requires its own type of substrate.

If installed horizontally or diagonally over bare studs or gypsum board, no further preparation of the surface is needed. The strips are attached to the wall in the tongue area, as with hardwood flooring, except that with wall applications the nails penetrate each stud.

Vertical installations require the addition of nailing surfaces. The two types of nailing surfaces are blocking and furring. (See Figure 5.10.) Blocking involves filling in horizontally between the studs with 2- to 4-inch pieces of wood in order to make a nailing surface. Blocking also acts as a fire stop. Furring features thin strips of wood nailed across the studs.

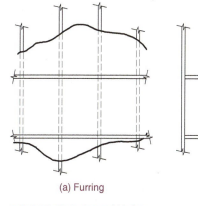

(a) Furring   (b) Blocking

FIGURE 5.10 Furring and blocking.

When wood is to be used on an outside wall, a vapor barrier such as a polyethylene film is required. In addition, wood should be stored for several days in the area in which it is to be installed so it may reach the correct moisture content. Some manufacturers suggest several applications of a water-repellent preservative to all sides, edges, and especially the porous ends (this is particularly important in high-humidity installations).

There are several suggested finishes for wood walls: wax, which adds soft luster to the wood; or a sealer and a matte varnish, for installations that will require cleaning. Paneling may also be stained, but it is important to remember that if solid wood is used, the natural beauty of the wood should be allowed to show through.

Plywood Paneling

Plywood is produced from thin sheets of wood veneer called plies, which are laminated together under heat and pressure with special adhesives. This process produces a bond between plies that is as strong as or stronger than the wood itself.

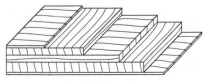

Veneer Core

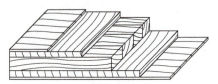

Lumber Core

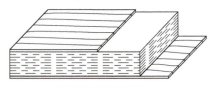

Particleboard Core

FIGURE 5.11 Types of plywood.

Plywood always has an odd number of layers that are assembled with their grains perpendicular to each other. As illustrated in Figure 5.11, plywood may also have a lumber core, a veneer core, a medium-density fiberboard core, or a **particleboard** core (see page 133 for information on particleboard); however, lumber core plywood is virtually never used today in fine architectural woodworking. The face veneer is the best side, with the back veneer being a balancing veneer.

The Architectural Woodwork Institute (AWI) is a not-for-profit organization that represents the architectural woodwork manufacturers located in the United States and Canada. The discussion in this section would not be possible without the assistance and cooperation of AWI.

The side of the plywood panel with the best-quality veneer is designated as the face, and the back may be of the same or of lesser quality, depending on its projected uses.

AWI's *Architectural Woodwork Quality Standards* provide for three grades of plywood panel construction: economy, custom, and premium.

- *Economy grade.* Generally used for projects such as utility areas and mechanical rooms—to produce woodwork items that are not intended to be seen by the public.
- *Custom grade.* Offers substantial control over installation, materials, and quality of work; generally used for high-quality architectural woodwork.
- *Premium grade.* Generally used in projects requiring the highest level of work quality, installation, and materials.[10]

TYPES OF VENEER CUTS

According to the AWI, *wood-veneer slicing* is an important factor in the various visual effects obtained. It is noted that two veneer slices from the same species will provide totally different appearances—even though they have similar color values. Leaves of veneer remain in sequential **flitch** as a log segment is sliced. The veneer options, illustrated in Figure 5.12, are detailed here.

- *Rotary sliced.* This veneer is extremely wide. It is created by mounting the log centrally in the lathe and turning it against an extremely sharp blade, providing an effect similar to that of unraveling a paper roll. A void variegated grain marking results from the slice and follows the annular growth rings of the log.
- *Plain sliced, also referred to as flat sliced.* This veneer creates a prismatic figure. It is created through mounting a half log with the heart side floating against the blade plate; the slice is made parallel to a line through the log's center.
- *Quarter sliced.* The quarter log is mounted on the guide plate to provide for striking of growth rings at approximate right angles. The result is a series of stripes; these stripes are varied in some voids and straight in others. The quarter-sliced cut is often used with oak, as it can result in limitless quantities of medullary ray.
- *Rift sliced.* This type of cut is used only with oak species. It produces a comb-grain effect, also known as a rift effect, through slicing in a direction perpendicular to the oak's medullary rays; a slicer or lathe can be used to accomplish the effect.[11]

Other decorative veneer patterns may be obtained by using the crotch, burl, or stump of the tree. The crotch pattern is always reversed so that the pointed part, or V, is up. Burl comes from a damaged area of the tree, where the tree has healed itself and grown over the injury; it is a very swirly pattern. Olive burl is frequently used in contemporary furniture.

MATCHING OF ADJACENT VENEER LEAVES

Leaves, as with the effect of different veneer cuts, can alter the appearance of a given panel or an entire installation. To create a particular appearance, the veneer leaves of a flitch are edge-glued together in a pattern such as:

- *Random-match.* While this is a match type, its intent is to provide an unmatched appearance. This is accomplished through joining veneer leaves out of flitch sequence.

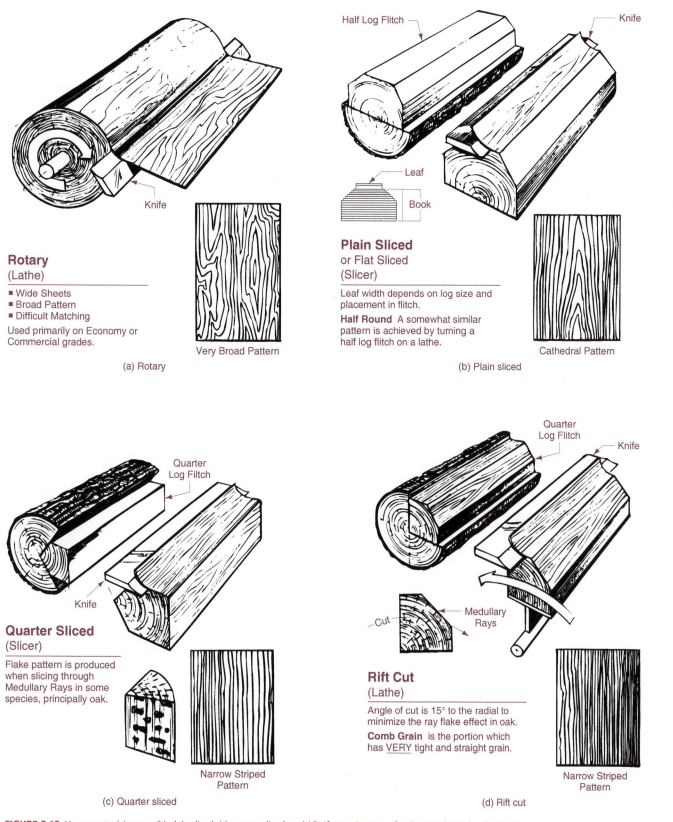

Rotary
(Lathe)

- Wide Sheets
- Broad Pattern
- Difficult Matching

Used primarily on Economy or Commercial grades.

Very Broad Pattern

(a) Rotary

Plain Sliced
or Flat Sliced
(Slicer)

Leaf width depends on log size and placement in flitch.

Half Round A somewhat similar pattern is achieved by turning a half log flitch on a lathe.

Cathedral Pattern

(b) Plain sliced

Quarter Sliced
(Slicer)

Flake pattern is produced when slicing through Medullary Rays in some species, principally oak.

Narrow Striped Pattern

(c) Quarter sliced

Rift Cut
(Lathe)

Angle of cut is 15° to the radial to minimize the ray flake effect in oak.

Comb Grain is the portion which has VERY tight and straight grain.

Narrow Striped Pattern

(d) Rift cut

FIGURE 5.12 Veneer cuts: (a) rotary, (b) plain sliced, (c) quarter sliced, and (d) rift cut. *Courtesy of Architectural Woodwork Institute.*

Veneers from a number of different logs can be utilized to manufacture a single panel set.

- ***Slip-match.*** This match type repeats flitch characteristics among the pieces. It is accomplished through joining veneer leaves in a side-by-side fashion—to match the order in which they have been taken from the flitch. Grain or color match at joints is the focus of this match type, and it should be noted that this match type might not be appropriate for some hardwood species, as the pattern will not be effective. Rift-sliced and quarter-sliced veneers can easily be slip-matched.

- **Book-match.** A **book-match,** which results in color shading and solid match for grain and color at joints, is true to its namesake, as every other veneer leaf is flipped as the leaves are sequentially removed from the flitch—much as a person would turn the pages of a book. To accomplish this match type, one leaf is placed loose-side-up, while the next is placed loose-side-down. This process continues through completion. It should be noted that unwanted color variation can naturally result from this process, but may be reduced through appropriate finishing methods.[12]

MATCHING OF WOOD VENEER LEAVES WITHIN A PANEL FACE

As slicing moves forward, the individual veneer leaves within a sliced flitch will naturally be wider or narrower, resulting in a change in veneer leaves in each panel face as use occurs. The "lay-up" of the leaves in the panel must be addressed through necessary specifications, which are detailed here. (See Figure 5.13.)

- **Balance-match.** The key to balance match is to utilize veneer leaves that have the same width prior to edge trimming. A single panel might be made of an odd or even leaf quantity, and it is not necessary for distribution to remain the same among panels in a sequenced set.

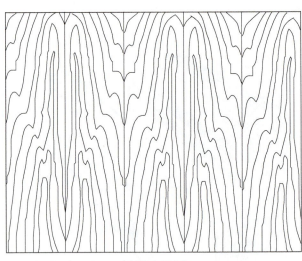

(a) Book-Match

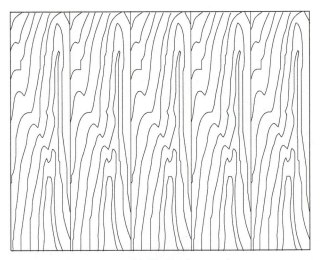

(b) Slip-Match

(c) Random-Match

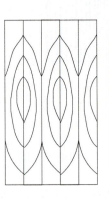 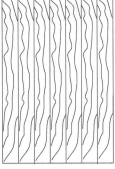 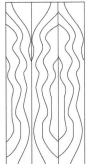

(d) Balance-Match

FIGURE 5.13 Matching of veneers: (a) book-match; (b) slip-match; (c) random-match; (d) balance-match.

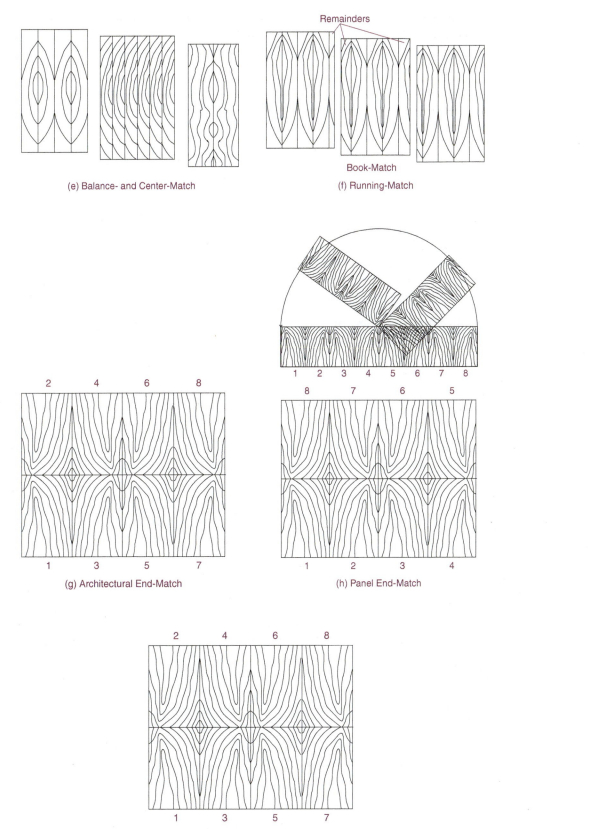

(e) Balance- and Center-Match

Remainders

Book-Match

(f) Running-Match

(g) Architectural End-Match

(h) Panel End-Match

(i) Continuous End-Match

FIGURE 5.13 (continued) (e) balance- and center-match; (f) running-match; (g) architectural end-match; (h) panel end-match; and (i) continuous end-match.

- **Balance- and center-match.** The key to center-balance match is to utilize an even number of veneer leaves that have the same width prior to edge trimming. A veneer joint is placed in the middle of the panel, resulting in horizontal symmetry. It should be noted that some figure loss might occur through this match process.

- **Running-match.** The key to caution with this match type is that it is generally not "sequenced and numbered" to be utilized for adjacent panels, and the user should not anticipate horizontal grain sequence. For this match type, it is not required that all veneer leaves be of equal width. It should be noted that this match type is generally thought of as the most cost effective; of equal importance is the aspect that the match type generally does not provide the most desirable appearance, and while it is considered standard for custom grade, it must be specifically requested for any other grade.[13]

END-MATCHING OF WOOD VENEERS

This match type can be desirable when the user wishes to elongate the length of available wall veneers. Desired extension of long conference tables and high wall panels are often reasons for use of end-matching. As detailed here, there are three types of end-matching:

- **Architectural end-match.** To accomplish this match type, which holds misalignment of grain pattern to a minimum, leaves must be book-matched or slip-matched individually. First, they are matched end-to-end; then they are matched side-to-side. End and side are alternated. This produces highly desirable continuous grain patterns, as are often needed for extensive length and width.

- **Panel end-match.** To accomplish this match type, which results in a generally blended appearance with some misalignment of grain pattern, leaves must be slip-matched—or book-matched—on panel subassemblies. Subassemblies are end-matched. This match type is sometimes sought out to meet the needs of a limited budget.

- **Continuous end-match.** To accomplish this match type, which results in sequenced grain pattern, leaves must be book-matched—or slip-matched—individually, with separate panels stacked vertically or horizontally in sequenced order. It should be noted that each label is representative of a full panel.[14]

SPECIALTY OR SKETCH MATCHES OF WOOD VENEERS

For those going into the retail interior design field, this information has been included to enable the correct identification of various patterns that are used in furniture.

There are regional variations in the "names" of the following veneer leaf-matching techniques, drawn as squares for simplicity. It is strongly recommended that the design professional use both names and drawings to define the desired effect, using a rectangle, polygon, circle, ellipse, or other shape. Rift-sliced, quarter-sliced, and highly figured veneers are generally used for these specialty matches. The different matches of veneer cause the reflection of light to vary from adjoining leaves, bringing "life" to the panel. Due to the inherent nature of the veneering process, alignment at corners might vary. (See Figure 5.14.)

- **8-Piece sunburst.** Made of eight or more veneer leaves cut at the appropriate angle with the grain radiating from the center. These veneer leaves are then book-matched, assembled, and trimmed for final size.

- **Box-match.** Made of four leaves with the grain running parallel to the perimeter of the panel. The leaves are cut at the appropriate angle and end-matched.

- **Reverse or end-grain box.** Made of four leaves with the grain running at right angles to the perimeter of the panel. The leaves are cut at the appropriate angle and book-matched.

- **Diamond-match.** Made of four leaves with the grain running 45° to the perimeter of the panel and surrounding the center. The leaves are cut at the appropriate angle and end-matched.

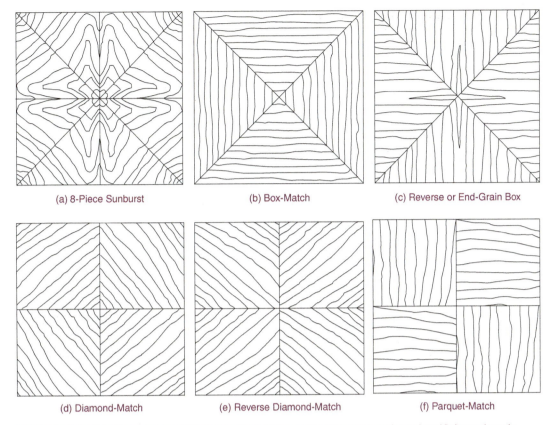

(a) 8-Piece Sunburst   (b) Box-Match   (c) Reverse or End-Grain Box

(d) Diamond-Match   (e) Reverse Diamond-Match   (f) Parquet-Match

FIGURE 5.14 Special table top veneers: (a) 8-piece sunburst; (b) box-match; (c) reverse or end-grain box; (d) diamond-match; (e) reverse diamond-match; (f) parquet-match. *Drawings courtesy of Architectural Woodwork Institute.*

- **Reverse diamond-match.** Made of four leaves with the grain running 45° to the perimeter of the panel and radiating from the center. The leaves are cut at the appropriate angle and book-matched.

- **Parquet-match.** Made by dividing the panel into multiple equal-size pieces and cutting the veneer to the same size. Each veneer leaf is joined at right angles to the adjoining piece of veneer.

Wood-Veneer Wall Surfacing

The design professional must specify the following:

- Species of veneer
- Method of slicing (plain, quarter, rotary, or rift)
- Matching of veneer leaves (book, slip, or random)
- Matching of a veneer face within a panel face (running, balanced, or center-balanced)
- Matching between panels (nonsequenced, sequenced, or blueprint)
- End-matching
- Grain direction, if other than vertical
- Fire-retardant rating, if required.[15]

MATCHING OF PANELS WITHIN A ROOM

Premanufactured panel sets, with full or selectively reduced width utilization, are composed of a specific number of sequence-matched and numbered panels based on a per-room basis for net footage selected from a manufacturer's available inventory. Paneling used from room to room may vary in color and grain characteristics. (See Figure 5.15.)

a - Pre-manufactured Sets - Full Width

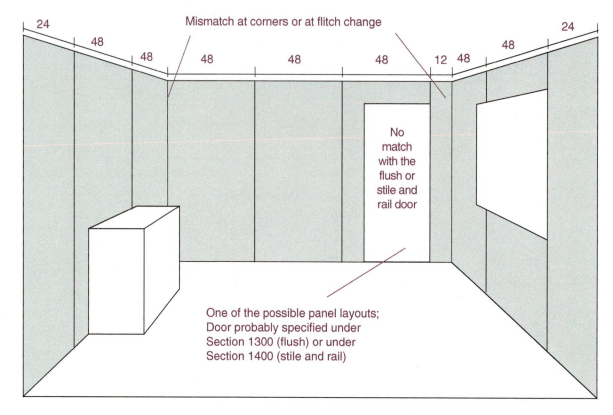

24 48 48 Mismatch at corners or at flitch change 48 48 48 48 12 48 48 24

No match with the flush or stile and rail door

One of the possible panel layouts;
Door probably specified under
Section 1300 (flush) or under
Section 1400 (stile and rail)

b - Pre-manufactured Sets - Selectively Reduced in Width

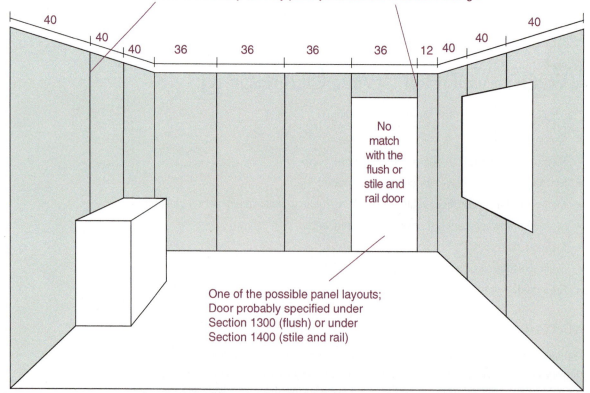

Some loss of continuity at every panel joint, corners or at flitch change

40 40 40 36 36 36 36 12 40 40 40

No match with the flush or stile and rail door

One of the possible panel layouts;
Door probably specified under
Section 1300 (flush) or under
Section 1400 (stile and rail)

FIGURE 5.15 Matching panels within an area. *Drawings courtesy of Architecture Woodwork Institute.*

c - Sequence-Matched Uniform Size Set

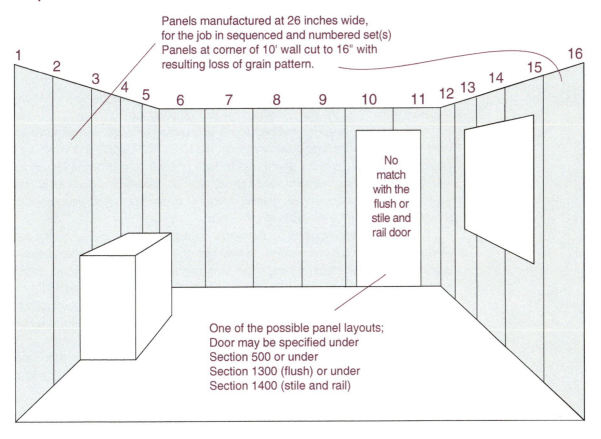

Panels manufactured at 26 inches wide,
for the job in sequenced and numbered set(s)
Panels at corner of 10' wall cut to 16" with
resulting loss of grain pattern.

No match with the flush or stile and rail door

One of the possible panel layouts;
Door may be specified under
Section 500 or under
Section 1300 (flush) or under
Section 1400 (stile and rail)

d - Blueprint-Matched Panels and Components

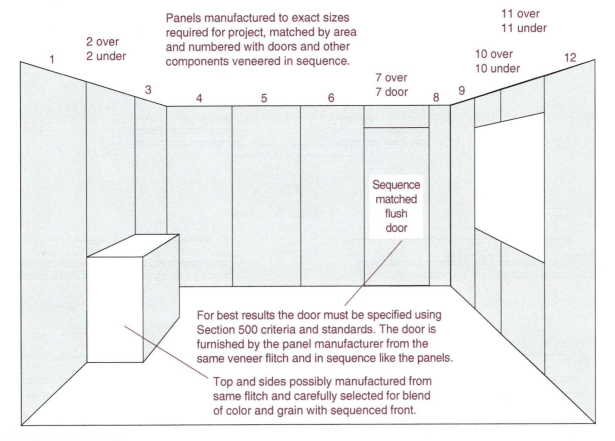

Panels manufactured to exact sizes
required for project, matched by area
and numbered with doors and other
components veneered in sequence.

2 over
2 under

11 over
11 under

10 over
10 under

7 over
7 door

Sequence
matched
flush
door

For best results the door must be specified using
Section 500 criteria and standards. The door is
furnished by the panel manufacturer from the
same veneer flitch and in sequence like the panels.

Top and sides possibly manufactured from
same flitch and carefully selected for blend
of color and grain with sequenced front.

FIGURE 5.15 (Continued)

Premanufactured sequence-matched panels are usually only available in 48" × 96" or 120" (1,219 mm × 2,438 mm or 3,048 mm) sheets in sets varying from 6 to 12 panels. If more than one set is required, matching between sets cannot be expected. Similarly, doors or components often cannot be fabricated from the same set, resulting in possible mismatch.

Made-to-order, sequence-matched panels are manufactured to exact sizes based on the project's net footage and height needs. The customer may request flitch samples from which to select the flitch to be employed, or the supplier may make the flitch selection if so requested; either way, the flitch must be large enough to do the job.

Made-to-order, blueprint-matched panels and components are manufactured to the exact sizes the manufacturer determines from the blueprints, clipping and matching each individual face to the project's specific needs. Each face will be matched in sequence with adjacent panels, doors, transoms, and cabinet faces as needed to provide for continuity. Again, unless specified otherwise, running match will be furnished. A single-source supplier should be specified for these types of components.

Panel width is set out based on the overall room dimension, as well as aspects such as window, door, and cabinet dimension. To maximize grain continuity, as is often desirable for appearance, balanced-match panels, rather than center-balanced-match panels, should be utilized. Center-balanced panels will minimize leaf-width variable from one panel to the next.[16]

Rooms treated with paneling always produce a feeling of permanency. Architectural paneling is as different from ready-made paneling as a custom-made Rolls Royce is from an inexpensive production car. Ready-made paneling is discussed later in this chapter.

There are several methods of installing panels for acoustical control. The panels may be floated or raised, and batten mouldings of wood, metal, or plastic may be used. (See Figure 5.16.)

Finishing

The AWI has specific standards for factory finishing of woodwork; therefore, its publication entitled *Architectural Woodwork Standards* should be consulted.

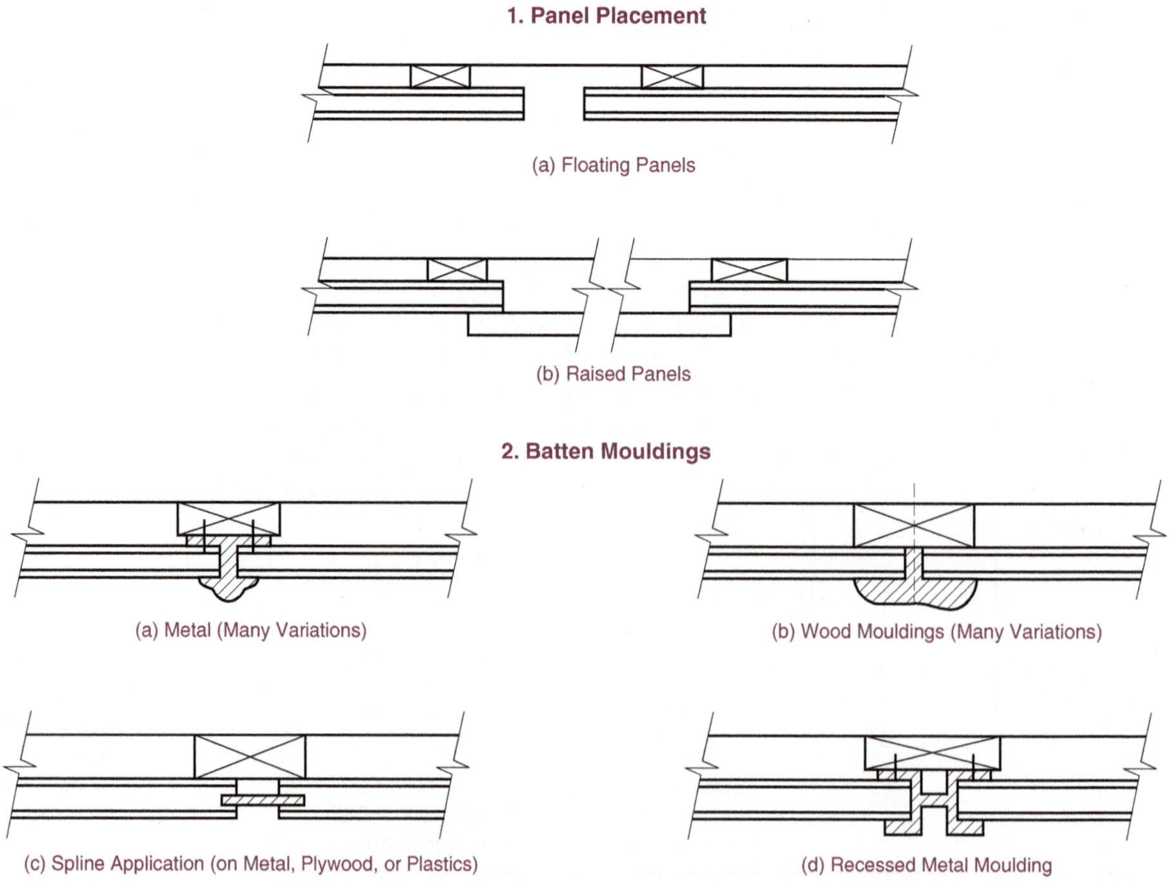

1. Panel Placement

(a) Floating Panels

(b) Raised Panels

2. Batten Mouldings

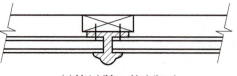

(a) Metal (Many Variations)

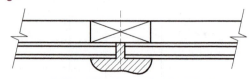

(b) Wood Mouldings (Many Variations)

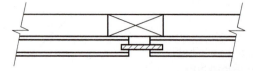

(c) Spline Application (on Metal, Plywood, or Plastics)

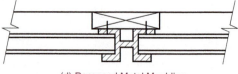

(d) Recessed Metal Moulding

FIGURE 5.16 Panel installation for acoustic control.

Prefinished Plywood

Prefinished plywood paneling varies from 1/4" to 1/2" thick. Standard panel size is 4 × 8 feet, although panels are also available in 7- and 10-foot heights. The face of the plywood is grooved in random widths to simulate wood strips. This feature also hides the joining, where each panel is **butted** up to the next, because outside edges are beveled at the same angle as the grooves. The finish on prefinished plywood paneling is clear acrylic over a stained surface.

Some plywood paneling features a wood grain reproduction on the plywood or a paper overlay applied to **lauan mahogany** plywood and then protected with an oven-baked topcoat.

INSTALLATION

As with all wood products, paneling should be stored in the room it will be installed in for 24 hours to condition for humidity and temperature. Paneling may be applied directly to the stud framing, but it is safer, from a fire hazard point of view, to install it over gypsum board. A 1/4" sound-deadening board used as a backing decreases sound transmission. Nails or adhesive may be used to install the panels. If nails are used, they may be color coated when exposed fasteners are acceptable, or countersunk and filled with colored putty.

MAINTENANCE

Prefinished plywood panels require frequent dusting in order to prevent a build-up of soil, which dulls the finish. Each manufacturer supplies instructions for maintenance of its particular product, which should be followed.

Particleboard

Particleboard (PB) is a composite panel product made of cellulose particles, which vary in size and are bonded through use of binder or synthetic resin. To provide a product that will best meet consumer needs, alterations may be made to manufacturing methods, resin levels, particle geometry, and board density. For desired changes related to performance needs, additives may be utilized during manufacturing. These additives can increase fire retardancy, aid in moisture resistance, and provide improved **dimensional stability.**

Hardboard is a composite panel that offers uniform appearance, density, and thickness without grain. It is resistant to elements such as swings in humidity and temperature and problems such as abrasion, marring, and scuffing. The primary materials used in the manufacturing process are inter-felted lingo-cellulosic fibers, which are consolidated through heat and pressure. During manufacturing, additional materials may be incorporated in order to ameliorate properties such as strength, durability, abrasion, and moisture resistance.

Medium Density Fiberboard (MDF) is a composite panel item that offers many options for designing the final product, as MDF panels of an array of dimensions and physical properties are available. These panels are often used to make mouldings, laminate flooring, kitchen cabinets, furniture, and door parts. MDF is generally made of cellulosic fibers bonded to a synthetic resin through heat and pressure. Additional materials may be added during manufacturing to provide desirable attributes.

Experts note a number of advantages of MDF, as compared to high-density fiberboard, plank wood, and particleboard. For example, MDF works well in bathrooms and other high-humidity locations, as its mild reaction to moisture tends to obviate swelling. Additionally, MDF, which is made of fine uniform wood fibers, is extremely smooth, resulting in a low "tear out." This provides a smooth cut, rather than a jagged edge, upon sawing.

Additionally, it offers the ease and economy of requiring only a coat of primer and two coats of paint.[17]

MARLITE SLATWALL

Typically, Marlite Slatwall is a horizontal support system with grooved slatwall panels, horizontal non-inserted grooves, and 3" vertical groove spacing. Optional groove treatments include vinyl or metal inserts. Groove spacing can be customized to the desired merchandise spacing. Grooves may be painted to match, contrast, or harmonize with panel surfaces. The slatwall panels are used in 3/4" thick wood panels with assorted hooks, brackets, and acrylic accessories that fit into grooves easily and securely.

Volta dimensional panels are sculpture for walls. MDF panels are carved in contiguous flowing patterns to create bold, exciting vertical works of art. (See Figure 5.17.) Volta is ideal for focal areas, special accent walls, and retail fixturing.[18]

INSTALLATION

Displaywall panels may be applied directly to open studs or over drywall. Care must be taken to prevent moisture penetration through the walls. Some hardboard is available in a stamped grille-type pattern or with holes. The grille types are framed with wood and used for dividers. The perforated board is useful for hanging or storing items. Special hooks and supports are available for this purpose and are easily installed and removed for adjustment.

Thicknesses of hardboard vary from 1/8" and 3/16" to 1/4". The 1/8" and 3/16" thicknesses must be installed over a solid backing, such as gypsum board. Panels are glued or nailed to the substrate.

MAINTENANCE

To remove surface accumulation such as dust and grease, a lint-free soft cloth dampened with furniture polish containing no waxes or silicones may be used. More stubborn accumulations may require wiping with a soft cloth dampened in a solution of lukewarm water and a mild detergent. The hardboard must be wiped dry with a clean, dry cloth immediately following this procedure. (An inconspicuous area or scrap paneling should be used for experimental cleaning.)

Decorative Laminate

This product is often mistakenly referred to as Formica, which is the brand name of a manufacturer of decorative laminate.

Laminate for walls may be thinner than the one for floors. The vertical surface of decorative laminate may be 0.050-inch (general purpose) or 0.030-inch (vertical surface). The 0.030-inch vertical surface type is not recommended on surfaces exceeding 24 inches in width. Decorative laminate for walls is often installed on the job site.

Balancing or backing laminates are used to give structural balance and dimensional stability. They are placed on the reverse side of the substrate to inhibit moisture absorption through the back surface. Laminates will not promote the growth of bacteria.

There are other specialty types of decorative laminate. Where antistatic properties are required, a standard-grade laminate is available. Most manufacturers of high-pressure

FIGURE 5.17 Windswept Volta panels shown with painted finish. *Photograph courtesy of Marlite.*

decorative laminate **(HPDL)** produce a fire-resistant type that, when applied with approved adhesives to a fire-resistant core, results in wall paneling with Class 1 or A flamespread rating.

INSTALLATION

When decorative laminates are to be used on a wall, 3/4-inch hardwood-faced plywood or particleboard should be used as a core. The use of an expansion-type joint is suggested. To permit free panel movement and to avoid visible fastenings, AWI recommends that panels be hung on the walls, utilizing metal panel clips or interlocking wood wall cleats.

MAINTENANCE

To clean the surface, use a damp cloth or sponge and a mild soap or detergent. Difficult stains such as coffee or tea can be removed using a mild household cleaner and baking soda, mixed to achieve a paste consistency. Using a stiff nylon bristle brush, scrub the affected area (approximately 15 to 20 strokes). Do not scrub so as to mar, damage, or scratch the surface finish. If spots remain, use an all-purpose cleaner or bathroom cleaner.

For stubborn stains, a paste of baking soda and water should be applied to the stain with a soft bristle brush. The last resort is undiluted household bleach such as Clorox, followed by a clean-water rinse. Use of abrasive cleansers or special cleansers should be avoided because they may contain abrasives, acids, or alkalines.

Metallic laminates other than solid polished brass may be cleaned as described previously. The surface of metallic laminates, however, should always be wiped completely dry with a clean soft cloth after washing. Stubborn smudges may be removed with a dry cloth and thin, clean oil. For solid polished brass surfaces, only glass cleaners free of petroleum products should be used. The surface may be touched up with Fill 'n Glaze and a good grade of automobile wax. The manufacturer's instructions must be followed carefully during application.

Porcelain Enamel

Porcelain enamel is baked on 28-gauge steel, then laminated to 3/16″ to 21/32″ gypsum board or hardboard. It comes in many colors and finishes for use in high-abuse public areas such as hospitals and food processing and preparation areas. It is also available with writing board surfaces that double as projection screens. Widths are from 2 to 4 feet, and lengths are from 6 to 12 feet. Weight varies from 1.60 to 2.7 pounds per square foot. Porcelain enamel is also used for toilet partitions in public rest rooms.

Glass

Glass is one of the oldest—and once most valuable—known materials used in construction. While formed pieces of colored glass were once graced with the value of precious stones, glass is, of course, much more common today.

Manufacturing results in three primary glass types:

1. Sheet glass, also known as window glass, is manufactured by drawing out molten glass and then exposing both sides to open flame. Because it is not treated subsequent to being manufactured, it often exhibits waviness and distortion.

2. Plate glass is cast in a solid plate, typically through a roller process, and offers polished and ground surfaces. This provides surfaces that are essentially parallel and plane.

3. Float glass, a less costly and more recent player on the glass scene, is manufactured through molten glass being floated over molten metal. Float glass and plate glass can easily and effectively be substituted for one another. *Textured glass, slumped glass,* and *formed glass* are terms commonly used to describe float glass. To add dimensional texture and/or designs to the glass, float glass is placed atop specially sculpted molds and then kiln-fired in accordance with individually determined firing schedules.[19] Of course, one disadvantage of glass is that it is breakable, but there are products specially made to reduce this problem.

Insulating glass consists of two or three sheets of glass separated by either a dehydrated air space or an inert gas-filled space, together with a **desiccant.** Insulating glass limits heat transference and, in some areas of the country, may be required by the building codes in all new construction for energy conservation purposes. It also helps eliminate the problem of condensation caused by a wide difference in outside and inside temperatures.

There are various types of safety glass. The one with which we are most familiar is **tempered glass,** which is used for windshields and in entry doors and shower doors. In tempered glass, a heavy blow breaks the glass into small grains rather than sharp, jagged slivers. Another type of tempered glass, which has a wire mesh incorporated into its construction, can break under a blow but does not shatter.

Laminated glass can control sound, glare, heat, and light transmission. It offers security and safety through high resistance to breakage and penetration. In interior areas where transparency is desired, laminated acoustical glass is effective in reducing sound transmission. When exterior sounds (traffic, airplanes, etc.) are present and distracting, laminated acoustical glass may be used. Acoustical glass may be clear or colored.

Another form of glass used for energy conservation is a laminated glass with a vinyl interlayer that, depending on the color of the interlayer, may absorb or transmit light in varying degrees. The tinted glass may have a bronze, grey, green, blue, silver, or gold appearance; these tints cut down on glare in a manner similar to sunglasses or the tinted glass in an automobile. Where 24-hour protection is required, such as in jewelry stores, banks, and detention areas, a security glass with a high-tensile polyvinyl butyl inner layer is effective. There are even bullet-resistant glasses on the market.

FIGURE 5.18 This installation of "Curves" by Livinglass was Interiors & Sources's 2009 Readers' Choice Awards Winner: Glass Products. *Photograph courtesy of Livinglass Inc.*

Livinglass produces "Curves," a decorative laminated glass whose name is based on its options of curved profiles. (See Figure 5.18.) The company states that this product is made of completely recycled resin and real glass. It further advises that the use of real glass in lieu of plastic provides for simple cleaning that does not result in discoloration or scratching. Other features of Livinglass Light glass include:

- LEED credits
- Available in thickness starting at 1/2"
- Impact-resistant safety glass
- Class A Class I fire rated
- UV, water, and chemical resistant
- Antimicrobial and sanitary
- Resists scratching, fading, and discoloration[20]

For those involved in historical restorations, Bendheim Corporation offers Restoration Glass. This glass is handmade using the original cylinder method, yet the glass easily meets today's tougher building codes. It is available in two levels of distortion: full, for thicker and more distorting effects, and light, for thinner and less distorting effects. Restoration Glass is available in laminated form if safety glass is required.

Office configurations are always changing. ZWall incorporates the intelligent use of steel, glass, and aluminum; substantial gauge of materials; and the built-in ability to easily transform existing products into something altogether different. ZWall offers a broad range of standard finish materials plus the flexibility to incorporate custom specifications. ZWall's unique integrated horizontal support rails allow off-module attachment and support of virtually any office system furniture.

Glass Tile

Oceanside Glass offers a matte finish option for its handcrafted glass tile in addition to its popular light-capturing iridescent and richly translucent non-iridescent finishes. The matte finish is available in all colors across all seven of the company's versatile lines of mosaics, field, decorative accent pieces, and trim. According to product designer Feras Irikat, "Handcrafted glass tile looks dramatically different in a matte finish, offering designers even more options than before. Dimensional relief pieces in particular take on an entirely different character." (See Figure 5.19.)

INSTALLATION

The makers of Oceanside Glass tile provide detailed instruction regarding appropriate grout and setting material. The company advises that its tile is paper-face mounted primarily because a great quantity of its colors are transparent; thus, this mounting provides a cover for the mesh. The company further advises that the paper-facing allows for alignment of small mosaic pieces, though some manual tile straightening might be required after removal of the paper.[21]

FIGURE 5.19 Elevations Extrados in Incense, an unusual shape for glass tile, was used as an interesting backsplash in this kitchen. The tiles are made from recycled glass. *Photograph courtesy of Oceanside Glass.*

Mirror

The mirrors used two thousand years ago by the Egyptians, Romans, and Greeks were highly polished thin sheets of bronze. Today, many of these metal mirrors may be seen in museums. The method of backing glass with a metallic film was known to the Romans, but it was not until 1507 that the first glass mirrors were made in Venice. Plate glass was invented in France in 1691, enabling larger pieces of glass to be manufactured. The shapes of mirrors used in various periods of design should be studied by interior designers, such as those of Robert and James Adam. Mirrors are no longer just accessories hung on the wall for utilitarian or decorative purposes. Walls are often completely covered with these highly reflective surfaces.

Quality mirrors are made of float glass and are silvered on the back to obtain a highly reflective quality. Also used in certain circumstances are two-way mirrors, which permit viewing from one side but not from the other (which appears to be an ordinary mirror). These two-way mirrors have many uses, such as in apartment doors, child observation areas, department stores, banks, and prison security areas.

Mirrors used on wall installations may be clear and brightly reflective or greyed or bronze hued. The latter are not as bright, but do not noticeably distort color values. The surface may also be antiqued, which produces a smoky, shadowy effect. Mirrored walls always enlarge a room and may be used to correct a size deficiency or to duplicate a prized possession, such as a candelabra or chandelier. Mirrored walls may also display all sides of a piece of sculpture or double the light available in a room.

Mirrors are available for wall installations in many sizes, ranging from large sheets to small mosaic mirrors on sheets similar to mosaic tile. Sometimes a perfect reflection is not necessary and the mirrors may be in squares, **convex** or **concave,** acid etched, engraved, or beveled.

MIRROR TERMINOLOGY

The following terminology was provided by the North American Association of Mirror Manufacturers.

- *Acid etch.* A process of producing a specific design or lettering on glass, prior to silvering by cutting into the glass with a combination of acids. This process may involve either a frosted surface treatment or a deep etch. This process can also be done on regular glass.

- *Antique mirror.* A decorative mirror in which the silver has been treated to create a smoky or shadowy effect. The antique look is often heightened by applying veining on the silvered side in any one or more of a variety of colors and designs.

- *Backing paint.* The final protective coating applied on the back of the mirror, over copper, to protect the silver from deterioration.

- *Concave mirror.* Surface is slightly curved inward and tends to magnify reflected items or images.

- *Convex mirror.* Surface is slightly curved outward to increase the area that is reflected. Generally used for safety or security surveillance purposes.

- *Edge work.* Among numerous terms and expressions defining types of edge finishing, the five in most common usage are listed here.

  - *Clean-cut edge.* Natural edge produced when glass is cut. It should not be left exposed in installation.

  - *Ground edge.* Grinding removes the raw cut of glass, leaving a smooth satin finish.

  - *Seamed edge.* Sharp edges are removed by an abrasive belt.

  - *Polished edge.* Polishing removes the raw cut of glass to give a smooth-surfaced edge. A polished edge is available in two basic contours.

  - *Beveled edge.* A tapered polished edge, varying from 1/4" to a maximum of 1 1/4" thick, produced by machine in a rectangular or circular shape. Other shapes or ovals may be beveled by hand, but the result is inferior to machine bevel. Standard width of bevel is generally half an inch. (See Figure 5.20.)

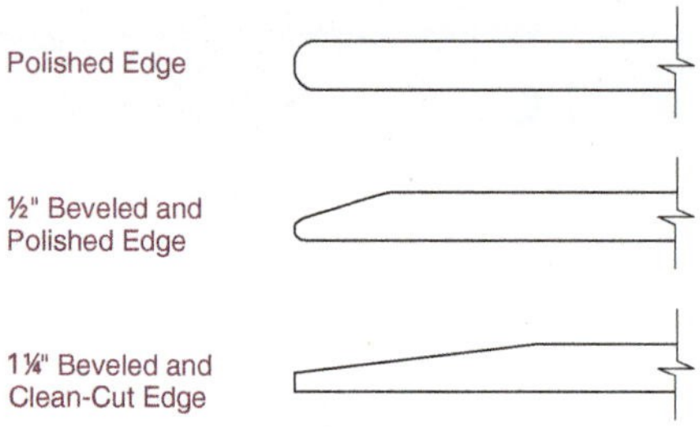

- *Electro-copper-plating.* Process of copper-plating by electrolytic deposition of copper on the back of the silver film. This protects the silver and assures good adherence of the backing paint.

- *Engraving.* The cutting of a design on the back or face of a mirror, usually accomplished by hand on an engraving lathe.

- *Finger pull.* An elongated slot cut into the glass by a wheel, so that a mirrored door or panel, for instance, may be moved to one side.

- *First-surface mirror.* A mirror produced by deposition of reflective metal on the front surface of glass, usually under vacuum. Its principal use is as an automobile rear-view mirror or transparent mirror.

- *Framed mirror.* Mirror placed in a frame that is generally made of wood, metal, or composition material and equipped for hanging.

- *Hole.* Piercing of a mirror, usually 1/2 inch in diameter and generally accomplished by a drill. Often employed in connection with installations involving rosettes.

- *Mitre cutting.* The cutting of straight lines by use of a wheel on the back or face of a mirror for design purposes. Available in both satin and polished finishes.

- *Rosette.* Hardware used for affixing a mirror to a wall. A decorative rose-shaped button used in several places on the face of a mirror.

Polished Edge

½" Beveled and
Polished Edge

1¼" Beveled and
Clean-Cut Edge

FIGURE 5.20 Mirror bevels.

- **Sand blasting.** Engraving or cutting designs on glass by a stream of sand, usually projected by air.

- **Shadowbox mirror.** Mirror bordered or framed at an angle on some or all sides by other mirrors, creating multiple reflections of an image.

- **Stock-sheet mirrors.** Mirrors of varying sizes over 10 square feet, and up to 12 square feet, from which all types of custom mirrors are cut. Normally packed 800 to 1,000 square feet to a case.

- **Transparent mirror.** A first surface mirror with a thin film of reflective coating. To ensure most efficient use, the light intensity on the viewer's side of the mirror must be significantly less than on the subject's side. Under such a condition, the viewer can see through the mirror as through a transparent glass, while the subject looks into a mirror.

INSTALLATION

Both mastic and mechanical devices, such as clips or rosettes, should be used to install a mirror properly. Clips are usually of polished chrome and are placed around the outside edges. Rosettes are clear plastic fasteners and require a hole to be drilled several inches in from the edge so the mirror will accept the fastening screws and rosettes. Because of the fragile quality of the mirror, their use should be limited to areas where the likelihood of breakage is minimal.

Ceramic Tile

Ceramic tile is frequently used on walls when an easily cleaned, waterproof, and durable surface is desired. One use of ceramic tile is as a **backsplash** in the kitchen or as a counter top. When ceramic tile is used for these purposes, the grout may be sealed by use of a commercial sealer or by using a lemon oil furniture polish. Ceramic tile is also used for the surrounds of showers and bathtubs and for bathroom walls in general. (See Figure 5.21.) These three uses are probably the most common ones, but ceramic tile may also be used on the walls in foyers and hallways, in various styles (plain, patterned, or displaying a logo), and as a heat-resistant material around fireplaces and stoves. If walls are completely covered with ceramic tile, there will be no need for trim pieces. In bathrooms or kitchens, however, or any area where tiling will not be continued from wall to wall or from ceiling to floor, trim pieces must be added. The type of tile trim used will vary with the method of installation. A thin-set installation will require a surface bullnose. With the thick-set method, a separate piece of trim is used to finish off the edge and corners.

A bullnose for thick-set installations has an overhanging curved piece, whereas a bullnose for thin-set installations is the same thickness as the surrounding tiles but has a curved finished edge. For bath and shower installations, angle trims for the top and inside edges are used, and for walls meeting the floor, a cove is used.

Crossville states that it offers the appearance and texture of marble in its Empire Porcelain Stone line. The company further states that Empire offers a broad color palette, a variety of shapes and sizes, a choice between polished and unpolished finishes, and 20 percent SCS-certified recycled content.[22]

INSTALLATION OF CERAMIC, METAL, AND MIRROR TILE

Because of the force of gravity, mortar cement cannot be troweled directly onto the wall without sagging. To prevent this sagging, a metal lath, similar to the one used for a plaster wall, is attached to the solid backing and then troweled with mortar. The metal lath acts as a stabilizing force. The backing may be wood, plaster, masonry, or gypsum board. This procedure is equivalent to the thick-set method of floor installation. For wall use over gypsum

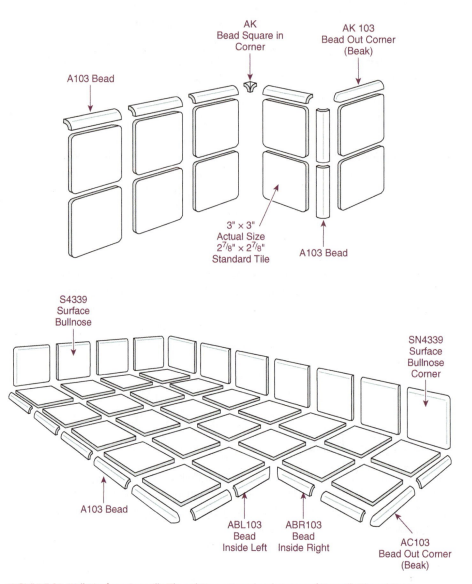

FIGURE 5.21 Wall trim from Crossville Tile and Stone. *Reproduced courtesy of Crossville Tile and Stone.*

board, plaster, or other smooth surfaces, an organic adhesive may be used. This adhesive should be water-resistant for bath and shower areas. (See Table 5.2.)

The Handbook of Ceramic Tile Installation, available from the Tile Council of America, is the nationally accepted guideline for tile installation, even for materials other than ceramic tile. The Council offers the following installation advice:

- When the lights are located at the wall/ceiling interface or mounted directly on the wall, use wall-washer and cove type light to produce dramatic room lighting effects.

- The coordination of proper backing surfaces, proper use of installation materials and methods, and location of light fixtures can help avoid shadows and other undesirable effects that occur with ceramic tiles. Shadows can also occur when light shines at an angle through windows and doors from side lighting interior walls and floors.[23]

Metal

Stamped metal is generally used for ceilings; however, it can also be used on walls. A product that can be used for this purpose is MetalCast. This premium product can be less costly than conventional metal castings. It provides a metal finish cast face and includes a gypsum composite

Table 5.2 | Wall Tiling Installation Guide

Simplest methods are indicated; those for heavier services are acceptable. Very large or heavy tiles may require special setting methods. Consult ceramic tile manufacturer.

Service Requirements	Wall Type (numbers refer to *Handbook* method numbers)					
	Masonry or Concrete	Page	Wood Studs	Page	Metal Studs	Page
Commercial Construction—Dry or limited water exposure: dairies, breweries, kitchens	W202 W221*, W223	46 49	W223 W231 W243 W244C, W244F W245, W246	49 50 51 52 53	W223 W241 W242, W243 W244C, W244F W245, W246	49 50 51 52 53
Commercial Construction—Wet: gang showers, tubs, showers, laundries	W202 W211, W215 W221* W246	46 48 49 53	W231 W244C, W244F W245, W246 B411 B414	50 52 53 58 61	W241 W244C, W244F W245, W246 B411 B419, B425 B414, B415 B420	50 52 53 58 59 61 62
Residential & Light Construction—Dry or limited water exposure: kitchens and toilet rooms, commercial dry area interiors and decoration	W215 W221*, W223	48 49	W222*, W223 W243 W244C, W244F W245, W246 W247, W260	49 51 52 53 54	W222* W242, W243 W244C, W244F W245, W246 W247, W260	49 51 52 53 54
Residential & Light Construction—Wet: tub enclosures and showers	W202 W211 W223	46 48 49	W222*, W223 W244C, W244F W245, W246 W247 B413 B412 B419, B425 B430 B415 B420, B426 B431 B421, B422	49 52 53 54 57 58 59 60 61 62 63 64	W222* W241 W244C, W244F W245, W246 W247 B413 B412 B419, B425 B430 B415 B420, B426 B431 B421, B422	49 50 52 53 54 57 58 59 60 61 62 63 64
Exterior (See notes on page 46.)	W201, W202	46	W244E W231	47 50	W244E W241	47 50

*Use these details where there may be dimensional instability and possible cracks developing in, or foreign coating (paint, etc.) on, the structural wall since these details include a cleavage membrane (15 lb. felt or polyethylene) between the wall surface and tile installation.

Source: Reproduced with permission of the Tile Council of North America.

backup. The finish has an appearance similar to that of buffed or antique burnished cast metal. (See Chapter 6 for more details on stamped metal.) The elements are 1/4" (6 mm) thick copper, brass, bronze, and nickel silver, and can be precisely manufactured into a variety of shapes.[24]

Perforated metal was developed for use in ventilation grilles, drainage grates, and similar applications. Today it has many interior uses; for example, it can be used instead of a solid wall, providing a feeling of privacy yet with a slight see-through quality. A partition made from perforated metal gives a sense of separation without the thickness of a solid wall. Another use of metal is for the doors of wood-framed kitchen cabinets. Perforated metal is made by stamping out holes of various sizes and shapes. The perforations can form almost any small geometrical pattern. A similar material is expanded metal, which, because of the manufacturing process, is always diamond shaped.

Acoustical Panels

Several manufacturers produce a mineral fiberboard or fiberglass panel that, when covered with fabric, absorbs sound and provides an attractive and individually designed environment. Because of the textured, porous surface of acoustical panels and the absorbent substrate, sound is absorbed rather than bounced back into the room. These panels may also be used as tack boards for lightweight pictures and graphics. In open-plan office areas, different colors of acoustical panels can be used to direct the flow of traffic through an open office and to differentiate between work areas. In addition to the acoustical qualities of these panels, there are two other beneficial features: (1) The panels are fire retardant, and (2), when installed on perimeter walls, there is a sound-insulating factor that varies with the thickness of board used. These panels are used where good speech privacy or speech intelligibility is important.

The acoustical panels may take the form of appliques in sizes of 2 × 4 feet or 2 × 6 feet, or they may cover the wall completely, in panel sizes of 24 or 30 inches × 9 feet.

FIGURE 5.22 For the walls of a lobby, FabriTRAK was used for soundproofing and sound control. *Photograph courtesy of FabriTRAK Inc.*

Vinyl- or fabric-faced acoustical panels may be designed for various types of installation; therefore, for use on an existing wall, only one side needs to be covered. For open-plan landscapes, both surfaces are covered to absorb sound from both sides. Some panels are covered on the two side edges for butted installation, whereas another portable type is wrapped on all surfaces and edges.

The FabriTRAK Wall System is a compilation of acoustic panel products that provide a sound control method while using fabric as an architectural finish. See Figure 5.22. It is a cost-effective system for creating and enhancing interior environments with form, function, color, and texture. The FabriTRAK system is designed to complement the architectural and design professional's creativity. The sound reduction profiles are recyclable, and the sustainable aspects of the system can be further enhanced with infills and fabrics that meet the LEED requirements of the U.S. Green Building Council.[25]

INSTALLATION

Installation is done by factory-trained installers; therefore, any needed adjustments can be made at the site. Because there are numerous types of acoustical panels, no single installation method covers all panels. Depending on the type of panel, panels may be attached to the wall by means of an adhesive and/or may have moulding concealing the seams. Manufacturers' recommended installation methods should be followed.

MAINTENANCE

Surface dirt is removed by vacuuming or light brushing. Spots can be treated with dry-cleaning fluid or with carpet shampoo. Damaged fabric panels can easily be replaced by recovering just the damaged panel. Be sure to order extra fabric so that repairs can be easily made.

Cork

Cork tiles or panels are available in a 12" × 36" size and in thicknesses of 1/2", 3/4", 1", and 1 1/2". They may be used in residential, commercial, educational, and institutional buildings. Because of its porous nature, cork can breathe and, therefore, can be used on basement walls or on the inside surface of exterior support walls without the risk of moisture accumulation. Because of the millions of dead-air spaces in the cork particles, cork also has good insulating properties.

INSTALLATION

Cork panels are applied by using a 1/8" × 1/8" notched trowel and the manufacturer-recommended adhesive.

MAINTENANCE

Vacuuming periodically with the brush attachment is recommended. A light, dust-free sealing coat of silicone aerosol spray will give dust protection; a heavier spray protects against dust and gives the surface a glossier finish, providing more light reflection. A heavy spray tends to close the pores of the cork, however, thus decreasing its sound deadening and insulating qualities. An alternative to the silicone spray is a 50–50 blend of clear shellac and alcohol.

Other Materials

Fixed Shoji panels can be used for walls or office partitions, as seen in Figure 5.23. Shoji panels have bamboo dividers framing Japanese rice paper.

QuarryCast is a molded "faux stone" with a sandstone look, available in a range of standard earthtone colors. It may be customized to meet a designer's criteria for color or texture; however, this option may be expensive for small quantities.

INSTALLATION

QuarryCast should be installed by a finish carpenter.

FIGURE 5.23 Office dividers are made with Shoji screens. Design © Cherry Tree Design. *Photograph courtesy of Cherry Tree Design.*

bibliography

Ackerman, P. *Wallpaper, Its History, Design and Use*. New York: Frederick A. Stokes Company, 1923.

Architectural Woodwork Institute. *Architectural Woodwork Quality Standards Illustrated*. 7th ed., Version 1.0. Reston, VA: Architectural Woodwork Institute, 2009.

Byrne, M. *Setting Tile*. Newton, CT: Taunton Press, 1996.

Pittsburgh Corning Corporation. *PC Glass Block Products Specification Guidelines*. Pittsburgh, PA: Pittsburgh Corning, 2005.

Plumridge, A., and W. Meulenkamp. *Brickwork, Architecture and Design*, New York: Harry N. Abrams, 1993.

glossary

Ashlar. Rectangular cut stone.

Backsplash. The vertical wall area between the kitchen counter and the upper cabinets.

Bond. Patterns formed by exposed surface of the brick.

Book-match. Process in which every other leaf is turned over, so the right side of a leaf abuts a right side and a left side abuts a left side.

Butt. Two pieces of material placed side by side so there is no space between the pieces.

Casing bead. A carved protective reinforcement strip to protect the edge from damage.

Cobble. Similar in appearance to fieldstone.

Compressive strength. Amount of stress and pressure a material can withstand.

Concave. Hollow or inward curving shape.

Convex. Arched or outward curving shape.

Course. One of the continuous horizontal layers of bricks, bonded with mortar.

Cramps. U-shaped metal fastenings.

Desiccant. Substance capable of removing moisture from the air.

Dimensional stability. Ability to retain shape regardless of temperature and humidity.

Drywall. Any interior covering that does not require the use of plaster or mortar.

Efflorescence. A powder or stain sometimes found on the surface of masonry, resulting from deposition of water-soluble salts.

Evacuated. Air is removed.

Feathering. Tapering off to almost nothing.

Fieldstone. Rounded stone.

Flitch Portion of a log from which veneer is cut.

Head. Horizontal cross-member supported by the jambs.

Header. End of an exposed brick.

Header course. Headers used every sixth course.

HPDL. High-pressure decorative laminate.

Jambs. Vertical member at the side of a door.

Laminated glass. Substance that breaks without shattering; glass remains in place.

Lauan mahogany. A wood from the Philippines that, although not a true mahogany, does resemble mahogany in grain.

Leaves. Individual pieces of veneer.

Load-bearing. A wall which supports any vertical load in addition to its own weight.

Medium Density Fiberboard (MDF). A composite panel item.

Mortar. A plastic mixture of cementitious materials, fine aggregate, and water.

Mortar stain. Stain caused by excess mortar on the face of brick or stone.

Nonferrous. Does not contain iron.

Particleboard. A composite panel made of various size cellulose particles

Raking light. Light shining obliquely down the length of a wall.

Reveal. A recessed space left between two adjoining panels for design purposes.

Rowlocks. Bricks laid vertically.

Rubble. Uncut stone.

Scratch coat. In three-coat plastering, the first coat.

Shiplap. An overlapping wood joint.

Soldier. A brick with the small end is vertical.

Stretcher. Brick with the largest dimension horizontal and parallel to the wall face.

Struck. Mortar joint where excess mortar is removed by a trowel.

Suction. Absorption of water by the gypsum board from the wet plaster.

Tambours. Thin strips of wood or other materials attached to a flexible backing for use on curved surfaces. Similar in appearance to a roll-top desk.

Tempered glass. Glass having two to four times the strength of ordinary glass as the result of being heated and then suddenly cooled.

Wythe. A continuous vertical section of masonry that is one unit in thickness.

endnotes

1. Stone Panels, www.stone-panels.com
2. Portland Cement Association, www.cement.org
3. Pittsburgh Corning, www.pittsburghcorning.com
4. Ibid.
5. National Gypsum, www.nationalgypsum.com
6. Ibid.
7. Ibid.
8. USG Corp., www.usg.com
9. Ibid.
10. *Architectural Woodwork Standards*, Edition 1, p. 172.
11. Ibid., p. 72.
12. Ibid., p. 73.
13. Ibid., p. 74.
14. Ibid., pp. 75–76.
15. Ibid., p. 174.
16. Ibid., pp. 176–178.
17. Composite Panel Association, www.pbmdf.com
18. Marlite, www.marlite.com
19. Moondaniglas, www.moondaniglass.com.au/technical.html
20. Livinglass www.livinglass.com
21. Oceanside Glass Tile, www.glasstile.com
22. Crossville Tile, www.crossvilleinc.com
23. Tile Council of North America Inc., www.tileusa.com
24. FormGlas, www.formglas.com
25. FabriTRAK, www.fabritrak.com

Ceilings

In this chapter, you will:

- Analyze the social and physical influences affecting historical changes in ceilings
- Recognize appropriate selection, composition, and maintenance of a variety of types of ceiling materials
- Illustrate knowledge of principles of acoustical design related to ceilings
- Identify specific products that work optimally for specific uses
- Explain the history of beams and the relevance of this history to modern use

Early Greeks and Romans used lime stucco for ceilings, on which low, medium, and high **reliefs** were carried out. Italians in the fifteenth century worked with plaster, and in England, Henry VIII's Hampton Court featured highly decorative plaster work ceilings. In the Tudor and Jacobean periods, the plaster work for ceilings had a geometric basis in medium and high relief. This style was followed by the classicism of Christopher Wren and Inigo Jones

FIGURE 6.1 A change from the patterned ceilings of the past, this contemporary ceiling in the Houston Toyota Center has a shiny finish. *Photo courtesy of Chelsea Decorative Products.*

(an admirer of Palladio). In the late eighteenth century, the Adam brothers designed and used cast plaster ornaments for medallions with **arabesques, patera,** and urns.

Stamped tin ceilings used in the nineteenth and early twentieth centuries disappeared from use in the 1930s but are now staging a comeback. (See Figure 6.1.) In private residences, tin ceilings were occasionally used in halls and bathrooms. These stamped metal ceilings are very suitable for Victorian restoration work; in addition, cornice mouldings are available. In commercial buildings, metal ceilings were used to comply with the early fire codes.

Today, the ceiling is not merely a flat surface over our heads that is painted white. Instead, the ceiling is an integral part of a room that affects space, light, heat, and sound. In addition, the ceiling's design should reflect the room's overall ambience. There are many ways to achieve this integration, such as beams for a country or Old World appearance, a stamped ceiling for a Victorian ambience, or an acoustical ceiling for today's noisier environments. A wood ceiling for contemporary warmth can be achieved by using WoodScenes painted finishes from Chicago Metallic. Ceiling treatments are limited only by the designer's imagination.

Plaster

There are times when the ceiling should be an unobtrusive surface in a room. If this is the case, plastering is the answer. The plaster surface may be smooth, highly textured, or somewhere in between. A smooth surface will reflect more light than a heavily textured one of the same color.

The plaster for a ceiling is applied in the same manner as for walls, although scaffolding must be used in the application process so the surface will be within working reach. It will take longer to plaster a ceiling than it will to plaster a wall area of similar size because of the overhead reach.

The ornately carved ceilings of the past are obtained today using one of three means:

1. Precast plaster, either in pieces or tiles

2. Molded polyurethane foam

3. Wood mouldings, mainly used as **crown mouldings**

Urethane foam mouldings are discussed in detail in Chapter 7. The Monarch ceiling panels from Chicago Metallic are glass-reinforced gypsum panels with ornately intricate patterns, detailed after turn-of-the-century styling, to provide today's modern interior with a distinguishing sense of elegance and refinement.

Gypsum Board

The main difficulty with installing gypsum board for ceilings is the board's weight. Ceiling panels are 1/2" thick and are specially designed to resist sagging; they are equal to a 5/8" wallboard, installed perpendicular to framing. Gypsum board requires more labor and scaffolding, however, and may be applied to a flat or curved surface. Spacing is 6 to 8 inches apart, whether using nails or screws. The seams and screw holes are filled in the same manner as for gypsum board walls. The surface may be perfectly smooth, lightly textured, or heavily textured. A smooth surface not only reflects the most light but also shows any unevenness of ceiling joists. Wallpaper may also be used on the ceiling.

Beams

While technically not a ceiling treatment, beams are probably the oldest form of ceiling construction. In this method, the ceiling beams of the lower floor become the floor joists of the room above. Colonial New England houses had hand-hewn timbers that ran the length of the room; a larger **summer beam** ran across the width. The area between the beams was covered by the floor boards of the room above or, in the case of a sloping ceiling, the wood covering the outside of the roof timbers. Later, these floorboards were covered with plaster and the timbers were left to darken naturally. The plaster in between the timbers had a rough or troweled surface. Today, instead of plaster, a plank ceiling is sometimes used in combination with beams.

The beams in early American homes were made of one piece of wood 12" or more square; today, beams of this size are difficult to obtain. However, iLevel from Weyhauser produces Parallam PSL, which is available in dimensions up to 11" × 19" and lengths up to 60 feet. These beams are made from 3-foot-long to 8-foot-long veneer strands that are dried and then bonded using adhesives via a patented microwave pressing process. Today, beamed ceilings are often used for a country setting with an Old World or contemporary feeling. (See Figure 6.2.) In southwestern style homes, rounded wood is used to imitate the **vigas** of the original adobe homes. These beams are sometimes filled in with smaller round pieces of wood called latillas.

There are several methods of imitating the solid, heavy look of hand-hewn beams. For example, box beams may be built as part of the floor joists or as a surface addition. To make a box beam appear similar to a hand-hewn beam, the surface must be treated to avoid the perfectly smooth surface of modern lumber.

In contemporary homes, **laminated beams** are used. These consist of several pieces of lumber (depending on the width required) glued together (on the wider surfaces). Because of this type of construction, laminated beams, which are commonly referred to as "lam" beams, are very strong.

FIGURE 6.2 Aged Wood is used on the ceiling of this entry way of the Blue Sky Grille at the Pepsi Center in Denver, Colorado. *Photograph courtesy of Aged Woods.*

Wood

A natural outgrowth of a beamed ceiling is to use wood planks or strips to cover ceiling joists. With the many types of wood available on the market today, wood ceilings are used in many homes, particularly contemporary ones.

Almost all types of strip flooring or solid wood for walls may be used on a ceiling. Because of the darkness of wood, which gives the appearance of a lower ceiling, this is more suitable for a cathedral or shed ceiling.

Acoustical Ceilings

RESIDENTIAL

Because the ceiling is the largest unobstructed area in a room, sound is bounced off its surface without much absorption. Just as light is reflected from a smooth, high-gloss surface, so sound is reflected or bounced off the ceiling. Uncontrolled reverberations

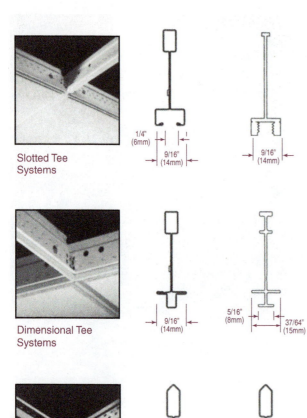

Slotted Tee Systems

1/4" (6mm) 9/16" (14mm) 9/16" (14mm)

Dimensional Tee Systems

9/16" (14mm) 5/16" (8mm) 37/64" (15mm)

Exposed Tee Systems

15/16" (24mm) 9/16" (14mm)

Concealed Grid System

3/4" (19mm) 15/16" (24mm)

Clean Room Grid System

1-1/2" (38mm)

FIGURE 6.3 Suspension systems. Each type gives a different look to the ceiling. *Photographs courtesy of Armstrong Ceilings.*

transform sound into noise, muffling music and disrupting effective communication. Textured ceiling tiles help reduce this reverberation and are often used in both residential and commercial interiors.

Acoustical ceilings, however, do not prevent the transmission of sound from one floor to another. The only answer to sound transmission is mass—the actual resistance of the material to vibrations caused by sound waves.

Sound absorption qualities may be obtained by using different materials and different methods. The most well-known is the acoustical **tile** (12-inch square) or **panel** (larger than 1 square foot) composed of mineral fiberboard. Other materials, such as fiberglass, metal, plastic-clad fiber, and fabric, may also be used. Sound absorption properties are produced by mechanical dies that perforate the mineral fiberboard after curing. Metal may also be perforated to improve its acoustical qualities if backed with an absorptive medium. An acoustical ceiling installation would be suitable in a basement play room.

INSTALLATION

In private residences, any of three installation methods may be used:

1. If the tiles are to be used over an existing ceiling, they may be cemented to that ceiling provided the surface is solid and level.

2. Tiles have interlocking edges that provide a solid joining method as well as an almost seamless installation. If the existing ceiling is not solid or level, furring strips are nailed up so that the edges of the tile may be glued and stapled to a solid surface.

3. A suspended ceiling may be used, which consists of a metal spline suspended by wires from the ceiling or joists. (This is the method used in commercial applications.) The tiles are laid in the spline so that the edges of the panels are supported by the edge of the T-shaped spline. The splines may be left exposed or they may be covered by the tile. (See Figure 6.3.) There are two advantages to using a suspended ceiling:

- Damaged panels are easily replaced.
- The height of the ceiling may be varied according to the size of the room or other requirements.

With an exposed spline, it is easy to replace a single panel; the damaged panel is merely lifted out. However, if the spline is covered, the damaged panel or panels are removed. When replacing the last panel, the tongue is removed.

MAINTENANCE

A soft gum eraser should be used to remove small spots, dirt marks, and streaks from acoustical tiles. For larger areas, or larger smudges, a chemically treated sponge rubber pad or wallpaper cleaner is used. The sponge rubber pad or wallpaper cleaner must be in fresh condition. Nicks and scratches may be touched up with colored chalks. Dust is removed by brushing lightly with a soft brush or clean rag or by vacuuming with a soft brush attachment.

Acoustical tiles must not be soaked with water. They should be washed through light application of a sponge dampened with a mild liquid detergent solution: 1/2 cup detergent in 1 gallon of water. After the sponge is saturated, it should be squeezed nearly dry and then lightly rubbed on the surface to be cleaned using long, sweeping, gentle strokes. The strokes should be in the same direction as the texture if the tile is ribbed or embossed.

Surface openings must not be clogged or bridged when acoustical tiles are painted. A paint of high hiding power should be used because it is desirable to keep the number of coats to a minimum (paint greatly affects the noise reduction coefficient [NRC] of the acoustical material). Some paint manufacturers provide specific formulations that have high hiding power and low combustibility and are not likely to bridge an opening in the tile. The paint must be applied as thinly as necessary.

COMMERCIAL

Acoustical ceiling products have become a mainstay of commercial installations. Movable office partitions are prevalent today, so audio privacy is necessary. In this day of electronic word processors and data processing equipment, office din is somewhat less than in the days of noisy typewriters, but telephones and voices still cause distracting sounds. Productivity is increased in a quieter environment, although a noiseless environment is easily disrupted.

FIGURE 6.4 Gensler Architects of Santa Monica, California, used MetalWorks Custom Plank System for Club Nokia in Los Angeles. *Photograph courtesy of Armstrong World Industries.*

The advantages of a residential suspended acoustical ceiling also apply to commercial installations; however, the major reason for using a suspended ceiling in commercial work is the easy access to wiring, telephone lines, plumbing, and heating ducts. (See Figure 6.4.)

When looking through the technical information on acoustical ceilings, the designer will find several of the following acronyms.

- *NRC.* The noise reduction coefficient (**NRC**) is a measure of sound absorbed by a material. The NRC of different types of panels may be compared; the higher the number, the more sound reduction is indicated. For purposes of comparison, tests must be made at the same **Hertz (Hz)** range.

- *STC.* The sound transmission class (**STC**) is a single number rating that is used to characterize the sound-insulating value of a partition (wall or ceiling). A partition prevents sound from being transmitted from one area to another; the STC rating denotes approximately how much the sound will be reduced when traveling through the partition. The higher the rating, the less sound will be transmitted through the wall or floor/ceiling.

- *CAC.* The ceiling attenuation class (**CAC**) refers to the sound attenuation ability of ceiling systems. The CAC rates how much sound will be reduced when it is transmitted through the ceiling of one room into an adjacent room through a shared **plenum.** A higher rating indicates that the material will allow less sound transmission.

- *LR.* Another characteristic often included in acoustical mineral fiberboard charts is light reflectance (**LR**), which indicates the percentage of light reflected from a ceiling product's surface. This LR varies according to the amount of texture on the ceiling's surface and the value of the color. Some ceiling panels have a mineral fiber substrate with a needle-punched fabric surface.

i-ceilings allow architects and others to integrate sound and wireless systems into the ceiling plane without the systems being visible from below. The new "interactive" products thus create more effective commercial interiors by increasing speech privacy and providing easier access to information and people.

One example of i-ceilings is Armstrong's i-Ceilings Wireless Systems, which has been designed to enhance reliable Internet and data network access as well as wireless telephone access from any location inside a building. The Antenna Panel is a standard Armstrong ceiling panel with the antenna already imbedded inside. Armstrong offers the PRIVACY Series, P-25 Model, which it states offers sound-masking capability "with more predictable performance than plenum-based systems." Armstrong states that this model offers better speech privacy and enhanced paging and background music.[1]

The Antenna and Sound Panels both look just like ordinary ceiling panels so that they blend in with the overall ceiling. This makes the interior space more aesthetically pleasing by eliminating unsightly speakers and surface-mounted antennas.

COMMERCIAL INSTALLATION

The traditional approach to lighting is **luminaries** recessed at specific intervals in the acoustical ceiling. The fixtures are often covered by lenses or louvers to diffuse the light. Today, not only lighting but also heating and cooling are often incorporated into acoustical installations. This is done in several ways. The heating and cooling duct may be spaced between the modules in one long continuous line or individual vents may be used. In one interesting innovation, the entire area between the suspended ceiling and the joists is used as a plenum area, with the conditioned air entering the room through orifices in the individual tiles.

One word of warning: If you are replacing a ceiling that may contain asbestos, OSHA has some very stringent regulations and safety precautions that must be strictly adhered to.

To create vaults, transitions, and curved islands, you might consider CurvGrid with EZ-Flex panels. These panels do not require cutting or tools; instead, they offer integral bend-and-twist tabs for use in installation. The company states: "the patented primary carrier reduces labor-intensive hanger drops by more than 50 percent versus competitive systems." These panels may be purchased in a variety of colors—in standard sizes of 2' × 4', 2' × 6', and 2' × 8', as well as custom sizes.[2]

Eurostone has a unique, sculptured stone look that is intrinsic to the material it is made from, primarily volcanic perlite. This volcanic stone is formed and fired in specially designed kilns at 960°F using a special inorganic binder to bond the stone particles together. These tiles are unaffected by water or high humidity, have no measurable sag, and have excellent dimensional stability. They may be installed in high humidity areas such as showers, swimming pools, and saunas, and also used in exterior soffits, canopies, and entrance ways. Eurostone tiles will not support the growth of bacteria or fungus. Therefore, it's ideal for use in schools, medical facilities, and hospitals.[3]

Metal

Metal ceilings were originally introduced in the 1860s as a replacement for the ornamental plasterwork that decorated the walls and ceilings of the most fashionable rooms of the day. Once in place, it was discovered that metal ceilings offered two important benefits: (1) Unlike plaster, the metal could withstand rough use, and (2) metal could be more easily maintained than plaster, which would flake, crack, and peel. The W.F. Norman Corporation uses 88-year-old dies to produce metal plates for ceiling and wall coverings. Styles include Greek, Colonial, Victorian, Empire, Gothic, Oriental, and Art Deco. Many of today's metal ceilings are actually steel, which can be prepainted or made of copper, brass, or chrome.

Stamped metal ceilings now come in 1 foot squares, 1' × 2', 2' × 4', or 2' × 8' and are installed by tacking the units to furring strips nailed 12" apart. The METALWORKS Open Cell system is designed to be durable and mask the plenum, while offering completely accessible options for open ceilings through an aesthetically pleasing product.[4]

Not all metal ceilings have to be flat. For example, Armstrong Ceilings offers a range of curved metal panel sizes and finish options through its RH200 Curved Plank System.

Chicago Metallic Corporation's CurvGrid provides a curve/wave look using standard 15/16" T-bar painted on all sides. Geometrix 3-D metal ceiling panels are made of lightweight aluminum panels and lend unique perspective and unexpected dimension to ceiling space. (See Figure 6.5.) Geometrix is available with high recycled content (HRC). HRC Specialty Ceiling Panels and Trim are classified as containing over 50 percent total recycled content.[5]

Other Ceiling Materials

A vinyl-coated, embossed aluminum, bonded to a mineral fiber substrate, results in an easily maintained, corrosion-resistant, and durable ceiling product. Grease vapor concentrations may be wiped clean with a sponge or a mild detergent solution; these types of ceilings are suitable for commercial kitchens, laboratories, and hospitals.

To create a ceiling that is easy to wipe clean, or for use in very moist areas such as bathrooms and showers, ceramic tile may be installed. Ceramic tile is also used in restaurant kitchens.

Baffles are fabric-covered fiberglass panels hung from a ceiling by means of wire attached to eyelets installed in the top edge of the panel. Baffles are not only functional, but decorative too, with a sound rating of NRC 0.80. Baffles hung perpendicular to a ceiling are an established and highly effective way to create additional sound-absorbing surfaces, especially in interiors lacking sufficient surfaces for wall-mounted panels. Baffles can be used for signage, and different colors can denote areas or departments within a larger space.

Not all acoustical ceilings are flat. Many are **coffered** in 2- to 4-foot square modules. These panels may or may not include luminaries.

Mirrors are not recommended for ceilings.

FIGURE 6.5 The Geometrix ceiling is also used on the back wall, creating a three-dimensional effect. *Photograph courtesy of Chicago Metallic Corp.*

bibliography

Rather, Guy Cadogan. *Ceilings and Their Decoration*. London, England: T. Werner Laurie, 1978.

glossary

Arabesque. Elaborate scroll designs that are either carved or in low relief.

CAC. Ceiling attenuation class. The CAC rates how much sound will be reduced when it is transmitted through the ceiling of one room into an adjacent room through a shared plenum.

Coffered. Panels are inserted below the level of the rest of the ceiling giving a two dimensional effect.

Crown moulding. The uppermost moulding next to the ceiling.

Hertz (Hz). Unit of frequency measurement, one unit per second.

Laminated beam. Several pieces of lumber glued to form a structural timber.

LR. Light reflectance. The amount of light reflected from the surface.

Luminaries. A complete lighting fixture, with all components needed to be connected to the electric power supply.

NRC. Noise reduction coefficient. The average percentage of sound reduction at various Hertz levels.

Panel. A ceiling unit larger than one square foot.

Patera. A round or oval raised surface design.

Plenum. The space between a suspended ceiling and the floor above.

Relief. A design that is raised above the surrounding area.

STC. Sound transmission class. A number denoting the sound-insulating value of a material.

Summer beam. A main supporting beam in early New England homes, in the middle of the room, resting on the fireplace at one end and a post at the other.

Tile. Ceiling tile (12 inches square).

Vigas. The round wooden poles used in exposed ceilings of south-western style homes and extending outside.

endnotes

1. Armstrong World Industries, www.armstrong.com/commercialceilingsna
2. Chicago Metallic Corp., www.chicago-metallic.com
3. Armstrong World Industries, www.armstrong.com/commercialceilingsna
4. Ibid.
5. Chicago Metallic Corp., www.chicago-metallic.com

Other Components

In this chapter, you will:

- Explain appropriate selection, composition, and maintenance of a variety of items, including mouldings, doors, and locks

- Distinguish between door and hardware needs for hospitals and other types of structures

- Recognize how to install and maintain appropriate items for establishing and maintaining building security

- Develop an understanding of specifications for doors—and understand the importance and practical application of this understanding

- Examine the importance of industry-specific regulations related to a variety of components

Mouldings

To an interior designer, trim and mouldings are what icing is to a cake: They cover, enhance, and decorate a plain surface. Basically, heavily carved or ornate trim is used in a traditional setting, whereas simpler trim is used where a contemporary ambience is desired.

Materials for trim and mouldings should be constructed from easily shaped stock. Both pine and oak are used when wood trim is desired, and both provide details that are easily discernible and smooth. Trim should always be **mitered** at the corners; that is, the joint should be cut at a 45° angle. Also available are medium density fiberboard (MDF) mouldings for painted interior trims and solid surface materials, such as Corian and Wilsonart Solid Surface, which are also used for counters. Depending on thickness, these materials are fairly easy to shape.

Bases are a type of moulding that are universally used to finish the area where the wall and floor meet. There are several reasons for using a base or skirting:

- It covers any discrepancy or expansion space between the wall and the floor.
- It forms a protection for the wall from cleaning equipment.
- It may be a decorative feature.

The word *base* is used to describe all types of materials, including those mentioned earlier as well as vinyl or rubber.

Baseboard is the term used for wood bases only. When a plain baseboard is used, the wood should be sanded smoothly on the face—and particularly on the top edge—to facilitate cleaning. In addition, the exposed edge should be slightly beveled to prevent breaking or chipping. Traditional baseboards have a shaped top edge with a flat lower part. This design may be achieved with one piece of wood 3 1/2" to 7" wide or may consist of separate parts, with a base moulding on top of a square-edged piece of lumber. A **base shoe** may be added to either type. Traditional one-piece baseboards are available as stock mouldings from the better woodworking manufacturers. (See Figure 7.1.)

For residential use, windows come prefabricated with the **brickmould** or exterior trim attached. The interior **casing** (the exposed trim) may be flat or moulded and is applied after the window and walls have been installed and the windows **caulked,** a crucial step for energy conservation. The interior casing usually matches the baseboard designs, although the size may vary.

Doors, particularly for residential use, often come **prehung.** After installation of the door frame, the space between the jamb and the wall is covered by a casing. This casing matches the profile of the one used around the windows, with the casing's width determined by the size, scale, and style of the room.

Crown and **bed mouldings** are used to soften the sharp line where the ceiling and walls meet. Cove mouldings also serve the same purpose; the difference is that crown mouldings are more intricately shaped (see Figure 7.2), and cove mouldings have a simple curved face. Cove mouldings may be painted the same color as the ceiling, thus giving the ceiling a lowered appearance. **Cornice** mouldings may be ornate and made up of as many as seven separate pieces of wood.

Chair rails are used in traditional homes to protect the surface of walls from damage caused by the backs of chairs. These rails may be simple strips of wood with rounded edges, or they may have shaped top and bottom edges, depending on the style of the room. The installed height of chair rails should be between 30 and 36 inches. When chair rails are to be

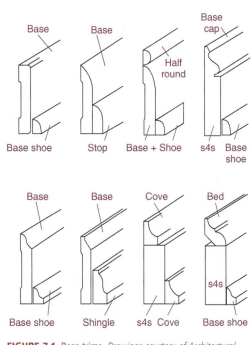

FIGURE 7.1 Base trims. *Drawings courtesy of Architectural Woodwork Institute.*

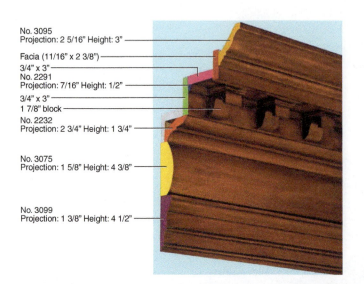

No. 3095
Projection: 2 5/16" Height: 3"

Facia (11/16" x 2 3/8")

3/4" x 3"
No. 2291
Projection: 7/16" Height: 1/2"

3/4" x 3"
1 7/8" block

No. 2232
Projection: 2 3/4" Height: 1 3/4"

No. 3075
Projection: 1 5/8" Height: 4 3/8"

No. 3099
Projection: 1 3/8" Height: 4 1/2"

FIGURE 7.2 This crown moulding is made up of nine separate pieces of moulded wood. *Photograph courtesy of Driwood Moulding Company.*

painted, they should be made of a hard, close-grained wood. If they are to be left natural, they should be of the same material and should be finished in the same manner as the rest of the woodwork.

When plywood panels are used on walls, the edges are sometimes covered with a square-edge batten. In more traditional surroundings, a moulded batten is used.

Picture mouldings, as the name implies, are used to create a continuous projecting support around the walls of a room for picture hooks. Picture moulding has a curved top to receive the picture hook. Of course, when pictures are hung by this method, the wires will be visible; nonetheless, this method is still used in older homes, museums, and art galleries, where frequent rearranging is required. No damage is done to the walls, as it is with the modern method of hanging pictures. Picture moulding is placed just below or several inches below the ceiling. Wherever the placement, the ceiling color is usually continued down to the top of the moulding.

An infinite variety of patterns may be used for mouldings. They may be stock shapes and sizes or shaped to the designer's specifications by the use of custom-formed shaper blades. This latter method is the most expensive but does achieve a unique moulding.

Wood mouldings may be covered with metal in many finishes (including bright chrome, brass, copper, or simulated metal) for use as picture frame moulding, interior trim, and displays.

All the mouldings discussed thus far have been constructed of wood. When a heavily carved cornice moulding is required, the material may be a **polymer.** Focal Point makes a polymer moulding by direct impression from the original wood, metal, or plaster article. This direct process gives the reproduction all the personality, texture, and spirit of the original, but with several advantages:

- The mouldings are much less expensive than the hand-carved originals.
- They are lighter weight and therefore easier to handle.
- They may be nailed, drilled, or screwed.
- They are receptive to sanding.
- They help save on installation costs because, in many cases, the original moulding consisted of several pieces, but modern technology reproduces multiple mouldings in a one-piece strip.

Focal Point is authorized to reproduce architectural details for the Victorian Society in America, for Colonial Williamsburg, and for the Historic Natchez Foundation.

When ceiling medallions were first used as **backplates** for chandeliers, they were made of plaster. However, polymer reproductions today are more lightweight than plaster and easier to ship. The medallions are primed white at the factory, ready to paint, or factory stained with Focal Finish, which offers 10 hand-applied finishes available on more than 30 medallion styles.[1] The use of medallions is not limited to chandeliers; they may also be used as backplates for ceiling fans. Focal Point's Quick Clips medallion installation system locks medallions into place with ease.

Other materials used in ornate ceiling cornices include gypsum with a polymer agent that is reinforced with glass fibers for added strength. A wood fiber combination may also be used.

Lightweight, QuarryCast, or glass-reinforced gypsum and cement cast architectural products, including all types of mouldings mentioned previously, are used internationally. Round or tapered column covers, with capitals and base, are also available. (See Figure 7.3.)

Other reproductions from the past include the dome and the niche cap. When first designed, they were made of plaster or wood, which was hand carved. Domes and niche caps can provide a touch of authenticity in renovations; in fact, many of Focal Point's designs have been used in restorations of national historical landmarks. Niche caps have a shell design and form the top of a curved recess that usually displays sculpture, vases, flowers, or any other prized possession.

FIGURE 7.3 Over 57,000 pieces of QuarryCast, MetalCast, and Glassfiber Reinforced Gypsum (GRG), representing virtually every column, wall panel, moulding, and so on, are visible in these photographs. *Photo courtesy of Formglas.*

Stair brackets are another form of architectural detail and are placed on the finished **stringer** for a decorative effect. (See Figure 7.4.)

Doors

An entry door makes a first impression, whether for a private residence or a business. Doors for residential use may be constructed of wood, metal, or fiberglass. Doors should be selected according to their usage.

- *Standard duty.* Typically involves doors where frequency of use is low; requires the lowest minimum performance standards.
- *Heavy duty.* Typically involves doors for moderate usage; requires intermediate minimum performance standards.
- *Extra heavy duty.* Typically involves doors where use is considered heavy and frequent; requires the highest minimum performance standards.[2]

In commercial applications, however, doors must be guaranteed not to burn for 1 to 1½ hours because of fire codes. When selecting an entrance door, check the exterior of the building to make sure that the design is compatible. Look for a door that meets Energy Star guidelines to ensure that it is energy efficient.

WOOD DOORS

Flush doors are perfectly flat and smooth, with no decoration. There are several methods of constructing a flush door. A honeycomb hollow core is used for some interior residential flush doors. The core of the door is made of 2- to 3-inch-wide solid wood for the **rails** and 1 to 2 inches of solid wood for the **stiles,** with an additional 20-inch-long strip of wood, called a *lock block*, in the approximate hardware location. The area between the solid wood is filled with a honeycomb or ladder core. (See Figure 7.5.) In less expensive doors, this core is covered by the finish veneer. More expensive doors have one or two layers of veneer before the finish veneer is applied. Thus, a flush door may be of three-, five-, or seven-ply construction.

Better-quality flush doors are constructed with a lumber core, also known as *staved wood*. In addition, wood blocks are used in place of the honeycomb or ladder core of the hollow core door. The staved or lumber core may or may not have the blocks bonded together. With staved core doors, the inside rails and stiles are narrower than in other flush doors because this type of construction is more rigid. Species used for face veneers include hardwoods, such as oak, mahogany, cherry, and maple, and softwoods, such as pine and fir. If the door is to be painted, a "paint-grade" wood door made of softwood should be specified.

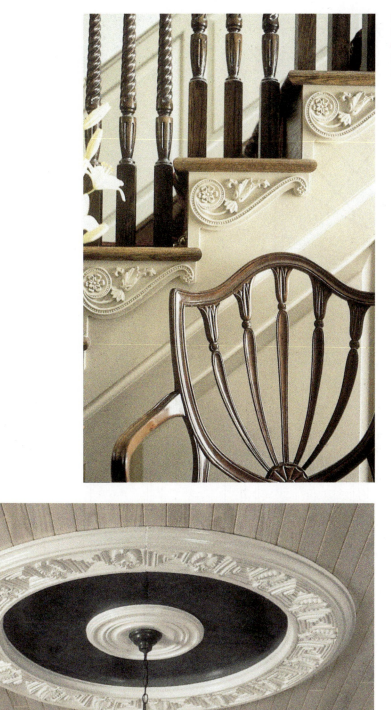

FIGURE 7.4 Top, the Woodlawn Stair Bracket from Focal Point Architectural Production. Below, the d'Evereux Rim from Focal Point's National Trust for Historic Preservation Collection. *Photos courtesy of Focal Point Architectural Products, Inc.*

Another method of door construction utilizes a particleboard or flakeboard core with a crossband veneer to which the face veneer is attached. A particleboard door core is warp resistant and solid, has no knots or voids, and has good insulation properties and sound resistance (thereby limiting heat loss and transfer of sound waves).

Flush doors for commercial installations may have a high-pressure decorative laminate (HPDL) as the face veneer or, for low maintenance, a photogravure or vinyl covering similar to the paneling discussed in Chapter 5.

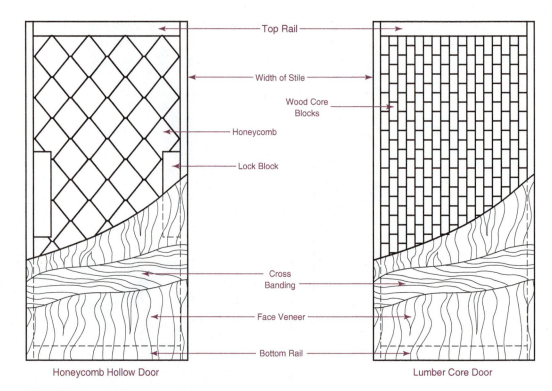

FIGURE 7.5 Door construction.

Honeycomb Hollow Door

Lumber Core Door

Top Rail

Width of Stile

Wood Core Blocks

Honeycomb

Lock Block

Cross Banding

Face Veneer

Bottom Rail

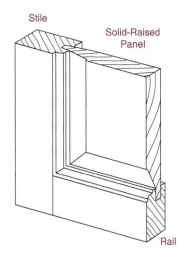

Stile

Solid-Raised Panel

Rail

Solid Ovola Sticking

Stile

Rim-Raised Panel

Rail

Solid Ogee Sticking

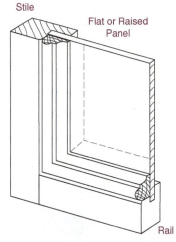

Stile

Flat or Raised Panel

Rail

Applied-Raised Moulding

FIGURE 7.6 Paneled doors.

Commercial installations of doors do not always require a moulding; the doors are merely set into the wall. In other words, the wall meets the door jamb.

There are three methods of achieving a paneled look in doors (see Figure 7.6). Several use a particular **sticking** (distinct shape of moulding):

1. The first method uses a solid ornate **ogee sticking;** in other words, the stiles and rails are shaped so the moulding and stile or rails are all one piece of wood.

2. The second method is the same as the first but uses a simpler **ovolo** sticking.

3. The third method uses a **dadoed** stile and rail, and the joining of panel and stile is covered by a separate applied moulding. If the panel is large, it will be made of plywood and a moulding will be used; if the panel is under 10 inches in width, it may be made of solid wood. (In premium grade, solid lumber is not permitted.)

Paneled doors reflect different periods, as do paneled walls. When period paneling is used, the doors should be of similar design.

There are an infinite number of designs for paneled doors. (See Figure 7.7.) Panels may be horizontal or vertical, small or large, curved or straight, wood or glass.

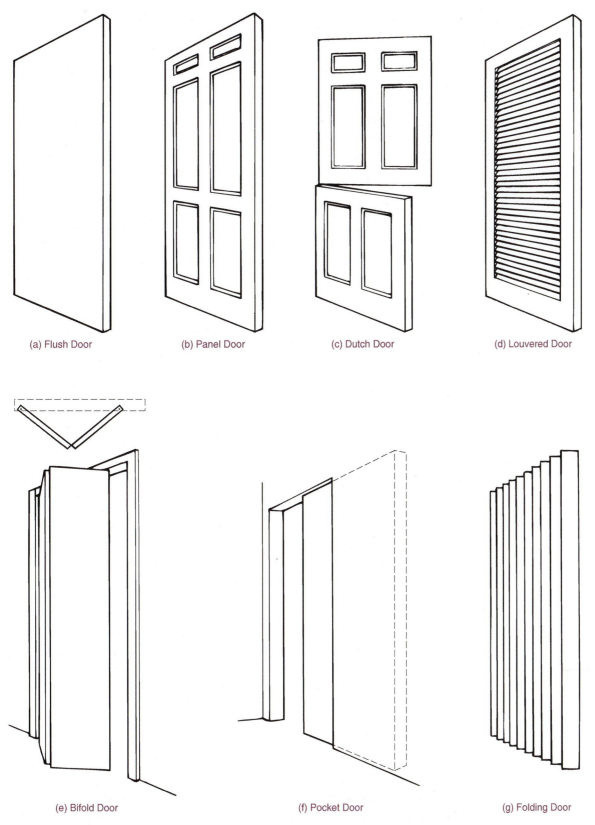

(a) Flush Door   (b) Panel Door   (c) Dutch Door   (d) Louvered Door

(e) Bifold Door   (f) Pocket Door   (g) Folding Door

FIGURE 7.7 Types of doors.

Dutch doors for residential use consist of an upper and lower part. Special hardware joins the two parts to form a regular door or, with the hardware undone, the top part may be opened to ventilate or give light to a room, with the lower part remaining closed. (It also keeps children and pets inside.) Dutch doors are used commercially as a service opening. In some cases, a shelf is attached to the top of the bottom half of the door.

Louvers are used in doors to provide ventilation, such as in cleaning or storage closets, or to aid in air circulation. Louvers are made of horizontal slats contained within stile-and-rail frames. Louvers may be set into wood or metal doors, with the louver at the top and/or bottom, or the center may be all louvered. Some louvers are visionproof, some are adjustable, and others may be lightproof or weatherproof.

One of the most common residential uses for a louvered door is a bifold door for a closet. For a narrow opening, a bifold door consists of two panels; larger openings require a double set of doors opening from the middle. The center panel of each pair is hung from the track, and the outer panels may or may not pivot at the jamb.

A pocket door, or recessed sliding door, requires a special frame and track that is incorporated into the inside of the wall. The finished door is hung from the track before the casing is attached. The bottom of the door is held in place by guides that permit the door to slide sideways while preventing back and forth movement.

Folding or accordion doors are used where space needs to be divided temporarily. Folding doors operate and stack compactly within their openings. The panels may be wood-veneered lumber core or particleboard core with a wood-grained vinyl coating. Each panel is 3 5/8 inches or less in width, and folding doors are available in heights up to 16 feet 1 inch. Folding doors operate by means of a track at the top to which the panels are attached by wheels. The handle and locking mechanism are installed on the panel closest to the opening edge.

For an Oriental ambience, fixed or sliding **Shoji** panels are available; these are wood-framed with synskin inserts, which have an Oriental rice paper look. Pinecrest offers a wide variety of Shoji panels, standard or custom, both fixed and sliding.

GLASS DOORS

Patio doors are similar in construction and appearance to wood panel entry doors. French doors are often used in residences to open out onto a balcony or patio. They have wood or metal frames and may consist of one sheet of tempered or laminated safety glass, or may have multiple **lights** in each door. Whenever full-length glass is used, by law it must be tempered or laminated. French doors are most often installed in pairs and may open out or in.

When French doors or other styles of doors are installed in pairs, one is used as the primary door. The second one is stationary, with a flush bolt or special lock holding it tight at the top and bottom. To cover the joining crack between the pair of doors and to make the doors more weathertight, an **astragal** is attached to the interior edge of the stationary door. Both doors may be used to enlarge the opening. If double doors are used, the astragal is on the exterior edge of the secondary door. Another style of a patio door is the sliding type.

Glass doors for residential use may be comprised of solid wood core, aluminum or vinyl, or fiberglass or steel (when sliding and hinged patio doors are considered). Steel and fiberglass doors are foam filled for increased thermal performance. Commercial glass doors must also be made of tempered or laminated glass and are subject to local building codes. The door may be all glass, framed with metal at the top and/or bottom, or framed on all four sides. Because of the nature of an all-glass door, the most visible design feature is the hardware.

METAL DOORS

Most metal doors are made of steel, although some are available in aluminum. In the past, metal doors had a commercial or institutional connotation, but today many interior and exterior residential doors and many bifold doors are made of metal. Exterior metal doors were shunned in the past because wood exterior solid core doors had better insulating qualities. The use of polystyrene and polyurethane as a core has provided residential metal exterior doors with similar insulating qualities, and it is not as susceptible to temperature changes and warping as is the wood door.

Surfaces may be factory coated with rust-resistant primer to be painted on site; alternatively, surfaces may be vinyl or baked-on polyester finishes embossed with wood grain patterns. Some metal doors are given a wood-fiber coating that can be stained. Higher-end models are actually laminated with a real-wood veneer. Steel doors have a less convincing wood grain than fiberglass doors.

FIBERGLASS DOORS

Fiberglass or fiberglass-composite doors are an alternative to wood. Fiberglass offers six times the energy efficiency as conventional wood doors. Models are available where both the door and sidelite swing open, so large furniture and appliances can pass easily through. An adjustable threshold gives a weather-tight seal, protecting the home from the elements. A **transom** may also be added.

American Style Collection fiberglass entry doors were inspired by early 1900s residential architecture. The collection complements many popular home designs, including Arts and Crafts, Bungalow, Cottage, and Colonial Revival styles.[3]

Made with Therma-Tru's patented AccuGrain technology, these doors provide the look of high-grade wood with all of the durability of fiberglass. The advantage of these collections is that the various components—door stile, side lights, and transoms—may be selected to personalize the entry way. (See Figure 7.8.)

FIGURE 7.8 This entry door is part of the Classic-Craft Oak Collection from Therma-Tru Doors. Decorative glass is encased between two panes of tempered glass for energy efficiency and easy cleaning. *Photo courtesy of Therma-Tru Corp.*

SPECIALTY DOORS

For commercial use there are several specialty core requirements: fire-rated, sound-rated, X-ray, bullet-resistant, and electrostatic-shielded. Fire doors have an incombustible material core with fire-retardant rails and stiles covered by a wood veneer or high-pressure decorative laminate. These doors are rated according to the time they take to burn. Depending on materials and construction, this time will vary between 20 minutes and 1 1/2 hours. Local building codes should be consulted before specifying.

Sound-rated doors have sound transmission class (STC) ratings. Bullet-resistant and electrostatic-rated doors must meet the manufacturer's standards.

For exterior use, a wood door must be of solid construction. Hand-carved doors are available for exterior use, but manufacturer's specifications must be studied carefully because a door that appears to be hand carved may actually be moulded to imitate hand carving at less expense.

SPECIFICATIONS FOR DOORS

Most doors are available prehung (i.e., assembled complete with frames, trim, and sometimes hardware). The bored hole in these doors is ready for installation of the lock. This bored hole must have a **backset** that corresponds to the selected hardware. Most prehung doors come predrilled with a 2 3/8" hole; however, most designer-type hardware looks better with a 2 3/4" backset or even more. The 2 3/8" backset, with knob-type hardware, can sometimes result in scraped knuckles.

Handing describes the direction the door opens and placement of the handle. When standing outside, look at the closed door.

- *If door swings in:*
  - Handle on right = left-hand door
  - Handle on left = right-hand door

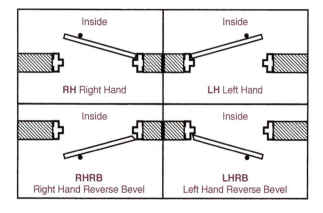

FIGURE 7.9 Door handing.

- **If the door swings out:**
  - Handle on right = right-hand door
  - Handle on left = left-hand door[4]

In the case of a pair of doors, hand is determined from the active leaf in the same way. If prehung doors are specified, door handing should be included. (See Figure 7.9.)

The following additional information should be provided when specifying doors:

- Manufacturer size—including width, height, and thickness.
- Face description—species of wood, type of veneer (rotary or sliced).
- If not veneer, then laminate, photogravure, vinyl coating, or metal.
- Construction—cross banding thickness, edge strips, top and bottom rails, stiles, and core construction.
- Finishing—prefinished or unfinished.
- Special detailing—includes specifying backset for hardware and any mouldings.
- Special service (e.g., glazing, fire doors, and so on).
- Warranty—differs for interior and exterior use.

Reinforced strike plate areas are a good security measure, and increasing the distance from the lockset to the deadbolt spreads the impact load from potential break-ins, thereby increasing security. Check the frame of the door to be sure it's strong, tight, and well-constructed.

Door Hardware

Most of the following material is adapted, by permission, from the *Tech Talk* bulletin, "Butts and Hinges," published by the **Door and Hardware Institute (DHI)** bulletin. This technical material has been simplified for ease of understanding.

HINGES

The two parts of a hinge consist of metal plates known as **leaves** that are joined by a **pin** that passes through the **knuckle** joints. **Countersunk** holes are predrilled in the leaves. **Template hardware** has the holes drilled accurately to conform to standard drawings, thus assuring a perfect fit. Template **butt hinges** have the holes drilled in a crescent shape. (See Figure 7.10.)

Door hardware, in general, is not an issue unless it does not work properly. For example, the door unit will not function properly if the proper hinging device is not specified.

There are hinges that will meet all types of applications. The standards developed by the Builders Hardware Manufacturers Association (BHMA) and promulgated through the American National Standards Institute (ANSI) are extremely helpful in making the correct selection of the proper hinge. These standards include ANSI/BHMA A156.18-2006.

The following eight points are intended to assist the contractor in proper hinge selection.

1. **Determine the Type of Hinge**

   Several pieces of information are needed to select the proper type of hinge: What is the door material (wood or hollow metal)? What is the frame material (wood or hollow metal, channel iron)?

   The four classifications of hinges are as follows:

   1. **Full mortise.** Both leaves are **mortised,** one leaf to the door and one leaf to the frame (wood door [WD] or hollow metal [HM] with wood frame [WF] or hollow metal frame [HMF]).
   2. **Half mortise.** One leaf is mortised to the door, and the other is surface applied to the frame (HM with channel iron frame [CIF]).

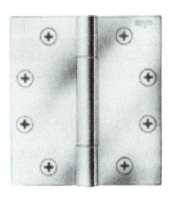

Full Mortise

Half Mortise

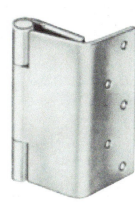

Half Mortise Swing Clear

Full-Mortise Swing Clear

Full Surface

Half Surface

Full-Surface Swing Clear

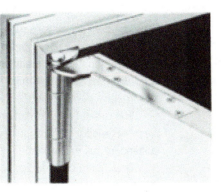

Pivot Reinforced

Half-Surface Swing Clear

FIGURE 7.10 Types of hinges.

3. **Full surface.** Both leaves are applied to the surface, one to the door and the other to the frame (metal core door [MCD] or HM with CIF).

4. **Half surface.** One leaf is mortised to the frame and the other is surface applied to the face of the door (WD x WF or MCD x HMF).

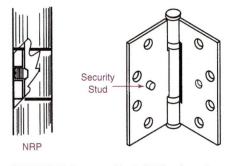

NRP

FIGURE 7.11 Nonremovable pin (NRP) and security stud. *Drawings courtesy of Door and Hardware Institute, "Butts and Hinges," Tech Talk, by H. Matt Bouchard, Jr. AHC.*

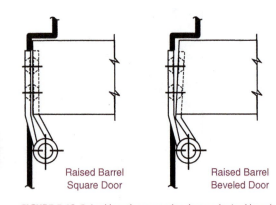

Raised Barrel
Square Door

Raised Barrel
Beveled Door

FIGURE 7.12 Raised barrel square-edge door and raised barrel bevel-edge door. *Drawings courtesy of Door and Hardware Institute, "Butts and Hinges," Tech Talk, by H. Matt Bouchard, Jr. AHC.*

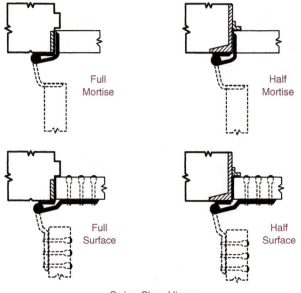

Full
Mortise

Half
Mortise

Full
Surface

Half
Surface

Swing Clear Hinges

FIGURE 7.13 Swing clear hinges. *Drawings courtesy of Door and Hardware Institute, "Butts and Hinges," Tech Talk, by H. Matt Bouchard, Jr. AHC.*

There is really no problem identifying the uses of the full mortise and the full surface. However, the half mortise and the half surface are sometimes difficult to keep straight. There is one easy way to remember what type of door the hinge is used for. You need only to remember *what the hinge is called*; this will tell you *what is done to the door*. For example, a half mortise hinge is *mortised to the door* and surface applied to the frame. A half surface hinge is *surface applied to the door* and mortised to the frame.

Several features are available for the full mortise hinge that must be indicated before going further. One point that must be made when discussing the classification of hinges is the term *swaging*. **Swaging** is a slight offset to the hinge leaf at the barrel. This offset permits the leaves to come closer together when the door is in the closed position. If the hinge were to be left in the natural state after the knuckle was rolled, the hinge would be referred to as **flatback**. A flatback hinge has a gap between the leaves of approximately 5/32". This allows heat and air conditioning to escape, as well as creates an unsightly gap between the door and the frame. The standard swaging on standard weight and heavyweight full mortise hinges provides 1/16" clearance between the leaves when the leaves are in the closed position.

Two additional features that are commonly used are the nonremovable pin (NRP) and the security safety stud (Sec Std.). (See Figure 7.11.) The nonremovable pin has a small set screw in the body of the barrel and is tightened down against the pin. In most cases the pin has a groove in the position where the set screw makes contact, allowing the set screw to seat. The set screw is positioned so it cannot be reached unless the door is opened. If pin removal is necessary, the set screw merely is removed and the pin tapped from the bottom in the usual manner.

The security safety stud is another feature which places a stud on one leaf and a locking hole on the other leaf. When the door is closed the stud is anchored into the opposite leaf. Even if the hinge pin is removed, the door is secure because the leaves are locked together.

One important point must be made here. Both these features are intended as *deterrents only*. If someone wants to gain entry through a door badly enough, eventually that person will get through!

Another special function available is the *raised barrel* hinge, which is used when the door is set back *into the frame*.

There are three different types of applications: jamb surface mount, raised barrel for square-edge door, and raised barrel for bevel-edge door. On the jamb surface mount application the door is mounted to accommodate both hinge leaves or what sometimes is referred to as a *double mortised*. The jamb surface mount may be applied to either a square- or a bevel-edge door.

The raised barrel for square-edge door and raised barrel for bevel-edge door application are mortised into the frame and door as a standard full mortise hinge. (See Figure 7.12.)

Depending on the depth of the frame, all three of these applications may restrict the degree of opening.

Another special feature is the *swing clear* type. (See Figure 7.13.) This is used mostly in hospitals and institutional buildings when the passage area must be the full width of the opening. One such use would be an 8-foot-wide corridor that requires a full opening for the passage of two beds or carts. With the use of swing clear hinges, this passage can be accomplished.

The hinges are designed to swing the door completely clear of the opening when the door is opened at a 95° angle. The standard way to

Other Components

164

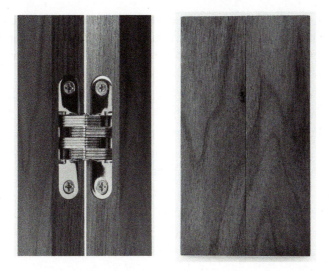

FIGURE 7.14 Soss Invisible Hinge: "Beautiful when open; invisible when closed." *Photograph courtesy of Grass America, Inc. & Universal Industrial Products.*

accomplish this degree of opening is to build a pocket in the wall to accept the door. This allows the door to be concealed in the wall and not obstruct the flow of traffic.[5]

Soss Invisible Hinges from Universal Industrial Products (see Figure 7.14) are available for light-, medium-, and heavy-duty applications. They are also available for metal cabinet applications. A phrase from the Soss Web site aptly describes how a Soss hinge appears in its various positions: "Beautiful when open; invisible when closed."

Concealed hinges for cabinets are different in construction from concealed door hinges. They are not visible from the outside of the cabinet but are surface mounted on the inside of the cabinet door.

2. *Select the Proper Weight and Bearing Structure*

Because of the large variety of door sizes and weights, hinges are divided into three groups:

1. Heavy weight/ball bearing

2. Standard weight/ball bearing

3. Standard weight/plain bearing

3. *Determine the Size of the Hinge*

Two factors determine the weight and structure of the hinge; several bits of information will be necessary:

1. Door height, width, thickness, and weight

2. Trim dimensions

A general rule of thumb is one hinge for every 30" of door height or fraction thereof.

• Doors up to 60" in height—two hinges

• Doors over 60" but not over 90" in height—three hinges

• Doors over 90" but not over 120" in height—four hinges

4. *Determine the Type of Material*

There are three base materials from which hinges are manufactured: steel, stainless steel, and brass. Each base material has different qualities.

1. *Steel* has great strength but is a corrosive material. If the atmosphere in which steel is used is not stable, it will begin to rust. The best application for steel is in a controlled environment, such as inside a building where the temperature and humidity are controlled.

2. *Stainless steel* also has great strength. It is rust resistant and has decorative value in that it can be polished to a satin or bright finish. Other considerations may be geographical, such as on the seacoast or in industrial areas where acids or atmospheric conditions exist.

3. *Brass* is noncorrosive, rust resistant, and very decorative. However, it has less strength than the steel or stainless steel material. Brass is often used where appearance is of great concern. Brass may be polished and plated in many various finishes.

   Both steel and stainless steel hinges may be used on listed or labeled door openings (fire rated). Brass material may not be used on fire-rated or labeled openings because of its low melting point.

5. **Determine the Type of Finish**

   All steel and brass material hinges can be plated to match the available finishes that are listed in ANSI/BHMA A156.18, *Materials and Finishes.* Most finishes are lacquered to resist oxidation or tarnishing of the finish. This will be extremely helpful during the specification process.

6. **Determine Handing**

   The hand of a hinge is determined from the outside of the door to which it is applied. Usually if the locked side of the door opens away (into the area) to the right, it takes a right-hand hinge (also referred to as RH). If it opens to the left, it takes a left-hand hinge (LH). (See Figure 7.9.)

7. **Determine Pin and Tip Style**

   There are a variety of tips from which to choose. (See Figure 7.15.) The standard in the industry is the **flat bottom tip.** This type of tip is normally furnished unless something else is specified. The *flush/concealed tip,* which is concealed inside the knuckle, is the second most commonly used tip. The *hospital tip,* which is used primarily in secure areas such as hospital mental wards and law enforcement detention centers, prevents hanging any objects on the tip of the hinge.

   Decorative type tips, such as *acorn, ball, steeple,* and *urn,* are also available from most manufacturers.

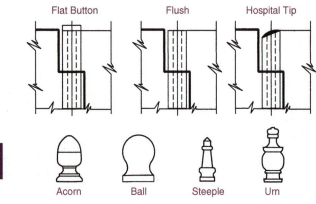

FIGURE 7.15 Pin and tip style. *Drawings courtesy of Door and Hardware Institute, "Butts and Hinges," Tech Talk, by H. Matt Bouchard, Jr. AHC.*

8. **Electric Hinges**

   Over the past 15 years, hinge manufacturers have made some changes that have revolutionized the hardware industry. With the introduction of electric hinges, we now have the ability to monitor the position of the door, transfer power, and incorporate both functions into the same hinge. With this, we now have the ability to electrify other hardware items such as locks and exit devices.

   Electric hinges can be modified—either exposed on the surface of the hinge or concealed in the hinge. When concealed, the modifications are not visible and normally go undetected by personnel using the openings.

   Electrically modified hinges are for low-voltage power transfer only (50 volts or less). Normal modifications are made to full mortise hinges. Monitoring can be supplied on a half surface hinge, however, when the need arises.

   Most manufacturers require the use of a mortar box or jamb box to protect the wire terminations on the inside of the frame. If this box is not used, the grout that may be poured into the frame will destroy the wiring and usually will void the product's warranty.

   The spring comes in two basic types: *single acting* (full mortise, half surface) and *double acting* (full mortise, half surface). Most likely, the only time the designer will need this type of hinge is when designing a restaurant where this type of hinge is used for the entrance and exit doors of the kitchen.

The smooth operation resulting from the use of continuous hinges, a relatively new concept in hanging doors, extends the life of the door opening. This type of hinge is usually of a continuous geared type, or the traditional piano hinge, which are similar to traditional hinges in that they have a rolled knuckle and pin. (See Figure 7.16.) These hinges distribute the weight of the door along the full height of the door frame; thus, the localized stress normally found with butt hinges and pivots is removed.[6]

LOCKS

The needs of the client and the expected usage of a lock will determine what type of lock will be selected. For residential uses, security is probably the foremost criterion, whereas for a commercial installation, heavy usage will necessitate not only a secure lock but also one built to withstand constant use.

There are three weights or grades of locks: (1) heavy duty (most expensive); (2) standard duty; and (3) light duty or builders grade (least expensive). The first two types are made of solid metal with a polished, brushed, or antique finish. The light duty grade has a painted or plated finish that may wear off.

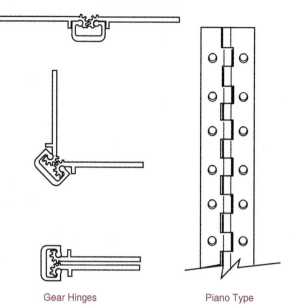
Continuous Hinges

Gear Hinges   Piano Type

FIGURE 7.16 Continuous hinges, gear hinges, and piano-type hinges. *Drawings courtesy of Door and Hardware Institute, "Butts and Hinges," Tech Talk, by H. Matt Bouchard, Jr. AHC.*

Types of Locks

The Door and Hardware Institute describes the four types of locks as follows (see Figure 7.17):

1. **Bored type.** These types of locks are installed in a door having two round holes at right angles to one another, one through the face of the door to hold the lock body and the other in the edge of the door to receive the latch mechanism. When the two are joined together in the door, they comprise a complete latching or locking mechanism.

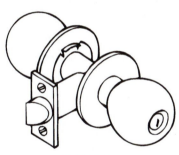
Bored Lock

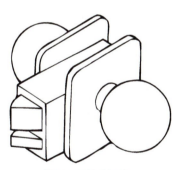
Preassembled Lock

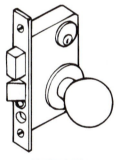
Mortise Lock

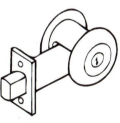
Bored Deadbolt

Bored Lever Handle Lock

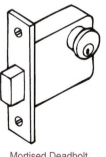
Mortised Deadbolt

FIGURE 7.17 Types of locks.

Bored type locks have the keyway (cylinder) and/or locking device, such as push or turn buttons, in the knobs. They are available in three weights: heavy, standard, and light duty.

The assembly must be tight on the door and without excessive play. Knobs should be held securely in place without screws, and a locked knob should not be removable. **Roses** should be threaded or secured firmly to the body mechanism. The trim has an important effect in this type of lock because working parts fit directly into the trim. The regular backset for a bored lock is 2 3/4 inches, but it may vary from 2 3/8 to 42 inches.

2. *Preassembled type.* The preassembled lock is installed in a rectangular notch cut into the door edge. This lock has all its parts assembled as a unit at the factory; when installed, little or no disassembly is required. Preassembled type locks have the keyway (cylinder) in the knob. Locking devices may be in the knob or in the inner case. The regular backset is 2 3/4 inches. Preassembled type locks are available only in a heavy-duty weight.

3. *Mortise lock.* A mortise lock is installed in a prepared recess (mortise) in a door. The working mechanism is contained in a rectangular-shaped case with appropriate holes into which the required components (cylinder, knob, and turn-piece spindles) are inserted to complete the working assembly. The regular backset is 2 3/4 inches. Mortise locks are available in heavy-duty and standard-duty weights. **Armored** fronts are also available. Security, function, and handing are all factors to be considered with regard to mortise locks. To provide a complete working unit, mortise locks, except for those with **deadlock (deadbolt)** function only, must be installed with knobs, levers, and other items of trim.[7]

4. *Rim lock.* Rim locks were first used at the beginning of the eighteenth century and are attached to the inside of the door stile. They are used today in restoration work or in new homes of medieval English, Salt Box, or Cape Cod styles. Because rim locks are exposed to view, the case and other parts are finished brass. The lock achieves its function by means of various types of bolts. The bolt is a bar of metal that projects out of the lock into a strike prepared to receive it.

The traditional style of surface-mounted rim (or box) locks for doors has been authentically recreated by Baldwin and designed in cooperation with leading museums and historical foundations.[8]

Hardware

Hardware, in general, may be

- *Universal.* Used in any position (example: surface bolt).
- *Reversible.* Hand can be changed by revolving from left to right or by turning upside down or by reversing some part of the mechanism (example: many types of locks and latches).
- *Handed (not reversible).* Used only on doors of the hand for which designed (example: most **rabbeted** front door locks and latches.

Although the hardware item specified may be reversible, or even universal, it is good practice to identify the hand completely, in accordance with the convention stated here.[9]

The simplest type of door hardware is the passage set, in which both knobs are always free and there is no locking mechanism. An example would be the door between a living room, dining room, and a hallway. A **springlatch** holds this type of door closed.

Bathroom doors require a privacy lock. This type locks from the inside in several ways. Some have a push button located on the interior rose; some have a turn or push button in the interior knob; and others have a turnpiece that activates a bolt. In an emergency, all privacy locks have some means of opening from the outside, either with use of an emergency release key or a screwdriver.

When the type of use has been decided, the style of the handle, rose, and finish is selected. There are many shapes of knobs (e.g., ball, round with a semi-flat face, or round with a concave face, which may be decorated). Knobs may be made of metal, glass, porcelain, or wood. Grip handle entrance locks combine the convenience of button-in-the-knob locking with traditional grip handle elegance. Grip handles should be of cast brass or cast bronze. Interior colonial doors may have a thumb latch installed on the stile surface.

Lever handles are used in private residences and are easier for those with arthritic hands to operate. Levers are also the preferred type for ADA requirements; however, door latch and lock sets with door knobs are acceptable. The maximum torque for all door controls (e.g., latch and lock sets, door levers, etc.) is 8 foot-pounds, with 5 foot-pounds preferred.

When persons with low or no vision have access to areas that might be dangerous, such as a doorway leading down to stairs, the knob must be knurled or ridged to provide a tactile warning.

Schlage manufactures an access bow key with a variety of sizes. The standard bow is 1" across; Hotel bows are 1.5"; Access bows are 1.75"; and the Everest bows are 1.2" across. All Everest key control systems are patented and can only be copied by Schlage locksmiths. For recognition by people with low or no vision, the larger bow is easily identified. Schlage also stamps "DO NOT DUPLICATE" on any bow of all versions of its keys at no extra charge, when specified.

Locks, which include all operating mechanisms, come in numerous finishes, including brass, bronze, chrome, and stainless steel, in bright polish, satin, antique, or oil rubbed. Baldwin Hardware Company first produced brass hardware using physical vapor deposition (PVD), a process that uses low voltage ionization to create a stacked finish that is practically indestructible. This finish, when used on brass products from Baldwin, is called the Lifetime finish.[10]

Clear finishes take the color of the base metal in the product and may be either high or low luster. Applied finishes result from the addition (by plating) of a second metal, a synthetic enamel, or other material. The most popular of the plated finishes are the chromiums, both polished and satin.

Polished brass and bronze finishes are produced by buffing or polishing the metal to a high gloss before applying a synthetic coating. Satin brass and natural bronze finishes are obtained by dry buffing or scouring; the resultant finish is then coated.

Roses are used to cover the bored hole in the door and may be round or square, decorated or plain. Some locks, particularly the mortise type, have **escutcheon** plates instead of roses. These are usually rectangular in shape.

Strictly speaking, the door itself is only right or left hand; the locks and the latches may be reverse bevel. It is necessary, however, to include the term *reverse* and to specify in accordance with the conventions on pages 161–162. This will prevent any confusion regarding what side is the outside, which is especially important when different finishes are desired on opposite sides of the door.

All Schlage locks are reversible. The correct hand, however, should be shown for all pin tumbler locks (small cylindrical pins that form obstacles unless the proper key is used) so they may be assembled to assure that keyholes are in the upright position. Hand information is also necessary to ensure proper finish of latchbolt and strike for locks that are to be installed on reverse-bevel doors. The assembly must be followed correctly to determine the hand of the door. Some locks, however, must be ordered as right- or left-handed.

Security and Electronic Locking Systems

Security has become an important feature of lockset selection. Most companies manufacture a lockset for which a key must be used on the outside. The lock features simultaneous retraction of both the latch and the deadbolt from the inside by turning the knob or lever, providing panic-proof (emergency) exiting. Such locks are recommended by police and fire departments to provide compliance with life safety and security codes.

The technological advances of the twenty-first century have revolutionized the way we secure commercial and residential buildings. Typically, biometric ID technologies use physiological characteristics that are unique to each individual, such as fingerprints, face recognition, DNA, hand and palm geometry, iris recognition, and odor or scent. The system assigns each person a unique ID number, based on biological data. No two persons carry the same biological data. Therefore, biometrics offer the highest level of security available today.[11]

Schlage Recognition Systems brings the true security and convenience of biometric technology easily within reach of most access control applications. The HandKey II utilizes field-proven hand geometry technology that maps and verifies the size and shape of a person's hand all in less than one second.[12]

One of the advancements in the security market was the introduction of the deadbolt and door lock replacement system. This high-security, concealed system was ingeniously designed to provide the strength of multiple deadbolts or door locks but with the aesthetics and simplicity of a single lock.

These advances in security have expanded to the residential market as well. For instance, Smartcode with Home Connect technology, produced by Kwikset, enables the consumer to:

- Lock and unlock remotely by using a motor-driven deadbolt
- Monitor and control the door locks from anywhere in the world through the Internet or a smartphone
- Arm and disarm the home's security system right at the lock or via the Internet
- Schedule when codes are allowed to access your home
- Check the lock status through the Internet or a smartphone
- Control the door lock through a home automation touch panel or remote
- Receive an e-mail, phone call, or text detailing who unlocked the door and when
- Have peace of mind because of increased security and convenience[13]

The system can employ up to 30 codes of four to eight digits in length. The system also utilizes a tapered deadbolt, which compensates for door misalignment conditions, such as a warped door.

Door Controls

A door should be controlled at the desired limit of its opening cycle to prevent damage to an adjacent wall or column, to equipment, to the door, or to its hardware. This control is achieved by stops and holders, which may be located on the floor, the wall, or overhead.

Floor stops are available in varied heights, sizes, shapes, and functions. They may have a mechanism, such as a hook or friction device, to hold the door open at the user's option. The height of the door from the floor, shape of the stops, and location of the stops in relation to traffic are important considerations.

Wall stops or bumpers have the advantage of being located where they do not conflict with floor coverings or cleaning equipment. Thus, they do not constitute a traffic hazard.

For commercial installations, there are two commonly used types of floor holders—the spring-loaded "step-on" type and the lever or "flip-down" type. Neither type acts as a stop.

Overhead closers used in commercial installations may be either surface mounted or concealed. (See Figure 7.18.) These devices are a combination of a spring and an oil-cushioned piston that dampens the closing action inside a cylinder. Surface-mounted closers are more accessible for maintenance, but concealed closers are more aesthetically pleasing. An actuator for power operations consists of a round plate with the ADA symbol on it. This actuator provides less than a 5.0 lb. opening force on a 36" wide door. A three-second delay is required to provide safe passage for a disabled person.

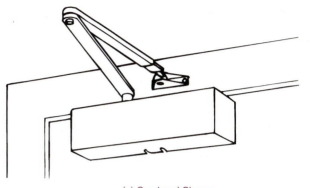
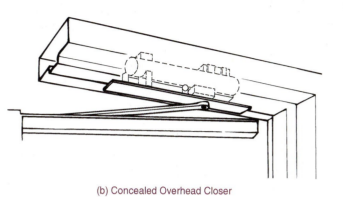

(a) Overhead Closer

(b) Concealed Overhead Closer

FIGURE 7.18 Overhead door controls.

In public buildings, all doors must open out for fire safety. A push plate is attached to the door, or a fire exit bar or panic bar is used. Slight pressure of the bar releases the rod and latch. For use by individuals with disabilities, this bar should be able to be operated with a maximum of 8 pounds of pressure.

An electronic eye is not a security measure but rather provides ease of access. When the beam is broken (i.e., someone steps in its path), the door opens. Locks that open without a key are frequently used for security purposes. For example, hotels use a specially coded plastic key card, similar to a credit card; the code is changed when each guest checks out. Numbered combinations may also be used. The combination may be changed easily, thus eliminating the need to reissue keys. More sophisticated systems can scan and identify the unique pattern of blood cells inside a person's eye; recognize fingerprints or the distinctive profile of a hand; or even respond to a voice whose digitized sound was previously stored in the system.

Plastic key cards and combination codes are also often used in restrooms of office buildings and other special areas where access is restricted to certain personnel. In some cases the key cards are also used for time card purposes.

To eliminate having to carry several keys for residential use, all the locksets for exterior doors may be keyed the same. This universal keying may be done when the locks are ordered, or a locksmith can make the changes later (but at a greater expense).

When specifying locksets, the following information must be provided: manufacturer's name and style number, finish, style of knob and rose, backset, wood or metal door, thickness of door, and door handing.

Lockset installation should be performed by a professional locksmith or carpenter to ensure correct fit (i.e., no door rattles or other fitting problems).

Hospital Hardware

Hardware for hospitals and health-related institutions includes items that might not be found in any other type of building. Because the hardware may be used by individuals who are aged, sick, or have disabilities, it must meet all the ADA requirements of safety, security, and protection and yet be operable with a minimum amount of effort.

Modifications of hinges may include hospital tips for added safety, special length and shape of leaves to swing doors clear of an opening, and hinges of special sizes and gauges to carry the weight of lead-lined doors. Hospital pulls are designed to be mounted with the open end down, allowing the door to be operated by the wrist, arm, or forearm when the hands are occupied.

bibliography

Buchard, Matt, Jr., AHC, "Butts and Hinges." *Tech Talk*. McLean, VA: Door and Hardware Institute, 1998.

Composite Panel Association. *Technical Bulletin, Particleboard and MDF for Shelving*. Gaithersburg, MD: Composite Panel Association, 1998.

glossary

Armored. Two plates are used to cover the lock mechanism in order to prevent tampering.

Astragal. Vertical strip of wood with weather stripping.

Backplate. An applied decorative moulding used on ceilings above a chandelier or ceiling fan.

Backset. The horizontal distance from the center of the face-bored hole to the edge of the door.

Base shoe. Moulding used next to the floor.

Bed moulding. Cornice moulding.

Brickmould. Exterior wood moulding to cover gap between a door or window and its frame.

Butt hinges. Two metal plates joined with a pin, one being fastened to the door jamb or frame and the other to the door.

Casing. The exposed trim moulding around a door or window.

Caulk. To fill a joint with resilient mastic. Also spelled *calk*.

Chair rail. Strip of wood or moulding that is placed on a wall at the same height as the back of a chair to protect the wall from damage.

Cornice. An ornamental moulding between the ceiling and the top of the wall.

Countersunk. Hole prepared with a bevel to enable the tapered head of a screw to be inserted flush with the surface.

Crown moulding. A moulding at the top of the cornice.

Dado. A groove cut in wood to receive and position another member.

Deadlock (Deadbolt). Hardened steel bolt with a square head operated by a key or turn piece.

Door and Hardware Institute (DHI). The organization that represents the industry.

Escutcheon. Plate that surrounds the keyhole and/or handle.

Flatback. A hinge that has a gap between the leaves of approximately 5/32 of an inch.

Flat bottom tip. Bottom of hinge is falt with the hinge.

Handing. The direction the door opens and placement of the handle.

Knuckle Cylindrical part of the hinge through which the pin passes.

Leaves. Flat plates of a pair of hinges.

Lights. Small panes of glass. Usually rectangular in shape.

Mitered. Two cuts at a 45° angle to form a right angle.

Mortised. Set into the surface.

Ogee sticking. A double curved shape resembling an S shape.

Ovolo. A convex moulding, usually a quarter of a circle.

Pins. The bolts of metal holding the leaves together.

Polymer. A high-molecular-weight compound from which mouldings are made.

Prehung. Frame and door packaged as one unit.

Rabbeted. A groove cut across the grain of the face of a member at an edge or end to receive the edge or end thickness of another member.

Rails. Cross members of paneling (walls or doors).

Rose. The plate, usually round, that covers the bored hole on the face of the door.

Shoji. Japanese room divider or window consisting of a light wooden frame covered with a translucent material, originally rice paper, but now a less vulnerable manmade material.

Springlatch. Latch with a spring rather than a locking action.

Sticking. The shape of moulding.

Stiles. Vertical members of paneling (walls or doors).

Stringer. A diagonal element supporting the treads and risers in a flight of stairs.

Swaging. A slight offset to the hinge at the barrel.

Template hardware. Hardware that exactly matches a master template drawing, as to spacing of all holes and dimensions.

Transom. The glass area above a door.

endnotes

1. Focal Point Architectural Products, www.focalpointproducts.com

2. Architectural Woodwork Standards, p. 209

3. Therma-Tru Doors, www.thermatru.com

4. Peachtree Doors and Windows, www.peachtreedoor.com

5. Basic Architectural Hardware, McLean VA: Door and Hardware Institute, 1985

6. "Butts and Hinges," *Tech Talk*, McLean VA: Door and Hardware Institute 1998, p. 1

7. Ibid.

8. Baldwin Hardware, www.baldwinhardware.com

9. Chown Hardware, www.chown.com

10. Baldwin Hardware, www.baldwinhardware.com

11. Ingersoll Rand, www.securitytechnologies.com

12. Ibid.

13. Kwikset, www.kwikset.com

8 Cabinet Construction

In this chapter, you will:

- Develop an understanding of design solutions affecting construction systems related to cabinets and drawers

- Examine the importance of industry-specific regulations related to cabinet and drawer construction and installation

- Recognize types of cabinets and their fabrication and installation methods, as well as maintenance requirements

- Distinguish between exposed surfaces and concealed surfaces—and understand appropriate construction methods related to each

- Demonstrate an understanding of the nature and value of integrated design practices related to cabinet and drawer construction

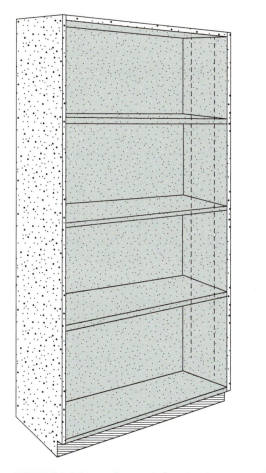

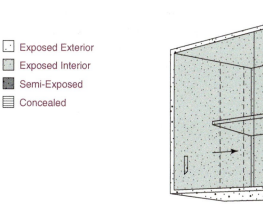

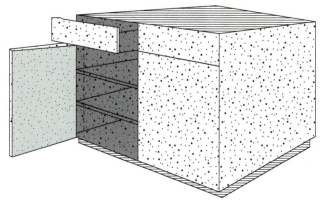

⬜	Exposed Exterior
▨	Exposed Interior
▓	Semi-Exposed
▤	Concealed

FIGURE 8.1 Cabinet surface terminology. *Drawings courtesy of the Architectural Woodwork Institute.*

To select or design well-made cabinet work, it is necessary to become familiar with furniture construction. By studying casework joints, specifiers will be able to compare and contrast similar items and make an informed decision on which piece of furniture, or which group of cabinets, offers the most value for the money.

The Architectural Woodwork Standards for cabinet construction are below.

ECONOMY GRADE defines the minimum quality requirements for a project's workmanship, materials, or installation and is typically reserved for woodwork that is not in public view, such as in mechanical rooms and utility areas.

CUSTOM GRADE is typically specified for and adequately covers most high-quality architectural woodwork, providing a well-defined degree of control over a project's quality of materials, workmanship, or installation.

PREMIUM GRADE is typically specified for use in those areas of a project where the highest level of quality, materials, workmanship, and installation is required.[1]

These may be mixed within a single project. Limitless design possibilities and a wide variety of lumber and veneer species, along with decorative laminates, factory finishes, and profiles, are available in all three grades of plywood panel construction as presented in Chapter 5.

When designing casework and specifying materials, several parts need definition. The Architectural Woodwork Institute (AWI) offers the following "Identification of Surfaces," which are illustrated in Figure 8.1.

Exposed Surfaces

Exposed exterior surfaces are all viewable exterior surfaces, including:

- All surfaces, including knee spaces, that can be seen when drawers and doors are closed

- The underside of cabinet bottoms higher than 42" (1,067-mm) above a finished floor, including the bottom of cabinets and the bottom periphery of light valances
- Cabinet tops lower than 80" (2,032-mm) above a finished floor; also included are cabinet tops 80" (2,032-mm) and higher that can be seen from an upper floor or building level
- The front edges of tops, bottoms, nailers, ends, stretchers, shelves, and divisions that can be seen
- Slanted cabinet tops that can be seen

Exposed interior surfaces are all viewable interior surfaces. These surfaces might be seen behind transparent doors or inside open casework, such as:

- Shelves—including edgebanding
- Partitions and divisions
- The inside surfaces of cabinet top components that are 36" (914-mm) or higher above a finished floor and the inside face of bottoms, backs, and ends, including pullouts
- Inside door faces and applied drawer fronts

Semi-exposed surfaces are inside surfaces that can be seen only when drawers or doors are open, including:

- Shelves—including edgebanding
- Divisions
- The inside face of inside backs, ends, and bottoms—including a bank of drawers and inside surfaces of cabinet top members that are 36" (914-mm) or higher above a finished floor
- The backs, bottom, sub-fronts, and sides of drawers
- The underside of cabinet bottoms that are between 24" (610-mm) and 42" (1,067-mm) above a finished floor
- Drawer stretchers, dust panels, and security panels

Concealed Surfaces

Concealed surfaces are interior or exterior covered surfaces or surfaces that generally cannot be seen, such as:

- Toe space—unless otherwise noted
- Stretchers, solid sub-tops, and sleepers
- The underside of cabinet bottoms that are set lower than 24" (610-mm) above a finished floor
- The flat tops of cabinets that are 80" (2,032-mm) or higher above a finished floor—unless the tops are able to be seen from an upper building level or floor
- The edges of adjustable shelves that cannot be seen
- The underside of drawer aprons, countertops, and knee spaces
- The faces of cabinet ends of adjoining units[2]

Drawers and Doors

Door and drawer fronts may use one of five different edge profiles (see Figure 8.2):

1. Square edge with thin applied band
2. Radius edge with thick applied band
3. Square edge with thick applied band

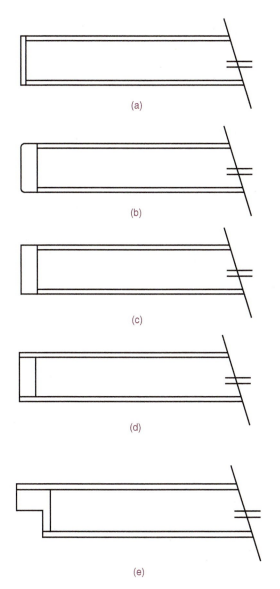

(a)

(b)

(c)

(d)

(e)

FIGURE 8.2 Common edge profiles: (a) square edge with thin applied band; (b) radius edge with thick applied band; (c) square edge with thick applied band; (d) square edge with inset band; (e) lipped edge with inset band. *Drawings courtesy of the Architectural Woodwork Institute.*

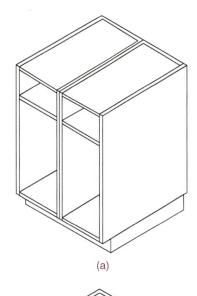

(a)

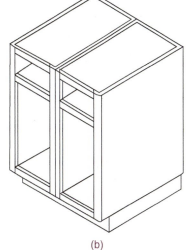

(b)

FIGURE 8.3 Construction types: (a) Type A, frameless and (b) Type B face-frame. *Drawings courtesy of the Architectural Woodwork Institute.*

4. Square edge with inset band

5. Lipped edge with inset band[3]

The construction type of the casework is identified as either Type A or Type B. (See Figure 8.3.) Type A is a frameless construction; the front edge of the cabinet body components are edgebanded. Type B is a face-frame construction; the front edge of the cabinet body components are overlaid with a frame.[4]

The interface style for cabinets and doors includes the following **overlay** styles, which differ depending on whether the construction type is Type A or Type B. (See Figure 8.4a and b.)

- *Flush overlay.* Drawer and door faces cover the body members of the cabinet; spaces are set between face surfaces to allow for operating clearance; default for either Type A or Type B casework.

- *Reveal overlay.* Drawer and door faces partially cover face frame or body members of the cabinet and allow space between the face surfaces in order to provide decorative reveals[5]

- *Lipped door.* Rabbet cut appears on three edges, with lip covering the gap between the case and drawer front

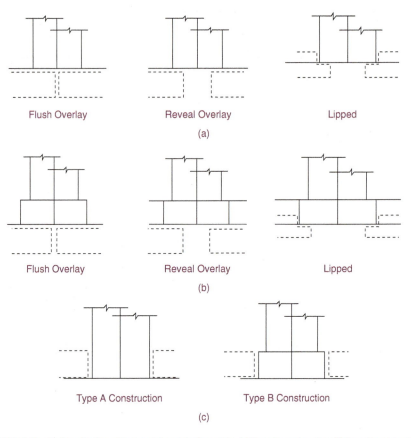

Flush Overlay   Reveal Overlay   Lipped

(a)

Flush Overlay   Reveal Overlay   Lipped

(b)

Type A Construction   Type B Construction

(c)

FIGURE 8.4 Terminology for the cabinet and door interface style: (a) Type A construction; (b) Type B construction; (c) Flush inset for Types A and B constructions. *Drawings courtesy of the Architectural Woodwork Institute.*

Drawer bottoms should always provide a minimum thickness of 1/4 inch and should be captured into dados on fronts, backs, and sides in order to allow for a bottom panel that is permanently locked into position.

Another interface style for cabinets and doors is flush inset, which is illustrated in Figure 8.4c.

Wood Cabinets

For a traditional type of paneling, stile-and-rail construction is used, which consists of a panel that may be flat, raised, or have a beveled edge. The vertical side strips are called **stiles,** and the horizontal strips at the top and bottom are called rails.

Rails, stiles, and **mullions** may themselves be shaped into an **ovolo** or **ogee** moulding; or, to give a more intricate design, a separate moulding may be added. For raised panels under 10 inches in width, solid lumber may be used in custom grade. For premium grade or wider panels, plywood is used with an attached edge of solid lumber, which is then beveled.

The grain or patterned faces for stile-and-rail drawer fronts for all grades will run either vertically or horizontally for the entire project at the manufacturer's discretion. Doors will be vertical. (See Figure 8.5.)

Unlike the stile-and-rail doors and drawer fronts, the layout requirements of grained or patterned faces varies according to the grade of the plywood panel. (See Figure 8.6.)

For economy grades, the drawer fronts will run either vertically or horizontally for the entire project at the manufacturer's discretion. Doors will be vertical, and mismatch is allowed. For custom grades, the doors, drawer fronts, and false fronts will run and match vertically within each cabinet unit. For premium grades, the doors, drawer fronts, and false fronts will run and match vertically within each cabinet unit and match across multiple cabinet faces in one elevation; at the cathedral grain, the crown will point up and run in the same direction

FIGURE 8.5 Stile-and-rail doors and drawer fronts for all grades. *Drawings courtesy of the Architectural Woodwork Institute.*

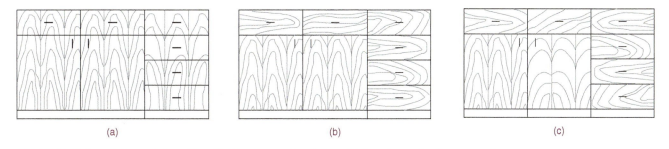

(a)   (b)   (c)

FIGURE 8.6 Flush panel doors and drawer fronts for the various grades of plywood: (a) premium grade; (b) custom grade; (c) economy grade. *Drawings courtesy of the Architectural Woodwork Institute.*

for the entire project. The manufacturer may specify blue print or sequence matching of the door, drawer fronts, and false fronts.

Panels are assembled all in one by means of mortise and/or **dowel joints.** At the joining of the panel and the stiles and rails, a small space is left to allow for the panel's natural expansion and contraction. This type of construction is known as *floating panel construction* and is recommended in areas where there are great variations in humidity. Panels that are glued have no allowance for this expansion and contraction and may split if movement is excessive. (See Figures 8.7 and 8.8.)

Because the detail and design options in this type of paneling are virtually unlimited, the AWI suggests that the following minimum information be provided for proper estimation and specification:

- Panel layout
- Grain patterns and relationships
- Stile-and-rail construction
- Moulding details
- Panel construction
- Joinery techniques[6]

Drawer Guides

Drawer guides, an important feature of well-made casework, may be constructed of wood or metal. If wood is selected, both male and female parts should be made of wood. Wood drawer guides are found mainly in wood furniture and are usually centered under the drawer, but they may also be attached to the side of the case, with the drawer sides being dadoed to accommodate the wood guide. The reverse procedure may also be used, with the guide attached to the drawer side and the frame dados receiving the guide. Paste wax should be applied to the wood guides to facilitate movement.

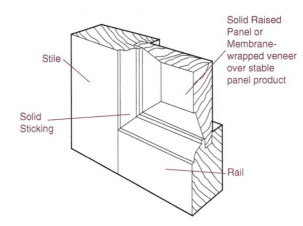

Stile

Solid Raised
Panel or
Membrane-
wrapped veneer
over stable
panel product

Solid
Sticking

Rail

Solid Raised Panel - Figure 400-15

Stile

Rim Raised Panel

Solid
Sticking

Rail

Rim Raised Panel - Figure 400-16

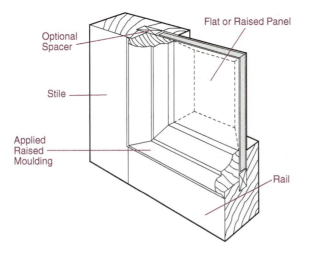

Optional
Spacer

Flat or Raised Panel

Stile

Applied
Raised
Moulding

Rail

Applied Moulding - Figure 400-17

FIGURE 8.7 Panel cabinet doors. These examples illustrate three styles of raised-panel and flat-panel doors. Applied moulding can be used for glass inserts as well. *Drawing courtesy of the Architectural Woodwork Institute.*

DRAWER SLIDE SELECTION GUIDE

The type of metal drawer slide selected depends on several factors: travel, width of drawer, action, and load factors.

Table 8.1 serves as both a checklist and a starting point for the discussion of a wide variety of drawer slide systems. While by no means exhaustive, the characteristics described are

Spline Joint
Used to strengthen and align faces when gluing panels in width or length, including items requiring site assembly.

Stub Tenon
Joinery method for assembling stile- and rail-type frames that are additionally supported, such as web or skeleton case frames.

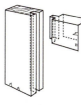

Haunch Mortise and Tenon Joint
Joinery method for assembling paneled doors or stile- and rail-type paneling.

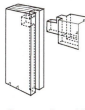

Conventional Mortise and Tenon Joint
Joinery method for assembling square-edged surfaces such as case face frames.

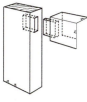

Dowel Joint
Alternative joinery method serving same function as Conventional Mortise and Tenon.

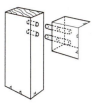

French Dovetail Joint
Method for joining drawer sides to fronts when fronts conceal metal extension slides or overlay the case faces.

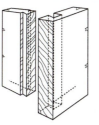

Conventional Dovetail Joint
Traditional method for joining drawer sides to fronts or backs. Usually limited to flush- or lipped-type drawers.

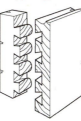

Drawer Lock-Joint
Another joinery method for joining drawer sides to fronts. Usually used for flush-type installation but can be adapted to lip- or overlay-type drawers.

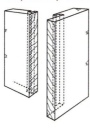

Exposed End Details
Illustrates attachment of finished end of case body to front frame using a butt joint and a lock mitered joint.

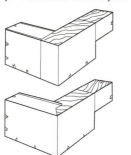

Through Dado Conventional joint used for assembly of case body members. Dado not concealed by application of case face frame.

Blind Dado Variation of Through Dado with applied edge "stopping" or concealing dado groove.

Stop Dado Another method of concealing dado exposure. Applicable when veneer edging or solid lumber is used. Exposed End Detail illustrates attachment of finished end of case body to front frame using butt joint.

Dowel Joint Fast becoming an industry standard assembly method, this versatile joinery technique is often based on 32 mm spacing of dowels.

FIGURE 8.8 Detail nomenclature. *Drawing courtesy of the Architectural Woodwork Institute.*

Table 8.1 Drawer Slide Selection Guide

Degree of Extension	• STANDARD EXTENSION—All but 4–6" of drawer body extends out of cabinet • FULL EXTENSION—Entire drawer body extends out to face of cabinet • FULL EXTENSION WITH OVERTRAVEL—Entire drawer body extends beyond the face of cabinet
Static Load Capacity	• 50 Pounds—Residential/Light Commercial • 75 Pounds—Commercial • 100 Pounds—Heavy Duty • Over 100 Pounds—Special Conditions, Extra Heavy Duty
Dynamic Load Capacity	• 30 Pounds; 35,000 cycles—Residential/Light Commercial • 50 Pounds; 50,000 cycles—Commercial • 75 Pounds; 100,000 cycles—Heavy Duty
Removal Stop	• INTEGRAL STOP—Requires ten times the normal opening force to remove drawer • POSITIVE STOP—Latch(es) which must be operated/opened to remove drawer
Closing	• SELF-CLOSING/STAY CLOSED—Drawer slides will self-close with their related dynamic load when the drawer is 2" from the fully closed position and not bounce open when properly adjusted
Metal Sided Systems	In recent years several hardware manufacturers have developed "drawer systems" of one type or another, nearly all proprietary. In addition to the above criteria, the following should be considered for these systems prior to approval for use. • POSITIVE STOP—Drawer must stop within itself and not rely on the drawer front to stop it • PULLOUT STRENGTH—Systems must demonstrate sufficient strength of attachment of front to sides—design professional should evaluate and approve individually

Source: Table reproduced with permission of the Architectural Woodwork Institute.

Cabinet Construction

182

often considered the most important by the client, the design professional, and the woodwork manufacturer. The selection of the slide characteristics will affect the usefulness of the cabinets. Careful consideration should be given to avoid "overspecifying" for the purpose intended. It is advisable that the owner and the design professional involve an AWI/AWMAC member manufacturer in the design and selection process early in the project. Dimensions use the inch-pound convention.

According to Knape and Vogt (KV), each drawer slide model has unique performance characteristics that are determined by the intended application for which it is designed. There are many different slides available for a variety of applications; contractors should choose the slide that best fits their application.

Length

Slide length is typically driven by drawer box construction. Slide length does not have an impact on overall application performance.

Travel

Travel is the maximum extension compared to the closed length. Most slides are either 3/4 or full travel; however, special extension lengths are available with modified travel. In general, the longer the travel, the less load a slide can carry.

- A 3/4 travel slide has extension to approximately 75 percent of its length.

- A full travel slide has extension approximately equal to its length.

- An over travel slide extends beyond its length.

Width

Drawer width affects the rigidity of the installation. In wide drawers, the slides have the potential to rack from side to side. Excessive racking can degrade performance and shorten slide life.

Action

The type of sliding mechanism used to carry the load affects its slide performance, motion, noise, and overall operation. KV slides use rollers, ball bearings, friction fits, or any combination in achieving movement. In general, better performance requires more rollers or ball bearings to support and distribute large loads.

Size

In addition to a slide's load rating, the physical size of the application is a consideration. Drawers having unusual width, depth, or height require careful consideration to determine which slide best suits the application.

Operating Clearance

Drawer slides operate within a specified clearance (the space between the drawer and the case). The clearance must be strictly held within the specified tolerances. When the clearance is too wide or too narrow, the slide experiences additional forces and stresses that reduce its expected performance and life.

KV designates drawer slides in "Pound Class" categories and uses dynamic (rather than static) loading to determine load ratings.

The "Pound Class" categories are used within the slide industry as general guidelines for drawer slide selection. However, these categories are not the same as actual load ratings, which vary based on slide length, application, and casegoods construction.

Static Loads

A **static load** is a resting load without any motion. Static load capacity is significantly higher than dynamic load capacity.

Dynamic Loads

A **dynamic load** is a load in motion. When a dynamic load gains momentum, it induces more stress and fatigue. Slides must withstand more forces when in motion than when static.

Dynamic loads affect the life and performance of any slide. Other factors affecting performance are:

- An evenly or unevenly distributed load
- A centered or off-centered load
- The load's center of gravity relative to the slide's centerline of travel
- The number of lifecycles required
- The speed or frequency of the cycles
- The length of cycle stroke
- The percent of travel
- The stopping force and distance[7]

The common types of slide mounting include side mount, center mount, and concealed bottom mount. Side mount applications require adequate side clearance and drawer side height. Center mount applications have a limited selection and are typically classed as utility slides. Concealed bottom mount applications are prevalent in the kitchen cabinet industry and allow for slide concealment with the proper drawer box construction.

Common slide features include "stay closed," "self-closing," and "soft-closing." Stay closed slides have a built-in feature to prevent unintentional opening. Self-closing slides have a built-in feature that will close a drawer without assistance from 1.5 to 3 inches of closure. Soft-closing slides have a built-in feature similar to self-closing with the added benefit of a controlled soft closure.

Cabinet Hardware

According to the AWI, architectural cabinet hinges will usually be furnished from the manufacturer's stock, unless otherwise specified. Table 8.2 highlights the four most common hinge types.

Table 8.2 — Hinge Selection Guide

Hinge Type	Butt	Wraparound	Pivot	European Style
Applications	Conventional Flush with Face Frame	Conventional Reveal Overlay	Reveal Overlay Flush Overlay	Conventional Flush without Face Frame Reveal Overlay Flush Overlay
Strength	High	Very High	Moderate	Moderate
Concealed when closed	No	No	Semi	Yes
Requires mortising	Yes	Occasionally	Usually	Yes
Cost of hinge	Low	Moderate	Low	Moderate
Ease of installation	Moderate	Easy	Moderate	Very Easy
Easily adjusted after installation	No	No	No	Yes
Remarks	Door requires hardwood edge	Exposed knuckle and hinge body	Door requires hardwood edge	1. Specify degree of opening 2. No catch required on self-closing styles

CONCEALED 35-MM CUP HINGE INSTALLATION REQUIREMENTS

The 35-mm cup **concealed hinges** require plastic insertion dowels to receive the screws of the hinge and 5-mm "Euroscrews" to attach the baseplate. The attachment of hinge bodies to particleboard or fiberboard doors with wood screws in the absence of the plastic insertion dowels is not acceptable in premium or custom grades. Manufacturers may use other solutions to assure long-term functionality, as agreed to between the buyer and the seller.[8] (See Figure 8.9.)

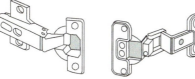
FIGURE 8.9 Concealed hinge style. *Courtesy of the Architectural Woodwork Institute.*

Grass offers a European-type hinge with a lifetime warranty. There are two different methods of installation: slide-on and snap-on.

Exposed hinges, which have visible knuckles, are usually used for traditional type cabinets. In contrast, the European-type hinge is completely hidden from view.

A piano hinge or continuous hinge is used on drop-leaf desks and on the doors of some fine furniture. Because piano hinges are installed the whole length of the edge, they support the door's weight of the door in an efficient manner.

Cabinet doors and drawers may be designed without pull hardware by using a finger pull either as part of the door or drawer construction, or by adding a piece of shaped wood, plastic, or metal to the front of the door. It is necessary to design these finger pulls in such a manner that the doors or drawers open easily (without someone breaking his or her finger nails).

Cabinet pull hardware consists of knobs (rounded or square) or handles (ranging from simple metal strips to ornately designed ones). The material from which this hardware is constructed may be wood, porcelain, plastic, or metal. It is necessary to select hardware that is compatible with the design of the cabinets or furniture. For traditional or period cabinets, authentic hardware should be chosen.

Some form of catch is needed to hold cabinet doors shut (see Figure 8.10). There are five different types of catches: **friction,** roller, magnetic, **bullet,** and touch catch. A friction catch, when engaged, is held in place by friction. A roller catch features a roller under tension that engages a recess in the **strike plate.** The magnet is the holding mechanism of a magnetic catch. In a bullet catch, a spring-actuated ball engages a depression in the plate. A touch catch releases automatically when the door is pushed. Many of these catches have elongated screw slots that enable the tension of the catch to be adjusted. Some hinges are spring loaded, eliminating the need for a catch.

Shelves

For shelves, or when the case body is exposed, the following construction methods are used: *Through dado* is the conventional joint used for assembly of case body members, and the dado is usually concealed by a case face frame. *Blind dado* has an applied edge "stopping"

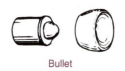

Bullet

Roller

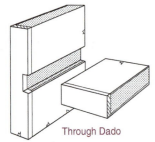

Through Dado

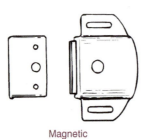

Magnetic

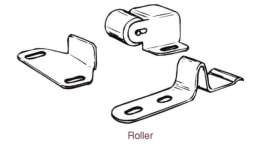

Roller

FIGURE 8.10 Cabinet catches.

Blind Dado

Stop Dado

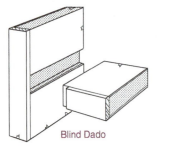

Dowel Joint

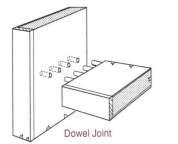

Euro. Screw

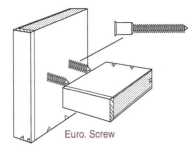

FIGURE 8.11 Through dado, blind dado, stop dado, dowel, and Euroscrew methods of shelf attachment. *Drawing courtesy of the Architectural Woodwork Institute.*

or concealing the dado **groove** and is used when the case body edge is exposed. **Stop** *dado* is applicable when veneer edging or solid lumber is exposed. (See Figure 8.11.)

Depending on their purpose, the span and thickness of shelves can vary. The following standards have been established by AWI:

- Closet and utility shelving ends and back cleats that support clothes rods or hooks should be 3/4 inch x 3 1/2 inch minimum.
- Closet and utility shelving ends and back cleats that do not support clothes rods or hooks should be 3/4 inch x 1 1/2 inch minimum.
- The thickness will be specified by the designer in relation to the anticipated load. If not specified, the shelf thickness should be a minimum of 3/4 inch.[9]

To increase a shelf's visible thickness, a dropped edge or applied piece of wood, called an **apron,** is used.

Particleboard (PB) and **Medium Density Fiberboard (MDF)** are often specified for shelves, and designers should be aware of fairly specific applications. For many common shelving applications, use Table 8.3. It is designed to quickly determine the amount of load that can be carried on either a PB or MDF shelving system. It is important to understand that the loads shown in the table are in units of pound per square foot (psf). This means that the load is evenly distributed over a one (1) square foot (144 inches) area of shelf. The distribution area can be in any shape. For example, it can be 12 inches square, 8 by 18 inches, or any combination of dimensions that equals 144 square inches. Kitchen cabinets, for example, normally will be designed for a uniform load of 15 pounds per square foot (psf), closets 25 psf, and books 40 psf.

The *Technical Bulletin, Particleboard and MDF for Shelving* may be obtained from the Composite Panel Association. Figure 8.1 gives common shelf nomenclature and displays some possible support situations.

To use Table 8.3, the first step is to determine the estimated shelf loading, then select the desired combination of shelf span, product type, and shelf thickness for the shelf design. The allowable spans, limited to a maximum of 36 inches. are found directly across from the shelf load values.

Shelf loads can vary greatly, and the amount a shelf deflects (or bends) depends on three factors: (1) the load, (2) the shelf span, and (3) the panel thickness. When heavy loads are anticipated, such as a bookshelf, which can easily reach 50 psf, it is important to note that the load acts only on the area where the object makes contact with the shelf. Potential shelf

Table 8.3 — Maximum Shelf Span in Inches for Uniform Loading

Maximum Shelf Spain (IN.)[1,2]

	Single Span[3]						Multiple Span[4]					
	Particleboard			Medium Density Fiberboard (MDF)			Particleboard			Medium Density Fiberboard (MDF)		
SHELF LOAD	SHELF THICKNESS			SHELF THICKNESS			SHELF THICKNESS			SHELF THICKNESS		
PSF[5]	1/2"	5/8"	3/4"	1/2"	5/8"	3/4"	1/2"	5/8"	3/4"	1/2"	5/8"	3/4"
50	13"	17"	20"	15"	19"	22"	13"	17"	20"	20"	25"	29"
45"	14"	18"	21"	16"	19"	23"	14"	18"	22"	21"	25"	30"
40	15"	18"	21"	16"	20"	24"	15"	19"	23"	21"	26"	31"
35	15"	19"	22"	17"	21"	25"	16"	20"	24"	22"	28"	33"
30	16"	20"	23"	18"	22"	26"	18"	22"	27"	23"	29"	34"
25	17"	21"	25"	19"	23"	28"	19"	24"	29"	25"	31"	36"
20	18"	22"	27"	20"	25"	30"	22"	27"	33"	27"	33"	36"
15	20"	25"	29"	22"	27"	33"	25"	32"	36"	29"	36"	36"
10	23"	28"	34"	25"	31"	36"	30"	36"	36"	34"	36"	36"

[1]For shelves 12 inches or less in depth with continuous support along the back edge of the shelf, the allowable span can be doubled.

[2]A maximum overhang beyond bracket or support not to exceed 6 inches may be added to these spans.

[3]Single Span: shelf simply supported (not fixed or fastened) at its ends only. (see Figure 1)

[4]Multiple Span: shelf simply supported at its ends with a center support. Span lengths refer to the distance from support to support, not the total shelf length. (see Figure 1)

[5]psf. = pounds per square foot

Source: Courtesy of Composite Panel Association. Table 1 of Technical Bulletin "Particleboard and MDF for Shelving."

stress must be considered carefully. It is recommended that the designer use the maximum concentrated load as the shelf loading value rather than the average of all objects to be loaded on the shelf. A bathroom scale can be used to estimate anticipated loads.

Table 8.3 was designed to limit deflections to a percentage of the shelf span. For example, a shelf with a 24" span can be expected to deflect a maximum of 0.10", while a 36" span will deflect 0.15" (slightly more than 1/8").[10]

When shelves are to be installed permanently, some form of **dado** may be used for positioning. The type used depends on the frame construction. Another permanent installation uses a wood quarter round on which to rest the shelf. If, however, the shelves are to be adjustable, there are several methods of support. The type used in fine china cabinets is a metal shelf pin. A number of blind holes, usually in groups of three, are drilled 5/8" apart in two rows on each interior face of the sides. The metal shelf pins are then inserted at the desired shelf level.

Metal shelf standards have slots every inch, with two standards on each side running from top to bottom of the shelf unit. Four adjustable metal clips are inserted at the same level into these slots. The metal strips may be recessed or surface mounted. This style allows for unlimited adjustment. (See Figure 8.12.)

For workshop and other informal shelving, metal brackets are attached to the back wall surface instead of to the sides.

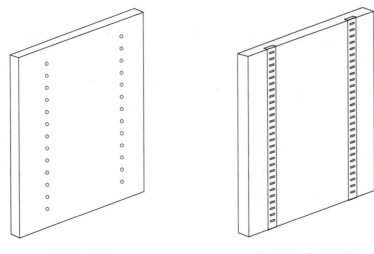

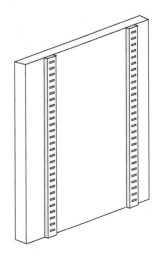

Multiple Holes Recessed Standards Surface Standards

FIGURE 8.12 Adjustable shelves. *Drawing courtesy of the Architectural Woodwork Institute.*

bibliography

Architectural Woodwork Institute. *Architectural Woodwork Standards*. 1st ed. Potomac Falls, VA: Architectural Woodwork Institute, 2009.

Composite Panel Association. *Technical Bulletin, Particleboard and MDF for Shelving.* Gaithersburg, MD: Composite Panel Association, 1998.

glossary

Apron. A flat piece of wood attached vertically along the underside of the front edge of a horizontal surface; may be for support (as in bookshelves) or decorative.

Bullet catch. A spring-actuated ball engaging a depression in the plate.

Butt hinge. The hinge is at right angles when open. (See Table 8.2.)

Concealed hinge. Arrangement in which all hinge parts are concealed when the door is closed.

Concealed surface. Part of the construction of the cabinet. Never visible when cabinet is finished. (See Figure 8.1.)

Dado. A cross-grained rectangular or square section.

Dowel joint. A joint, usually right angle, using dowels for positioning and strength.

Dynamic loads. A moving load, as opposed to static.

Exposed exterior and interior surface. (See Figure 8.1.)

Exposed hinge. Arrangement in which all hinge parts are visible when the door is closed.

Flush overlay. Cabinet construction in which door and drawer faces cover the body members of the cabinet with spaces between face surfaces sufficient for operating clearance. The door and frame are level and the frame is completely visible when the door or drawer is closed.

Friction catch. When engaged, the catch is held in place by friction.

Groove. A square or rectangular section cut with the grain.

Lipped door. A door with an overlapping edge; it partially covers the frame.

Medium density fiberboard (MDF). Engineered board consisting of wood fibers.

Mullion. Vertical member between panels.

Ogee. A double curved shape resembling an S shape.

Overlay. The door is on the outside of the frame; when closed, the door hides the frame from view.

Ovolo. A convex moulding, usually a quarter of a circle.

Particleboard (PB). Generic particleboard.

Pivot hinge. Hinge leaves are mortised into the edge of the door panel and set in the frame at the top of both the jamb and door. Some of this type of hinge pivots on a single point. (See Table 8.2.)

Reveal overlay. Cabinet construction in which the door and drawer faces partially cover the body members or face frames of the cabinet with spaces between face surfaces creating decorative reveals.

Semi-exposed surface. Surface only visible when door is open.

Static load. A resting load without any motion. Static load capacity is significantly higher than dynamic load capacity.

Stile. Vertical pieces on paneling.

Stop. A metal, plastic, or wood block placed to position the flush drawer front to be level with the face frame.

Strike plate. Metal plate attached to the door frame, designed to hold the roller catch under tension.

endnotes

1. *Architectural Woodwork Standard*, Edition 1, p. 172.
2. *Architectural Woodwork Standard*, 1st ed., 2009, p. 249
3. Ibid., p. 250
4. Ibid., Glossary, p. 380
5. Ibid., p. 252
6. Ibid.
7. Knape & Vogt, www.robertscoinc.biz
8. *Architectural Woodwork Standard*, 1st ed., 2009
9. Ibid.
10. Composite Panel Association, *Technical Bulletin Particleboard and MDF Shelving*. Composite Panel Association, Gaithersburg, MD 20879

9 Kitchens

In this chapter, you will:

- Analyze the social and physical influences affecting historical changes in kitchen design
- Develop an understanding of how to select and apply appropriate materials and products for the kitchen, based on properties and performance criteria such as cost, lifecycle, and ergonomics
- Identify the kitchen work triangle and be able to effectively lay out and specify kitchen furniture, equipment, and fixtures
- Explain the importance of industry-specific regulations and federal law related to aspects of kitchen design such as energy conservation and recycling
- Recognize that a certified kitchen designer has technical knowledge of construction techniques and systems used in new construction and light exterior and interior remodeling—including plumbing, heating, and electrical—and understand why this knowledge is important in kitchen design

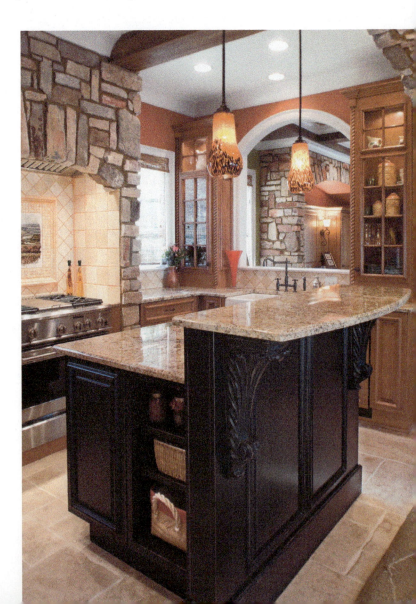

The kitchen has undergone many changes over the years. In the Victorian era, the cast iron cookstove was the primary means of cooking and heating. Although an improvement over the open fire used in Colonial days, much time and labor were required to keep it operating. The coal or wood used by the stove had to be carried into the house, and the stove required blacking to maintain its shiny appearance. In winter, the heat radiating from the cookstove heated the kitchen and made it a gathering place for the family. In summer, however, the fire had to be lit to use the stove-top for cooking and the oven for baking, which made the kitchen feel like a furnace. (These traditional wood- or wood/coal-burning cookstoves are still available. Some models use gas or electricity but retain the look of a traditional cookstove.)

In addition to the cookstove, the only other pieces of furniture in the kitchens of the past were tables, chairs, and a sink. All food preparation was done on the table or on the draining board next to the sink. There were no counters as we know them today and no upper storage cabinets. All food was stored in the pantry or in a cold cellar. Today, the kitchen has once again become a gathering place for the family. Much family life is centered around the kitchen, not only for food preparation, but also for entertaining and socializing.

Kitchens of every shape and size can benefit from an efficient **work triangle.** (See Figure 9.1.) The imaginary lines—which trace the most used paths in the room—stretch from stove, sink, and refrigerator to one another. Designers from the National Kitchen and Bath Association offer these recommendations for the work triangle.

- Each leg should be between 4 and 9 feet
- All three legs should total between 12 and 26 feet.
- No cabinet should intrude into a leg by a distance of greater than 12 inches.
- The major traffic flow in the room should not progress through the triangle.

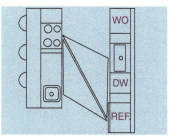
U-Shaped Triangle

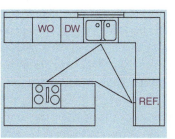
Broken U-Shaped Triangle

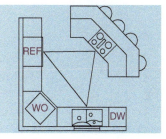
Broken U-Shaped Attached Seat Triangle

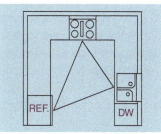
Single Wall Island Triangle

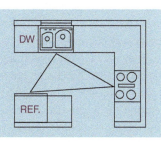
L-Shaped Island Triangle

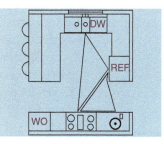
L-Shaped Island Triangle 2

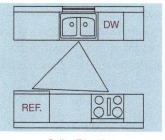
Galley Triangle

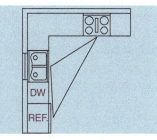
L-Shaped Triangle

FIGURE 9.1 Work triangles. *Drawing courtesy of Kohler.*

FIGURE 9.2 Approach for the sink. The touch of a button raises and lowers the sink height from 28 to 36 inches. At its lower positions, the height is ideal for seated use or wheelchair heights. Raised to 36 inches, it matches the counter height of standard base cabinets. *Photos courtesy of Populas Furniture by AD-AS.*

By utilizing these image examples, contractors can locate their kitchen's floor plan and determine the best layout for the room.[1]

In addition to an efficient work triangle, adequate lighting and adequate storage are important. The type of kitchen desired depends on the availability of space, lifestyle, and ages and number of the family members. The limiting factors in kitchen design are expense and space. The best utilization of space will create a functional and enjoyable working area. Kitchens are becoming larger and now account for almost 10 percent of the total square footage of a single-family home. They also feature more cabinetry and counter space. Barrier-free products are increasing in importance. Tim Carter has some very important tips on designing a kitchen for physically impaired clients in his Barrier Free Kitchen Checklist for Planning & Design, which includes ergonomic height-adjustable computer workstations, office furniture, healthcare tables, ergonomic desks, therapy tables, and home appliances. (See Figure 9.2.)

Lifestyle involves several factors. One is the manner of entertaining. Formal dinners require a separate formal dining room, whereas informal entertaining may take place just outside the work triangle, with guest and host or hostess communicating while meals are being prepared. If entertaining is done outside the home of a working host or hostess, then the kitchen may be minimal in size. Such things as how the grocery shopping is done also affect the type of cabinets. If grocery shopping is done twice a month, for example, the pantry space should be increased to allow for storage of foodstuffs.

A small kitchen will appear larger with an open plan (that is, without a wall dividing it from the adjacent room). It will also appear larger with a vaulted ceiling. Other factors also need to be considered when planning a kitchen. A young couple with small children, for example, might require a family room within sight of the kitchen. In addition, teenagers like to be near food preparation areas for easy access to the refrigerator and snacks. Some cooks prefer to work from a pantry and therefore do not need a lot of upper cabinets, whereas others prefer to have a bake center and work from both the upper and lower cabinets. Figure 9.3 is an example of a small city kitchen.

One style gaining in popularity on the West Coast is the double island kitchen. One island is for cleanup, prep, and periodic storage. The other island is the primary workstation, encasing the dishwasher, sink, and stove top. A long wall might have a double oven side by side versus top and bottom configurations.[2]

FIGURE 9.3 A limited space can still be well designed and efficient.

A number of years ago Ellen Cheever, Certified Kitchen Designer (**CKD**), ASID, gave the following work simplification techniques for planning a kitchen, which are still important today.

1. Build the cabinets to fit the cook.
2. Build the shelves to fit the supplies.
3. Build the kitchen to fit the family.

Floor Plans

Infinite variations are available on basic kitchen floor plans. The simplest of all kitchen floor plans is the one-wall, otherwise known as **pullman, strip,** or **studio.** Here, all appliances and counter space are contained on one wall. When required, folding doors or screens are used to hide the kitchen completely from view. This minimal kitchen is not designed for elaborate or family meals.

The **corridor kitchen,** or two-wall plan, utilizes two parallel walls and doubles the available space over the one-wall plan. The major problem with this design is through traffic. If possible, for safety's sake, one end should be closed off to avoid this traffic. The width of the corridor kitchen should be between 5 and 8 feet. A narrower width prevents two facing doors from being opened at the same time. For energy conservation, the refrigerator and stove should not face each other directly (as shown in Figure 9.3). In an L-shaped kitchen, work areas are arranged on two adjacent walls rather than on two opposite walls; the advantages of this layout are that there is no through traffic and all counters are contiguous. The L-shaped kitchen may also include an island or a peninsula. This island may simply be an extra work surface, may contain the sink or stove, or may include an informal eating area. If the island has a raised side facing an eating or seating area, the higher side will hide the clutter in the kitchen.

The U-shaped kitchen is probably the most efficient design. It has three walls of counter space with no through traffic. Depending on the location of the kitchen window, there are at least two walls or more of upper cabinets. The work triangle is easy to arrange in this design, with the sink usually at the top of the U, refrigerator on one side, and range on the other. The refrigerator is always placed at the end of the U to avoid breaking up the counter area and to provide easy accessibility to the eating area. The stove, range, or cooktop is on the opposite side but more centered in the U. Islands also work in a U-shaped kitchen provided that the passageways are more than 4 feet wide.

When planning any kitchen, thought should be given to the activities of each area. For example, the sink area serves a dual purpose. First, it is used for food preparation, such as washing and cleaning fruits and vegetables. Second, after the meal the sink is used for cleanup. In this age of the electric dishwasher, the sink area is generally used only for preliminary cleaning; however, in the event of a large number of dishes, sufficient space should be provided next to the sink, 18" on one side and 24" on the other, so a helper can dry the dishes. Counters are generally 36 inches high. However, they can vary from 42 to 45 inches for those who are standing to 30 to 32 inches for seated cooks and children.

Certain areas of the kitchen require a minimum amount of adjacent counter space. For example, the sink needs 24 to 36 inches of counter space on the dishwasher side and 18 to 36 inches on the other side. For cooktops, 18 to 24 inches should be allowed on either side. Regardless of the type of design, there must be at least 16 inches of counter space on the handle side of the refrigerator, which should be at the end of one side of the counter near the entrance to the kitchen. The refrigerator should not be placed in such a manner that the counter is broken up into small areas.

The refrigerator should be plugged into its own individual 115-volt electrical outlet on a circuit separate from those used for heating and cooking appliances. The refrigerator should be placed in an area that will not receive direct sunlight or direct heat from the home heating system. In addition, it should not be placed next to sources of heat, such as next to the range or dishwasher.

The cooking area is considered to be the cooktop area. Many wall ovens are now located in separate areas from the cooktop.

Kitchen Appliances

Only those appliances that are necessary to a kitchen floor plan (i.e., major appliances) will be discussed in this section. Mixers and toasters are outside the scope of this book.

Major appliance manufacturers must comply with PL. 94-163, a law enacted by Congress in 1975. This law provides that energy costs for appliances must be calculated as so much per **kilowatt-hour (kwh).** This information must be supplied on a tag attached to the front of the appliance. Consumers can then calculate their yearly energy cost by finding out their local kilowatt-hour rate. By using these figures, comparison shopping can be done. It is important to bear in mind that the higher the local rate the more important energy conservation features become.

Concerning energy conservation, the Energy Star program from the EPA is awarded to dishwashers and refrigerators that contribute to savings of both power and water. Significant savings can be realized by minimizing the amount of hot water needed. The water temperature in a dishwasher should be at least 140°F to clean the dishes. All models that are Energy Star qualified have an internal water heater which boosts the water temperature inside the dishwasher. This allows the thermostat on the household water heater to be turned down to 120°F, reducing water heating costs by 20 percent. By federal law, all dishwashers must have a no-heat drying option, resulting in a significant savings of energy. Refrigerators that qualify for the Energy Star program have improved insulation, meaning that the compressor needs to run less often. Heat from the compressor warms the kitchen, resulting in increased air conditioning and higher energy consumption.

The style of appliances selected may affect the style of cabinetry. For example, black appliances look better with white or light-colored wood cabinets, whereas freestanding Old World style stoves may look better with French country cabinetry.

Colored, white, and stainless steel appliances are available. If a change in the kitchen's decor is planned for the future, white is always a safe choice. All-black appliances are very popular in contemporary kitchens, with black glass fronts on **microwave ovens** and conventional ovens. White appliances may have some chrome accents. However, if totally white, they are more expensive than regular black or white appliances.

When selecting major appliances, it is important to remember that extra features increase an appliance's cost. Therefore, the selected features should be in line with the consumer's lifestyle.

The American Gas Association defines the various surfaces used on kitchen appliances. Porcelain enamel is most frequently used on surface tops and oven doors because it resists heat, acid, stains, scratches, yellowing, and fading. Baked enamel or electrostatically applied polyester is less durable than porcelain enamel because it is less resistant to stains and scratches; it resists chipping better than porcelain enamel.

Stainless steel is resistant to corrosion, dents, and stains and is easy to clean. It may turn dark, however, if it is overheated. Chrome-plated finishes are durable and will not dent easily. Excess heat may cause chrome to discolor over a period of time.

Elmira Stove Works creates custom kitchen appliances with vintage style and modern convenience (see Figure 9.4). The company offers a number of options that can be tailored to the consumer's specific requests.[3]

FIGURE 9.4 This Model 1944 Splashback mounts easily on the back wall between the range and hood, completing the color statement and protecting against splashes and stains. *Photograph courtesy of Elmira Stove Works.*

REFRIGERATORS

The most costly kitchen appliance to purchase and to operate is the refrigerator. By July 1, 2001, all refrigerators were required to use 10 percent less energy than previous models. The U.S. Department of Energy (DOE) has since issued a proposed new standard based on a joint recommendation submitted by efficiency proponents and manufacturers. The DOE found that technology options including improved compressor efficiency, brushless DC evaporator and condenser fan motors, and vacuum insulation panels (VIPs) could lead to cost-effective energy savings in the range of 20 to 30 percent, depending on the product class. The initial increased cost of such methods may be offset by better efficiency over a period of years. As with other appliances, the selection of a refrigerator depends on the consumer's lifestyle as well as the pocketbook.

For our purposes, the word *refrigerator* will be used instead of *refrigerator/freezer* because we assume that all refrigerators have some form of freezer section. There are a wide variety of features from which to select.

The three standard refrigerator styles are top freezer, bottom freezer, and side-by-side. An additional refrigerator style is the French door refrigerator, which offers a freezer on the bottom with a double door. As consumers consider refrigerator dimensions, they should be aware that the dimensions will be determined by the refrigerator's capacity and style. In addition, some refrigerator styles are available with a door whose opening direction can be reversed.

In terms of energy efficiency, the least efficient is generally the side-by-side style, and the most efficient is the top-freezer style, with the bottom-freezer style between them. A refrigerator with an in-door dispenser for ice and water is generally less efficient than its counterparts that lack this feature.[4]

Exterior refrigerator features include panel adapter kits, which are used on the refrigerator's face to match other appliances. Stainless steel is the latest and most expensive finish for appliances and usually adds $300 to $500 more to the appliance's cost.

Side-by-side refrigerators have separate vertical doors for the freezer and refrigerator sections; because the narrower doors have a shorter swing radius, they work well in a galley kitchen or across from appliances with doors. Side-by-side refrigerators are preferred by shorter users and those confined to a wheelchair. Often, this type of refrigerator comes with convenient water and ice dispensers in the door.

Refrigerators are sold by their storage capacity (in other words, by cubic feet of space). Although families and kitchens generally are getting smaller, the size of the refrigerator is staying around 16 to 17 cubic feet. This may be a result of working parents who have less time to grocery shop and need to stockpile food, or it may mean that people are entertaining frequently and need to keep food on hand for guests. The most energy-efficient refrigerator is in the 15- to 20-cubic-foot range, without an icemaker. Sizes of refrigerators vary from 13 cubic feet to 28 cubic feet. The actual food storage amount is probably several cubic feet less than advertised due to the method of calculation.

Today manufacturers classify sizes under the type of door or freezer location (one or two doors on the refrigerator or top or bottom freezer). To design the refrigerator as an integral part of the cabinetry, some manufacturers have recessed the refrigerator coils or placed them above the refrigerator, which makes the refrigerator flush with the edge of the counter; however, this type is considerably more expensive than the regular models. The refrigerator door can also be covered to match the cabinets, and it can have custom handles. Because this style has no bottom vent, the toe-kick panel can extend from the cabinet across the base of the refrigerator. For new construction, 37 inches of floor space should be allowed for the refrigerator, even if the planned unit is narrower, and accommodations for a water hook-up should be made even though the hook-up may not be used at the time.

Sub-Zero states that its units blend into surroundings "with almost no visible hinges, holes, or vents." The company also advises that the unit's 24" depth allows for flush installation with kitchen cabinets, which have the same depth. It should be noted that while

FIGURE 9.5 The 648PRO Model from the PRO48 line has glass-fronted doors for the refrigerator. *Photograph courtesy of Sub-Zero, Inc./Sub-Zero, Inc.*

FIGURE 9.6. This CoolDrawer Multi-Temperature Refrigerator is opened to show the food inside the drawer. *Image courtesy of Fisher & Paykel Appliances Inc.*

Sub-Zero units might be shallower than some other unit types, they can provide similar or greater capacity through increased width.[5] (See Figure 9.5.)

The most common refrigerator features include meat keepers, un-wrapped food sections, adjustable shelves, and humidity-controlled vegetable storage areas. Other interior features might include egg storage, handy cheese and spread storage, and glass shelves that prevent spilled liquids from dripping onto other shelves. The shelves on the doors of both the refrigerator and freezer may be fixed or adjustable. The latest feature is a door deep enough to hold gallon containers. Other features include frozen juice can dispensers, ice makers, and ice cream makers within the freezer compartment. An ice-water dispenser, with cubed and/or crushed ice that is accessible without opening the refrigerator door, may conserve energy and justify the additional expense, depending on frequency of use.

One manufacturer offers a third door for access only to the ice cube compartment. Another has a storage unit in the door that can be opened for access to snack items without opening the full-length refrigerator doors. Some companies offer see-through storage bins. The wine chiller holds up to 50 resting bottles of wine. Another appliance in this series is the icemaker, which produces up to 50 pounds of ice per day.

The CoolDrawer was the recipient of the 2010 Platinum award for excellence in design. It permits a variety of temperature settings to allow for many types of food and beverages, including wine, to be stored at appropriate temperatures.[6] (See Figure 9.6.)

Most manufacturers are interested in energy conservation, and efficiency has greatly improved over the past 15 years. However, convenience should also be taken into consideration. For example, a self-defrosting refrigerator consumes more energy than a manual defrost, but it is much more convenient.

Nylon rollers are provided for moving or rolling the refrigerator from the wall. If the refrigerator is to be moved sideways, a **dolly** should be used to avoid damaging the floor covering.

RANGES

Old-fashioned stoves have been replaced by **freestanding range** units, **drop-in range** units, or **slide-in range** units.

Freestanding ranges vary from 20 to 40 inches wide, but most are 30 inches wide. A freestanding range has finished sides and is usually slightly deeper than the 24-inch kitchen counter. This type of range may be considered if a change of residence will take place in the near future. Slide-in ranges usually measure 30 inches wide. Slide-ins fit into a space between cabinets, whereas drop-ins fit into cabinets connected below the oven. Slide-in models can be converted to freestanding by the addition of optional side panels and a backguard. Some ranges contain the cooking units, microwave, and/or oven in one unit; alternatively, the oven and cooktop may be in two separate units (often in two separate locations in the kitchen).

Many 30-inch ranges now come with a second oven above the cooktop surface, which may be another **conventional oven** or a microwave. An exhaust fan is incorporated beneath some of the microwave ovens. The cooking medium may be gas or electricity. Electric ovens can maintain even temperatures better than most gas-powered models. Some ranges have the cooking surface flush with the counter, whereas on others, the cooking surface is lowered an inch or so. The only difference is that if several large or wide pans are used at the same time, such as during canning or for large parties, the lowered surface is more restrictive. The flush surface permits the centering of the larger pans. The surface of ranges may be white or colored with porcelain-coated steel, stainless steel, tempered glass, or ceramic glass. (Note the raised cooking surface in Figure 9.3.)

For those who desire state-of-the-art technology combined with authentic nineteenth-century styling, old-fashioned-type ranges are now available with gas or electricity. Even wood- or coal-burning cookstoves are available. These decorative ranges conceal features such as self-cleaning convection ovens, digital clock timers, and exhaust vent systems. Several companies manufacture these types of products.

The U.S. Department of Energy estimates that the typical annual cost of operating an efficient gas range is about half the cost of operating an electric range. This only amounts to a dollar or two per month, however, so individual preference is more of a consideration.

ELECTRIC RANGES

There are several different types of element choices for electric ranges. The least expensive and most common is the coil element. The most expensive is the European solid disk of cast iron sealed to the cooktop, which some manufacturers refer to as a **hob.** With the solid-electric element, a red dot indicates that the element is thermally protected and will shut down if a pan boils dry. Some elements have a silver dot—a pan sensor that maintains a fairly constant preselected temperature, sometimes with a variance of 20°F. Electric elements heat quickly and can maintain low heat levels.

Another type of element is the radiant **glass-ceramic cooktop,** or smoothtop. When first introduced in 1966, these cooktops were white; now they are available in black or patterned greyish-white ceramic glass. The patterned surface shows smudges and fingerprints less than a shiny black surface. All these surfaces are heated primarily by conduction; however, some use halogen. Some smoothtops have quick-heating elements; for safety's sake, the indicator lights will stay on as long as the surface is hot. This type of cooktop has a limiter that cycles the burners on and off, restricting the temperature reached by the glass surface. Smoothtops should be cleaned with a special cream, which both cleans and shines the ceramic. These cooktops are usually 30 inches wide. Both radiant and induction methods require flat-bottomed pots of the same diameter.

Two newer methods of heating are halogen and induction, both of which are used for glass-ceramic cooktops. The halogen units have vacuum-sealed quartz glass tubes filled with halogen gas that filters out the white light and uses infrared as a heating source. The surface becomes a bright red when turned on. Halogen units provide the option of instant on and instant off, and the surface unit itself does not get hot. The only heat the glass top may retain is absorbed from a hot pan.

Induction elements are the most expensive type. Induction cooktops use magnetic coils below the ceramic-glass surface to generate heat directly in the pot or pan rather than the cooking surface. When induction-type smoothtops sense overheating, they beep and shut off the power to that burner. Because of the method of heating, induction units turn off the power when a pot is removed. Induction models use electronic touchpads and take the cake for quick heating and energy efficiency.

For greatest efficiency, all cooking utensils used on an electric range must be flat bottomed to allow full contact with the cooking unit, although induction units will work with slightly warped pans. Usually there are four cooking units, but some of the larger glass cooktops have five or even six units.

Some electric ranges have the controls and clock on a back panel. On separate cooktops, controls are in the front or at the side of the cooktop. On electric ranges, controls may be divided left and right, with the oven controls in between, giving a quick sense of which control works which elements. Controls on the latest cooktops are electronic touchpads.

Cooktops now have concealed or visible hinges that make it easy to clean under the cooktop, the area where the overflow from drip bowls ends up. Porcelain drip bowls, which are much easier to clean than the shiny metal bowls, can be cleaned in the oven during the self-cleaning cycle.

GAS RANGES

Gas cooktops can be made of porcelain-coated steel or stainless steel. One advantage of using gas is that it is easier to moderate temperature changes. However, installation must be done by a professional. Conventional gas burners have grates that hold the pan above the flame. These grates should be heavy enough to support the pan and be easy to clean. Propane burns a little cooler than regular gas. Sealed gas burners are fused to the cooktop, and there are no drip pans; all spills remain on the glass surface, making cleanup easier.

Newer gas ranges have pilotless ignition systems that light the cooking unit automatically from either a spark ignition or a coil ignition. By eliminating the standard, always-burning pilot light, these ranges reduce the gas needed for cooking by 30 percent, keep the kitchen cooler, and prevent pilot outage caused by drafts or other conditions. Electricity must be run to the range to operate the pilotless ignition. In case of electricity failure, the burner may be lit by a match; however, as a safety precaution, the oven cannot be used by lighting a match. If electricity cannot be run to the pilotless range, models with pilot lights are still available. One of the latest trends is the use of multi-burner restaurant-type gas ranges, with six or even eight burners in home kitchens. (Truly commercial ranges are not permitted in a private residence because of the excessive heat generated.) These freestanding ranges are very useful when catering for a large crowd or for the gourmet cook. Gas appliances produce exhaust gases that are better expelled by using an exhaust fan. To make the gas flame easier to modulate, Wolf is introducing dual stacked burners with sealed burner pans to make cleaning easier.

OVENS

Electric ovens come in 24-, 27-, and 30-inch widths; however, some 30-inch ovens require a 33-inch cabinet. Ovens come in two types: self-cleaning **(pyrolytic action)** or standard. Self-cleaning ovens have a special cleaning setting that is activated by the timer for the required length of time. This cleaning cycle runs at an extremely high temperature and actually incinerates any oven spills, leaving an ash residue. One of the excellent byproducts of a self-cleaning oven is that, because of the high temperatures required to operate the cleaning cycle, the oven is more heavily insulated than is customary and so retains heat longer and uses less energy when baking. Gas ovens that are self-cleaning are now available. At the low end of the price range is the standard oven which requires the use of spray-on oven cleaners. These are becoming hard to find because most ovens are now self-cleaning.

Ovens cook by one of three methods: radiation, convection, or microwave. Radiant baking is the method used in most ovens.

The company producing Jenn-Air states that it utilizes a fan in the interior of the oven cavity for the purpose of circulating warm air. This differs from the process of using radiant heat within a conventional oven. Jenn-Air further advises that its processes increase roasting and baking speeds. The location of the heating element at the top and bottom of the oven—with the fan located in the back of the unit—provides efficient use of space and produces juicy meats. It offers the ability to bake three racks of items rather than the conventional one or two racks. Jenn-Air wall **convection ovens** provide six convection modes: Convect Bake, Convect Roast, Convect Broil, Convect Pastry, Convect Slow, and Convect Frozen Pizza. An additional True Convect V2 Convection mode taps only the convection elements and fans.[7] It should be noted that convection ovens are generally more costly than other types of oven units.

Built-in ovens are required when using a separate cooktop. These may be single conventional oven units or double oven units with one a conventional type and the other a microwave. Sizes available are 24, 27, and 30 inches. The 24- and 27-inch ovens fit into a standard 27-inch cabinet, but not all 30-inch models fit into a 30-inch cabinet. Some require a 30-inch opening, which only a 33-inch cabinet provides.

Electric ovens may have a solid door, a porcelain enamel door with a window, or a full black glass window door. The porcelain enamel is available in many colors. Controls may be operated by knobs or electronic touchpads. Electric ovens require the door to be left ajar when the broiling models are in use; otherwise, food will roast. Many new ovens turn off automatically after 12 hours (this is a good safety feature).

Sometimes double ovens are used, but they do not offer the advantage of waist-level shelves (which are better for physically impaired individuals). Timers for ovens vary in length from 99 minutes to 10 hours. Warming drawers are becoming more prevalent in upscale kitchens. (See Figure 9.7.) These thermostatically controlled drawers are designed to keep hot foods hot or crisp prior to serving, and they may also be used for proofing bread.

Gaggenau produces the programmable WS 261 warming drawer, which allows for temperatures from 100°F to 175°F. This product includes a convection fan for even heat distribution and an integrated baseplate heating function, which permits cups and plates to be completely preheated. It also allows for the reheating of food and beverages without the occurrence of cold spots.[8]

MICROWAVE OVENS

Microwave cooking activates the molecules in food about 2 1/2 billion times per second. The friction between molecules produces the heat. Today, most microwave ovens are operated by means of touch controls that electronically monitor the amount of energy from full power to a warming setting or defrost cycle.

FIGURE 9.7 Warming drawer by Wolf Appliance, Inc. *Photograph courtesy of Wolf Appliance, Inc.*

Microwave ovens may be programmed to cook whole meals on a delayed-time basis. Some feature recipes that are available at a touch, and others use a meat probe to produce meat that is rare, medium, or well done.

A microwave's size refers to the cooking cavity. Originally microwaves were designed to sit on a countertop. Today, most medium-sized models are specifically designed to be mounted over the range (OTR), with built-in recirculating exhaust fans, or under specially sized cabinets (UTC), without a vent. Sizes vary from 0.5 cubic foot to 1.3 cubic feet. Microwave ovens are rated by watts, from 600 to 1,000 watts. The greater the wattage, the more quickly the oven heats food. In other words, cooking time needs to be increased for the lower wattage microwaves. The feature used most frequently on a microwave oven is the defrost cycle.

Unlike regular ovens, microwave cooking time varies with the amount of food to be cooked; four potatoes require about 70 percent less energy when microwaved, but 12 potatoes bake more efficiently in a conventional oven. For safety's sake, some microwaves have child lockouts with keypad releases.

VENTILATION FANS

All exhaust systems should move a minimum of 200 cubic feet per minute. There are many methods of venting cooking fumes from the kitchen. Ducted fans may be either updraft or downdraft. With updraft, the hood over the cooking surface collects the heat, odors, and fumes and exhausts them to the outside. This method takes up some space in the cabinet over the cooking surface.

Some manufacturers have a raised vent at the back of the cooktop, which may not always completely exhaust fumes from the front burners, particularly if the pans are very high. A split downdraft consists of two vents on each side of the cooktop surface.

For cooktops that are in the center of the room there are chimney style island hoods that ventilate upwards. For outside walls, an exhaust fan that vents directly outdoors may be used. Ductless or recirculating systems have a **charcoal filter** that filters out odors.

DISHWASHERS

Dishwashers are typically 24" wide and are usually installed adjacent to the sink so that the plumbing connections are easily made. Dishwashers discharge the dirty water through the sink containing the garbage disposal. It is recommended that the sink drain plugs be inserted during dishwasher operation to prevent noise transfer through drains. Special dishwasher features can include adjustable or removable tines; shelves; racks built to accommodate tall glasses, stemware, and odd shaped and tall items; or convertible racks for multiple uses.

A small closed basket for baby bottles and rings is also available on some dishwasher models. The controls for the dishwasher are usually on the front; however, some dishwashers have the controls in the top of the door and are not visible when the dishwasher door is closed.

Another alternative is the 18" wide dishwasher, which is suitable for couples or residences with limited space.

The U.S. EPA, through the Energy Star program, awards manufacturers whose dishwashers can help save money on utility bills through superior designs that require less money and less energy to get the dishes clean and dry. Construction includes more effective washing action, energy efficient motors, and other advanced technology such as settings that determine the length of the wash cycle and the temperature of the water necessary to clean the dishes. A list of manufacturers who qualify is found on www.energystar.org/manufacturers .asp. Note that Energy Star does not endorse the manufactured products, companies, or opinions included therein.

The most desirable features in dishwashers are quiet operation, energy and water conservation, and versatile loading. Available features in dishwashers include a heavy-duty cycle for cleaning heavily soiled pots and pans, a regular cycle for normal soil, rinse and hold for a small number of dishes requiring rinsing, and low-energy wash cycles. If the utility company offers lower off-peak rates, a delay-start feature may be desirable.

Dishes may be dried by the heated cycle, or, for energy efficiency, a no-heat drying cycle may be programmed. To save water and energy, it is best not to rinse dishes before putting them into the dishwasher because a soft food disposer or filtration system is built in. Some foods, such as eggs, rice, pasta, and cooked cereals, may need rinsing.

Racks and even dividers are now adjustable, allowing for large-size dishes or wider items that do not fit over the fixed dividers. Some dishwashers have a separate rack on top for silverware, making the silverware easier to get at, easier to clean, and more scratch resistant. A small drop-down rack provides a second rack; this enables two rows of cups to be washed in the same space. Water-saver dishwashers are now available that use only 6 gallons.

Consumers need to choose which features are the most important for them. With an open plan house, sound deadening would be the most important feature; for large parties, capacity would be best. Raising the dishwasher another 6 inches can save the consumer stress on the back when loading or unloading dishes. This higher counter might be part of a cookbook storage area.

TRASH COMPACTORS

Trash compactors vary in width from 12 to 18 inches and reduce trash volume by 75 percent in less than one minute. In today's society, in which trash disposal has become an expensive service, trash compactors reduce the volume of trash considerably. They may make trash less biodegradable, however, because of its compacted volume.

Trash compactors can be used to crush recyclable aluminum cans and plastic bottles, making them less bulky. Be aware, however, that some recycling depots require that the cans be in their original condition. For this reason, trash compactors may be becoming obsolete in some parts of the United States. Where recycling is not required, trash compactors can still be used in the conventional manner.

Sinks

Kitchen sinks are constructed of stainless steel, enameled cast iron, enameled steel, or manufactured materials (usually compression-molded modified acrylic). Each material has its pros and cons.

Stainless steel sinks give a contemporary look to a kitchen and are less likely to cause breakage if dishes are accidentally dropped into them. Finishes may be satin or gloss.

Any water spots will leave a spot on the shiny surface, however. In addition, heat from the hot water dissipates more rapidly with a metal sink than with a porcelain enamel one. When selecting a stainless steel sink, the lower the number of the gauge, the thicker the metal will be. Undercoating absorbs sound, protects against condensation, and helps maintain sink water temperature. Like all kitchen sinks there is a great variety of sizes, depths, and number of bowls in stainless steel. (See Figure 9.8.)

Some sinks even come with an integral draining board. Porcelain enamel sinks show stains easily, and a scouring powder is usually required to remove these stains. The porcelain may become chipped when hit with a heavy object. Enameled cast iron sinks provide a colorful touch in the kitchen, whereas enameled steel sinks are low cost and lightweight but also less durable than the other types. Sinks made of solid surface materials are easily cleaned,

FIGURE 9.8 Elkay undermount sink.

but colors are limited and require an experienced installer, which raises the cost. Porcelain sinks are made from high-fired clay with an enamel finish, a combination that is used more in Europe than in the United States. Porcelain sinks are highly chip resistant but can break when a heavy object is dropped into them.

Composite or quartz acrylic is the latest material for kitchen sinks. This material produces a color-through sink impervious to stains and scratches. Composite sinks are made from a combination of natural materials and synthetics.

Some kitchen sinks, such as stainless steel sinks and those designed to be used with a metal rim, are flush with the counter. In this style, any water spilled on the counter may be swept back into the sink. Self-rimming sinks are raised above the surface of the counter; in this style, any water spilled must be mopped up. Some self-rimming sinks have predrilled holes, which must be ordered to suit the type of faucet to be used. The old standard had three holes, or four holes if a spray or soap dispenser was to be used. With the increasing use of single-lever faucets with self-contained pull-out sprays, only one hole may be needed. Some models of stainless steel sinks have knockout holes started in their undersides for extra accessories. An extra hole may be needed for a water purifier, hot water dispenser, cold water dispenser, or soap/lotion dispenser. Under-mounted, flush-mounted, and integral or molded sinks have the faucets on the counter. Very contemporary kitchens have sinks with wall-mounted faucets. When the faucet is pointed down it is called a **bib** (like an outside hose faucet.)

Single-compartment sink models should be installed only where there is minimum space. One-bowl models do not provide a second liquid disposal area if the bowl is in use.

Designer Susan Dossetter prefers to use two **farmhouse sinks** next to each other: "I like two sinks side by side, one becomes a receptacle for dirty pots and pans while you keep working in the other, and I love the fact that it's so deep you can't see the dirty dishes from across the room."[9] A more contemporary design of the farmhouse sink is shown in Figure 9.9; however, it is not as deep as the original farmhouse sinks.

L-shaped double models are used in corner installations. A single-bowl sink, called a bar sink or hospitality sink, is often placed in a separate area of the kitchen, usually in an island. These sinks typically have a high arc bar faucet. In triple sinks one of the bowls is usually shallower and smaller than the other two and may contain the garbage disposal unit. Some sinks have small colanders for draining pastas or cleaning vegetables, or have fitted wooden cutting boards. Other sinks have a ribbed area for draining dishes. Instead of the normal square or rectangular sinks, they may be D-shaped, have lower divides between sinks, different depths, and so on.

Corian, when used as a material for kitchen sinks, may or may not be an integral part of the counter.

FIGURE 9.9 Elkay farmhouse sink.

The width of a kitchen sink varies between 25 and 43 inches. Some sinks with attached drain boards are almost 50 inches wide. New sinks have the drain at the rear, which means there is a flat area for food preparation and more accessible storage space under the sink.

Accessories for sinks may include a fitted cutting board, where waste material may be pushed off one corner into the sink. In addition, wire or plastic colanders are useful for holding food or vegetables that require rinsing. The company that makes the adjustable sink, Accessible Designs Adjustable Systems, Inc. (AD-AS), also makes adjustable ranges and adjustable storage cabinets.

MAINTENANCE

Kitchen sinks should only be cleaned with mild powders or paste cleaners. Steel wool or heavy-duty abrasive powders should not be used. A mirrored-finish stainless sink can be cleaned with a special automotive polishing compound to maintain its sheen.

KITCHEN FAUCETS

Faucets do not come with the kitchen sink and can sometimes be as expensive as the sink itself. Brass and copper are the latest finishes for kitchen faucets.

Moen developed a new copper finish in response to the growing use of copper cookware and accessories by gourmet chefs and today's style conscious homeowner. The mixing type of valve, with which hot and cold may be blended with one handle, allows one-handed operation. Single-handle faucets meet ADA requirements. Several manufacturers provide lifetime warranties on their valves. Another type of ADA-approved handle is the wristblade handle. One problem is that the handle may be accidentally turned on when in the hot position, which may lead to a burn. To prevent burns, the water heater should be set at 120°F. Most kitchen faucets have a hose attached for spraying the sink and washing vegetables. A gooseneck faucet is higher than normal and may be used for the kitchen; however, it is more frequently used in a bar sink.

Kohler Co. is a world leader in products for the kitchen and bath as well as home furnishings, which it markets under the brand names of Kohler plumbing. Several hot water dispensers on the market provide very hot water (about 190°F) for making hot drinks and instant soups. The extra hole in the sink may be used for these dispensers as well as for purified water. The latest innovation from Kohler is the wall- or deck-mounted articulating faucet, as shown in Figure 9.10.

The Karbon Articulating Kitchen Faucet, developed to lock water flow as needed, includes a variety of moveable joints. The faucet can be placed low in the sink for preparation and cleaning; it can also be completely extended to fill large pots. When the faucet is not being used, it can be folded away so as not to interfere with other uses.[10]

Another faucet type, the Pilar Pull-Down Kitchen Faucet with Touch$_2$O Technology, can be turned on and off through a touch at any point on the handle or spout.[11]

The Delta Trinsic Pull-Down Kitchen Faucet with Touch$_2$O Technology is an innovation on the forefront of design and technology. Water turns on and off with just a touch anywhere on the spout or handle. The Delta Champagne Bronze faucet finish uses PVD (physical vapor deposition) technology, which is designed not to corrode, tarnish, or discolor. Finish molecules are embedded deep in the faucet's surface, creating a bond that is virtually indestructible.

The innovative ONO from KWC has a highflex hose that can be guided in any direction, but when at rest—with or without the spray holder—it always retains its shape. Lightly actuating the lever on the spray automatically switches the integrated vacuum diverter over from spout operation to a needle spray. As soon as the adjustment lever is released, the water comes out of the swivel spout again.[12]

Because of increasing awareness of water conservation, plumbing manufacturers are now making 2.5- to 2.7-gallons-per-minute flow kitchen faucets. European faucets are often called **taps.**

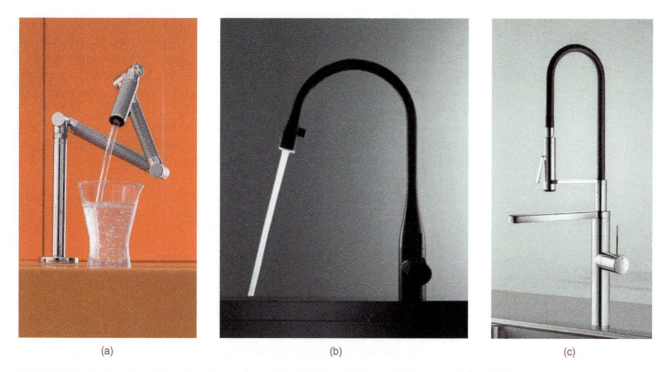

(a)   (b)   (c)

FIGURE 9.10 (a) Kohler's Karbon Articulating Kitchen Faucet. (b) The Delta Trinsic Pull-Down Kitchen Faucet with Touch$_2$O Technology turns water on and off with a mere touch of the wrist or forearm. *Photo courtesy of Delta Faucet Company, www.deltafaucet.com.* (c) KWC ONO with highflex EVE 2, KWC. *Photograph courtesy of KWCAmerica.*

Kitchen Cabinets

Stock kitchen cabinets usually start at 15 inches wide and come in 3-inch increments up to 48 inches. The depth of lower cabinets is 24 inches and the depth of upper cabinets is 12 inches. Filler strips are used between individual cabinets to make up any difference in measurements.

Kitchen cabinets are usually made of all wood or wood with decorative laminate doors. Solid wood is required for raised panel designs. For dimensional stability, a medium density or multidensity fiberboard is used for the case and shelves; the edges are then banded with a wood veneer that matches the door and drawer fronts. The interior of the cabinets is often coated with a PVC plastic material that reflects light, making it easier to find items inside and easier to clean. Under-cabinet appliances are also popular and help clear the counter of clutter. When looking at the construction of kitchen cabinets, it would be wise to reread Chapter 8 on cabinet construction. All better quality cabinets will meet the criteria set forth in that chapter.

Since the kitchen is a very personal room, the style of cabinets selected for it should reflect the consumer's lifestyle. At one extreme are kitchens in which everything is hidden from sight (behind solid doors) and counters are empty. At the other extreme are kitchens with raised panel doors, shaped at the top, often with glass inserts, and shelves on which personal collections and/or kitchen utensils are displayed. Glass doors should be used with glass shelves for displaying decorative items, or the impact on the viewer is lost. (It is also important to consider what will be visible through the glass doors.) Another style of kitchen uses open shelves for the storage of dishes and glasses; a pantry is used for food storage. Most kitchens fall somewhere between these extremes; the overriding idea is that kitchens should be personalized for the client.

Wood cabinets may use flush overlay, reveal overlay, or, for more traditional styles, an exposed frame with a lipped door. The face surface of the door may be **plane,** have a flat or raised panel, or have mouldings applied for a traditional approach. Contemporary kitchens may have not only flush overlay doors, but flush overlay in combination with linear metal or wood decorative strips, which also function as drawer and door pulls. The traditional front frame cabinet construction and the European-style frameless construction (sometimes referred to as 32-mm cabinets) are both popular. They receive their name because 32 millimeters is the spacing of predrilled holes in the cabinet sides for shelf spacing. Shelves in all cabinets should be fully adjustable to accommodate the needs of the user. A well-stocked kitchen requires a minimum of 50 square feet of shelf space and a minimum of 11 square feet of drawer space. Pots and pans are more readily accessible if drawers, rather than base cabinet shelves, are used for storage.

When the frameless type of construction is used, it will have an opening 1 1/2" wider than that in conventionally constructed cabinets. A quality frameless cabinet is as strong as a face frame cabinet, with 1/2" thick sides and 1/4" thick back. There is very little cost difference between framed and frameless construction.

Many special features may be ordered for the custom-designed kitchen, which will add to the cost of the installation. However, these may be ordered to fit the consumer's personal and budgetary needs.

Following is a list of some of the available features.

- Base-sliding shelves make all items visible, which eliminates the need to get down on hands and knees to see what is at the bottom of a base unit.

- A bread box may be contained within a drawer with a lid to help maintain freshness.

- A cutting board, usually made of maple, that slides out from the upper part of a base unit is convenient and will help protect the surface of the counter from damage. However, a cutting board should not be placed directly over a drawer that might be needed in conjunction with the cutting board.

- Lazy Susans in corner units or doors with attached swing-out shelves utilize the storage area of a corner unit. Another use for the corner unit of the base cabinet is the installation of a 20-gallon water heater, which provides instant hot water for the kitchen sink and the electric dishwasher and prevents waste of water. A second water heater can be installed close to the bathroom to conserve energy; this avoids the need for someone to wait for the hot water to reach the bathroom.

- Dividers placed in drawers aid in drawer organization, and vertical dividers in upper or base units utilize space by arranging larger and flat items in easily visible slots (thus avoiding nesting).

- Bottle storage units have frames to contain bottles.

- Spice racks may be attached to the back of an upper door or built into a double-door unit. A special spice drawer insert allows for easy visibility of seasonings.

- Hot pads may be stored in a narrow drawer under a built-in cooktop.

- A tilt-down sink front may hold sponges, scouring pads, and so on.

- Wire- or plastic-coated baskets for fruit and vegetable storage provide easily visible storage.

- A wastebasket attached to either a swing-out door or a tilt-down door, or sliding out from under the sink, provides a neat and out-of-sight trash container.

- Appliance garages are built into the back of the counter and enclose mixers, blenders, and other small appliances. The garage may have tambour doors or may match the cabinets.

- Portable recycling units have been on the market for some time. Some states and cities have comprehensive recycling laws, and both custom and stock cabinets offer multibasket recycling units (the four-unit model is most popular). Manufacturers recommend putting one single recycling unit near the sink for compostables, and then two away from the food preparation area, one for aluminum cans and the other for bottles. Local building codes should be checked to see whether some type of venting is necessary for the cabinet under the sink.

- A mixer can be placed in a base unit; gas cylinders then raise or lower in and out of the cabinet.

Several kitchen cabinet companies publish brochures that will assist in kitchen planning. These brochures include questionnaires that cover such issues as height of primary user, type of cooking to be performed, and what the consumer may or may not like about the current kitchen plan.

Counter Materials

Counters may be made of the following materials: decorative laminate, ceramic tile, wood, marble, travertine, solid surface materials, solid surfacing veneer (SSV), stainless steel, granite, or slate.

DECORATIVE LAMINATE

Decorative laminate was one of the first materials to be used for counters, whether residential or commercial. However, with the introduction of other types of counter materials, decorative laminate is now used primarily for counters in the lower end of the cost spectrum. A decorative laminate surface is durable, but it is not a cutting surface and will chip if heavy objects are dropped onto it.

Installation

Postformed countertops must be constructed at the plant rather than at the job site, because heat and special forming fixtures are used to create the curved edge. The counter may be manufactured as a single unit, or each postformed side may be manufactured separately. By manufacturing each side separately, any discrepancy in the alignment of the walls can be adjusted at the corner joints.

For square-edged counters, the edge is applied first and then routed smooth with the substrate. The flat surface is then applied, and the overlapping edges are routed flush with the counter surface.

Maintenance

Decorative laminate may be cleaned with warm water and mild dish soaps. Use of abrasives or special cleansers should be avoided because they may contain abrasives, acids, or alkalines. Stubborn stains may be removed with organic solvents or two minutes of exposure to a hypochlorite bleach, such as Clorox, followed by a clean-water rinse. The manufacturer's specific instructions and recommendations for cleaning should be followed.

CERAMIC TILE

Ceramic tile is a popular material with which to cover kitchen counters. To facilitate cleaning, the **backsplash** may also be covered with tile. Ceramic tile is a durable surface; the most vulnerable part is the grout, which can absorb stains unless a stainproof grout is specified. A grout sealer or lemon furniture oil will also seal the grout's surface so stains will not penetrate. Around the sink area, the ceramic tile counter may be carried down the front to the top of the doors below. This style, which is reminiscent of old farmhouse kitchens, protects wood cabinets from water. Because of the hard surface of the tile, fragile items that are dropped on the counter will break; if heavy objects are dropped, the tile may be cracked or broken. Sufficient tile for replacements should be ordered when the counter is installed.

Installation

For countertops, 1/4" or 1/2" cementitious ceramic tile backer boards are a good substrate for tile. The backer board should be adhered to the countertop surface using a latex modified thinset mortar and screws or nails. It is recommended that the screws or nails be installed every 6" on center. The ceramic tile should be installed using a latex modified thinset mortar subsurface of 1 1/8" (5/8" minimum) thick exterior grade plywood.[13]

The remaining installation procedure is the same as for floors and walls.

Maintenance

Maintenance of ceramic tile counters is the same as that for ceramic tile floors.

WOOD

Wood counters are usually made of a hard wood, such as birch or maple, and are constructed of glued strips of wood that are then sealed and coated with a varnish. Unsealed wood will permanently absorb stains. Wood counters should not be used as a cutting surface because the finish will become marred. A special area may be set aside for cutting purposes or a slide-out bread board can be installed. Any water accumulating around the sink should be mopped up immediately, as a wood surface can become damaged from prolonged contact with moisture. Wood counters may be installed in a curved shape by successively adding a strip of wood, gluing it, and clamping it. When dry, another piece is added.

MARBLE

Marble has often been used as a material for portions of the countertop. Today, in some expensive installations, marble may be used for the entire counter area. Some people like to use a marble surface for rolling out pastry or making hand-dipped chocolates. As mentioned in the section on marble floors, marble may absorb stains. This tendency may cause unsightly blemishes on marble countertops. Heavy items dropped on a marble surface will crack it.

Maintenance

Stain removal from marble countertops is the same as for marble floors.

QUARTZ

Cambria, which is "certified by NSF International as a safe surface for food preparation,"[14] is preferred by some to granite, as Cambria is nonporous and considered stronger than granite.

Maintenance

Wipe with warm water. Unlike other countertops, there is no sealing, buffing, or reconditioning ever needed.

CONCRETE

A concrete counter may be poured on site or at the factory, usually with reinforcements added, and then allowed to cure. It is usually ground with diamond cutters and then sealed with several coats of epoxy.

Maintenance

Apply a good water-based liquid wax every nine months to a year.

FIGURE 9.11 The Jenn-Air Floating Glass series, a sleek alternative to stainless steel exteriors, is shown with custom Italian cabinetry. This award-winning design is by Ellen Cheever. *Photo courtesy of Ellen Cheever & Associates.*

TRAVERTINE

When travertine is used as a counter material, it must be filled. Maintenance of travertine countertops is the same as for marble floors.

GRANITE AND SLATE

Granite has become a very popular material for kitchen counters in upscale houses. However, granite will absorb stains; therefore, it should be sealed. Construction of the cabinets must be strong enough to support the extra weight of stone. Granite is one of the most bacteria-resistant kitchen surfaces, and it is not affected by citric acid, coffee, tea, alcohol, or wine.

Slate, when used as a counter material, also needs to be sealed. (See Figure 9.11.)

Maintenance

Maintenance of granite and slate countertops is the same as that for granite walls and slate floors.

SOLID SURFACE MATERIALS

DuPont Corian solid surface is one of the most versatile materials in the global marketplace today. Consumers and professionals from all over the world are increasingly discovering that Corian is a material with endless potential. It is

- Available in over 100 standard colors with unlimited customization.
- Stain resistant.
- NSF/ANSI Standard 51 Certified for food contact and Class I(A) fire rated.
- Durable: Tough and long-lasting.
- Renewable: Color runs all the way through, making restoration easy if necessary.
- Heat-resistant.
- Easy-to-clean and maintain: Smooth seamless appearance.
- Without grout lines to catch dirt and bacteria.
- A nonporous surface that does not promote the growth of mold and mildew when properly cleaned.
- GREENGUARD Certified as a low-emitting material.[15]

Other brands of solid surface materials are made of polyester, which resists tight radii. Dark colors may perform differently from light colors.

Solid surface materials may have thicker, built-up edges, made by using joint adhesive. These can be routed into a variety of decorative treatments, including bull-nose edges and "sandwich" inserts. Solid surface manufacturers may be able to supply custom colors for large projects.

Maintenance

Most stains on solid surface materials wipe off with a regular household detergent. Because of the solid composition of these materials, most stains stay on the surface and may be removed with any household abrasive cleanser or Scotch-Brite pad gently rubbed in a circular motion. Cigarette burns and cuts may be removed with very fine sandpaper, 120-140 grit, and then rubbed with a Scotch-Brite pad. If the surface was highly polished, repolishing may be required to blend the damaged area.

STAINLESS STEEL

All commercial kitchens have stainless steel counters because these counters can withstand scouring, boiling water, and hot pans. Stainless steel counters can be installed in private residences, if desired, providing a high-tech look.

Maintenance

One of the problems with stainless steel is that the surface may show scratches, and with hard water the surface shows water spots. Water spots may be removed, however, by rubbing the damp surface with a towel; in addition, scratches gradually blend into a patina. Apart from possible scratches and spots, stainless steel is extremely easy to maintain.

Floors

Kitchen floors may be made of ceramic tile, quarry tile, wood, laminate, or any type of resilient flooring (see Figure 9.11). The choice of flooring will depend on the consumer's needs and personal wishes. Some people find a hard-surfaced floor to be tiring to the feet, whereas others are not bothered by the hard surface. Wood floors need to be finished with a durable finish that will withstand any moisture that may be spilled accidentally. Resilient flooring may be vinyl, may or may not be cushioned, or may use the new rubber sheet flooring.

Walls

Kitchen walls should be painted with an enamel paint that is easily cleansed of grease residue. Crossville Tile has paired with Benjamin Moore to develop a fan deck of paint color combinations that complement Crossville's Color by Numbers collection.

The backsplash may be covered with the same decorative laminate as used on the counter, applied either with a cove or a square joint. Ceramic tile may be used in conjunction with a ceramic tile counter or with a decorative laminate one. Mirror may also be selected for kitchen walls; it provides reflected light and visually enlarges the appearance of the counter space. A completely scrubbable wallcovering is another alternative material for the backsplash.

Certified Kitchen Designers

A certified kitchen designer (CKD) is a professional who has proven knowledge and technical understanding regarding kitchens through a stringent examination process conducted by the Society of Certified Kitchen Designers, the licensing and certification agency of the American Institute of Kitchen Dealers. A CKD has technical knowledge of construction techniques and systems used in new construction and light exterior and interior remodeling, including plumbing, heating, and electrical.

A CKD will provide a functional and aesthetically pleasing arrangement of space depicted in floor plans and interpretive renderings and drawings. In addition to designing and planning the kitchen, the CKD supervises installations of residential-style kitchens.

An interior designer would be well advised to work with a CKD.

glossary

Backsplash. A protective area behind a counter.

Bib. A downward-facing faucet.

Charcoal filter. A frame that contains charcoal particles, which filter the grease from the moving air.

CKD. Certified kitchen designer.

Convection oven. Cooking appliance in which heated air flows around the food.

Conventional oven. Cooking appliance in which food is cooked by radiation.

Corridor kitchen. Two parallel walls with no contiguous area.

Dolly. Two- or four-wheeled cart used for moving heavy appliances.

Drop-in range. Range designed to be built into base units.

Farmhouse sink. Hand-made low-fired ceramic sink without an overflow, which is molded from clay and then fired and glazed. The apron is flush with the cabinet front.

Freestanding range. Range having finished sides.

Glass-ceramic cooktop. A smooth ceramic top used as a cooking surface in electric ranges.

Hob. Sealed solid element providing a larger contact area with the bottom of the pan and better control at low-heat settings.

Kilowatt-hour (kwh). A unit of energy equal to 1,000 watt hours.

Microwave oven. Device in which heat is generated by the activation of the molecules within the food by the microwaves.

Plane. A flat surface.

Postforming. Heating a laminate to take the shape of a form.

Pullman kitchen. A one-wall kitchen plan.

Pyrolytic action. An oven that cleans by extremely high heat, incinerating any residue to an ash.

Slide-in range. Similar in construction to a drop-in range, except that the top edges may overhang the side; therefore, this type must be slid in rather than dropped in.

Strip kitchen. One-wall kitchen plan.

Studio kitchen. One-wall kitchen plan.

Tap. European word for faucet.

Work triangle. An imaginary triangle drawn between the sink, refrigerator, and cooking area.

endnotes

1. Kohler, "Work Triangles," www.kohler.com
2. Kevin Henry, "The Evolution of the Modern Kitchen," *Pure Contemporary Magazine*, March 2005
3. Elmira Stove Works, www.elmirastoveworks.com
4. Dimensions Guide, www.dimensionsguide.com/refrigerator-dimensions
5. RefrigeratorPro, www.refrigeratorpro.com
6. Design Journal Magazine, www.adexawards.com
7. Jenn-Air, www.jennair.com
8. Gaggenau, www.gaggenau.visukomm
9. House Beautiful, www.housebeautiful.com
10. Kohler, www.kohler.com
11. Delta, www.deltafaucet.com
12. KWC, www.kwcamerica.com
13. Floorings Transformed, www.flooringstransformed.com
14. Cambria USA, www.cambriausa.com
15. Dupont, www.dupont.com

In this chapter, you will:

- Recognize appropriate selection, composition, and maintenance of a variety of items addressed within bathroom design

- Examine the importance of industry-specific regulations and federal law related to energy conservation in the functioning of bathroom fixtures

- Explain the importance of federal law related to aspects of public restroom design, with an emphasis on ADA Title III Accessibility Guidelines

- Assess the nature and value of integrated design practices related to bathroom planning

Ancient Greek cities featured large public baths where one could take a hot and cold bath and then get a rubdown with olive oil. Public bathing was also practiced by the Romans, who used aqueducts to bring the water to the people of Rome. Their bathing facilities consisted of dressing rooms, warm rooms, hot baths, steam rooms, recreation rooms (where the bather exercised), and cold baths, as well as a swimming pool. These bathing facilities were an early version of present-day spas. After the fall of the Roman Empire, during the Dark Ages, bathing became much less frequent. In the 1800s and early 1900s, one often reads the Saturday night bath was a ritual. A metal tub was brought into the heated kitchen, and hot water was poured in by hand. Almost 90 percent of the modernization of bathrooms has occurred in the past 25 years.

Today, people in the United States take more showers and baths than residents of any other nation. In fact, hotels in the United States were the first to provide bathing rooms, beginning during the late 1800s. The novelty quickly proliferated in hotels and homes throughout the nation until the practice of bathrooms became commonplace. By the late twentieth century, this enjoyment of bathrooms gave rise to concerns of water and energy conservation. As the decades moved forward and baby boomers grew older, it became clear that fixtures in modern bathrooms would need to rise to meet a variety of accessibility and safety needs.[1]

Because all bathrooms have the same three basic fixtures, it is the designer's challenge to create a bathroom that is not only unique but functional. Knowledge of the different materials used in these fixtures and the variety of shapes, sizes, and colors will help designers meet this challenge.

Planning a Bathroom

Eljer offers the following suggestions for planning a better bathroom: The size of the family needs to be considered. The more people who will use a bathroom, the larger it should be. There should also be more storage, more electrical outlets, and perhaps more fixtures. If the bathroom is to be used by several people at the same time, compartmenting can often add to utility.

The family schedule should also be considered. Where several people depart for work or school at the same time, multiple or **compartmented** bathrooms should be considered. Two lavatories will allow a working couple to get ready for work at the same time.

The most economical arrangement of fixtures is against a single **wet wall.** Economy, however, is not the only factor to be considered. Plumbing codes, human comfort, and convenient use require certain minimum separation between—and space around—fixtures. The minimum size for a bathroom is approximately 5 feet by 7 feet, although, if absolutely necessary, a few inches may be shaved off these measurements. Deluxe bathrooms may be very large and incorporate a seating area or an exercise room and/or a **spa.**

In a corridor-type bathroom, there should be 30 inches of aisle space between the bathtub and the edge of the counter or the fixture opposite. The bathtub should only be placed under the window if there is privacy and the walls and window frames are tiled to retain watertight integrity. This window location is often used in the master bathroom. There should be a minimum of 24 inches in front of a toilet to provide knee room. When walls are on either side of the toilet, they should be 36 inches apart. If the **lavatory** or bathtub is adjacent to the toilet, then 30 inches is sufficient.

The lavatory requires elbow space. Five feet is the recommended minimum length of a countertop with two lavatories. The lavatories should be centered in the respective halves of the countertop. For a sit-down **vanity,** the counter should be 7 feet long, with 24 inches between the edges of the lavatories for greatest comfort. Six inches minimum should be allowed between the edge of a lavatory and any side wall.

The location of the bathroom door is extremely important. The door should be located so it will not hit a fixture, because such poor placement would eventually cause damage both to the door and the fixture. A sliding pocket door may have to be used to prevent this.

All bathroom fixtures, whether tubs, lavatories, toilets, or **bidets,** come in white and in standard colors which are more expensive than white fixtures. High-fashion colors—even black—cost 40 percent or more than white fixtures. Care should be taken not to select fad colors that will become dated, because bathroom fixtures are both difficult and expensive to replace when remodeling. To obtain a perfect match, all fixtures should be ordered from the same manufacturer. Colors, even white, vary from one manufacturer to another.

Floors

Bathroom floors should be of a type that can be cleaned easily, particularly in the area of the bathtub, shower, and toilet. Ceramic tile may be used, but it should not be highly glazed because glazed tiles, when used on a floor, can be slippery when wet. Other types of flooring material that can be used for the tub area include wood with a good finish, laminate, or any of the resilient flooring materials.

Carpeting may be used in the master bath but is not suggested for a family bath because of a likelihood of excessive moisture, which may cause mold and mildew.

Walls

Wallcoverings are often used in bathrooms. Vinyls or vinyl-coated wallcoverings are recommended because they are easy to wipe dry and maintain. Bathroom walls should be treated (before applying wallcovering) to prevent possible mildew (see Chapter 2). Most of the manufactured materials used for counters can be used to cover vertical surfaces, either on the wall or as a shower enclosure. If an acrylic shower and tub **surround** is not used, ceramic tile is installed because of its vitreous quality.

Only semi-gloss paint or enamels that can withstand moisture should be used on bathroom walls.

Bathtubs

The typical tract home bathtub is 5 feet long, 30 inches wide, and (in less expensive styles) only 14 inches deep. Tubs that are 6-foot long are available, however, for those who like to soak. Tub height, measured from the floor, may vary (14, 16, or even 22 inches). The depth figures represent the outside tub measurements, allowing for the **overflow** pipe. A 14-inch tub height does not permit the drawing of a very deep bath. Tub heights of 14 inches are convenient for bathing children.

Many semi-custom homes feature 5' × 42" or 6' × 42" oval tubs in master baths, among other sizes. In fact there are so many sizes and shapes of tubs that there is no longer an "average" size.

Most state laws require that all bathtubs installed today have a **slip-resistant** bottom. Many tubs also come with a handle on one or both sides, which is extremely useful for the elderly or infirm.

The straight end of the bathtub contains the drain and the plumbing, such as faucets or **fittings,** and the overflow pipe; therefore, the location of the bathtub must be decided before the order is placed. Bathtubs may be ordered with a left or right drain, all four sides enclosed, the front and two sides enclosed, or the front and one side enclosed. For a completely built-in look, a drop-in model may be specified.

The drop-in model is sometimes installed as a sunken tub. Although a sunken tub may present a luxurious appearance, it can be difficult to get into and out of such tubs. In addition, sunken tubs can be difficult to clean; it often means lying flat on the floor to reach the interior. Furthermore, sunken or recessed tubs can represent a safety hazard in that small children may crawl into the bathtub and hurt themselves or, at the worst, drown.

Bathtubs are manufactured of several materials. The old standby is the porcelain enameled cast-iron tub, which was originally a high-sided bathtub raised from the floor on ball-and-claw feet with the underside exposed. This style is still available today in a modernized version. (See Figure 10.1.)

The porcelain enamel gives better color than other materials and is approximately 1/16″ thick; however, this finish can be chipped if a heavy object is dropped on it. Therefore, bathtubs should be kept covered with a blanket or a special plastic liner until construction has been completed.

FIGURE 10.1 Modernized version of the old-fashioned ball-and-claw bathtub. *Photograph courtesy of American Standard Brands.*

A cast-iron bathtub is the most durable bathtub available; however, it is expensive and heavy, often weighing as much as 500 pounds. Therefore, the floor should be strong enough to bear the combined weight of the tub, the tub full of water, and the bather. Formed steel tubs with a porcelain enamel finish were developed to provide a lightweight (about 100 pounds) tub that would be less expensive than cast iron. Formed steel tubs are ideally suited for upper story installations or for remodeling because they are easier to move into place than cast-iron tubs. A formed steel tub is noisier than a cast-iron tub, but a sound-deadening coating may be applied to the underside at extra cost. If the bathtub does not come with an insulated coating on the outside, a roll of fiberglass insulation can be wrapped around the tub. This insulation not only helps the tub retain heat longer, but it also helps reduce noise. Because of the properties of steel, formed steel bathtubs may flex; thus, they do not have as thick a layer of porcelain enamel as do cast-iron tubs.

Heavy-duty polyester reinforced with fiberglass and surfaced **gel coat** can be used for bathtubs. In specifying this type of tub, it is important to select a name brand. There are currently many poor-quality units on the market produced by a process that does not require a large investment. Consequently, the tubs can crack easily and lose their surface rapidly. Good maintenance practices and avoidance of abrasive cleansers are mandatory for polyester-reinforced tubs. Some manufacturers recommend using a coat of marine wax or a good automotive wax to restore the shine to dulled surfaces of gel coat tubs.

Another type of lightweight bathtub is acrylic reinforced with fiberglass. This type of bathtub does not have such a high gloss as the gel-coated ones; however, maintenance is easier. There are several advantages to acrylic-reinforced fiberglass bathtubs. First, they are much lighter weight than steel or cast iron, although they may not be as durable. Second, the tub surround can be cast as an integral part of the bathtub and can include such features as a built-in seat, soap ledges, and grab bars. The latter type of tub can be installed only in new construction, because the tub and surround are too large to be placed in a remodeled bathroom. For remodeling, there are molded tub units with wall surrounds in two, three, or four pieces that pass easily through doorways and join in the recessed bathtub area to form a one-piece unit.

Soaking tubs are also made from reinforced fiberglass. Instead of sitting or lying in the tub, one sits on a molded, built-in seat; the tub is then filled to the requisite depth. Some soaking tubs are recessed into the floor and the bather steps over the edge and down into the tub; others are placed at floor level and require several steps to reach the top. Soaking tubs should not be installed in every bathroom in the house, because it is impossible to bathe small children in such tubs and the elderly or infirm will find it too dangerous to enter and leave a soaking tub. A regular bathtub should be installed in at least one bathroom in the house.

Some think of the registered trademarked name Jacuzzi as interchangeable with the term *whirlpool bath,* but the two are not synonymous. The trademarked term is derived from the name of the whirlpool bath's inventor; therefore, use of the term Jacuzzi should be limited to reference of items manufactured by the Jacuzzi Luxury Bath company.

Air baths and whirlpool baths are, for the most part, bathroom fixtures that require draining each time they are used. To provide additional strength, a number of products, including Jacuzzi's, are made with vacuum-formed acrylic that is reinforced with a fiberglass material. Whirlpool jets in a Jacuzzi, which provide a circular bubble pattern in the water, are located throughout the bath fixture, with an eye toward focusing massage on a variety of muscle groups.[2]

One specific air massage system, the EverClean Air Bath System offered by American Standard, provides an antimicrobial additive. With a focus on hindering growth of mildew and mold in pipes, this additive is molded into air circulation components. The system also offers a heater and optional chromatherapy.[3]

Kohler offers BubbleMassage baths. The company advises that these baths "are designed to deliver a holistic, complete-body experience." The company further advises that the 120 jets along the bottom perimeter provide a cushion of bubbles moving in random motion, and the intensity and direction of bubbles can be controlled by the user.[4]

Most companies manufacture a corner bath, which can be either a plain bath or, more often, a whirlpool. The corner location gives a feeling of openness because the tub does not have walls surrounding it and is only used for bathing, not for showering.

Spas or hot tubs are similar to whirlpool baths but need not be drained after each use. They are equipped with heat and filtration systems. Because the same water is recirculated, daily testing and maintenance of the proper water chemistry are required. Spas may be installed outside in warmer climates or in an area other than the bathroom. They have many of the same features as the whirlpool baths but are larger (64 to 84 inches long, 66 to 84 inches wide, and 28 to 37 inches high). Spas come with factory-installed redwood skirts and rigid covers.

Tub surrounds and shower enclosures may also be reinforced fiberglass, as mentioned previously, or they may be decorative laminate, ceramic tile, solid ABS, or solid acrylic. Many of these surrounds and enclosures have integrated tubs with built-in whirlpool systems. The all-in-one type eliminates the need to caulk around the area where the tub and surround meet. Failure to install and caulk the tub surround properly is the major cause of leaks in the tub area. When designing a bathroom, the bathtub should be placed where an access panel can be installed to simplify future plumbing repairs. Access *must* be provided to any whirlpool equipment to facilitate future maintenance.

Ceramic tile is installed as described in Chapter 4. The substrate must be exterior-grade plywood or a special water-resistant grade of gypsum board. The backer board, mentioned in Chapter 4, also makes a suitable substrate. Particular attention must be paid to the application of the grout, because the grout makes ceramic tile a waterproof material. When a cast-iron tub is used, the extra weight may cause a slight sagging of the floor. Any space caused by this settling should be caulked immediately.

Showers

Showers may be installed for use in a bathtub or they may be in a separate shower stall. There should always be at least one bathtub in a house, but stall showers may be used in the remaining bathrooms. When used with a bathtub, the tub spout contains a **diverter** that closes off the spout and diverts the water to the showerhead. A bathroom with a shower instead of a tub is designated as a three-quarter bath.

Stall showers are 34" square; a slightly larger 36" square is recommended if space is available. These are minimum requirements; deluxe showers may be 48" square or even 60" × 36" wide. The larger ones usually include a seat.

Stall showers may be constructed entirely of ceramic tile; in other words, the sloping base and walls are all made of tile. When installing a ceramic tile shower area, particular attention should be paid to the waterproof base and to the installation procedures supplied by the manufacturer or the Tile Council of North America. Other stall showers have a **preformed base,** with the surround touching the top of the 5" to 6" deep base. This preformed base is less slippery than a base of a tile but not quite as aesthetically pleasing. Shower walls may be constructed of any of the solid surface materials.

The standard height of a showerhead is 66 inches for men and 60 inches for women, which puts the spray below the hairline. These measurements mean that the plumbing for the showerhead must break through the tub or shower surround. Therefore, it is recommended that the shower **feed-in** be 74 inches above the floor. When placed at this height, the showerhead should be adjustable so it can be used to wash hair or to hit below the hairline.

The Flipside handshower provides four distinct showering sensations, each with its own dedicated sprayface:

- Koverage provides a full-face spray for a superb performance for everyday use.
- Kotton releases a uniquely dense, soft, enveloping downpour of luxury spa spray.
- Komotion offers a full-face spray that delivers a drenching spray in an exhilarating, circular pattern that both relaxes and refreshes the senses for a deep sense of well-being.
- Kurrent delivers a targeted massage spray to ease away aches and pains and revitalize the body.[5]

A hand-held shower can easily be installed in any bathtub, provided the bathroom walls are covered with a waterproof material. This type of shower comes with a special diversion spout, and the water reaches the showerhead by means of a flexible metal line. One type of showerhead is hung on a hook at the required height. Another type is mounted on a 5-foot vertical rod and attached to the water outlet by means of a flexible hose. This full-range sliding spray holder or grab bar locks at any desired height. The spray holder is both adjustable and removable.

There are several advantages of hand-held showers. Such showers can be hung at a lower level for use by children and can be used to rinse the hair of young children without the complaint of "the soap is getting in my eyes." In addition, hand-held units may be used to clean and rinse the interior of the bathtub.

The In2ition Two-in-One Shower from Delta Faucet, which flows at 2.5 gallons per minute (gpm), gives you water any way you need it, anywhere you want it. (See Figure 10.2.) The showerhead features a detachable handshower, which can run separately from or simultaneously with the showerhead, providing the warmth and flexibility of two streams of water at once. Bathers can enjoy the comfort of water streaming from the showerhead position, while using the handshower to accomplish other tasks, such as bathing children, washing the pet, and keeping the shower clean.[6]

FIGURE 10.2 The In2ition Shower with H$_2$Okinetic Technology from Delta Faucet. *Photograph courtesy of Delta Faucet Company, www.deltafaucet.com.*

Showerheads that are more than 5 to 10 years old use between 3 and 8 gallons of water per minute. Replacing one of these with a model achieving a flow of 2.5 gallons per minute or less will save the average household almost 12,000 gallons of water annually. Water is a limited resource that should be conserved. In fact, some cities have mandated 2.5 gallon showerheads. However, water conservation does not have to mean a skimpy shower. Speakman Anystream showerheads will automatically adjust water flow to compensate for available pressure. By means of the spray-adjusting T-handle, output ranges from bracing needle spray to gentle rain.

There are several ways to keep water within the shower area. One way is to add a shower curtain hung from rings at the front of the shower. A shower curtain is a decorative feature; however, unless care is taken to ensure placement of the shower curtain inside the base when using the shower, water may spill over onto the floor, causing a hazard. Glass shower doors are also used (the type depends on local building codes). All shower doors

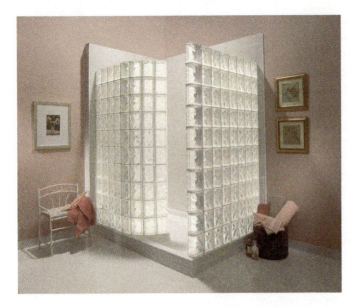

FIGURE 10.3 This walk-in shower is one of two designs in the Pittsburgh Corning Glass Block Shower systems which provide the custom-built glass block shower—without the "custom" hassle. *Photograph courtesy of Pittsburgh Corning Glass Block.*

are made of tempered glass, but some codes require the addition of a wire mesh. These glass doors may pivot, hinge, slide, or fold. The major maintenance problem with glass doors involves removing soap and hard water residue from the glass surface and cleaning the water channel at the base of the door. However, a water softener greatly reduces or even eliminates this residue. Some shower units are designed with close-fitting doors that completely enclose the front of the unit and become steam systems with a **sauna** effect. (See Figure 10.3.)

Master bathroom showers are often designed so no door or curtain is required. These shower stalls have walls placed in such a manner that the water is contained within the wet area.

Wheelchair-accessible stall showers are available and vary in size from 42" × 36" to 65" × 36", all with an interior threshold height of only 1/2". Units with integral seats have the seat placed toward the front of the enclosure for easier access. Hewi, Inc. manufactures a wide variety of accessories which will make a shower accessible, including a fold-up seat, hanging seats, and grab bars (all available in 12 colors).

Tub and Shower Faucets

The old-fashioned type of tub faucet is ledge mounted; the fitting is mounted on the edge of the tub or tub enclosure, usually with an 8-inch to 18-inch **spread.**

Tub/shower combinations may be of two different types: deck mounted or wall mounted. **Deck mounted** are used only for tubs. Both types are available in single or dual control (hot and cold water are controlled together or separately). A shower-only unit has wall-mounted controls, which may be single or dual control. Single controls regulate the temperature of the water more easily. Two choices are available with a tub/shower combination: two sets (one for the tub and the other for the shower), or one set with a diverter. The diverter in tub/shower combinations is most commonly a diverter-on-spout. After the water temperature is balanced, the diverter is pulled up to start the shower. To stop the flow of water to the showerhead, the diverter is pushed down. The handle diverter design has three handles; by twisting the middle handle, the water is diverted to the showerhead. The two other handles control the hot and cold water. This handle diverter has 8-inch **centers.**

Most showerheads are adjustable and change the flow of water to drenching, normal, or fine spray. Some showerheads have a pulsating flow that provides a massaging action. Conventional showerheads use from 6 to 8 gallons of water per minute. However, plumbing codes are being amended to make 2.7 gallons of water per minute at 60 psi the maximum amount of water that can be used. Antiscald controls are required by law on all showerheads. Many manufacturers have similar multi-jet showers.

Fast-flowing Roman tub valves feature high-flow 3/4" valves. This type of valve enables whirlpool baths to be filled rapidly, provided a large-capacity water tank is used. Like all other types of faucets, showerheads may come in white, brass, or a combination of brass and chrome.

Lavatories

Lavatories come in many sizes, shapes, and materials, according to personal and space requirements. Although many types of materials are used, most lavatories are made of vitreous china. All of the following materials may be used, however: glass, cast iron, stainless steel, sculpted marble, china or ceramic, wood, enameled steel, polished brass, or solid surface materials.

(a) (b)

FIGURE 10.4 (a) Kallos spun glass undercounter lavatory; (b) Vox Vessels square lavatory in White and Symbol with a tall single-control lavatory faucet in Polished Chrome. *Both photographs courtesy of Kohler.*

The latest trend, shallow hand washing lavatories, is available in the United States and Europe. In this style, there is no waste of water as in larger washbasins. (See Figure 10.4.)

Lavatories are usually round or oval, but they may also be rectangular, or even triangular for corner installations. Sizes range from 11" × 11" for powder rooms to 38" × 28".

Pedestal lavatories, a newer style of lavatory, are probably most suitable in a master bathroom because they do not provide the adjacent counter area usually needed in family bathrooms. They may be as streamlined or decorative as desired. To compensate for the lack of counter space, some pedestal lavatories are as large as 44" × 22", with a wide ledge surrounding the bowl area.

Built-in lavatories or sinks may be one of six types.

1. They may be self-rimming (where a hole is cut into the counter smaller than the size of the lavatory and the bowl is placed so the edge is raised above the level of the counter). With a self-rimming sink, water cannot be swept back into the bowl and must be mopped up.

2. For a flush counter and bowl installation, the lavatory may be installed with a flush metal rim. This is a popular and inexpensive style but can cause a cleaning problem at the juncture of the rim and the countertop.

3. The integral bowl and counter, such as those made of solid surface materials, is another option. With this type, which may be placed virtually anywhere on the vanity top, the countertop and bowl are seamed for a one-piece look, with the faucets usually mounted on the counter.

4. An old-fashioned wall-hung installation is quite often used in powder rooms or for wheelchair users.

5. The lavatory is installed under the counter. This type of installation is generally used with a tile, marble, or synthetic countertop. Under-the-counter installations are becoming very popular and require that the fittings be deck mounted.

6. The lavatory can be installed above the counter; this is a modern version of the pitcher and bowl set of the Victorian era.

Lavatories come punched with one hole or three holes. The single hole is for European-style single hole faucets. With single-control fittings and 4-inch centerset fittings, the third hole is for the **pop-up rod.** In wide-spread fittings, however, the third hole is used for the mixture of hot and cold water.

Some lavatories are punched with one or two extra holes. These holes are used as a shampoo lavatory and have a retractable spray unit. The second extra hole is for a soap or shampoo dispenser. Shampoo lavatories are extremely useful for a family with children because the bowl is usually installed in a 32″ high vanity (in contrast to the 36″ height of a kitchen sink). Some styles of shampoo lavatories feature spouts that swing away.

In imported brochures, lavatories are often referred to as **basins** or washbasins. Basins are available for very small bathrooms such as guest or powder rooms. They are triangular in shape, about 18″ in length, 6″ wide, and 6″ deep.

Lavatory Faucets

There are many types of lavatory faucets. For example, Alfred M. Moen invented the single-handle faucet after being burned by the sudden flow of hot water. **Center-fit** faucet fittings have been used ever since the 1980s. With these units, the two handles and spout are in one piece, with a 4-inch spread. The single-control unit (with a 4-inch spread) has a central control that regulates both temperature and rate of flow. This single-control unit may also work by means of a lever that, when pulled up, increases the flow of water and, when pushed down, decreases the flow. In European models the flow is started by moving a small pencil-thin lever. Temperature is controlled by moving the lever to the right for cold and to the left for warm or hot water. For arthritis sufferers, the lever faucet is easier to operate than a knob type.

Placement of the faucets depends on the sink's design. Some sinks have predrilled holes for the faucets, others require a deck-mounted style, and still others are wall mounted. Faucets must be ordered after the sink has been selected.

The popularity of center-fit faucets has been declining; spread-fit fittings now comprise 80 percent of the market, and their share is growing. Center-fit faucets may be making a comeback, however, as consumers look to the past. With spread-fit faucets, the hot and cold handles and the spout are independent of each other. To make installation and choice of faucet sets easier, the fittings should be joined by means of flexible connectors. If flexible connectors are not used, faucet choices may be limited to the spread of the holes in the selected lavatory. When center-fit fittings are used, a plate covers the center hole. When a spread-fit fitting is used, the center hole accommodates the spout. Mini-wide faucets offer the appearance of spread-fit faucets and fit the common 4-inch center fit. Mini-wides are more difficult to clean, however, because the faucets are very close together.

To conserve water, bathroom faucets are now set to a flow of 2 gallons per minute. Most manufacturers are now using a ceramic disc cartridge inside the faucet as they are considered very durable, especially with problem water. The cartridge helps prevent dripping, which can waste gallons of water a year.

Several companies are now manufacturing faucets designed as barrier-free products with water conservation in mind. When the faucet's electronic sensor beam is broken by the hands, water flows at the preset temperature. This typically results in savings of up to 85 percent over normal water usage. Additional energy savings are realized because hot water is conserved.

Faucets may be polished chrome, black chrome, polished brass, or even gold plated. A current trend is to use two different finishes on the same faucet, such as black chrome with polished chrome and/or polished brass, or wood and brass. Brushed nickel with brass is often used as well. In addition, two finishes are often used on what is known as the ring handle (circular handles with no extended part).

Usually chrome is the most durable finish, followed by colors and then brass. With the introduction of the PVD process, brass is now a viable choice. Delta, a Masco company, uses Brilliance on their brass bathroom fittings, with the pop-up drain (usually the first part of the faucet assembly to show wear) being coated also.

Translucent and metal handles have slight indentations to provide a non-slipping surface. The handles may also be of a lever type. The traditional shape for spouts is being re-placed by a more delicately curved or very organic geometric shape. The Roman-style faucets previously used for bathtubs are now being used for lavatories.

Pull-out spouts, which have previously been a feature of kitchen faucets, are now used for lavatories. **Wrist control** handles, which meet the standards of the Americans with Disabilities Act, do not require turning or pulling but are activated by a push or pull with the wrist rather than the fingers.

Toilets

In Europe, a toilet is often called a *water closet*. The plumbing trade frequently uses that term or *closet* when referring to what the layperson calls a toilet. In some areas of the United States, the toilet may also be called a *commode*. We will use the word *toilet* because this is the more common word; however, when talking to a plumber, *closet* is more correct. Toilet bowls and tanks are constructed of vitreous china, because only vitreous china can withstand the acids to which a toilet is subjected. Most toilets are designed with water-saving devices that are both economically and environmentally important.

There are two basic shapes to a toilet: regular (round bowl) and the elongated bowl. Most toilets do not come with a toilet seat; therefore, it is important to know the shape of the toilet before ordering a seat. Some special shape expensive toilets do, however, come with a seat. More space (usually 2 inches) is required for installing an elongated bowl toilet. Local building codes will provide space requirements.

Toilets may be wall hung, which leaves the floor unobstructed for easy cleaning, or floor mounted. Wall-hung toilets have a wall outlet; in other words, they flush through a drain in the wall. To support the weight of a wall-hung toilet, the contractor must use 6-inch studs and install an L-shaped unit called a chair carrier. Floor-mounted toilets flush through the floor or the wall. For concrete floor construction, wall outlets are suggested to eliminate the extra cost of slab piercing.

Another choice in the design of toilets is whether the tank and bowl should be a **low profile,** one-piece integral unit, or whether the tank and bowl should be in two pieces. An old-fashioned ambience can be created by using an overhead wall-hung tank with a traditional pull chain. In areas where condensation on the toilet tank is a problem, an insulated tank may be ordered.

All toilets are required to have a visible water turn-off near the bowl on the back wall in case of a faulty valve in the tank.

Toilets have different flushing actions, such as gravity flush or pressure assisted. Gravity flush uses nothing more than water weight to generate flushing pressure and will work with very low **water pressure** from the water supply system. The pressure-assisted system is described in the following text.

The 1992 National Energy Policy Act limited water use for new toilets to 1.6 gallons per flush, compared with the typical 3.5-gallon models. For a family of four, that meant a savings of more than 11,000 gallons of water per year. A European import even has double-handed flushers to vary how much water is used in each flush. However, when this new law went into effect, the new toilets were not very efficient and often resulted in double flushes, which defeated the purpose of the law. All the major plumbing manufacturers now use the *FLUSHMATE* vessel from the Sloan Valve Company.

The toilet actually contains a tank inside a tank. That is, the pressure-assist vessel resides within the tank of the toilet. This vessel holds all of the water used by the toilet. The pushing action of the pressure-assist vessel requires the bowl to be designed differently, which means a gravity toilet cannot be retrofitted with a pressure-assist vessel.[7] (See Figure 10.5.)

Toto now manufactures the DuoFitIn-Wall Tank System. This in-wall unit features a high-efficiency dual flushing system that optimizes water usage by enabling the user to choose 0.09 gallons per flush (gpf) for liquid waste and 1.6 gpf for solid waste. The system is universal height as the toilet bowl's rim height may be adjusted from 15" to 19" and it supports up to 880 lbs.[8]

FIGURE 10.5 Aquia Wall-Hung Dual-Flush Toilet. *Courtesy of Toto USA.*

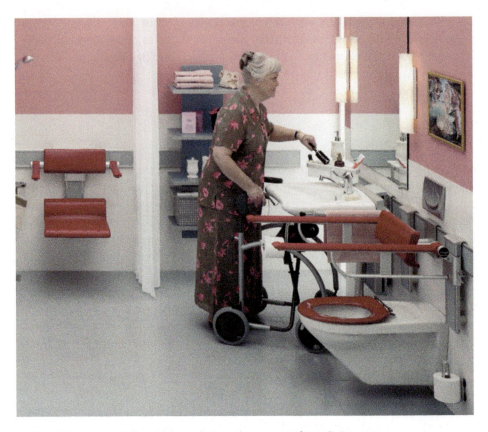

FIGURE 10.6 Barrier-free bathroom by Pressalit Care. *Photo courtesy of Pressalit Care, Inc.*

The contractor should allow 36″ × 36″ of clearance space in front of the toilet or bidet, as well as 16″ from the center of the fixture to an adjacent wall or fixture.

Toilets for elderly and disabled individuals have an 18″ high seat, whereas regular toilet seats are 15 1/2″ high. Higher toilets may also have a set of metal rails or armrests for extra support. The height of the seat on one-piece toilets may be less than 18 inches. (See Figure 10.6.)

Bidets

Although bidets are common in Europe, they are only now becoming an accepted fixture in American bathrooms, and only in more sophisticated types of installations. A bidet is generally installed as a companion and adjacent to the water closet or toilet and is used for cleansing the perineal area. Bidets do not have seats. The user sits astride the bowl, facing the controls that regulate water temperature and operate the pop-up drain and transfer valve. Water enters the bidet via the spray rinse in the bottom of the bowl. A bidet may also be used as a foot bath when the pop-up drain is closed.

When the fresh water supply is below or directly involved with piping, a **vacuum breaker** must be installed.

Countertops

The term *vanity cabinet* is not technically used in the architectural profession. Ready-made bathroom cabinets containing the lavatory are so often called and sold by this name, however, that this term is used to refer to the prefinished cabinet with doors underneath the countertop. Vanity cabinets may be ordered with or without a finished countertop. The lavatory is purchased separately. Other types of vanities come with the countertop and bowl molded in one.

A ready-made vanity is between 29 and 30 inches in height. For a master bathroom in a custom-designed house, the counter can be raised to suit personal requirements; however, some building codes state that at least one vanity in the house must be at the lower height.

Most custom-designed bathrooms have specially designed cabinets containing the lavatory with a storage area beneath. A bathroom countertop may be made of the same materials as a kitchen counter, although marble is more frequently used in bathrooms than in kitchens.

Solid surfacing materials for countertops, vanities, lavatory bowls, showers, and bathtubs are becoming increasingly popular because they are versatile and attractive.

Accessories

There should be 22 inches of towel storage allowed for each person, and towels should be within convenient reach of the bath, shower, and lavatory. Soap containers may be recessed into the wall, such as those used in the tub area. For the lavatory with a counter, a soap dish can be a colorful accessory. A toilet tissue dispenser should be conveniently placed next to the toilet. Many faucet manufacturers that make designer model faucets also make bath accessories to match.

Ground fault interrupter (**GFI**) electrical outlets must also be provided for the myriad of electrical gadgets used in the bathroom. All switches should be placed far enough away so they cannot be reached from a tub or shower area. (This is usually stated in local building codes.) All electrical switches should be at least 60 inches away from water sources.

Mirrors may be on the door of a built-in medicine cabinet, or they may be installed to cover the entire wall over the counter area. When used in the latter manner, mirrors visibly enlarge the bathroom. The top of the mirror should be at least 72 inches above the floor.

Special cabinets may contain pull-out laundry hampers, tilt-out waste baskets, drawer organizers for cosmetics and toiletries, and appliance garages for personal appliances.

Sussman Lifestyle Group offers the WarmaTowel, an amenity that adds comfort and cozy warmth to the bath experience. The towel warmer is all-brass construction and is matched with a stainless-steel built-in heater. WarmaTowel comes in a variety of floor, pivoting, and wall models and finishes. (See Figure 10.7.)

FIGURE 10.7 WarmaTowel towel warmers are the perfect complement to any luxury bath. Shown is a floor model.
Photo courtesy of Sussman Lifestyle Group, a division of Sussman-Automatic Corp.

Ventilating fans are required in bathrooms that do not have windows that can be opened.

Certified Bathroom Designers (**CBDs**) perform the same services for bathroom design as Certified Kitchen Designers (CKDs) do for kitchen design.

Public Restrooms

The previously discussed bathrooms were designed to accommodate one or two people at a time. In public restrooms, however, conditions and location may mean that the bathroom will be used by many people at the same time. (This includes not only people who can walk, but those who use wheelchairs and those who walk with impaired mobility.)

The ADA Title III requires all new construction of public accommodations and commercial facilities to meet or exceed ADA Accessibility Guidelines for Buildings and Facilities (ADAAG) specifications.

According to Bobrick Washroom Equipment Inc., public washrooms are one of the most critical building amenities with regard to accessibility and function for people with disabilities. With one in four persons becoming disabled sometime during their life, washrooms need to be responsive to a wide range of human needs and abilities, including people without disabilities, those using wheelchairs and walking aids, people with sight or hearing disabilities, people with impaired coordination, those with cardiac or pulmonary disorders, and even people affected by temporary illness, pregnancy, or advanced age. The ADA requires that all washrooms, whether newly constructed or remodeled, be usable by people with disabilities. This means that some of each type of fixture or feature must meet barrier-free requirements. All building plans, however, should be confirmed with local jurisdictions to ensure job compliance.[9]

Bobrick publishes a brochure, *Barrier-Free Washroom Planning Guide*, which includes diagrams to aid in making public restrooms accessible for wheelchair-bound individuals. (See Figure 10.8.) This planning guide also has specifications for water closets serving children ages 3 through 12, and also the forward and side reach of various ages of children.

Universal design can be accomplished in several ways, such as (1) using the same item for everyone, (2) positioning an item differently, (3) modifying or replacing a single manufactured feature of an item, or (4) replacing an item with one that is more adjustable or adaptable. Universal design eliminates radically different looking items and special labels (e.g., handicapped), as well as the stigma associated with them, while providing choices for all users.[10]

Public restrooms receive a great deal of physical abuse, most of which is not premeditated but occurs through normal wear and tear. Unfortunately, because vandalism does occur, fixtures and materials must be selected for durability. Bobrick manufactures a line of Maximum-Security Accessories that are mostly secured from the rear. A two-stall restroom in a small restaurant and multi-stall restrooms in a huge recreational facility must be designed differently with this potential for vandalism in mind.

Maintenance is another factor in the selection of materials and fixtures for public restrooms. Floors are usually made of ceramic tile or similar material and require a floor drain, not only for an emergency flooding situation, but also to simplify cleaning and disinfecting of the floor. For the hospitality areas, such as hotels, durable and functional commercial accessories are available.

LAVATORIES

To aid in cleaning the counter areas of public restrooms, vitreous china lavatories with flush metal rims are most frequently specified. Such lavatories allow quick cleaning of any excess water on the counter. White sinks are usually selected in restrooms for two reasons: (1) They are cheaper and (2) cleanliness is more easily visible.

Lavatories come with three holes punched in the top; however, soft or liquid soap dispensers may be installed in a four-hole sink. Alternatively, the soap dispenser may be

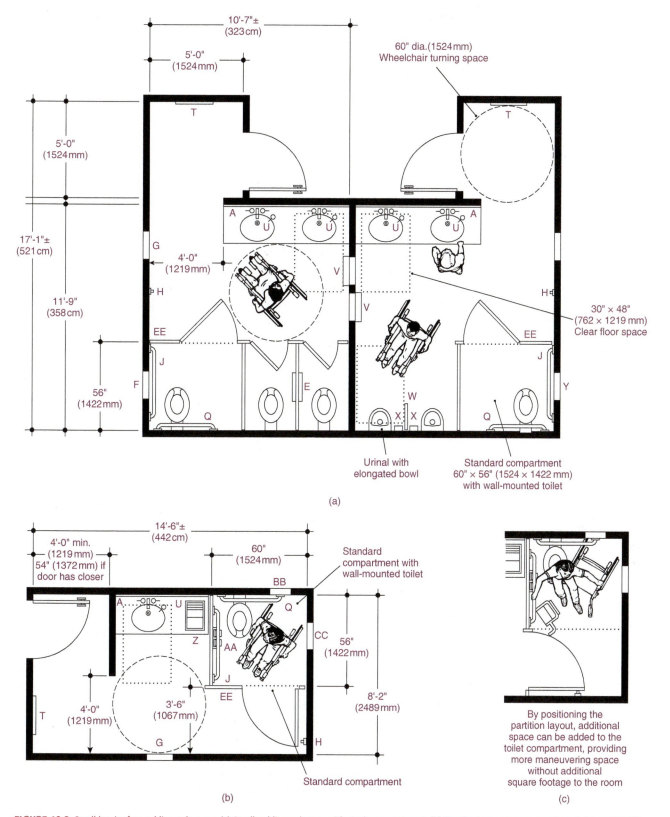

10'-7"±
(323 cm)

5'-0"
(1524 mm)

60" dia.(1524 mm)
Wheelchair turning space

5'-0"
(1524 mm)

T

T

A   U   U   U   A

G

4'-0"
(1219 mm)

V

17'-1"±
(521 cm)

H

V

H

30" × 48"
(762 × 1219 mm)
Clear floor space

11'-9"
(358 cm)

EE

EE

J

J

F

E

Y

56"
(1422 mm)

Q

W

X   X

Q

Urinal with
elongated bowl

Standard compartment
60" × 56" (1524 × 1422 mm)
with wall-mounted toilet

223

Bathrooms

(a)

14'-6"±
(442 cm)

4'-0" min.
(1219 mm)
54" (1372 mm) if
door has closer

60"
(1524 mm)

Standard
compartment with
wall-mounted toilet

BB

A   U

Q

Z

CC

56"
(1422 mm)

AA

J

T

4'-0"
(1219 mm)

3'-6"
(1067 mm)

EE

8'-2"
(2489 mm)

G

H

Standard compartment

By positioning the
partition layout, additional
space can be added to the
toilet compartment, providing
more maneuvering space
without additional
square footage to the room

(b)

(c)

FIGURE 10.8 Small barrier-free public washrooms. (a) Small public washroom with single compartment. (b) Standard compartment meeting minimum ADAAG requirements. (c) Standard alcove compartment that provides greater accessibility. By positioning the partition layout, space can be added to the toilet compartment, providing more maneuvering space without adding square footage to the room. *Courtesy of Bobrick Washroom Equipment Inc.*

attached to the wall above each lavatory or between two adjacent ones. For freestanding applications, wall-hung vitreous china lavatories may be specified.

A specially designed lavatory that meets ADA requirements must be installed to enable the seated person to reach faucet handles. Faucets, toilets, and washroom accessories meant to be used by physically disabled people must meet ADA specifications for controls and operating mechanism (push buttons, valves, knobs, and levers); in other words, *they must be operable with one hand, without tight grasping, pinching, or twisting of the wrist, and with a force that does not exceed 5 pounds of force.*

Because some wheelchair occupants are paraplegic, it is important to turn down the temperature of hot water to 110°F and wrap the waste pipe with some form of insulation. These measures will prevent inadvertent burns.

FAUCETS

Some companies specialize in manufacturing faucets designed to be used in public restrooms. These faucets are available with **metering devices,** usually of the push-button type, that can be adjusted to flow for 5 to 15 seconds. This metering conserves energy and water and prevents accidental flooding. Other faucets have an electronic eye; when the beam is broken, the faucet turns on and stays on as long as there is continuous motion (such as hands being washed) in the sensor field. By reacting to motion and not to beam obstructions, they can help conserve water, minimize vandalism, and reduce maintenance time. Common obstructions, like soap and water, will not disrupt normal operation. If the sensor is covered completely, the faucet will shut off in 12 seconds. Most electronic faucets have temperature controls to eliminate the chance of scalding.

Faucets manufactured for commercial use can be fitted with anti-vandal devices, which require special tools to dismantle.

TOILETS

Wall-hung toilets are often used in public restrooms to facilitate cleaning. The toilet seats on these toilets do not have lids and must have an open front. To aid in quicker maintenance and to avoid vandalism, toilets in public restrooms do not usually use a conventional tank, but instead have a **flush valve.** This valve requires greater water pressure than residential toilets, but uses less water and is easier to maintain. This type of valve is not used in private residences because it is too noisy. It may be operated by hand or sometimes by a foot pedal. Another electronic method of flushing activates the flushing mechanism automatically when there is no longer pressure on the seat.

Several different types of **urinals** may be used in the men's room. All are constructed of vitreous china, and all have integral flushing rims. One type is a stall urinal mounted on the floor. Others may be wall hung. A wall-hung unit with an elongated front is designed for use by the physically disabled and meets ADA requirements. Urinals can also have automatic flushing similar to the toilets mentioned before.

STALL PARTITIONS

There are many different styles of stall dividers and many different materials from which to select for them. The **pilasters** may be floor anchored, ceiling hung, overhead braced, or floor-to-ceiling anchored. Ceiling types minimize maintenance but require structural steel support in the ceiling. Stalls are 32" to 36" wide and 56" to 60" high. However, doors are 22" to 29" wide for in-swinging doors and 32" to 36" wide for out-swinging doors. The difference in the width measurement is made up by stiles which vary between 3 to 24 inches, depending on requirements. Doors of regular stalls open into the stall, whereas some wheelchair-accessible stalls have out-swinging doors that are 34" wide with an overall size of 60" wide by 59" deep.

Bobrick's *Barrier-Free Washroom Planning Guide* offers complete instructions regarding the size and location of stalls, toilets, lavatories, and all accessories. There is a great need for more stalls in ladies' rooms than in men's restrooms. Some architects are beginning to realize this need after seeing long lines outside the ladies' rooms at sporting events and other public affairs.

The material used for partitions may be galvanized steel primed and finished with two coats of baked enamel, stainless steel, seamless high-pressure decorative laminate, or even marble. All of these finishes come in a variety of colors and may be coordinated with the colors used for washroom accessories, vanity centers, shelves, and countertops.

When the design of restrooms dictates, entrance screens for privacy should be used. It is important to consider the direction the door opens and placement of mirrors to ensure privacy.

Urinal screens are used in men's restrooms. These screens may be wall hung, floor anchored, ceiling hung, or supported by a narrow stile going from floor to ceiling, in a similar manner to the stall partitions. Urinal screens are placed between each urinal or between the urinal area and other parts of the restroom.

ACCESSORIES

Washroom accessories must not project more than 4 inches into a clear access aisle if their leading edge is between 27 and 80 inches above the finish floor; if their leading edge is at or below 27 inches, then they may project any amount as long as the required minimum width of an adjacent clear access aisle is maintained. This standard is specifically designed to ensure detection by visually impaired people. It is recommended that all floor-standing and surface-mounted units projecting more than 4 inches be located in corners, alcoves, or between other structural elements so as not to be a hazard to visually impaired people or interfere with access aisles or wheelchair turning areas. Fully recessed accessories are the preferred choice throughout universally designed washrooms.

As was mentioned previously, soap dispensers may be installed on the lavatory rim itself. This type is preferable because any droppings from the dispenser are washed away in the bowl; the dry powder type usually leaves a mess on the counter area. To meet ADA standards, soap dispensers installed over lavatories must be mounted so their push buttons are no higher than 54 inches above the finished floor. Paper towel dispensers should be within easy reach of the lavatory, along with towel disposal containers. Sometimes both these accessories come in one wall-hung or wall-recessed unit. Another method of hand drying is the heated air blower. At the push of a button, heated air is blown out and the hands are rubbed briskly until dry. This type of hand dryer eliminates the mess of paper towel disposal; however, if the dryer breaks down there is no way for users to dry their hands. Newer hand dryers operate electronically, similar to automatic faucets; in other words, they start when the hands are positioned under the blower and turn off when the hands are removed. There are also automatic motion-controlled paper towel dispensers which spew out a sheet of paper towel.

Each toilet compartment requires a toilet tissue dispenser; an optional accessory is the toilet seat cover dispenser. In addition, a feminine product disposal accessory is necessary in each stall in a ladies' room. A napkin and tampon vending machine should be placed outside, near the toilet stalls. A hook for hanging pocketbooks and jackets is optional in toilet stalls. The preferred location for a hook is on the handle side of the door so no personal items are left behind. Another optional accessory in ladies' toilet stalls is a flip-down shelf that holds packages off the floor area.

In stalls for use by disabled individuals, stainless steel grab bars are required by law to be mounted on the wall nearest the toilet. They are 1 1/2 inch in diameter, 1 1/2 inches from the wall, and 33 inches from the floor. Local building codes vary, so it is important to consult the codes for exact measurements.

There are two methods of transfer for wheelchair-bound people, depending on their abilities. Those who are able to stand with support can pull themselves upright by means of the grab bars. Others have to use the side transfer method, in which the arm of the wheelchair is removed and the individuals lean across the toilet and pull themselves onto the seat. The side transfer method requires a larger stall, because the chair must be placed alongside the toilet; front transfer requires only the depth of the chair plus standing room in front of the toilet.

Another accessory, often installed in the larger stalls, is a baby changing station that folds down from the wall. It has straps to hold the baby while the mother is busy.

bibliography

Bobrick. *Barrier-Free Washroom Planning Guide*. Los Angeles, CA: Bobrick, 2005.

Mazzurco, Philip. *Bath Design*. New York: Whitney Library of Design, an imprint of Watson-Guptill Publications, 1986.

glossary

Basin. A European term for a lavatory.

Bidet. A sanitary fixture for cleansing the genitourinary area of the body.

CBD. Certified bathroom designer.

Center fit. Two handles and one spout mounted on a single plate.

Centers. Another way of saying "on centers"; in other words, the measurement is from the center of one hole to the center of the second hole.

Compartmented. Bathroom divided into separate areas according to function and fixtures.

Deck mounted. The faucets are mounted on a surface outside of the tub or lavatory.

Diverter. Changes flow of water from one area to another.

Feed-in. Where the rough plumbing is attached to the fittings.

Fittings. Another word for the faucet assembly; a term used by the plumbing industry.

Flush valve. Designed to supply a fixed quantity of water for flushing purposes.

Gel coat. A thin, outer layer of resin, sometimes containing pigment, applied to a reinforced plastic moulding to improve its appearance.

GFI. Ground fault interrupter. A special electrical outlet for areas where water is present.

Lavatory. The plumbing industry's name for a bathroom sink.

Low profile. A one-piece toilet with almost silent flushing action. There are almost no dry surfaces on the bowl interior.

Metering device. An object that releases a preset measured amount of water when the metering device is activated.

Overflow. A pipe in bathtubs and lavatories used to prevent flooding. The pipe is located just below the rim or top edge of these fixtures.

Pedestal. A lavatory on a base attached to the floor rather than set into a counter surface. The base hides all the waste pipes that are usually visible.

Pilaster. Vertical support member, varying in width.

Pop-up rod. The rod that controls the raising and lowering of the drain in the bottom of the lavatory.

Preformed base. Shower pan or base of terrazzo or acrylic.

Sauna. A steam bath of Finnish origin.

Slip-resistant. Special material on the bottom of the tub to prevent falls.

Spa. Whirlpool type bath for more than one person, with a heating and filtration system. Frequently installed outside in warmer climates.

Spread. Distance between holes of a bathtub or lavatory faucet.

Surround. The walls encircling a bathtub or shower area.

Urinals. Wall-hung vitreous plumbing fixtures used in men's rooms, with flushing device for cleaning purposes.

Vacuum breaker. A device that prevents water from being siphoned into the potable water system.

Vanity. Laypersons' term for a prefabricated lavatory and base cabinet.

Water pressure. Measured as so many pounds per square inch. Usually 30 to 50 psi.

Wet wall. The wall in which the water and waste pipes are located.

Wrist control. Long lever handles operated by pressure of the wrist rather than with fingers.

endnotes

1. Linda Trent, "Combining Kitchen and Bath Elements," *Interiors & Sources*, April 1994
2. Jacuzzi, www.jacuzzi.com
3. American Standard, www.americanstandard-us.com
4. Kohler, www.us.kohler.com
5. Ibid.
6. Delta Faucets, www.deltafaucet.com
7. Sloan Valve Co., www.sloanvalve.com
8. Toto, www.toto.com
9. Bobrick Washroom Equipment Inc., www.bobrick.com
10. Ibid.

Measurements

Metric Conversion Table

This simple metric conversion chart contains equivalents only for the linear measurements taken from the textbook.

Some other quantities such as gallons, pounds, square yards, and temperatures may be converted from the following figures:

To convert square yards to square meters multiply square yards by .80

To convert gallons to liters, multiply gallons by 3.8

To convert pounds to kilograms, multiply pounds by 0.45

To convert Fahrenheit to Celsius, subtract 32 from the Fahrenheit amount and multiply by 5/9

IN.	CM	IN.	CM	IN.	CM	FT	M
1/000	0.003	4	10.16	36	91.44	1	.31
1/16	0.16	4 1/4	10.80	37	93.98	2	.61
3/32	0.24	5	12.70	39	99.06	3	.91
1/8	0.32	6	15.24	40	101.60	4	1.22
5/32	0.40	7	17.78	42	106.68	5	1.52
3/16	0.48	8	20.32	44	111.76	6	1.83
1/4	0.64	9	22.86	46 1/2	118.11	7	2.13
5/16	0.79	10	25.40	48	121.92	8	2.44
3/8	0.95	11	27.94	52	132.08	9	2.74
7/16	1.11	12	30.48	54	137.16	10	3.05
1/2	1.27	14	35.56	55	139.70	12	3.66
5/8	1.59	15	38.10	59	149.86	15	4.57
3/4	1.91	18	45.72	60	152.40	22	6.71
7/8	2.22	19 1/2	49.53	64	162.56	25	7.62
1	2.54	20	50.80	66 1/2	168.91	28	8.53
1 1/16	2.70	22	55.88	72	182.88	37	11.28
1 1/4	3.18	23	58.42	78	198.12	64	19.51
1 1/2	3.81	24	60.96	82	208.28	66	20.12
2	5.08	27	68.58	84	213.36	100	30.48
2 1/4	5.72	29	73.66	90	228.60		
2 3/8	6.03	30	76.20	91	231.14		
2 3/4	6.99	30 1/2	77.47	96	243.84		
3	7.62	32	81.28				
3 1/8	7.94	33	83.82				
3 5/8	9.21	34	86.36				
3 7/8	9.84	35 3/4	90.81				

Note: Page numbers followed by f *and* t *indicate figures and tables respectively.*

Index